Helck

1

Story and Art by
Nanaki Nanao

Contents

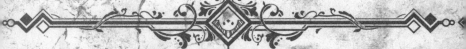

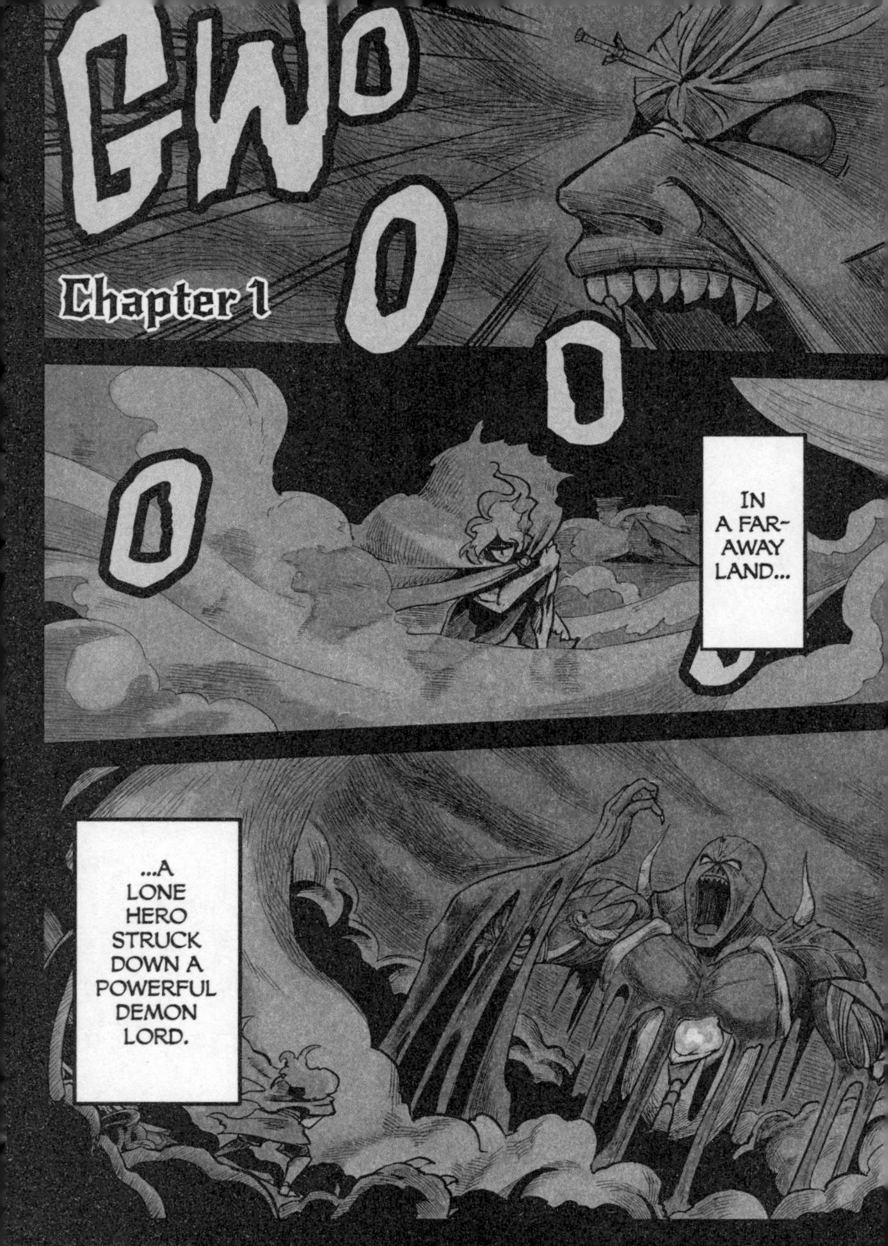
GWOOOOO
Chapter 1
IN A FAR-AWAY LAND...
...A LONE HERO STRUCK DOWN A POWERFUL DEMON LORD.

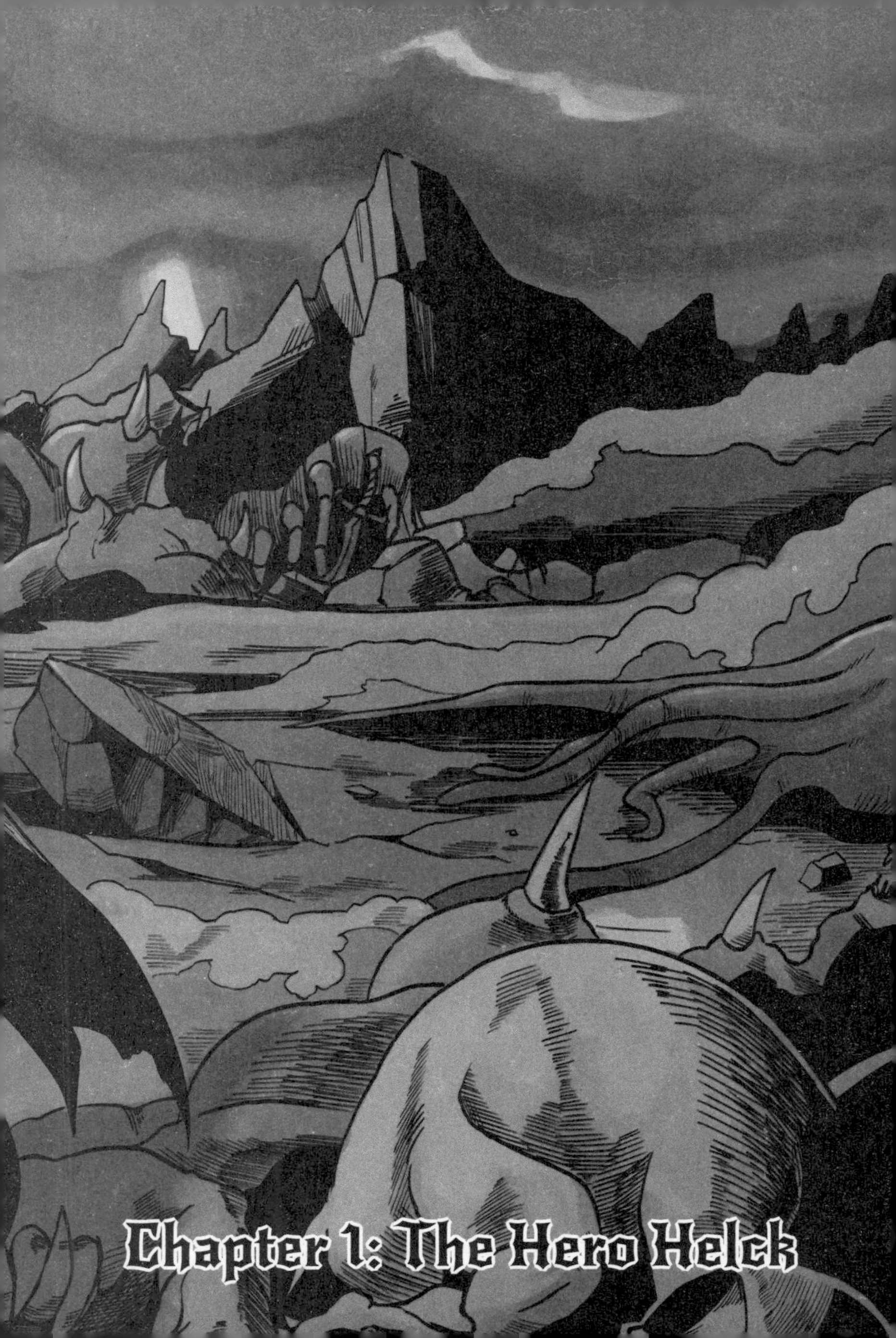
Chapter 1: The Hero Helck

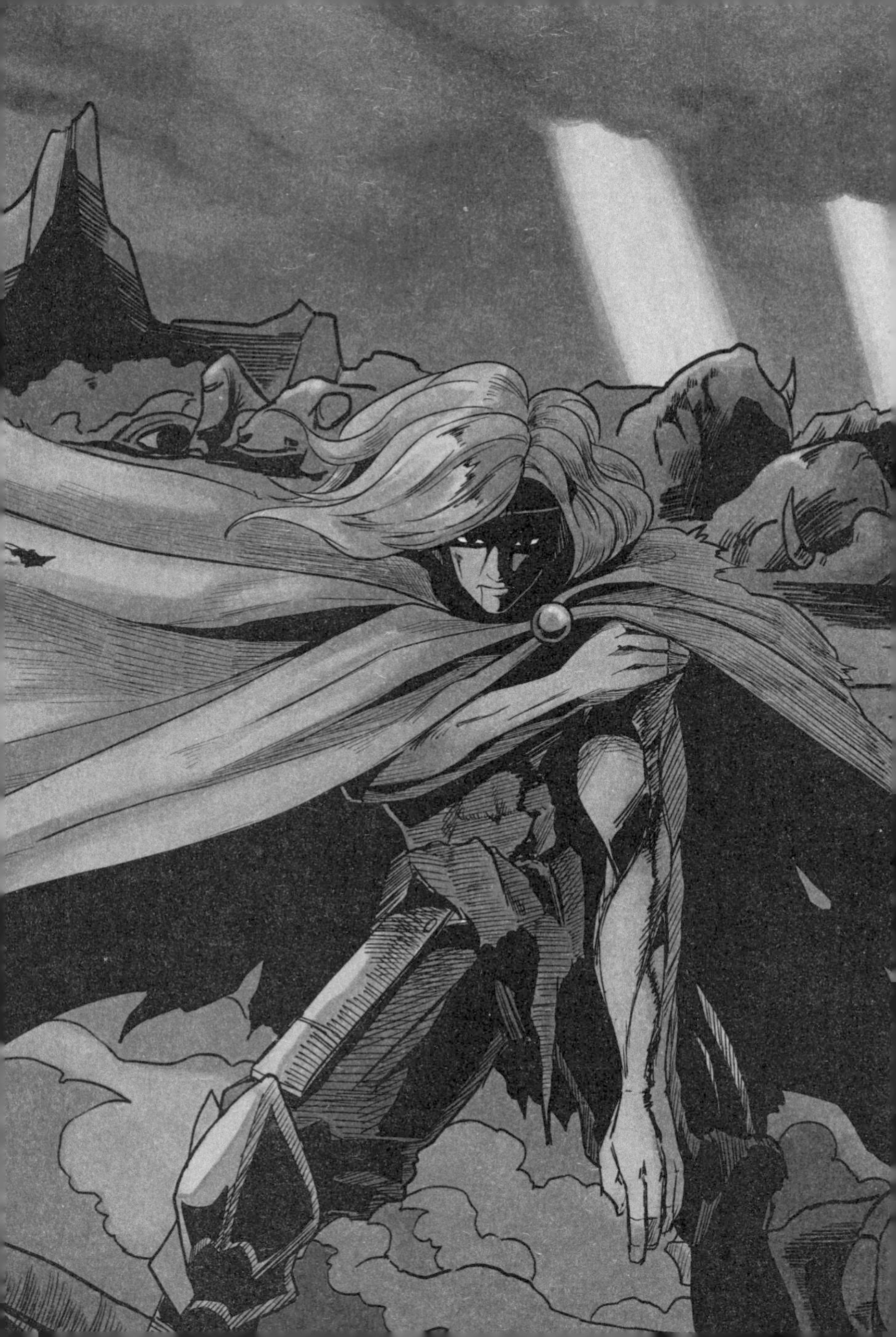

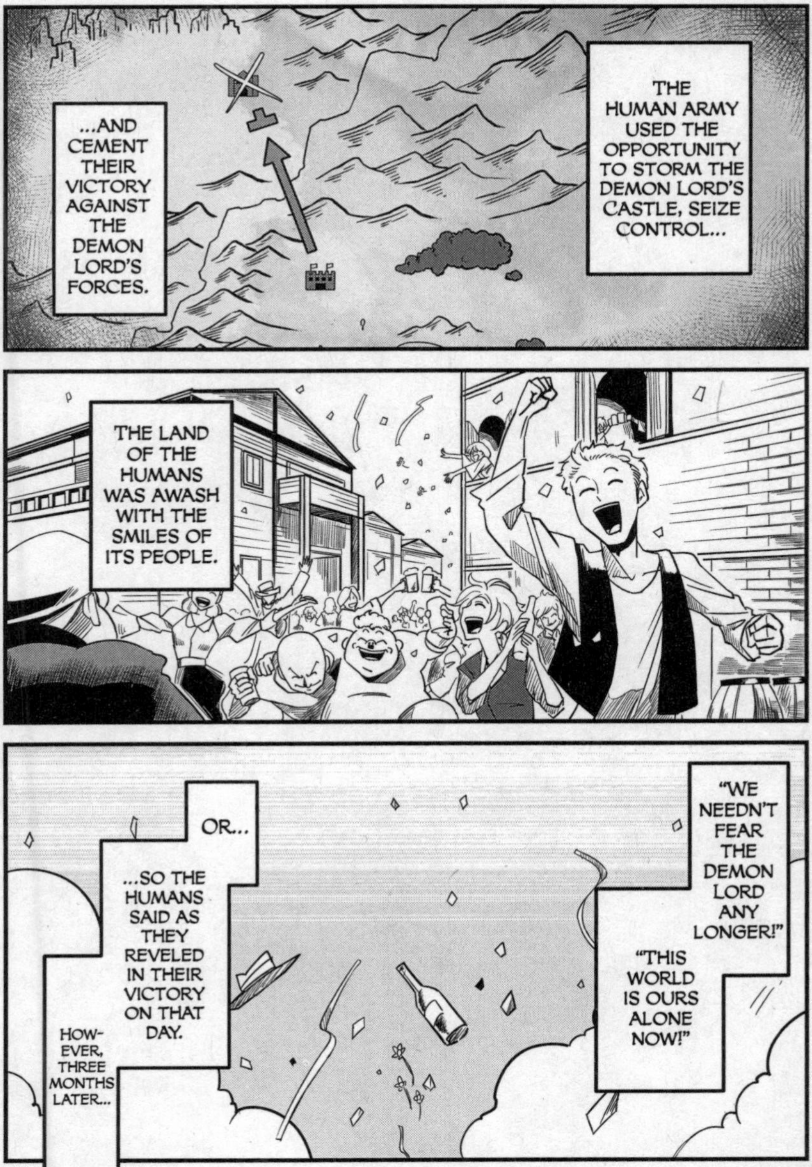
THE HUMAN ARMY USED THE OPPORTUNITY TO STORM THE DEMON LORD'S CASTLE, SEIZE CONTROL...
...AND CEMENT THEIR VICTORY AGAINST THE DEMON LORD'S FORCES.
THE LAND OF THE HUMANS WAS AWASH WITH THE SMILES OF ITS PEOPLE.
"WE NEEDN'T FEAR THE DEMON LORD ANY LONGER!"
"THIS WORLD IS OURS ALONE NOW!"
OR...
...SO THE HUMANS SAID AS THEY REVELED IN THEIR VICTORY ON THAT DAY.
HOW-EVER, THREE MONTHS LATER...

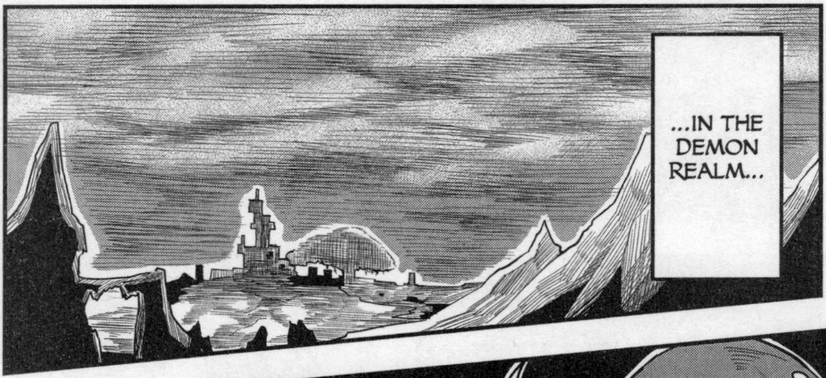
...IN THE DEMON REALM...

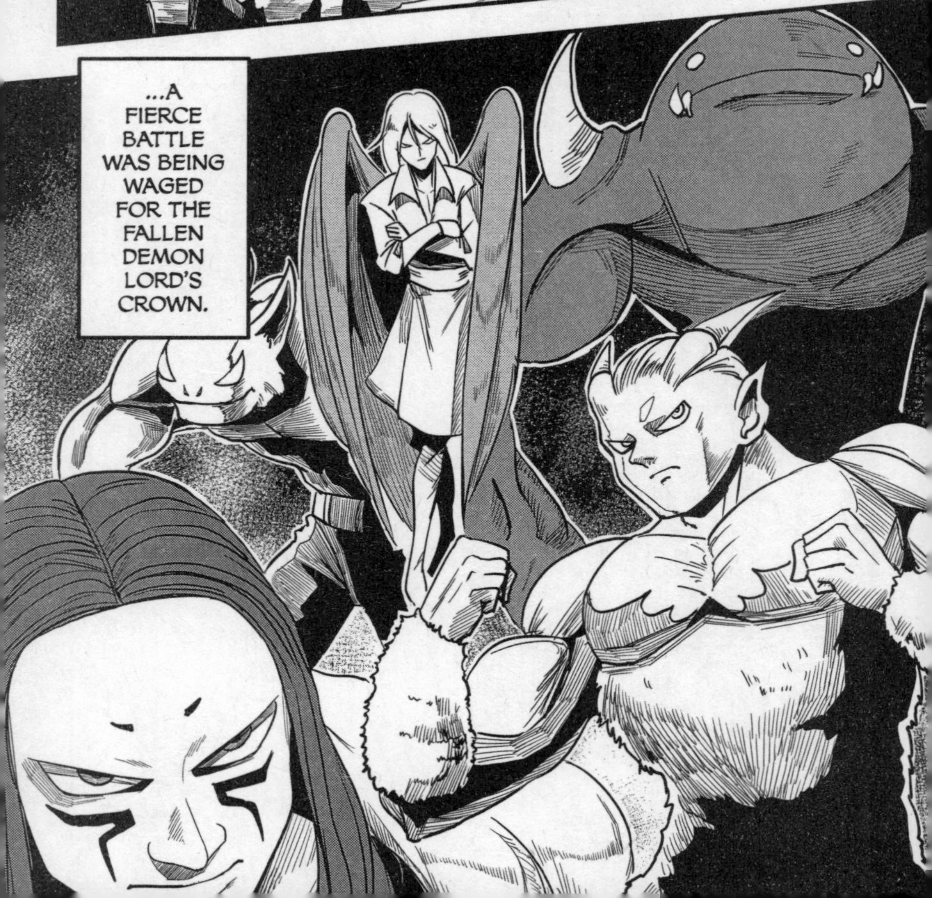
...A FIERCE BATTLE WAS BEING WAGED FOR THE FALLEN DEMON LORD'S CROWN.

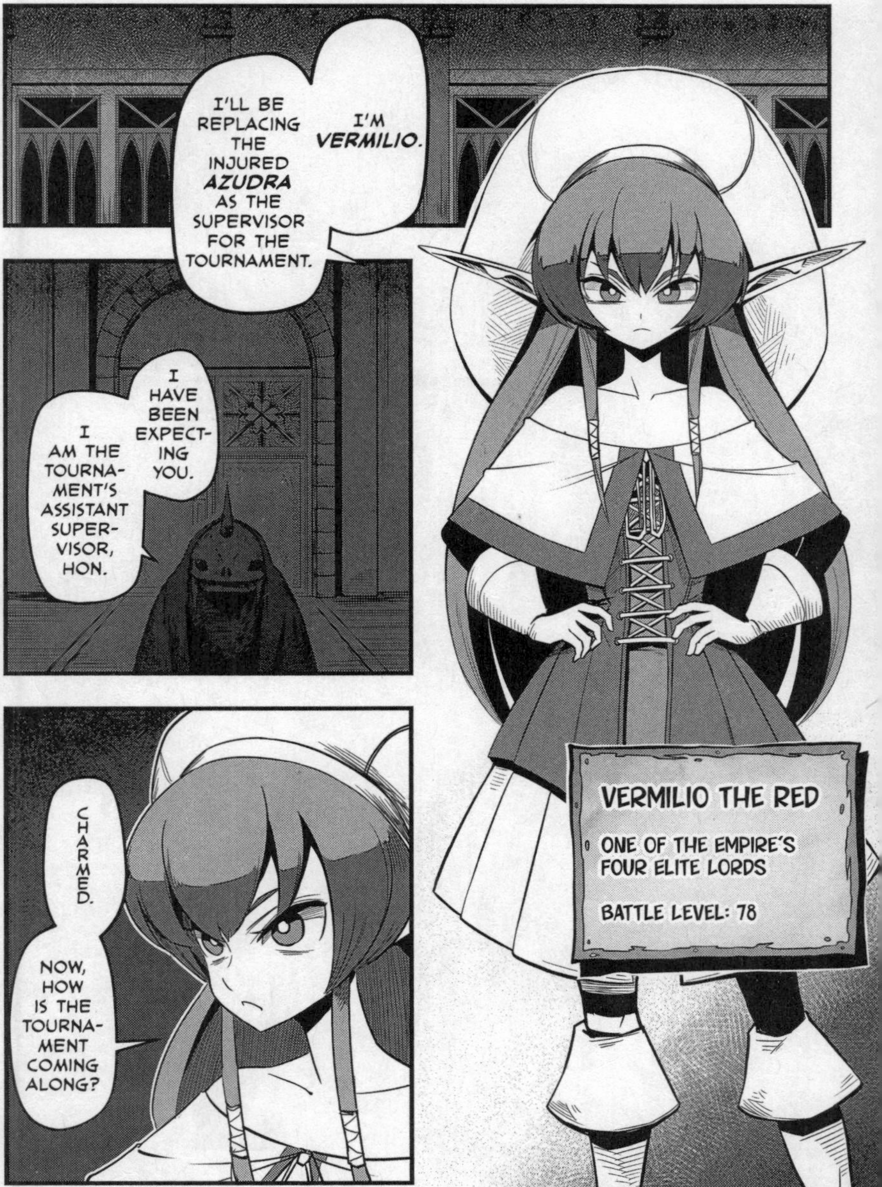
I'M VERMILIO.
I'LL BE REPLACING THE INJURED AZUDRA AS THE SUPERVISOR FOR THE TOURNAMENT.
VERMILIO THE RED
ONE OF THE EMPIRE'S FOUR ELITE LORDS
BATTLE LEVEL: 78
I HAVE BEEN EXPECTING YOU.
I AM THE TOURNAMENT'S ASSISTANT SUPERVISOR, HON.
CHARMED.
NOW, HOW IS THE TOURNAMENT COMING ALONG?

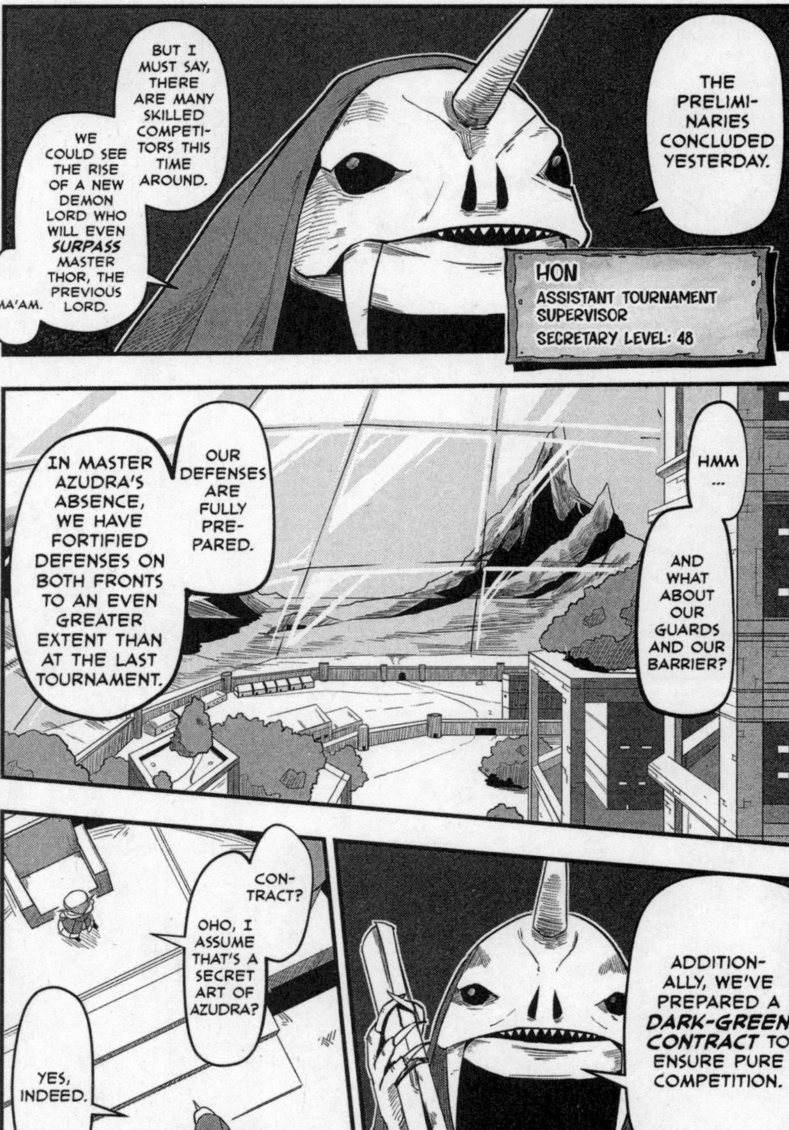
THE PRELIMINARIES CONCLUDED YESTERDAY.
HON
ASSISTANT TOURNAMENT SUPERVISOR
SECRETARY LEVEL: 48
BUT I MUST SAY, THERE ARE MANY SKILLED COMPETITORS THIS TIME AROUND.
WE COULD SEE THE RISE OF A NEW DEMON LORD WHO WILL EVEN *SURPASS* MASTER THOR, THE PREVIOUS LORD. MA'AM.
HMM ...
AND WHAT ABOUT OUR GUARDS AND OUR BARRIER?
OUR DEFENSES ARE FULLY PREPARED.
IN MASTER AZUDRA'S ABSENCE, WE HAVE FORTIFIED DEFENSES ON BOTH FRONTS TO AN EVEN GREATER EXTENT THAN AT THE LAST TOURNAMENT.
ADDITIONALLY, WE'VE PREPARED A ***DARK-GREEN CONTRACT*** TO ENSURE PURE COMPETITION.
CONTRACT?
OHO, I ASSUME THAT'S A SECRET ART OF AZUDRA?
YES, INDEED.

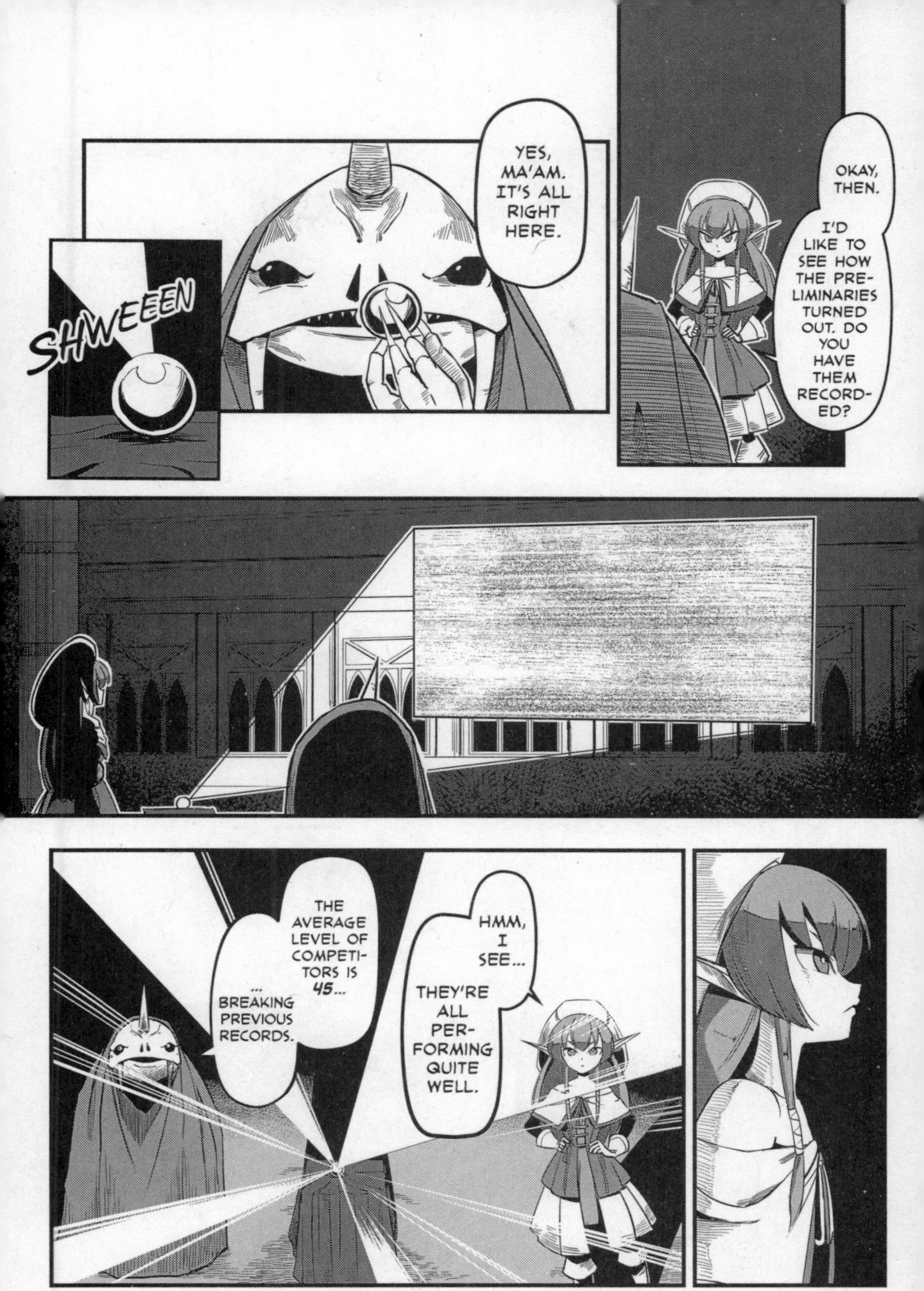
OKAY, THEN.
I'D LIKE TO SEE HOW THE PRE-LIMINARIES TURNED OUT. DO YOU HAVE THEM RECORD-ED?
YES, MA'AM. IT'S ALL RIGHT HERE.
SHWEEEN
HMM, I SEE...
THEY'RE ALL PER-FORMING QUITE WELL.
THE AVERAGE LEVEL OF COMPETI-TORS IS 45...
... BREAKING PREVIOUS RECORDS.

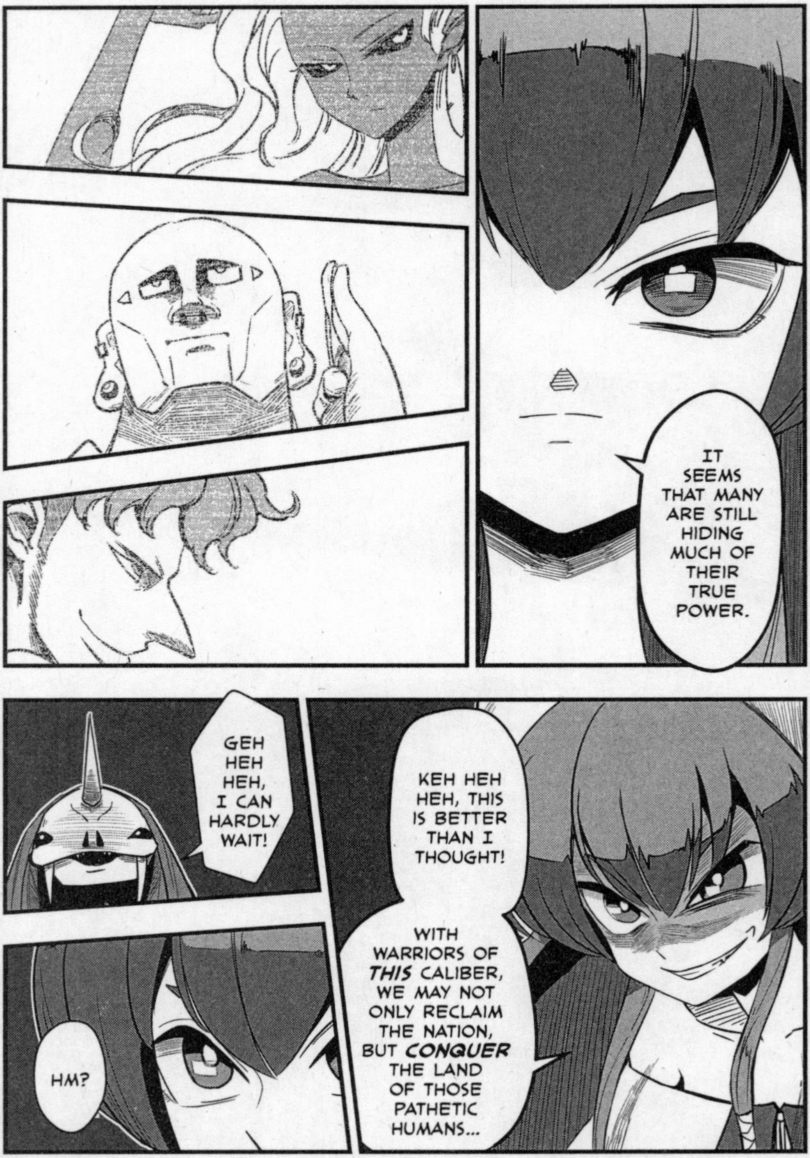
IT SEEMS THAT MANY ARE STILL HIDING MUCH OF THEIR TRUE POWER.
KEH HEH HEH, THIS IS BETTER THAN I THOUGHT!
WITH WARRIORS OF *THIS* CALIBER, WE MAY NOT ONLY RECLAIM THE NATION, BUT ***CONQUER*** THE LAND OF THOSE PATHETIC HUMANS...
GEH HEH HEH, I CAN HARDLY WAIT!
HM?

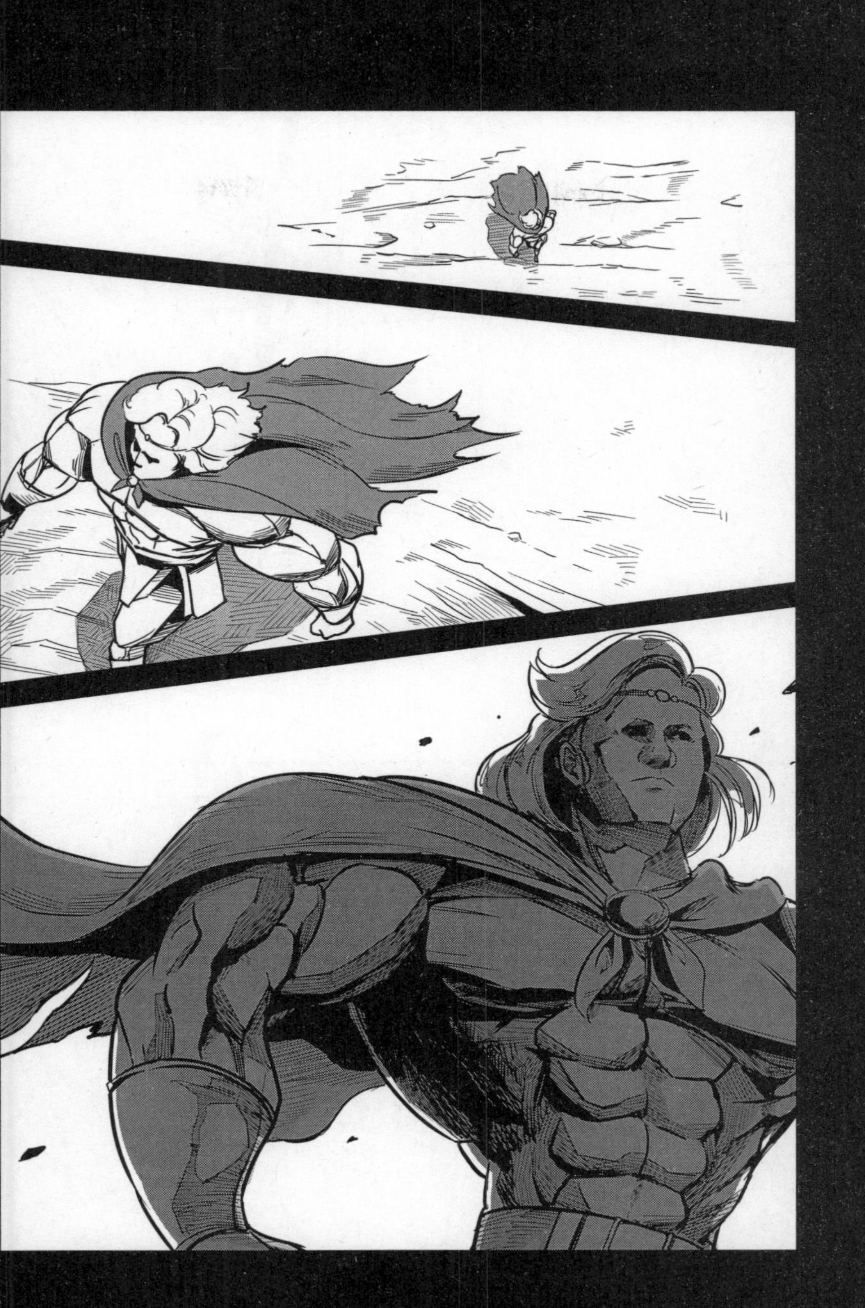

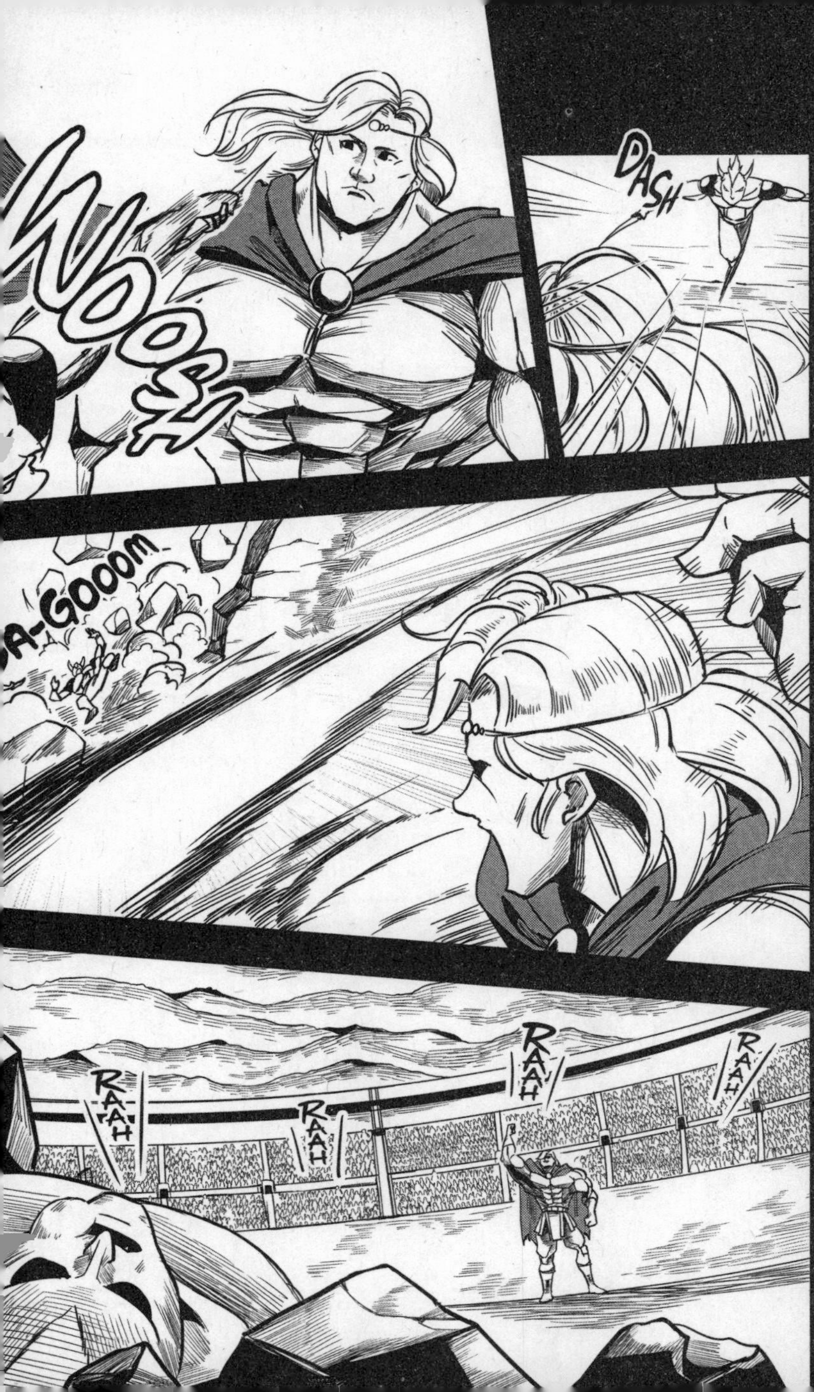
DASH
WOOSH
A-GOOOM
RAAH
RAAH
RAAH
RAAH

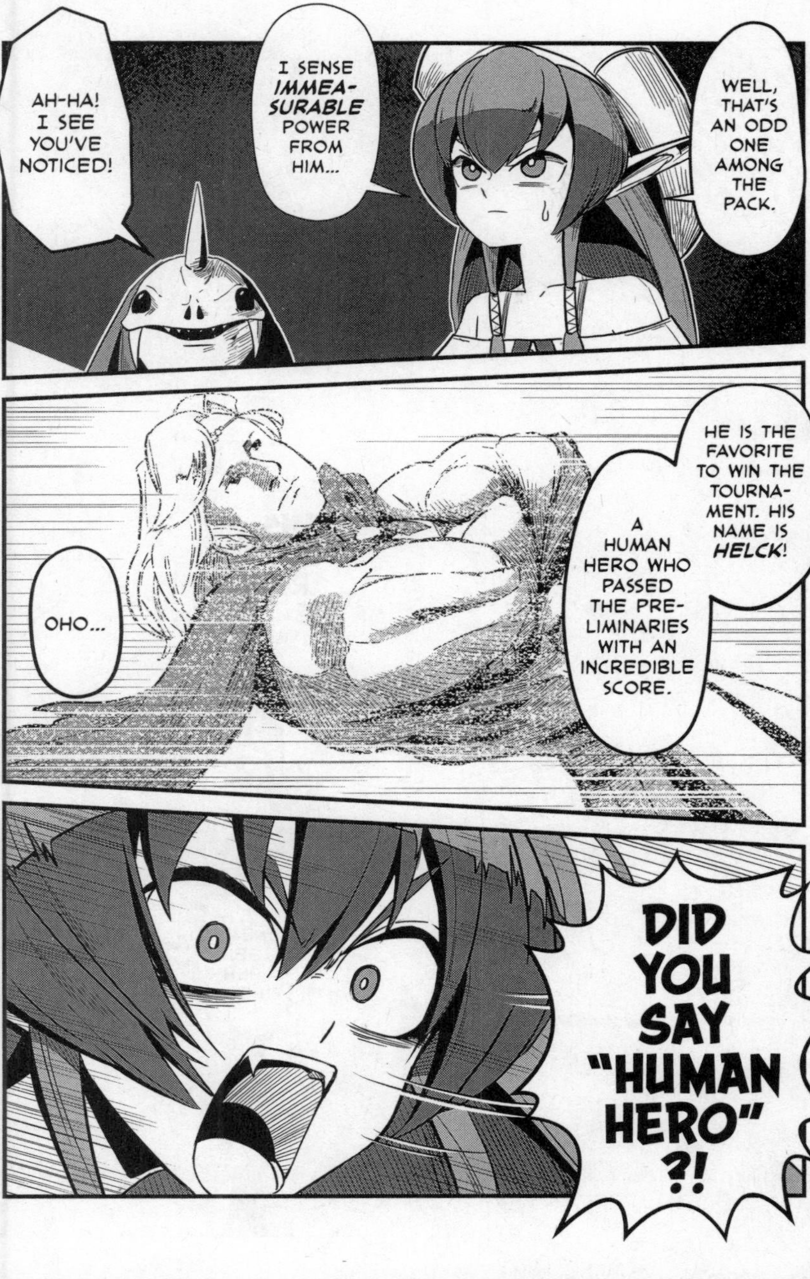
WELL, THAT'S AN ODD ONE AMONG THE PACK.
I SENSE IMMEASURABLE POWER FROM HIM...
AH-HA! I SEE YOU'VE NOTICED!
HE IS THE FAVORITE TO WIN THE TOURNAMENT. HIS NAME IS HELCK!
A HUMAN HERO WHO PASSED THE PRELIMINARIES WITH AN INCREDIBLE SCORE.
OHO...
DID YOU SAY "HUMAN HERO"?!

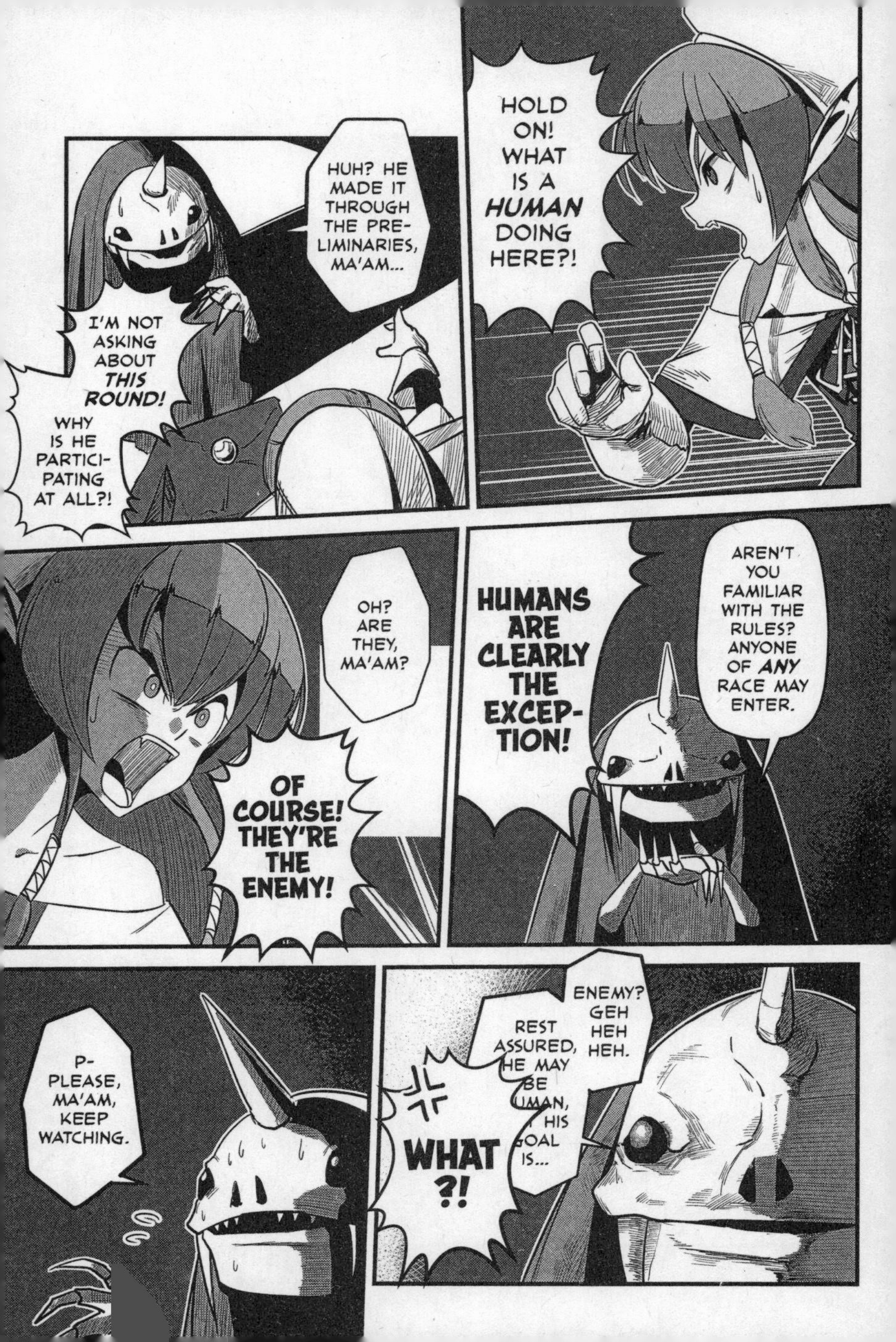
HOLD ON! WHAT IS A *HUMAN* DOING HERE?!
HUH? HE MADE IT THROUGH THE PRE-LIMINARIES, MA'AM...
I'M NOT ASKING ABOUT *THIS ROUND!*
WHY IS HE PARTICI-PATING AT ALL?!
AREN'T YOU FAMILIAR WITH THE RULES? ANYONE OF *ANY* RACE MAY ENTER.
HUMANS ARE CLEARLY THE EXCEP-TION!
OH? ARE THEY, MA'AM?
OF COURSE! THEY'RE THE ENEMY!
ENEMY? GEH HEH HEH.
REST ASSURED, HE MAY BE UMAN, T HIS OAL IS...
WHAT?!
P-PLEASE, MA'AM, KEEP WATCHING.

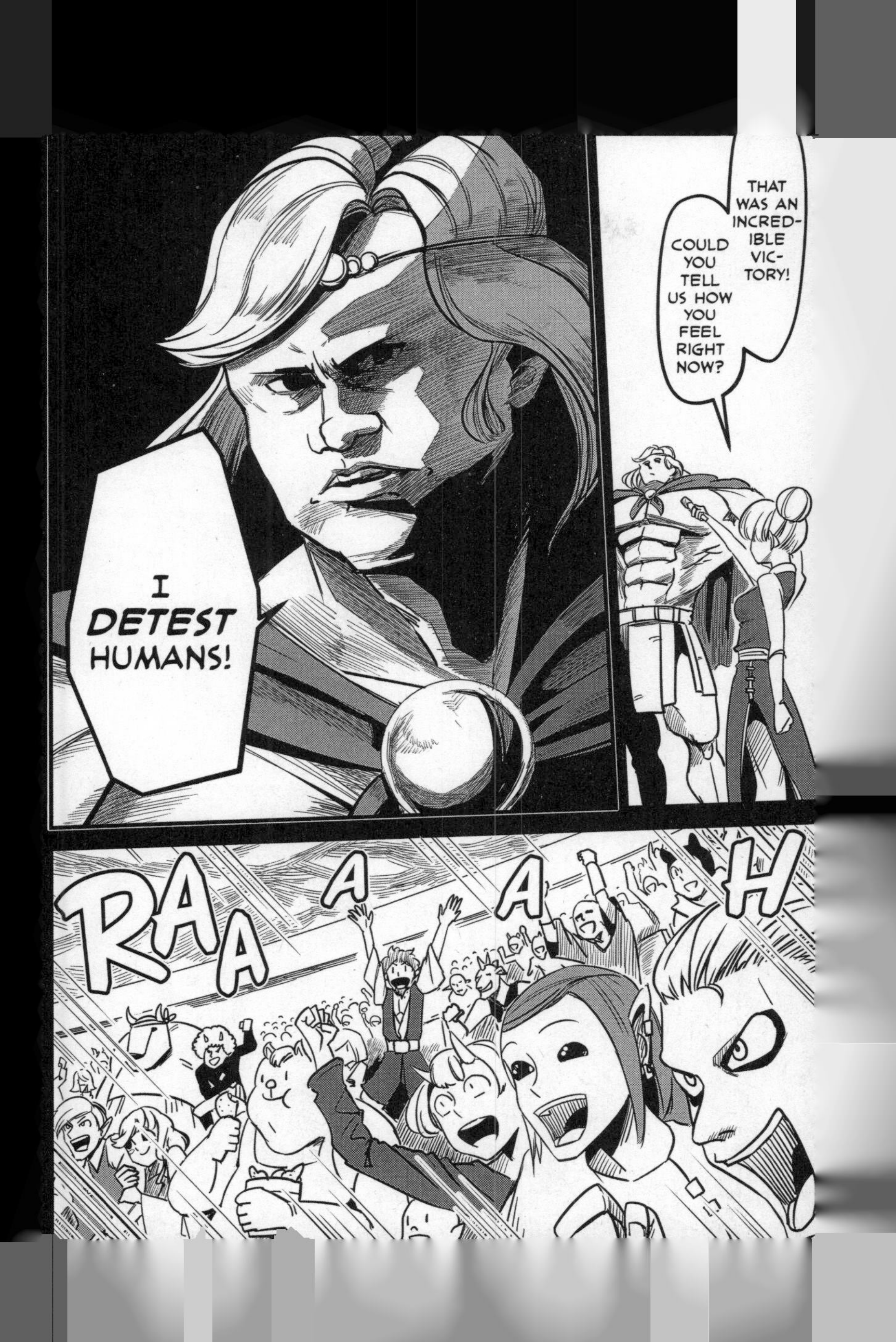
THAT WAS AN INCRED-IBLE VIC-TORY!
COULD YOU TELL US HOW YOU FEEL RIGHT NOW?
I *DETEST* HUMANS!
RAAAAH

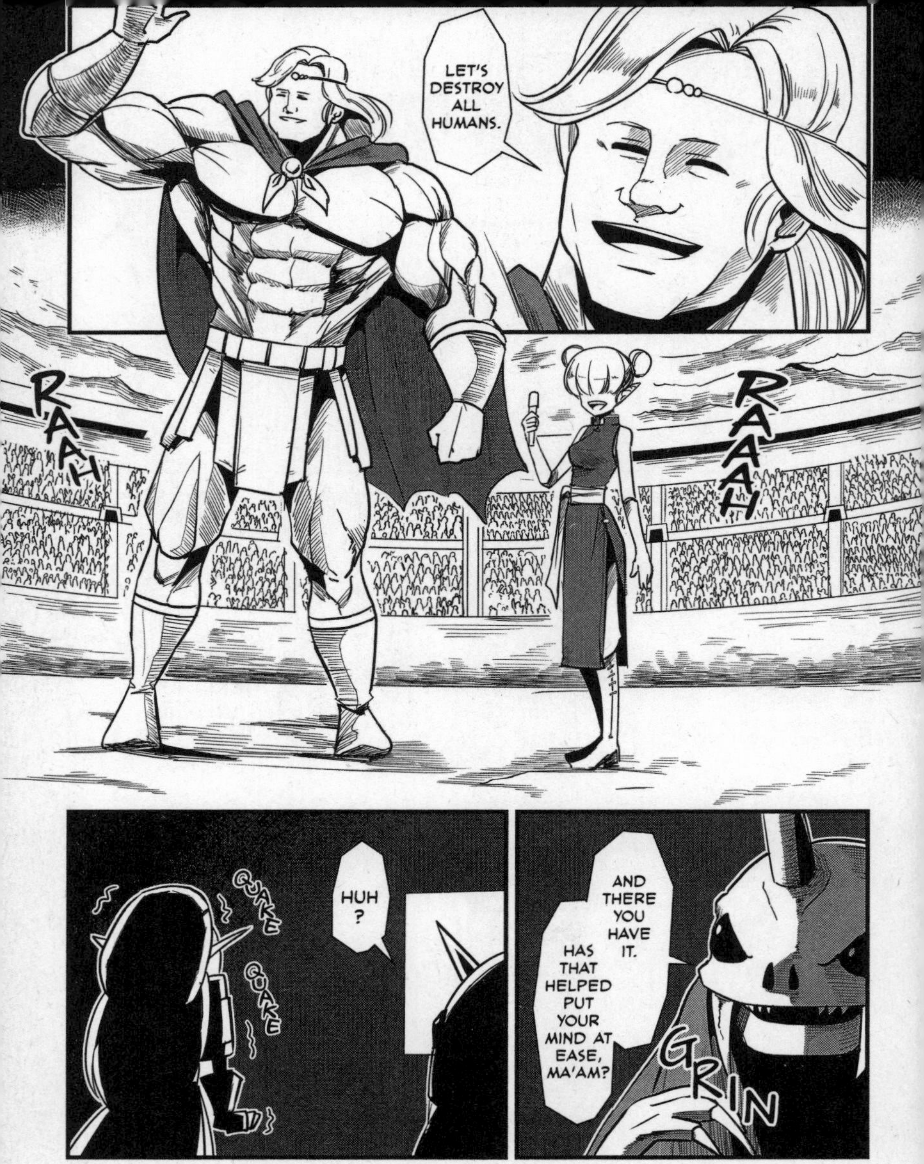

LET'S DESTROY ALL HUMANS.
RAAAH
RAAH
AND THERE YOU HAVE IT.
HAS THAT HELPED PUT YOUR MIND AT EASE, MA'AM?
GRIN
HUH?
QUAKE
QUAKE

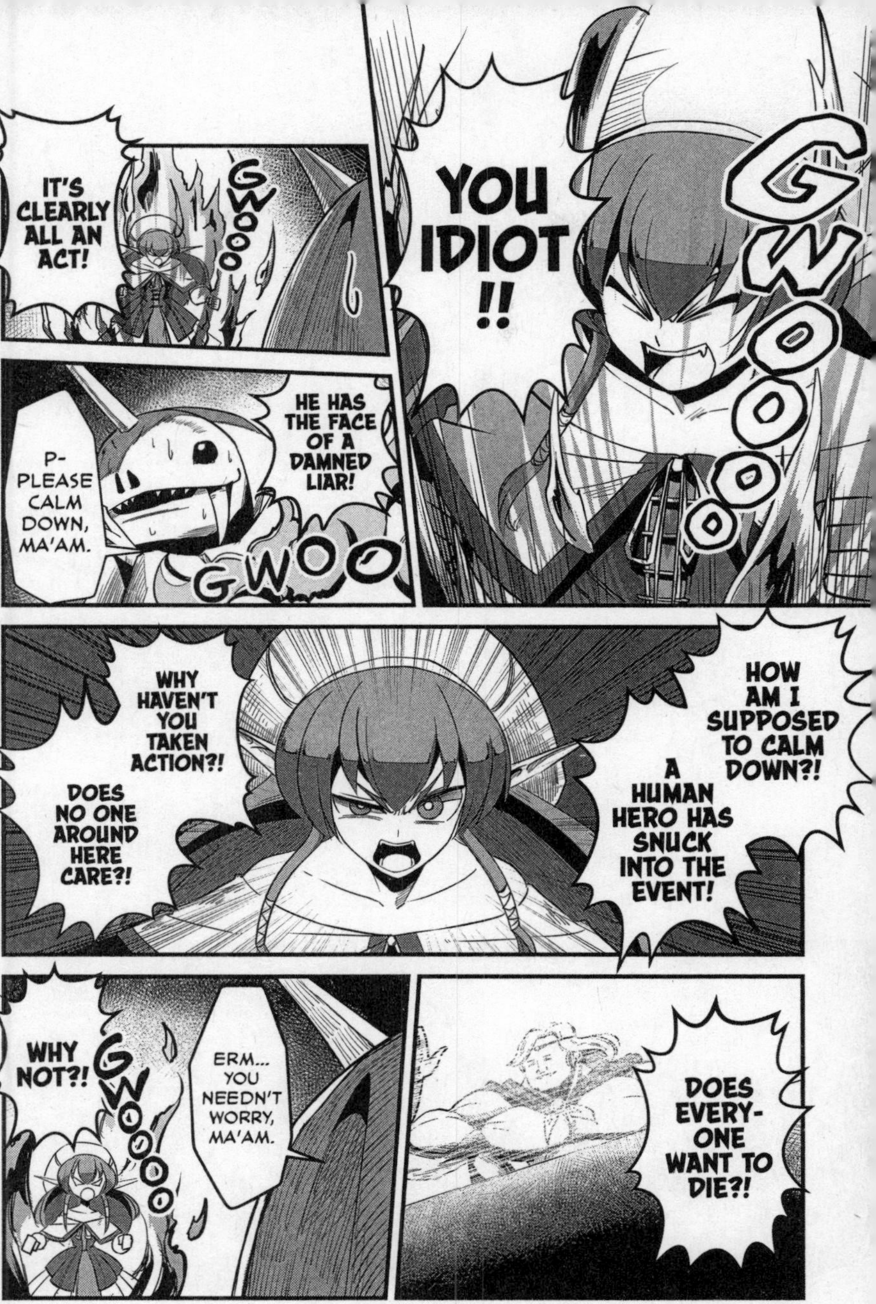
GWOOOOOOO
YOU IDIOT!!
GWOOO
IT'S CLEARLY ALL AN ACT!
HE HAS THE FACE OF A DAMNED LIAR!
GWOO
P-PLEASE CALM DOWN, MA'AM.
HOW AM I SUPPOSED TO CALM DOWN?!
A HUMAN HERO HAS SNUCK INTO THE EVENT!
WHY HAVEN'T YOU TAKEN ACTION?!
DOES NO ONE AROUND HERE CARE?!
DOES EVERY-ONE WANT TO DIE?!
ERM... YOU NEEDN'T WORRY, MA'AM.
GWOOOO
WHY NOT?!

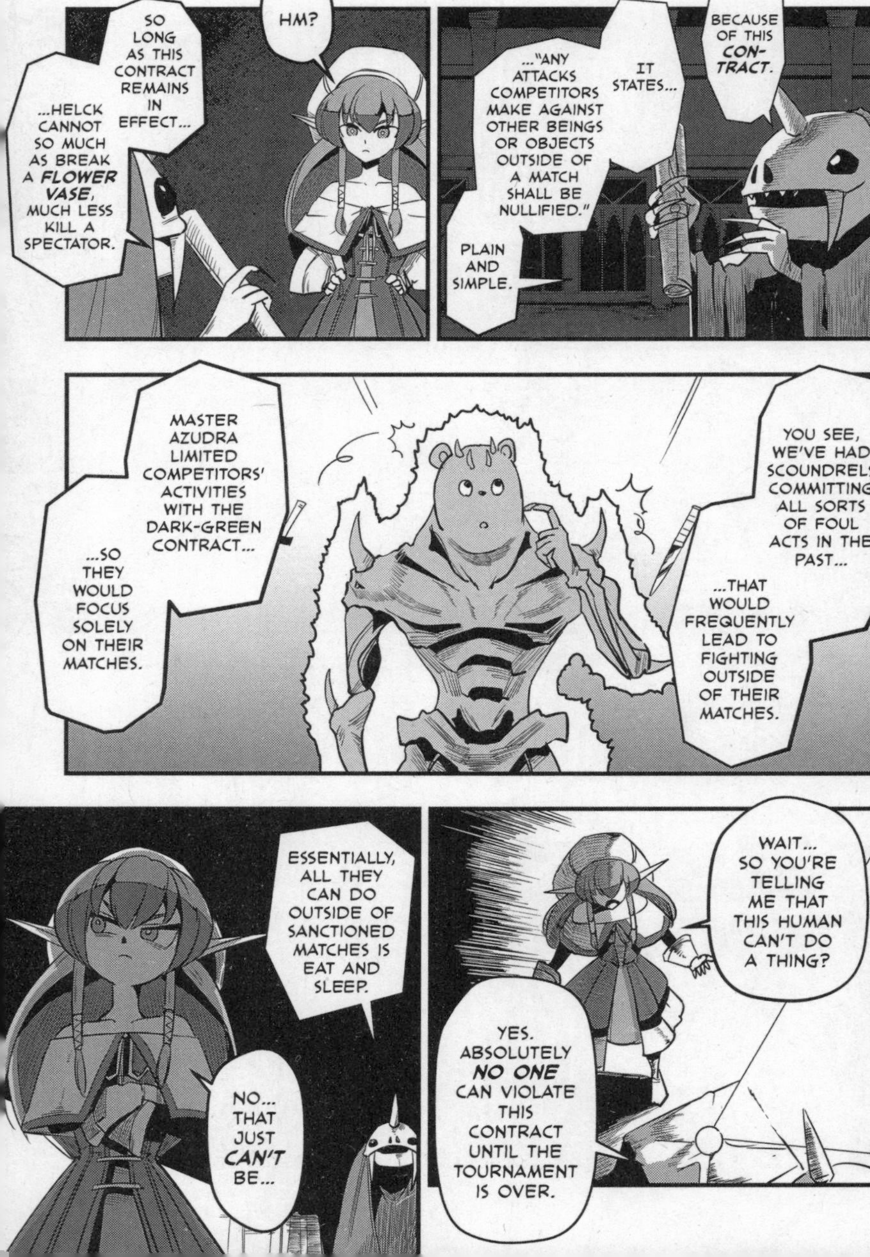
BECAUSE OF THIS CONTRACT.
IT STATES...
..."ANY ATTACKS COMPETITORS MAKE AGAINST OTHER BEINGS OR OBJECTS OUTSIDE OF A MATCH SHALL BE NULLIFIED."
PLAIN AND SIMPLE.
HM?
SO LONG AS THIS CONTRACT REMAINS IN EFFECT...
...HELCK CANNOT SO MUCH AS BREAK A FLOWER VASE, MUCH LESS KILL A SPECTATOR.
YOU SEE, WE'VE HAD SCOUNDRELS COMMITTING ALL SORTS OF FOUL ACTS IN THE PAST...
...THAT WOULD FREQUENTLY LEAD TO FIGHTING OUTSIDE OF THEIR MATCHES.
MASTER AZUDRA LIMITED COMPETITORS' ACTIVITIES WITH THE DARK-GREEN CONTRACT...
...SO THEY WOULD FOCUS SOLELY ON THEIR MATCHES.
WAIT... SO YOU'RE TELLING ME THAT THIS HUMAN CAN'T DO A THING?
YES. ABSOLUTELY NO ONE CAN VIOLATE THIS CONTRACT UNTIL THE TOURNAMENT IS OVER.
ESSENTIALLY, ALL THEY CAN DO OUTSIDE OF SANCTIONED MATCHES IS EAT AND SLEEP.
NO... THAT JUST CAN'T BE...

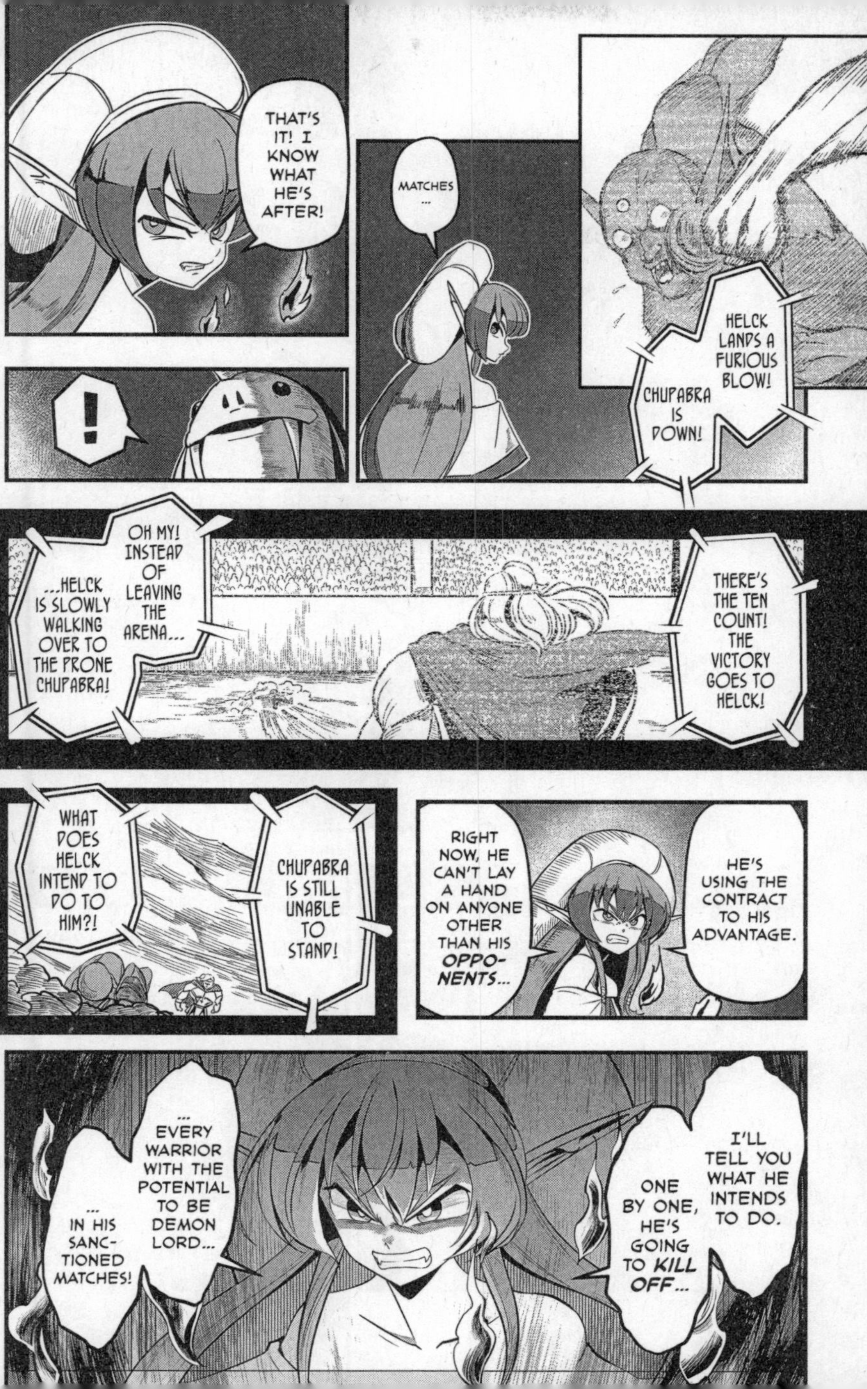
HELCK LANDS A FURIOUS BLOW!
CHUPABRA IS DOWN!
MATCHES ...
THAT'S IT! I KNOW WHAT HE'S AFTER!
!
THERE'S THE TEN COUNT! THE VICTORY GOES TO HELCK!
OH MY! INSTEAD OF LEAVING THE ARENA...
...HELCK IS SLOWLY WALKING OVER TO THE PRONE CHUPABRA!
HE'S USING THE CONTRACT TO HIS ADVANTAGE.
RIGHT NOW, HE CAN'T LAY A HAND ON ANYONE OTHER THAN HIS *OPPONENTS*...
CHUPABRA IS STILL UNABLE TO STAND!
WHAT DOES HELCK INTEND TO DO TO HIM?!
I'LL TELL YOU WHAT HE INTENDS TO DO.
ONE BY ONE, HE'S GOING TO *KILL OFF*...
... EVERY WARRIOR WITH THE POTENTIAL TO BE DEMON LORD...
... IN HIS SANCTIONED MATCHES!

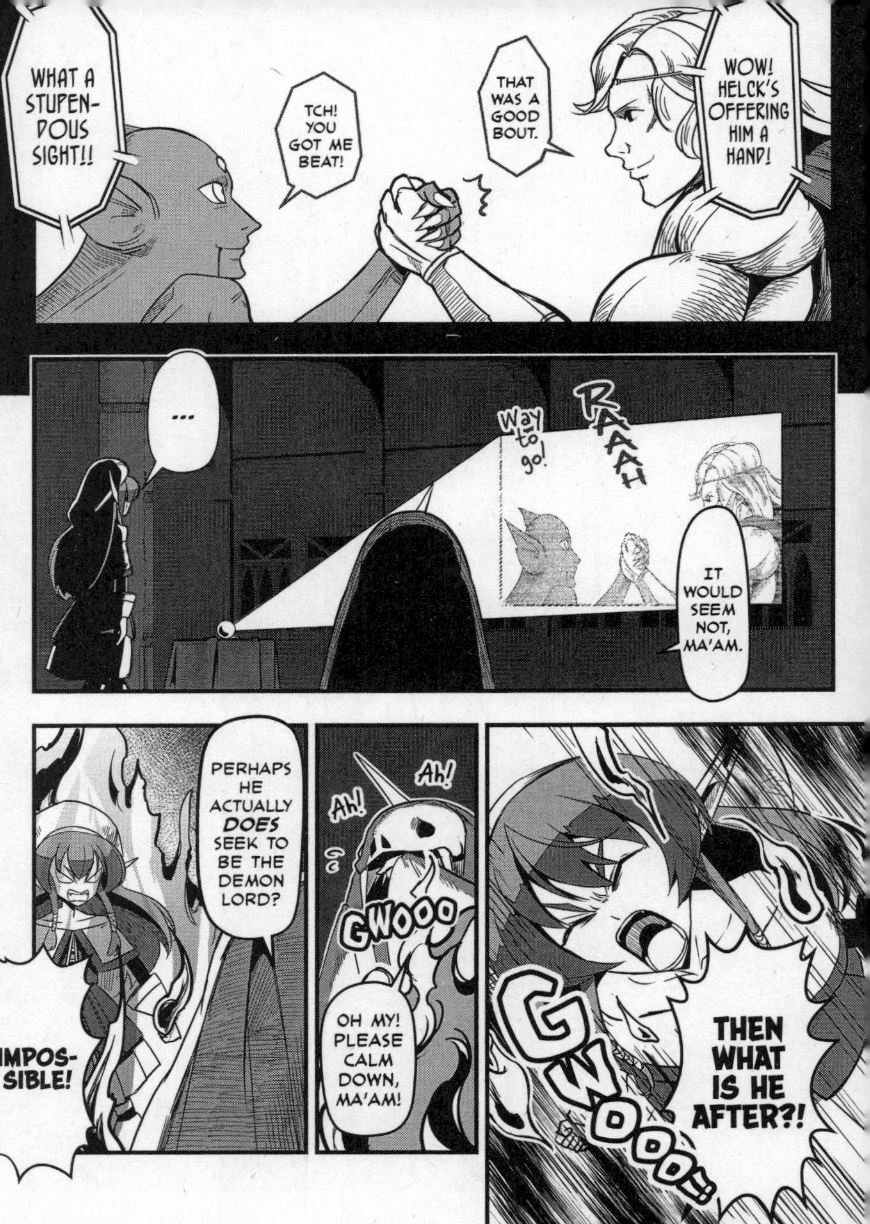
WOW! HELCK'S OFFERING HIM A HAND!
THAT WAS A GOOD BOUT.
TCH! YOU GOT ME BEAT!
WHAT A STUPEN-DOUS SIGHT!!
RAAAH
Way to go!
IT WOULD SEEM NOT, MA'AM.
...
GWOOOO!!
THEN WHAT IS HE AFTER?!
Ah!
Ah!
GWOOO
OH MY! PLEASE CALM DOWN, MA'AM!
PERHAPS HE ACTUALLY ***DOES*** SEEK TO BE THE DEMON LORD?
IMPOS-SIBLE!

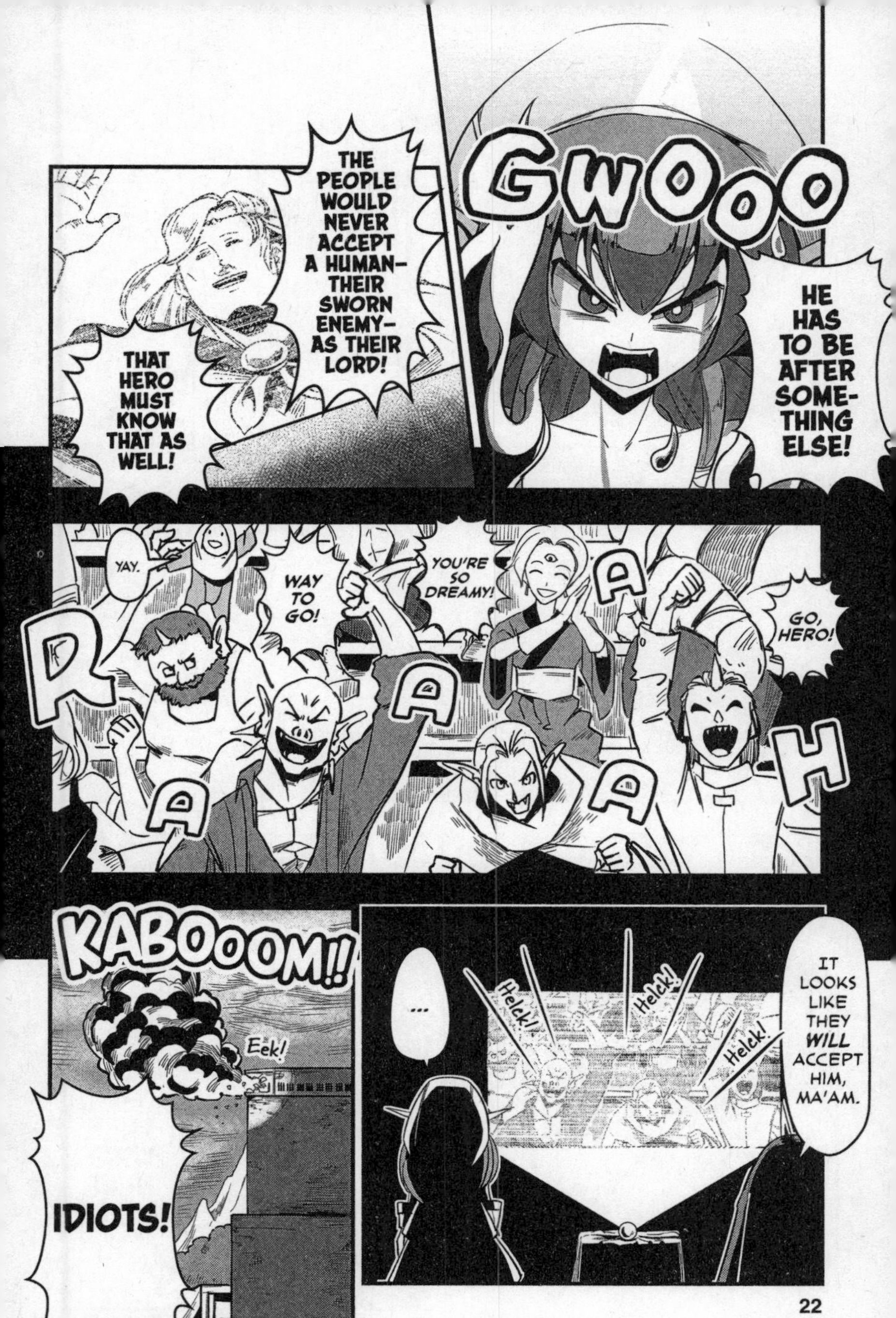
GWOOO
HE HAS TO BE AFTER SOME-THING ELSE!
THE PEOPLE WOULD NEVER ACCEPT A HUMAN—THEIR SWORN ENEMY—AS THEIR LORD!
THAT HERO MUST KNOW THAT AS WELL!
RAAAAAH
GO, HERO!
YOU'RE SO DREAMY!
WAY TO GO!
YAY.
IT LOOKS LIKE THEY WILL ACCEPT HIM, MA'AM.
Helck!
Helck!
Helck!
...
KABOOOOM!!
Eek!
IDIOTS!

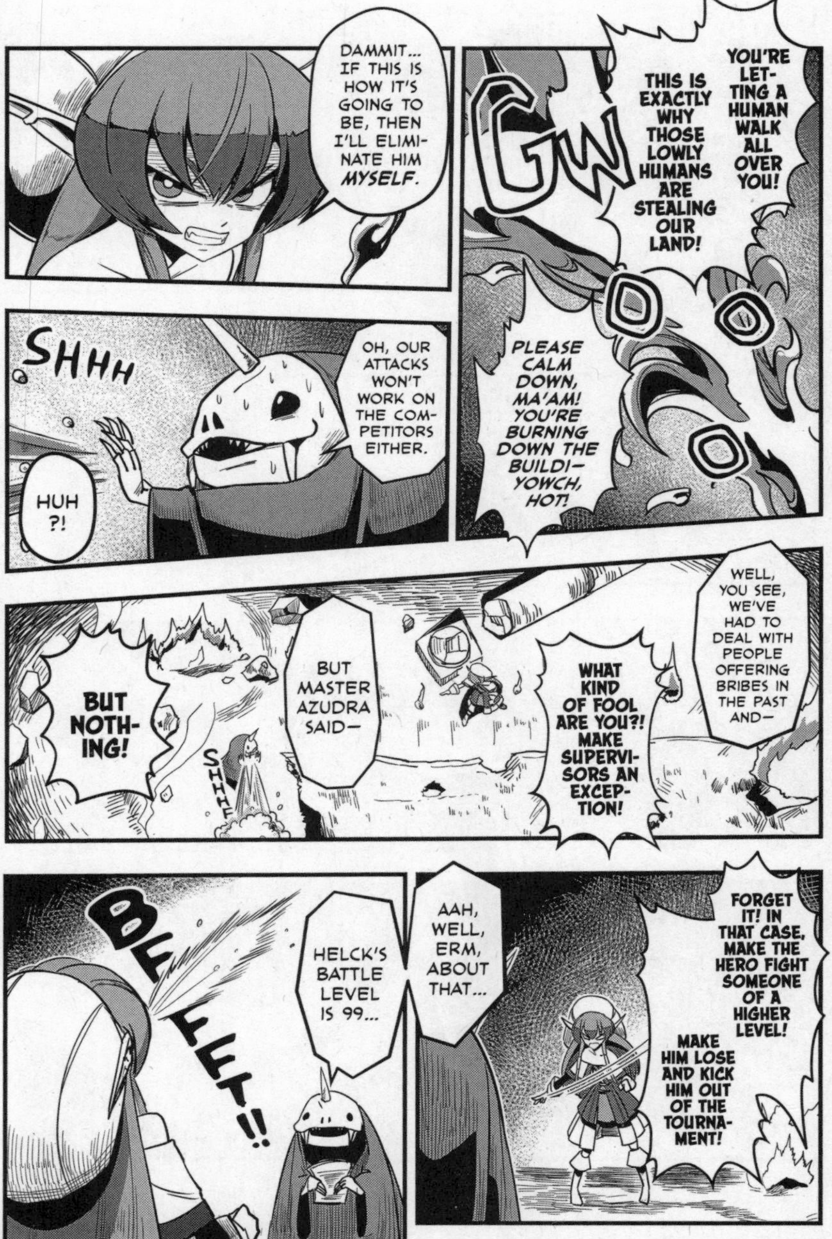
YOU'RE LETTING A HUMAN WALK ALL OVER YOU!
THIS IS EXACTLY WHY THOSE LOWLY HUMANS ARE STEALING OUR LAND!
GWOOO
PLEASE CALM DOWN, MA'AM! YOU'RE BURNING DOWN THE BUILDI— YOWCH, HOT!
DAMMIT... IF THIS IS HOW IT'S GOING TO BE, THEN I'LL ELIMINATE HIM MYSELF.
SHHH
OH, OUR ATTACKS WON'T WORK ON THE COMPETITORS EITHER.
HUH?!
WELL, YOU SEE, WE'VE HAD TO DEAL WITH PEOPLE OFFERING BRIBES IN THE PAST AND—
WHAT KIND OF FOOL ARE YOU?! MAKE SUPERVISORS AN EXCEPTION!
BUT MASTER AZUDRA SAID—
BUT NOTHING!
SHHHF
FORGET IT! IN THAT CASE, MAKE THE HERO FIGHT SOMEONE OF A HIGHER LEVEL!
MAKE HIM LOSE AND KICK HIM OUT OF THE TOURNAMENT!
AAH, WELL, ERM, ABOUT THAT...
HELCK'S BATTLE LEVEL IS 99...
BEFFT!!

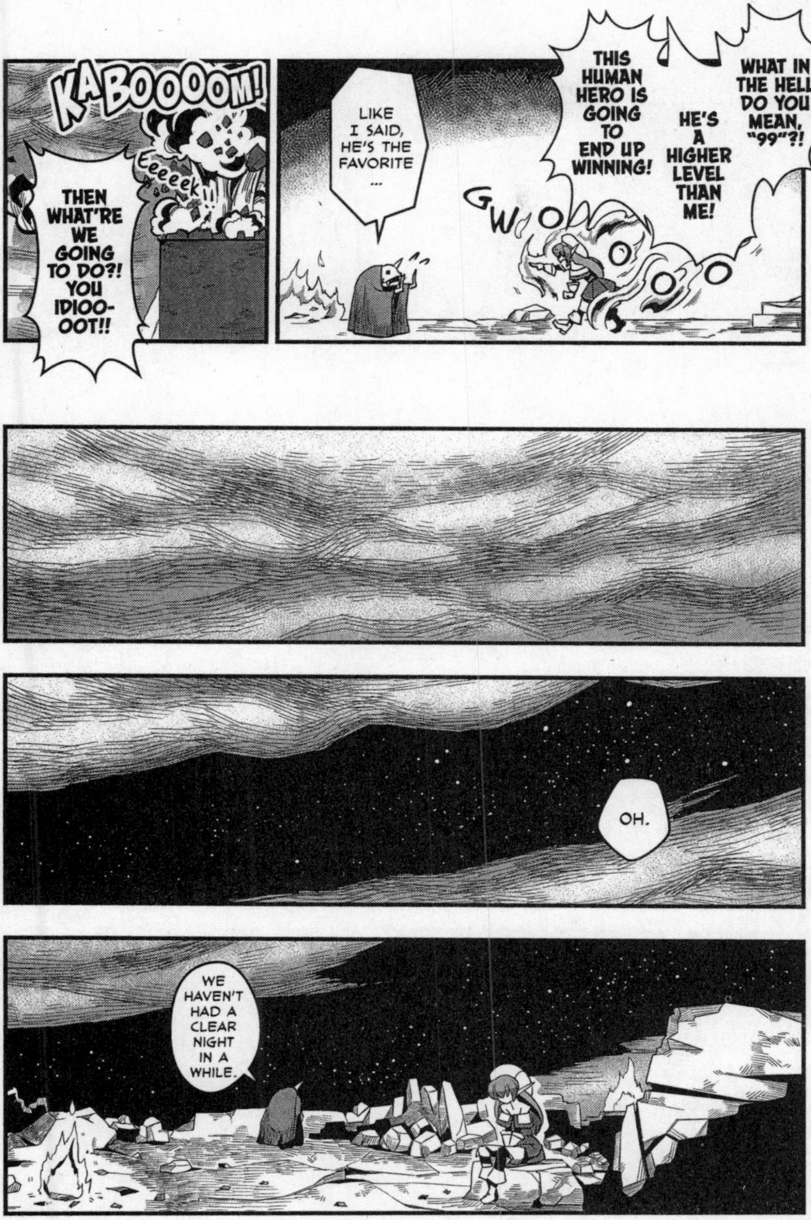

WHAT IN THE HELL DO YOU MEAN, "99"?!
HE'S A HIGHER LEVEL THAN ME!
THIS HUMAN HERO IS GOING TO END UP WINNING!
GWOOOOOO
LIKE I SAID, HE'S THE FAVORITE ...
KABOOOOM!
Eeeeek!!
THEN WHAT'RE WE GOING TO DO?! YOU IDIOOOOT!!
OH.
WE HAVEN'T HAD A CLEAR NIGHT IN A WHILE.

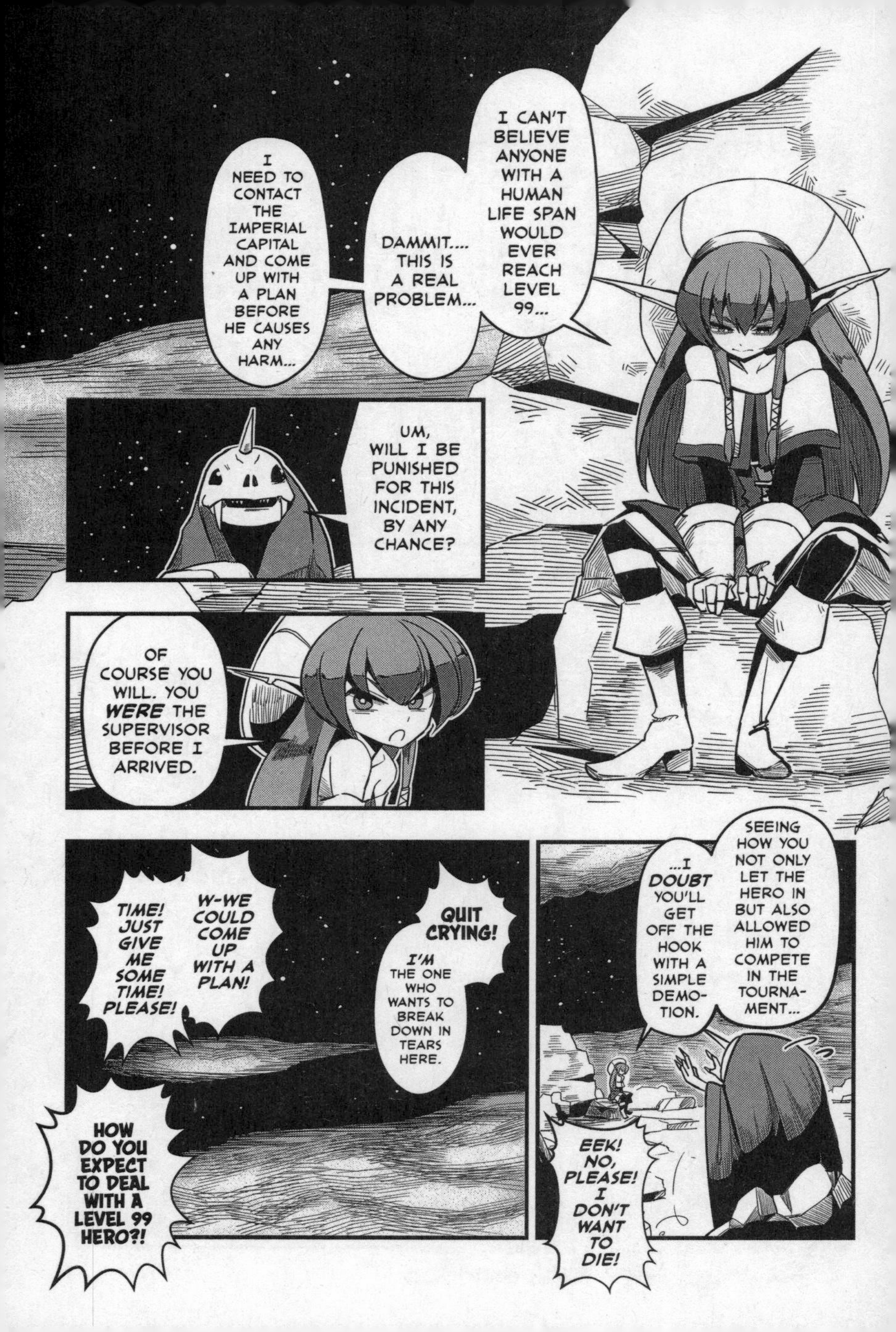
I CAN'T BELIEVE ANYONE WITH A HUMAN LIFE SPAN WOULD EVER REACH LEVEL 99...
DAMMIT.... THIS IS A REAL PROBLEM...
I NEED TO CONTACT THE IMPERIAL CAPITAL AND COME UP WITH A PLAN BEFORE HE CAUSES ANY HARM...
UM, WILL I BE PUNISHED FOR THIS INCIDENT, BY ANY CHANCE?
OF COURSE YOU WILL. YOU *WERE* THE SUPERVISOR BEFORE I ARRIVED.
SEEING HOW YOU NOT ONLY LET THE HERO IN BUT ALSO ALLOWED HIM TO COMPETE IN THE TOURNA-MENT...
...I *DOUBT* YOU'LL GET OFF THE HOOK WITH A SIMPLE DEMO-TION.
EEK! NO, PLEASE! I DON'T WANT TO DIE!
QUIT CRYING!
I'M THE ONE WHO WANTS TO BREAK DOWN IN TEARS HERE.
W-WE COULD COME UP WITH A PLAN!
TIME! JUST GIVE ME SOME TIME! PLEASE!
HOW DO YOU EXPECT TO DEAL WITH A LEVEL 99 HERO?!

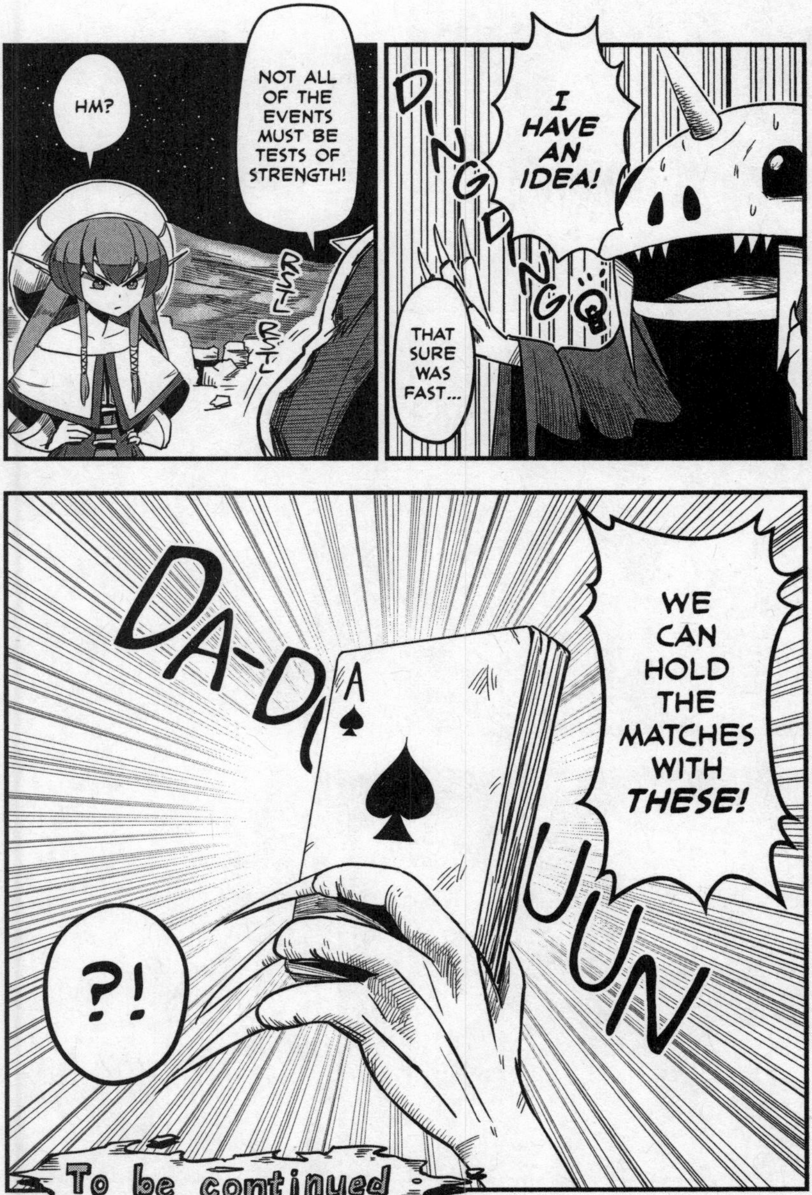

I HAVE AN IDEA!
DING DING
THAT SURE WAS FAST...
NOT ALL OF THE EVENTS MUST BE TESTS OF STRENGTH!
RSTL RSTL
HM?
WE CAN HOLD THE MATCHES WITH *THESE!*
DA-DUUUN
?!
To be continued

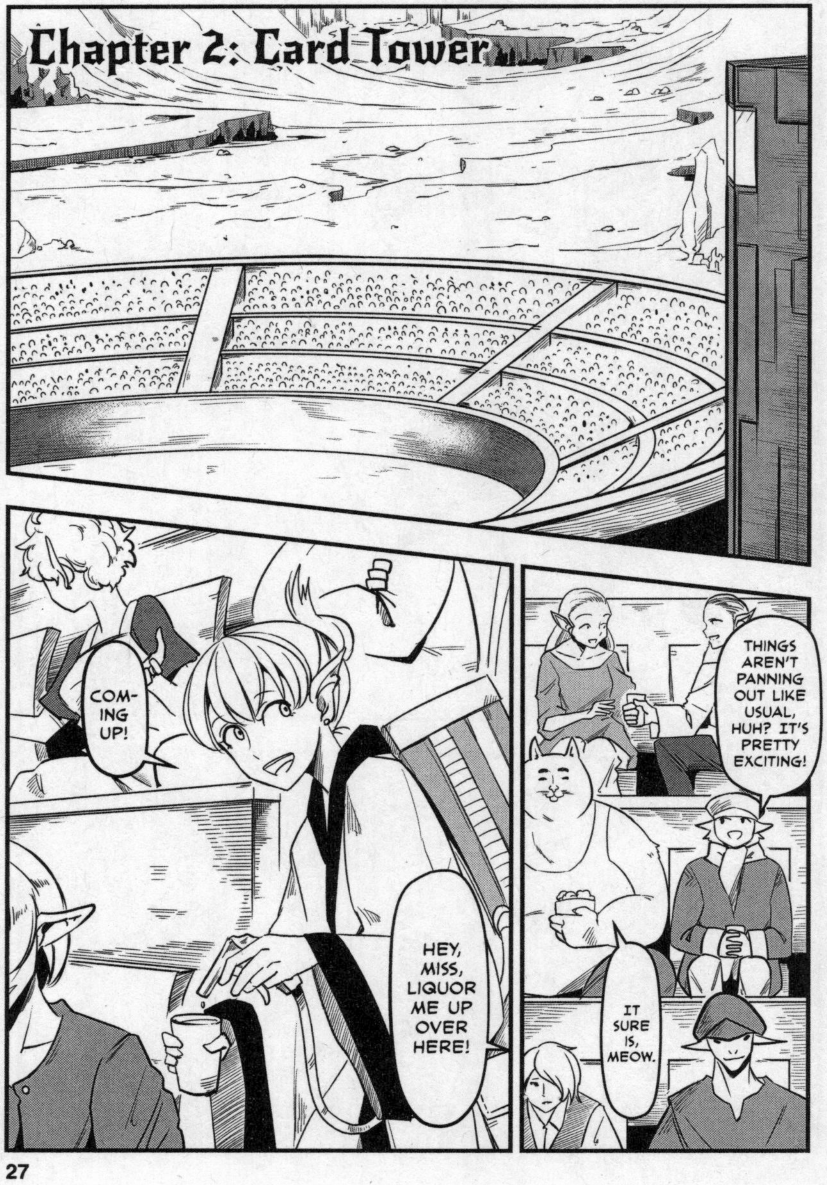
Chapter 2: Card Tower
THINGS AREN'T PANNING OUT LIKE USUAL, HUH? IT'S PRETTY EXCITING!
IT SURE IS, MEOW.
HEY, MISS, LIQUOR ME UP OVER HERE!
COM-ING UP!

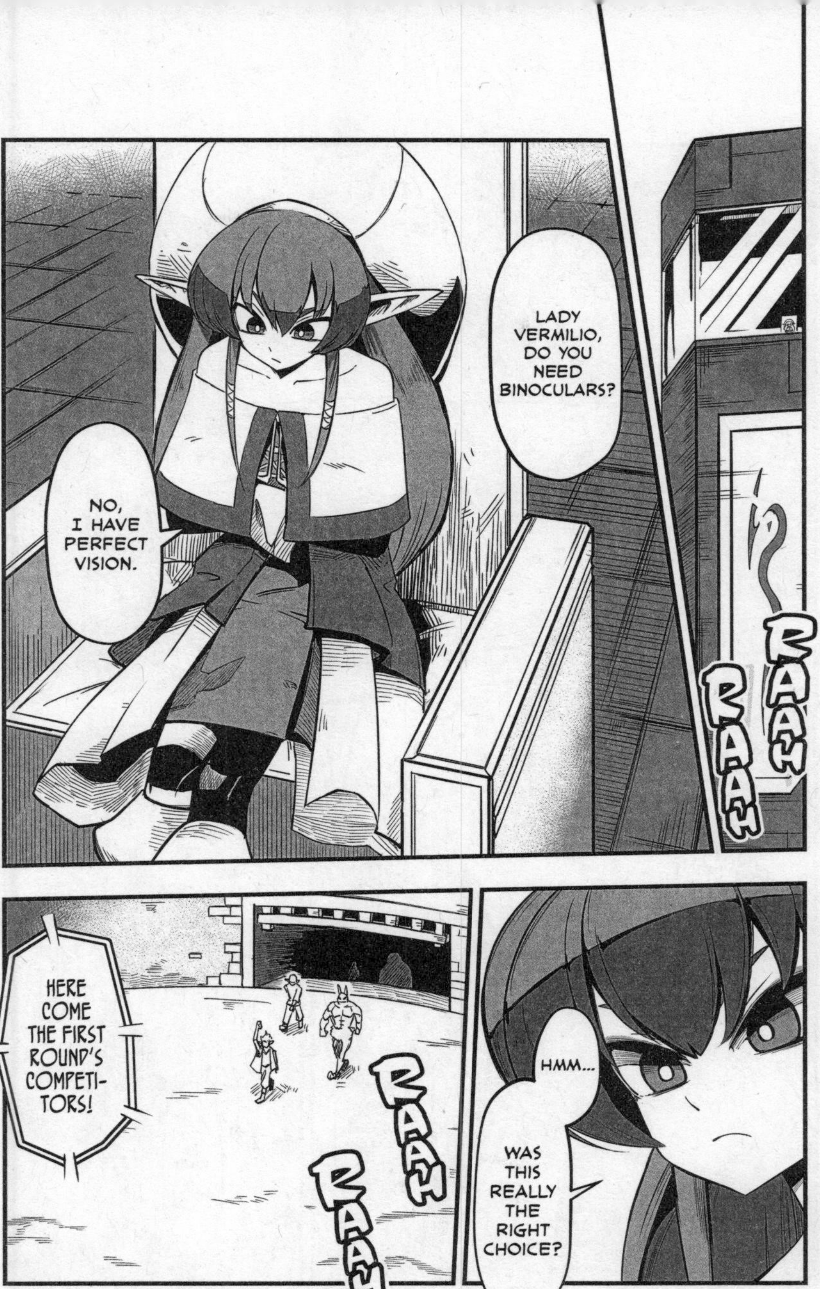
LADY VERMILIO, DO YOU NEED BINOCULARS?
NO, I HAVE PERFECT VISION.
RAAAH
RAAAH
HMM...
WAS THIS REALLY THE RIGHT CHOICE?
HERE COME THE FIRST ROUND'S COMPETI- TORS!
RAAAH
RAAAH

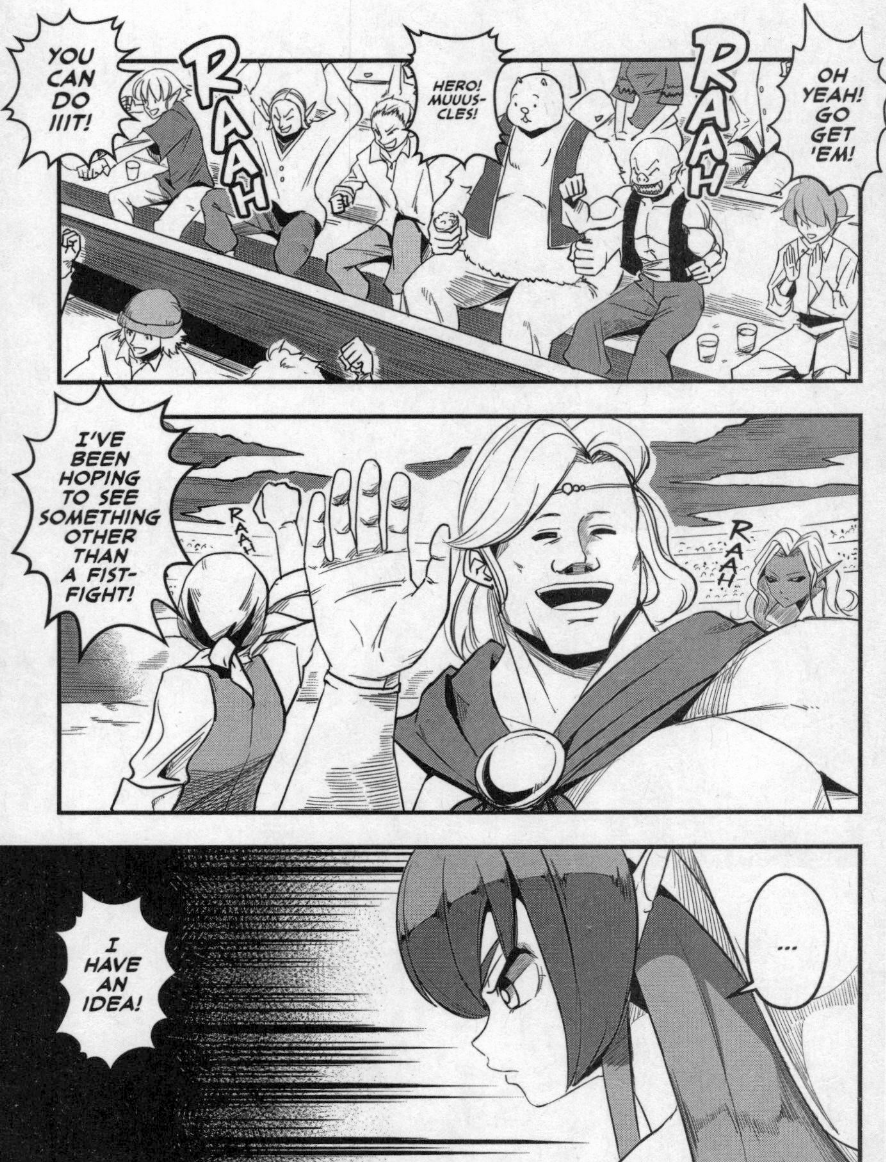

OH YEAH! GO GET 'EM!
RAAH
HERO! MUUUS-CLES!
RAAH
YOU CAN DO IIIT!
RAAH
I'VE BEEN HOPING TO SEE SOMETHING OTHER THAN A FIST-FIGHT!
RAAH
...
I HAVE AN IDEA!

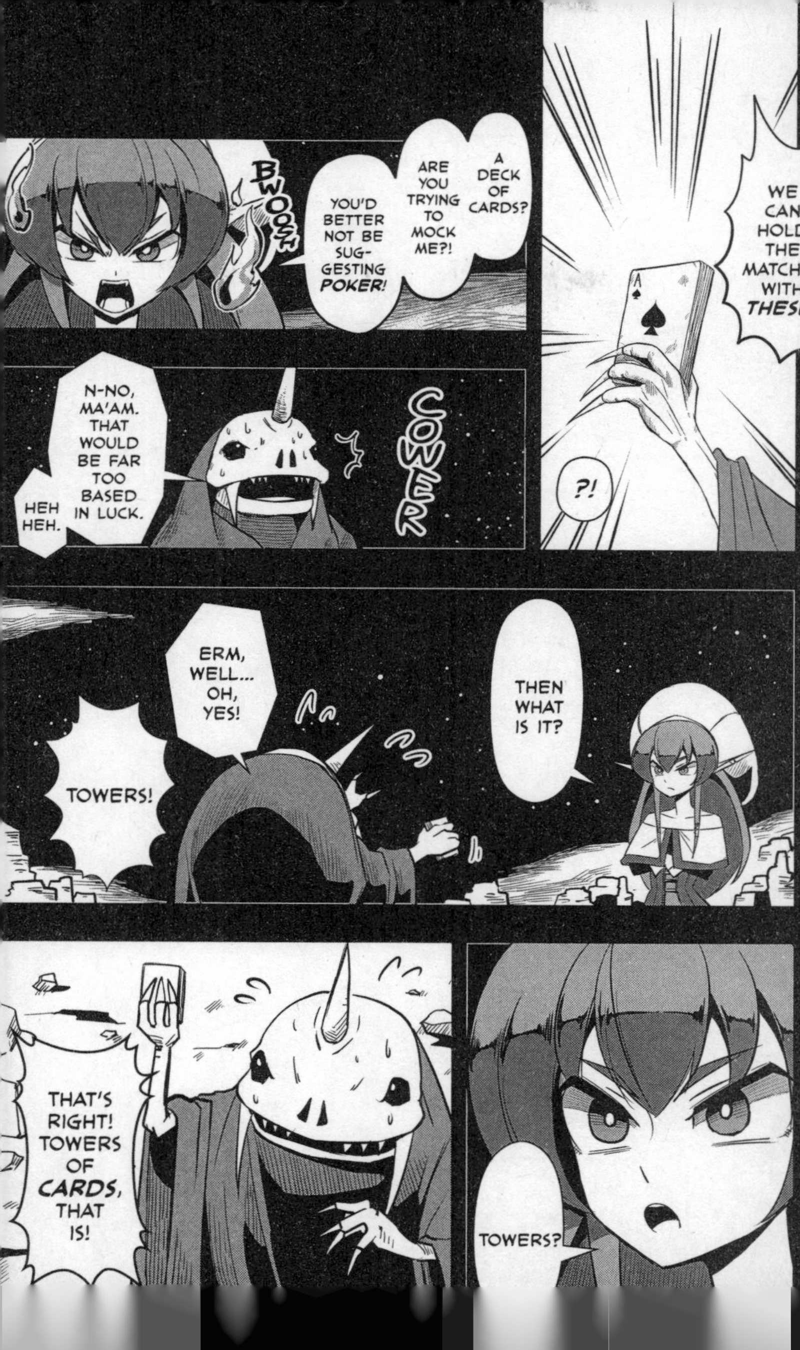
WE CAN HOLD THE MATCHES WITH *THESE!*
?!
A DECK OF CARDS?
ARE YOU TRYING TO MOCK ME?!
YOU'D BETTER NOT BE SUG-GESTING *POKER!*
BWOOSH
COWER
N-NO, MA'AM. THAT WOULD BE FAR TOO BASED IN LUCK.
HEH HEH.
THEN WHAT IS IT?
ERM, WELL... OH, YES!
TOWERS!
TOWERS?
THAT'S RIGHT! TOWERS OF *CARDS*, THAT IS!

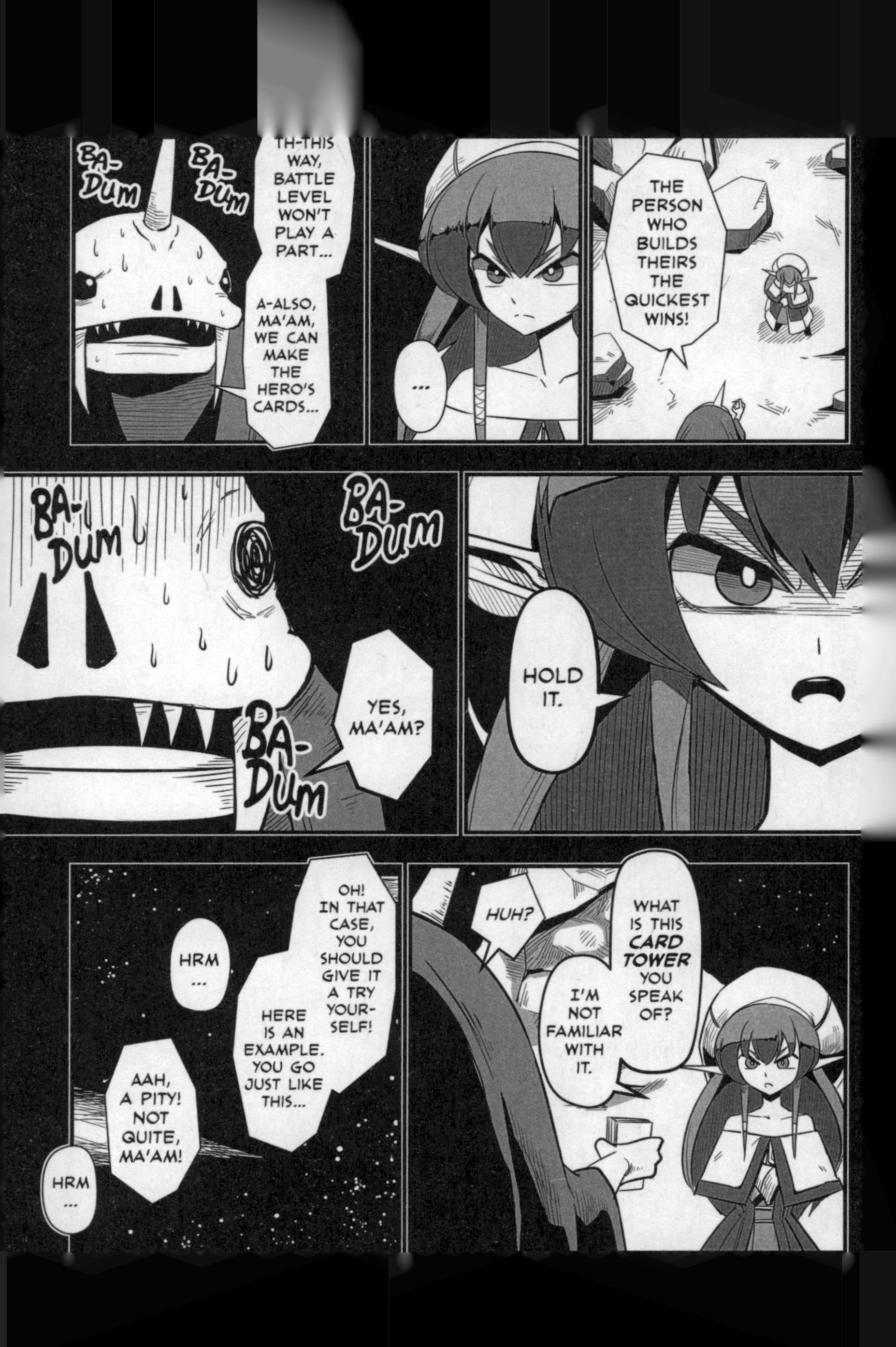
THE PERSON WHO BUILDS THEIRS THE QUICKEST WINS!
...
BA-DUM
BA-DUM
TH-THIS WAY, BATTLE LEVEL WON'T PLAY A PART...
A-ALSO, MA'AM, WE CAN MAKE THE HERO'S CARDS...
HOLD IT.
BA-DUM
BA-DUM
YES, MA'AM?
BA-DUM
WHAT IS THIS *CARD TOWER* YOU SPEAK OF?
HUH?
I'M NOT FAMILIAR WITH IT.
OH! IN THAT CASE, YOU SHOULD GIVE IT A TRY YOURSELF!
HRM...
HERE IS AN EXAMPLE. YOU GO JUST LIKE THIS...
AAH, A PITY! NOT QUITE, MA'AM!
HRM...

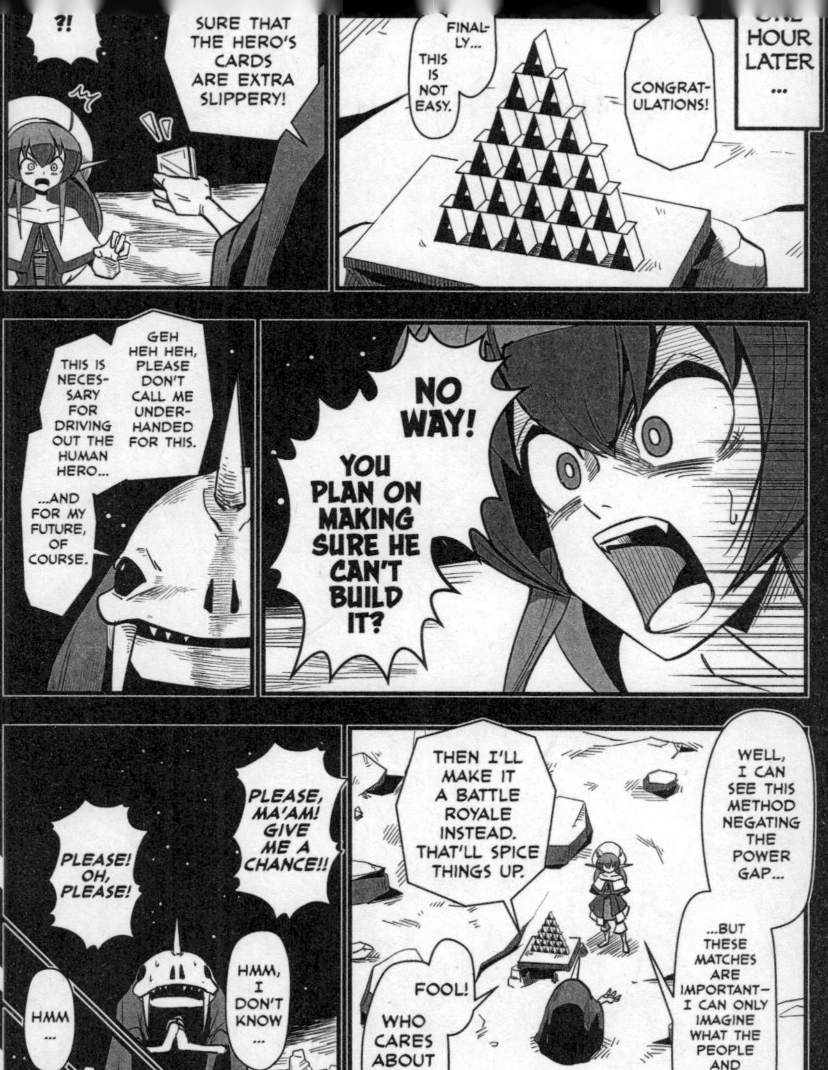
HOUR LATER …
CONGRAT-ULATIONS!
FINAL-LY… THIS IS NOT EASY.
SURE THAT THE HERO'S CARDS ARE EXTRA SLIPPERY!
?!
NO WAY!
YOU PLAN ON MAKING SURE HE CAN'T BUILD IT?
GEH HEH HEH, PLEASE DON'T CALL ME UNDER-HANDED FOR THIS.
THIS IS NECES-SARY FOR DRIVING OUT THE HUMAN HERO…
…AND FOR MY FUTURE, OF COURSE.
WELL, I CAN SEE THIS METHOD NEGATING THE POWER GAP…
THEN I'LL MAKE IT A BATTLE ROYALE INSTEAD. THAT'LL SPICE THINGS UP.
…BUT THESE MATCHES ARE IMPORTANT— I CAN ONLY IMAGINE WHAT THE PEOPLE AND FIGHTERS WOULD THINK…
FOOL!
WHO CARES ABOUT "SPICING THINGS UP"?!
PLEASE, MA'AM! GIVE ME A CHANCE!!
PLEASE! OH, PLEASE!
HMM, I DON'T KNOW …
HMM …

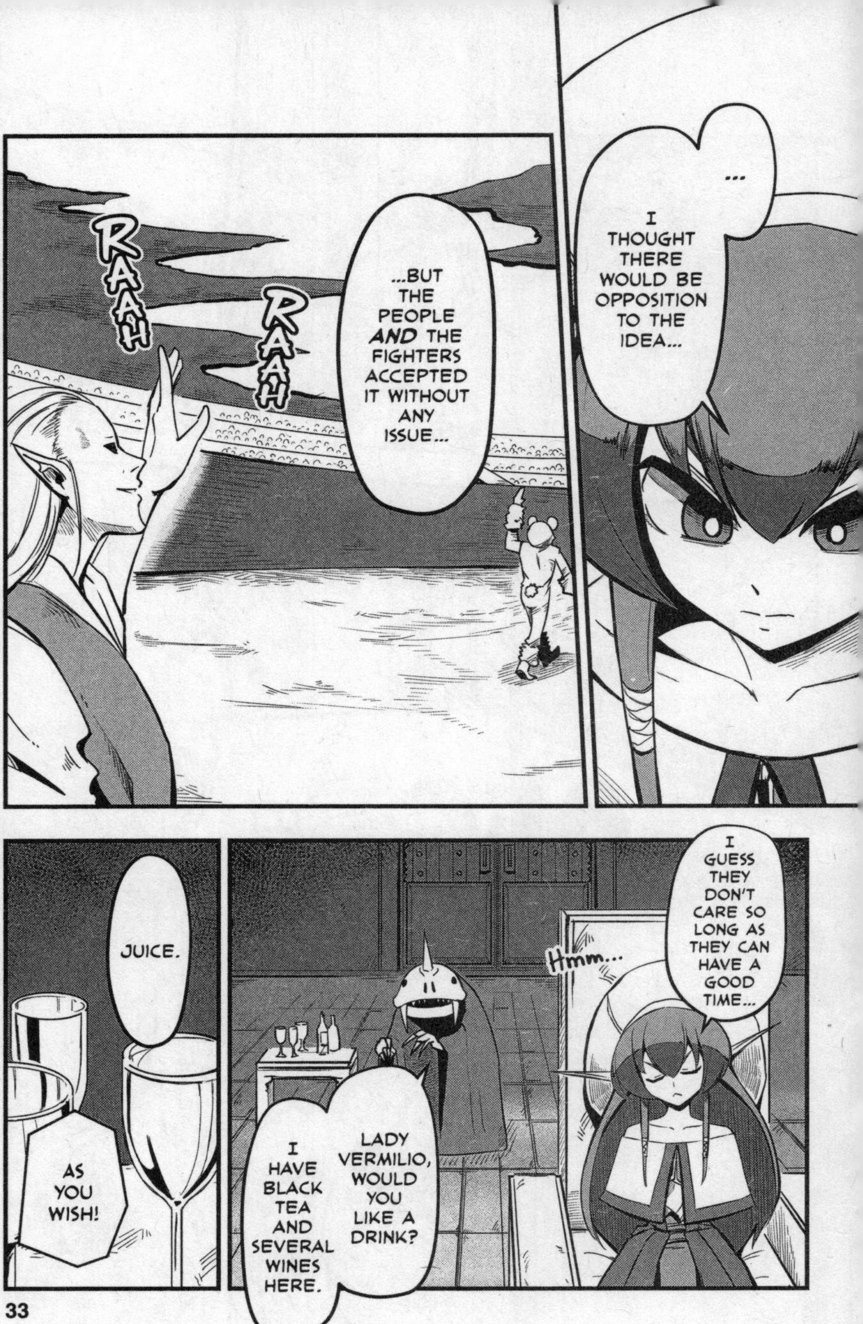
...
I THOUGHT THERE WOULD BE OPPOSITION TO THE IDEA...
...BUT THE PEOPLE AND THE FIGHTERS ACCEPTED IT WITHOUT ANY ISSUE...
RAAH
RAAH
I GUESS THEY DON'T CARE SO LONG AS THEY CAN HAVE A GOOD TIME...
Hmm...
LADY VERMILIO, WOULD YOU LIKE A DRINK?
I HAVE BLACK TEA AND SEVERAL WINES HERE.
JUICE.
AS YOU WISH!

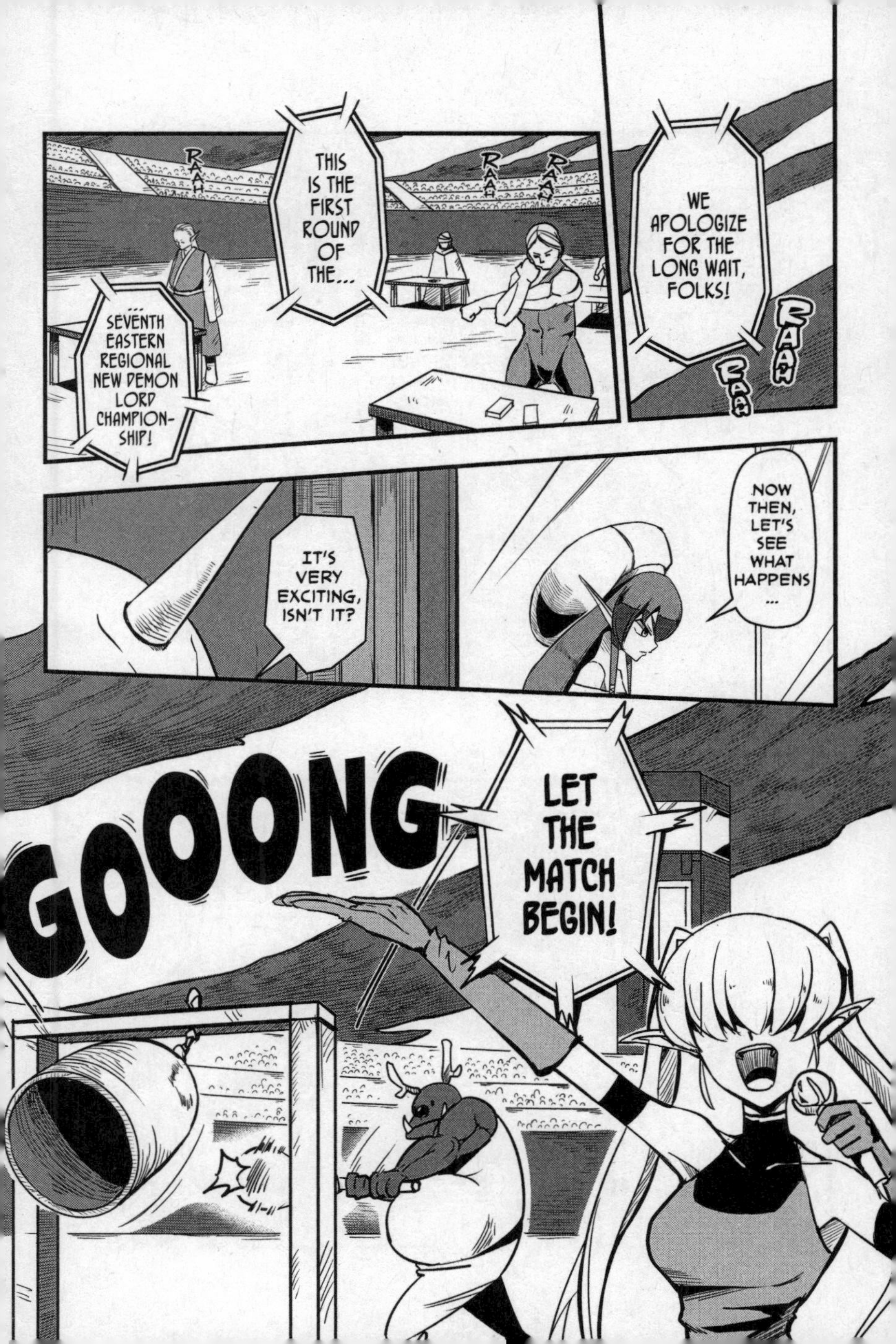

WE APOLOGIZE FOR THE LONG WAIT, FOLKS!
RAAAH
RAAH
RAAH
RAAH
RAAH
THIS IS THE FIRST ROUND OF THE...
...SEVENTH EASTERN REGIONAL NEW DEMON LORD CHAMPIONSHIP!
NOW THEN, LET'S SEE WHAT HAPPENS...
IT'S VERY EXCITING, ISN'T IT?
LET THE MATCH BEGIN!
GOOONG

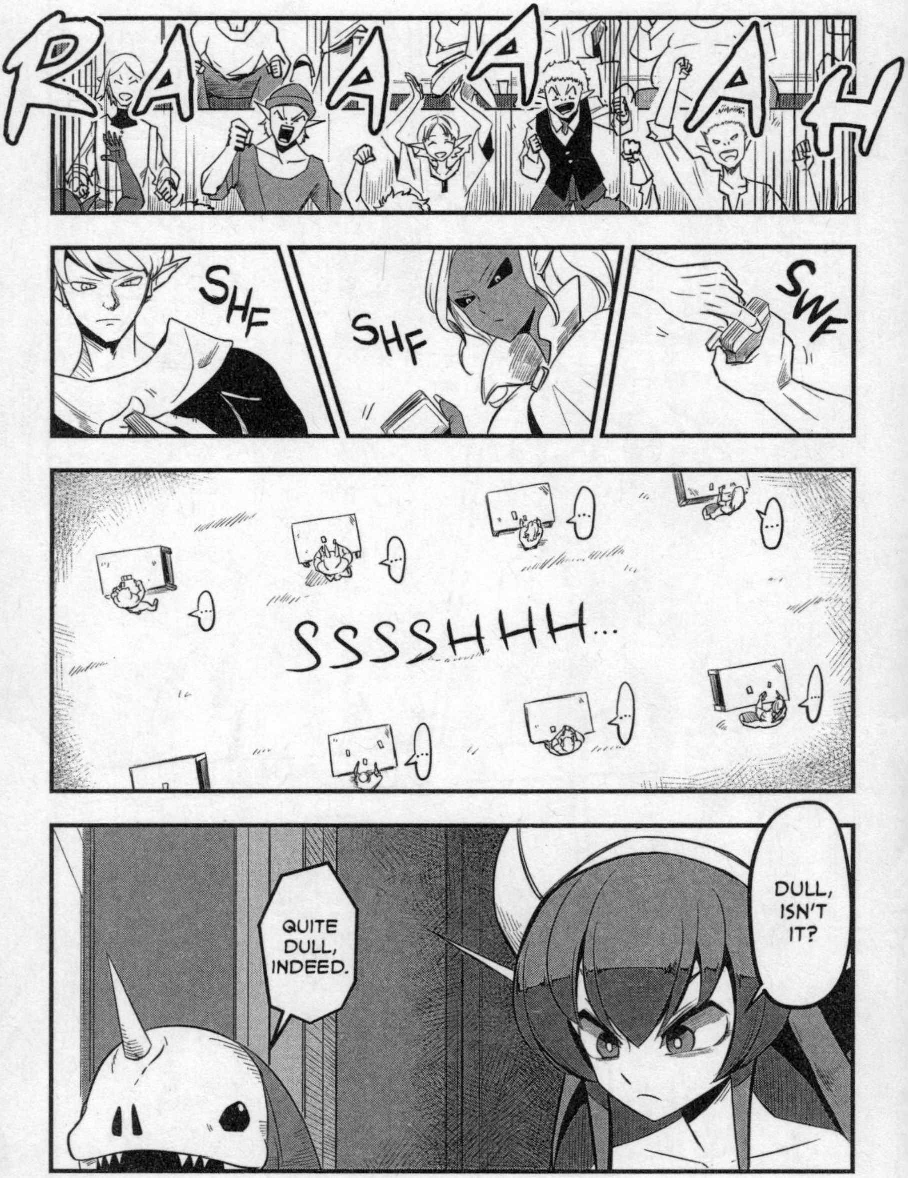
RAAAAAH
SWF
SHF
SHF
SSSSHHH...
DULL, ISN'T IT?
QUITE DULL, INDEED.

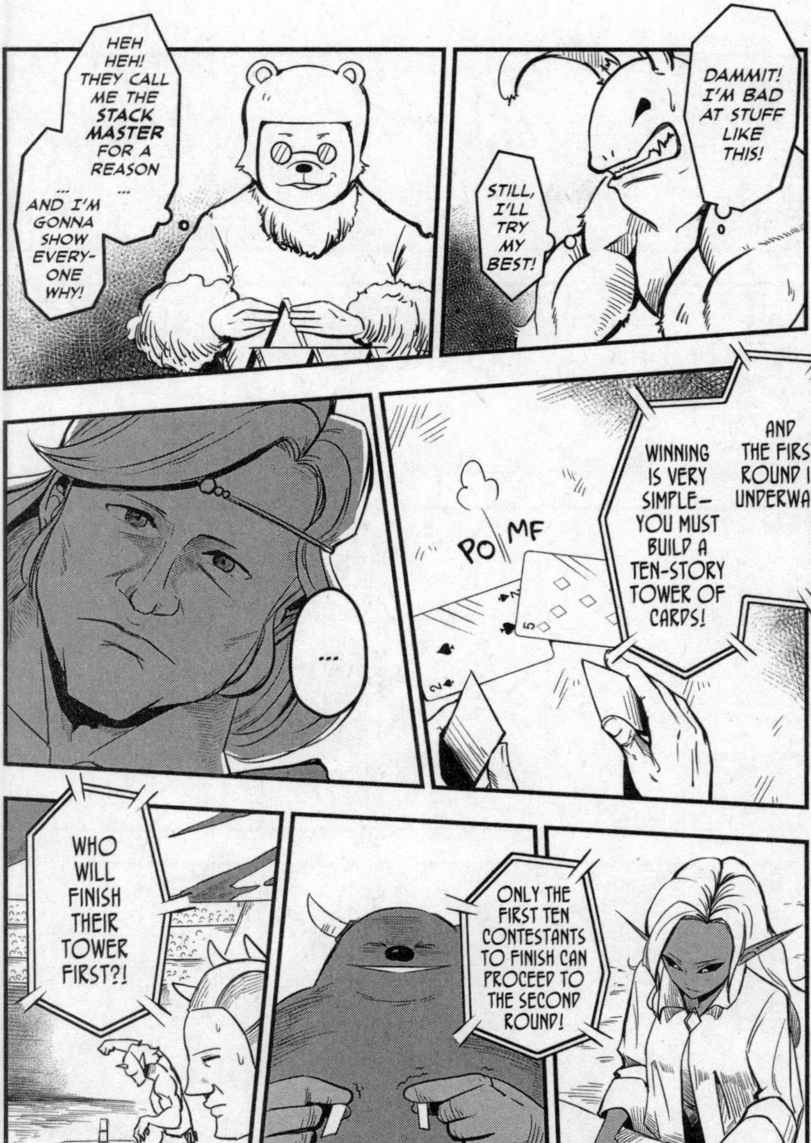
DAMMIT! I'M BAD AT STUFF LIKE THIS!
STILL, I'LL TRY MY BEST!
HEH HEH! THEY CALL ME THE STACK MASTER FOR A REASON ... ...
AND I'M GONNA SHOW EVERY-ONE WHY!
AND THE FIRST ROUND IS UNDERWAY!
WINNING IS VERY SIMPLE—YOU MUST BUILD A TEN-STORY TOWER OF CARDS!
POMF
...
ONLY THE FIRST TEN CONTESTANTS TO FINISH CAN PROCEED TO THE SECOND ROUND!
WHO WILL FINISH THEIR TOWER FIRST?!

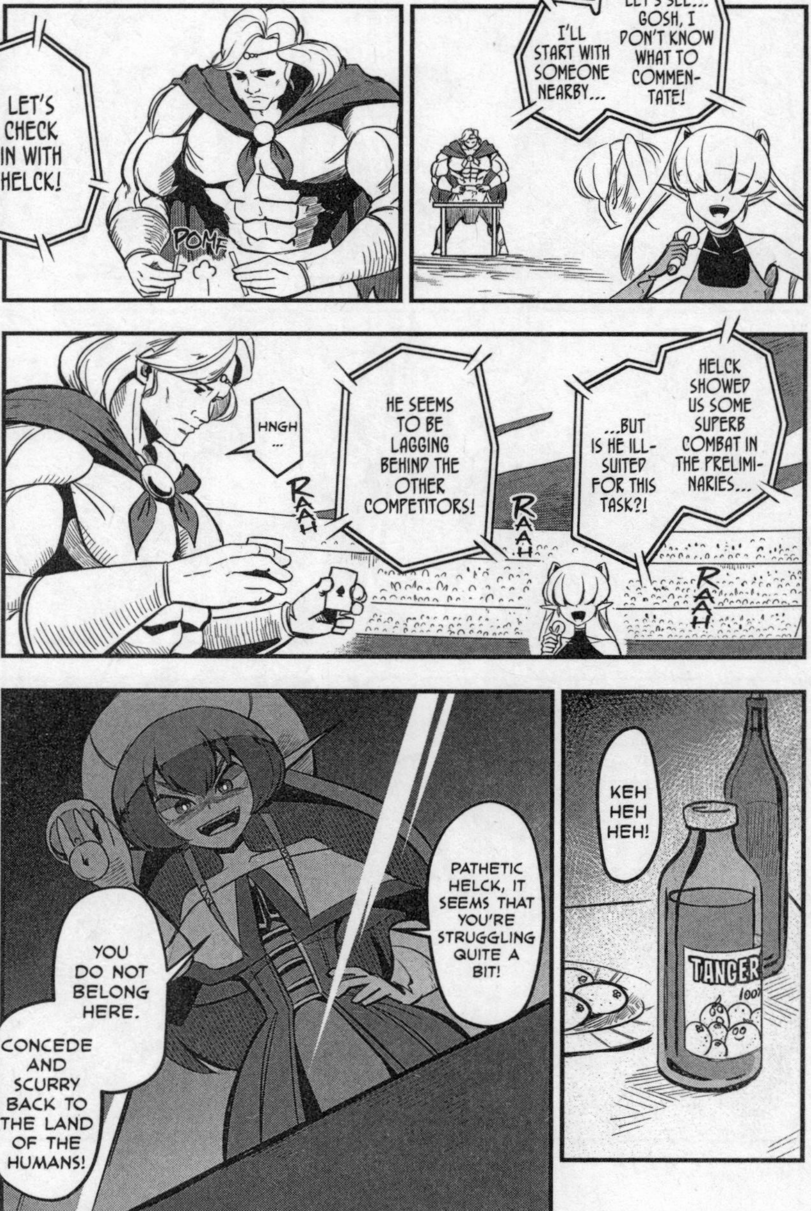
LET'S SEE... GOSH, I DON'T KNOW WHAT TO COMMENTATE!
I'LL START WITH SOMEONE NEARBY...
LET'S CHECK IN WITH HELCK!
POMF
HELCK SHOWED US SOME SUPERB COMBAT IN THE PRELIMINARIES...
...BUT IS HE ILL-SUITED FOR THIS TASK?!
RAAH
RAAH
HE SEEMS TO BE LAGGING BEHIND THE OTHER COMPETITORS!
RAAH
HNGH...
KEH HEH HEH!
TANGER
PATHETIC HELCK, IT SEEMS THAT YOU'RE STRUGGLING QUITE A BIT!
YOU DO NOT BELONG HERE.
CONCEDE AND SCURRY BACK TO THE LAND OF THE HUMANS!

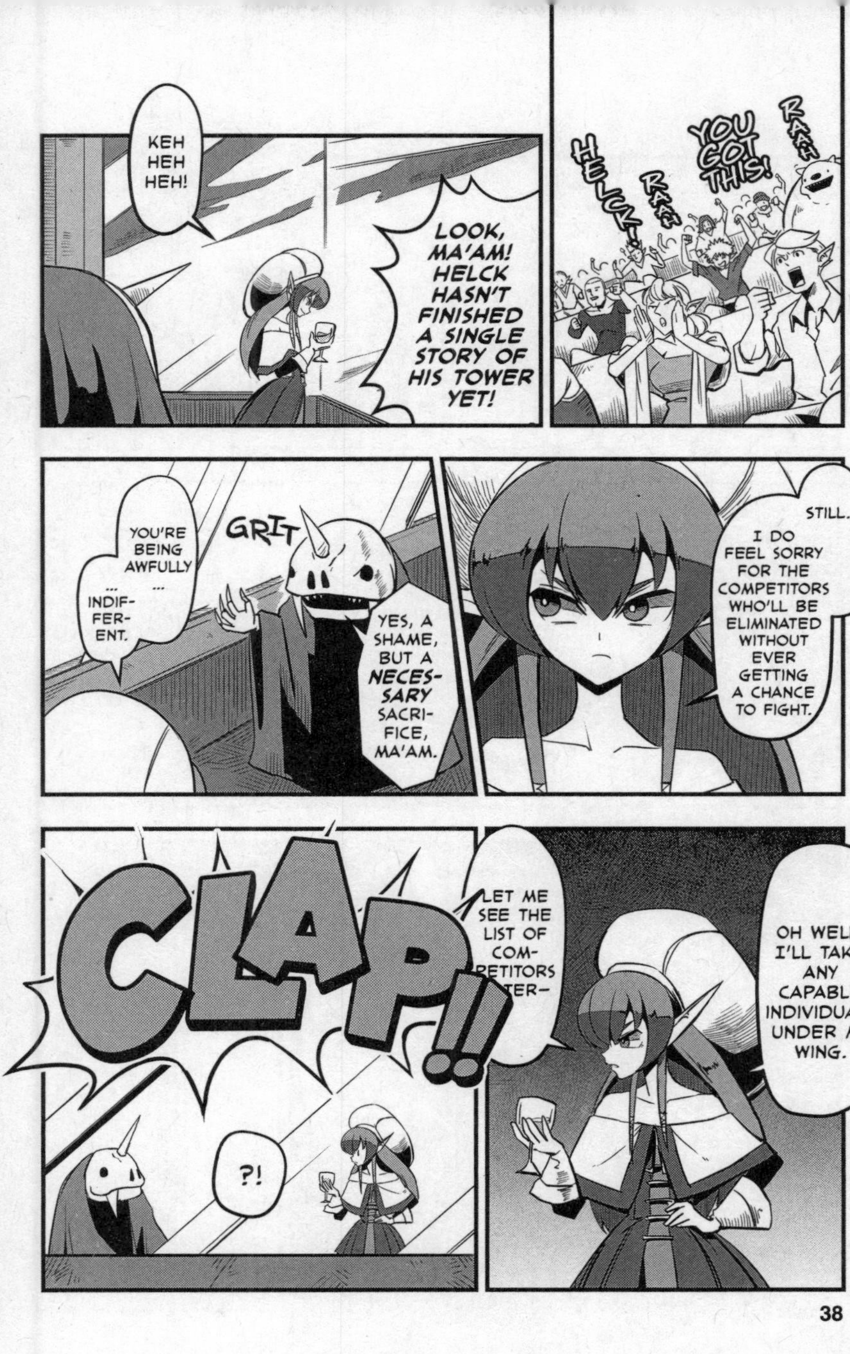
RAAH
YOU GOT THIS!
RAAH
HELCK!
KEH HEH HEH!
LOOK, MA'AM! HELCK HASN'T FINISHED A SINGLE STORY OF HIS TOWER YET!
STILL... I DO FEEL SORRY FOR THE COMPETITORS WHO'LL BE ELIMINATED WITHOUT EVER GETTING A CHANCE TO FIGHT.
YES, A SHAME, BUT A *NECES-SARY* SACRI-FICE, MA'AM.
GRIT
YOU'RE BEING AWFULLY ... ... INDIF-FER-ENT.
OH WELL. I'LL TAKE ANY CAPABLE INDIVIDUALS UNDER MY WING.
LET ME SEE THE LIST OF COM-PETITORS AFTER-
CLAP!!
?!

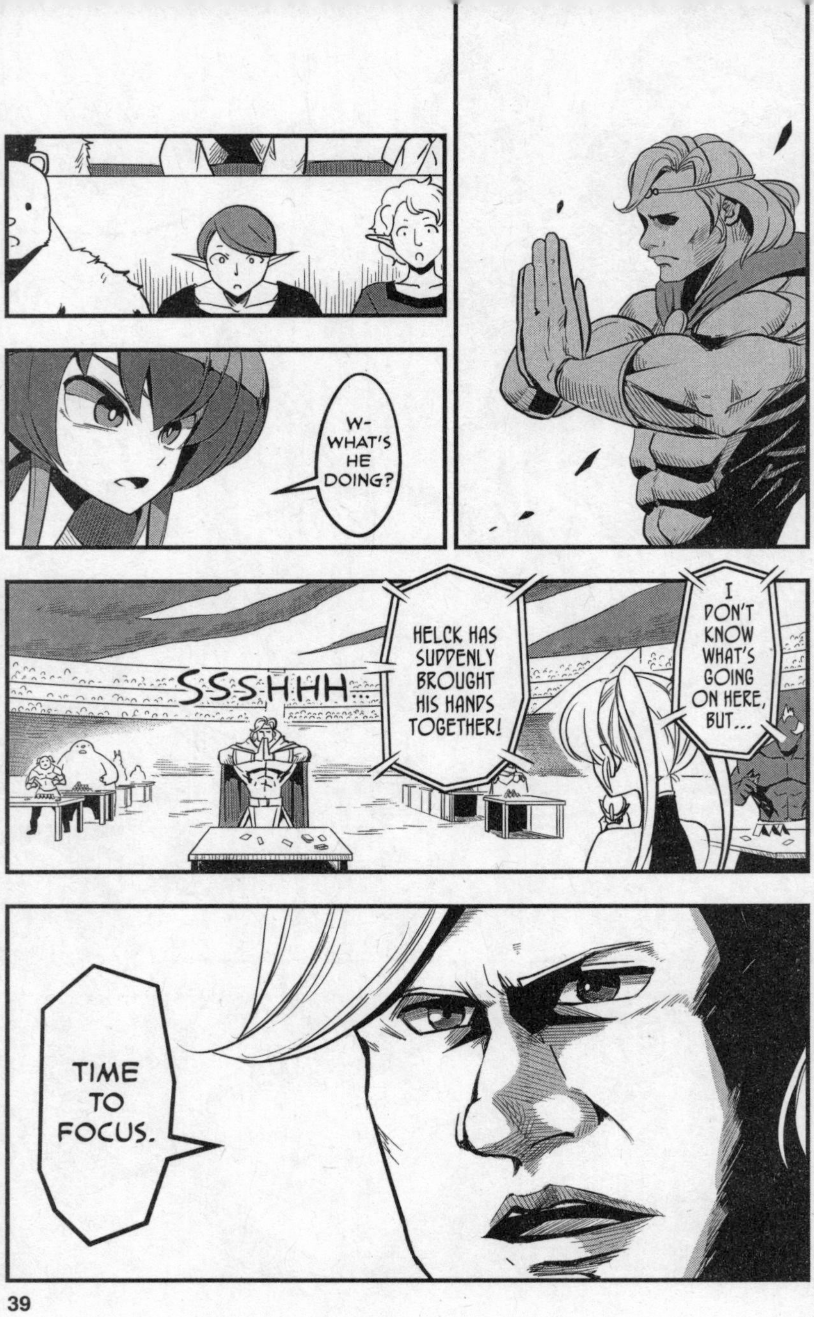
W-WHAT'S HE DOING?
I DON'T KNOW WHAT'S GOING ON HERE, BUT...
HELCK HAS SUDDENLY BROUGHT HIS HANDS TOGETHER!
SSSHHH...
TIME TO FOCUS.

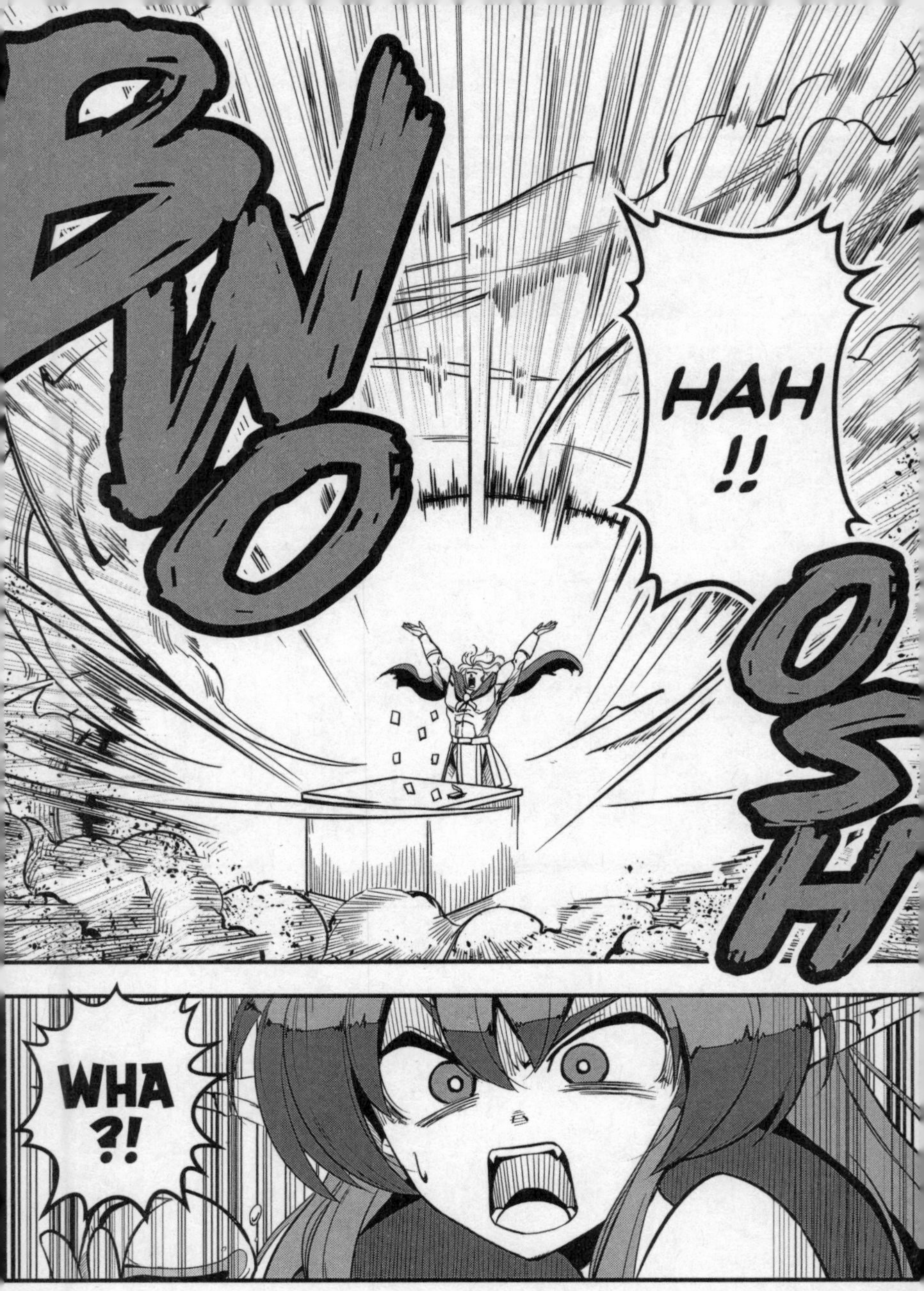
HAH !!
BWOOSH
WHA ?!

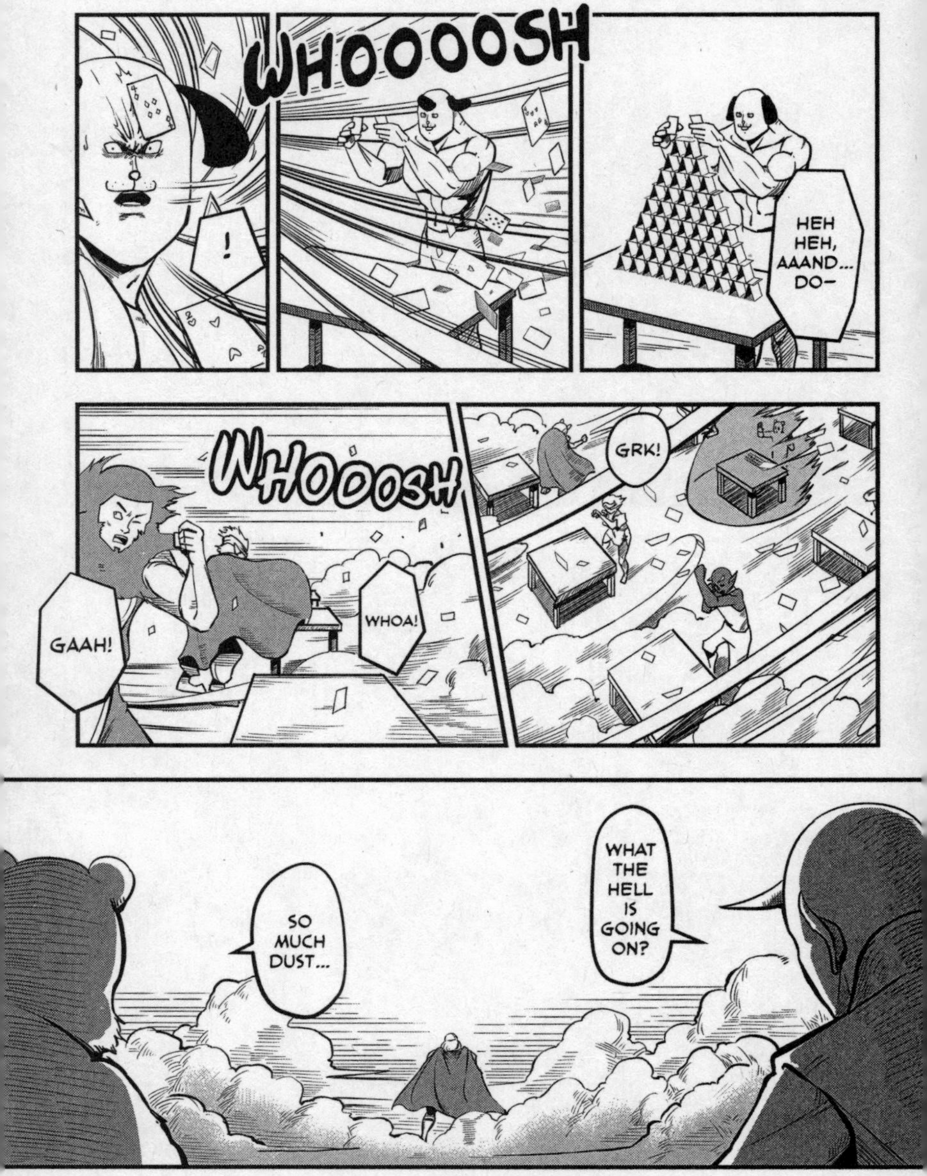
HEH HEH, AAAND... DO—
WHOOOOSH
!
GRK!
WHOOOSH
WHOA!
GAAH!
WHAT THE HELL IS GOING ON?
SO MUCH DUST...

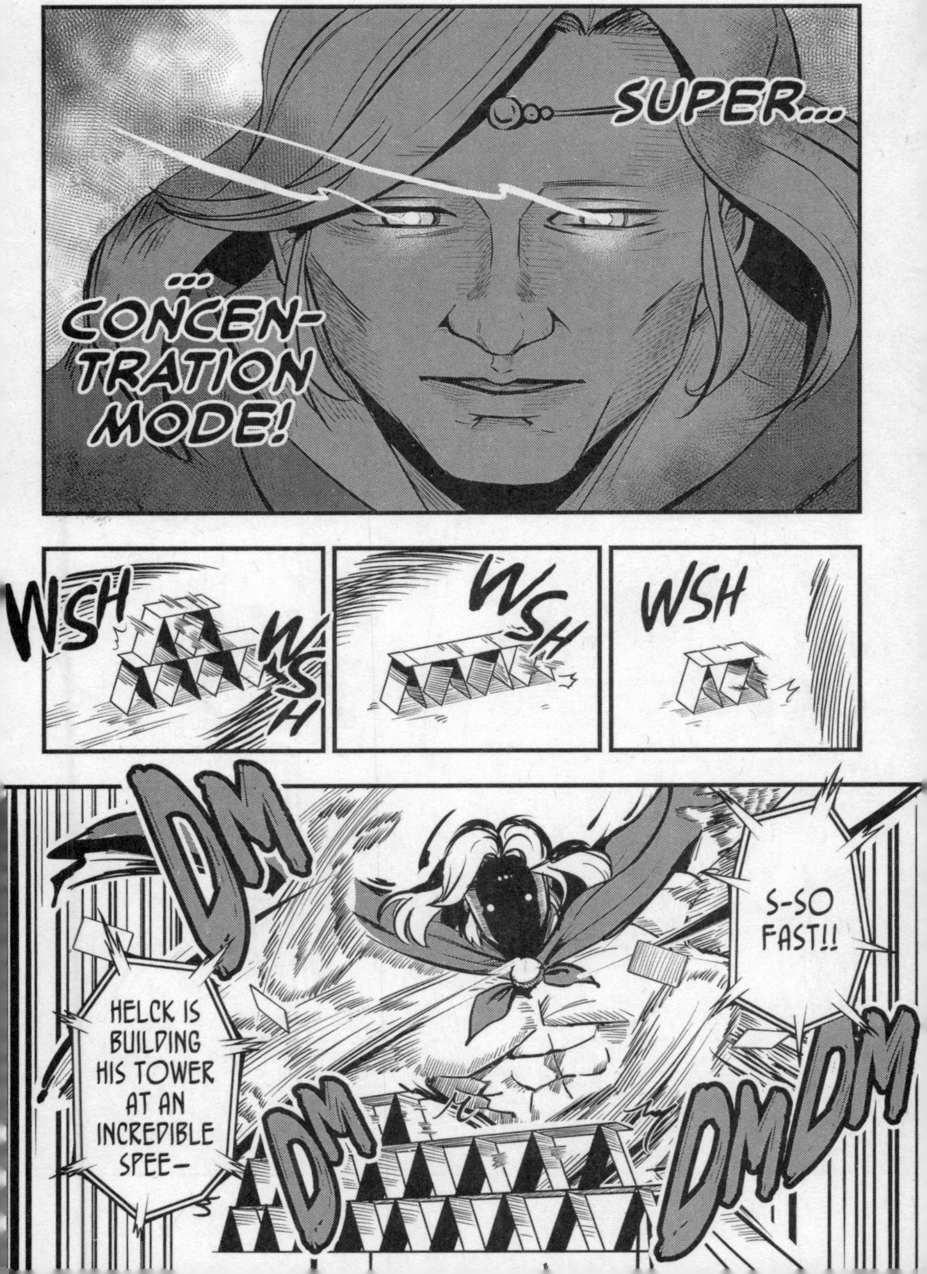
SUPER...
...CONCEN-TRATION MODE!
WSH
WSH
WSH WSH
S-SO FAST!!
DM DM
DM
HELCK IS BUILDING HIS TOWER AT AN INCREDIBLE SPEE—
DM

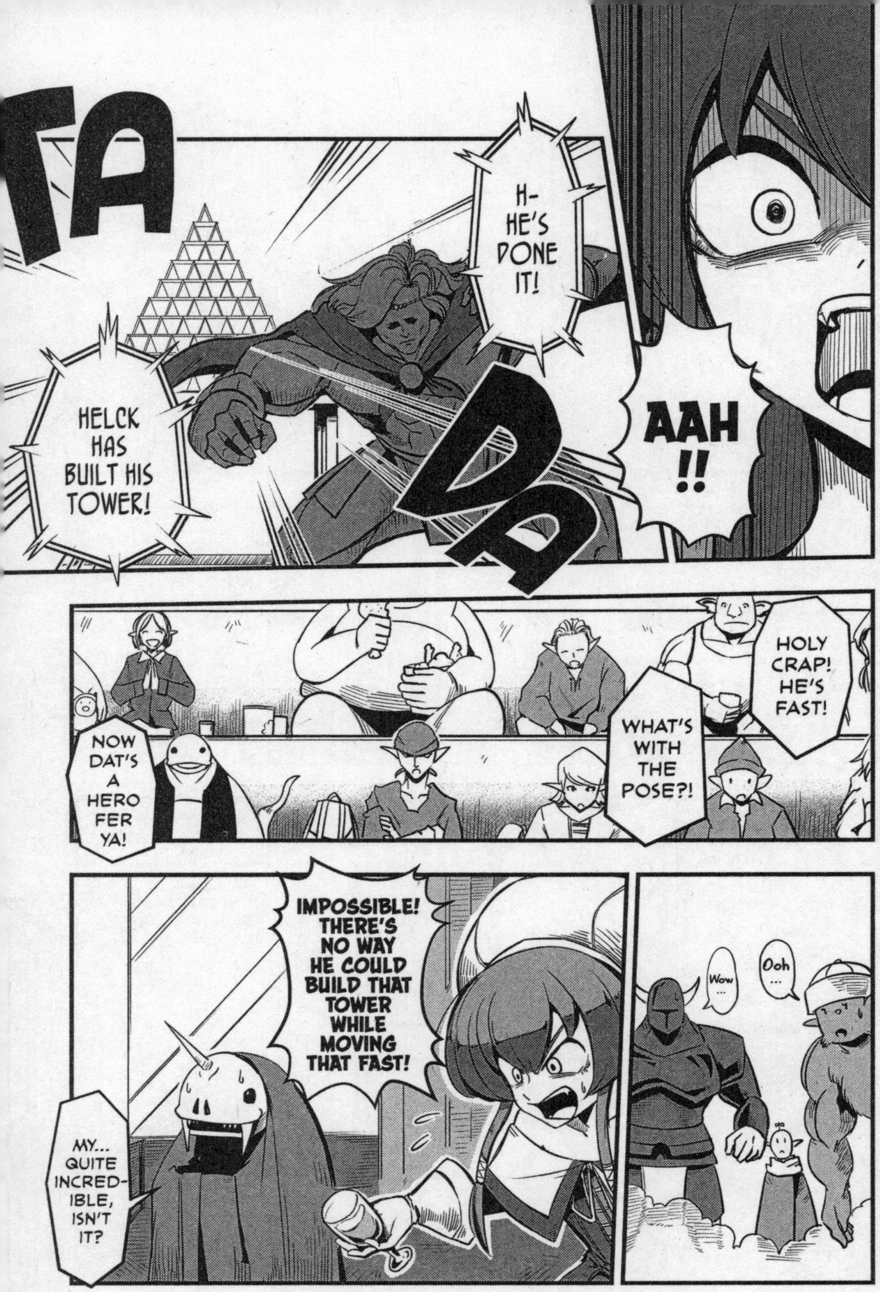
AAH!!
H-HE'S DONE IT!
TA DA
HELCK HAS BUILT HIS TOWER!
HOLY CRAP! HE'S FAST!
WHAT'S WITH THE POSE?!
NOW DAT'S A HERO FER YA!
Ooh...
Wow...
IMPOSSIBLE! THERE'S NO WAY HE COULD BUILD THAT TOWER WHILE MOVING THAT FAST!
MY... QUITE INCREDIBLE, ISN'T IT?

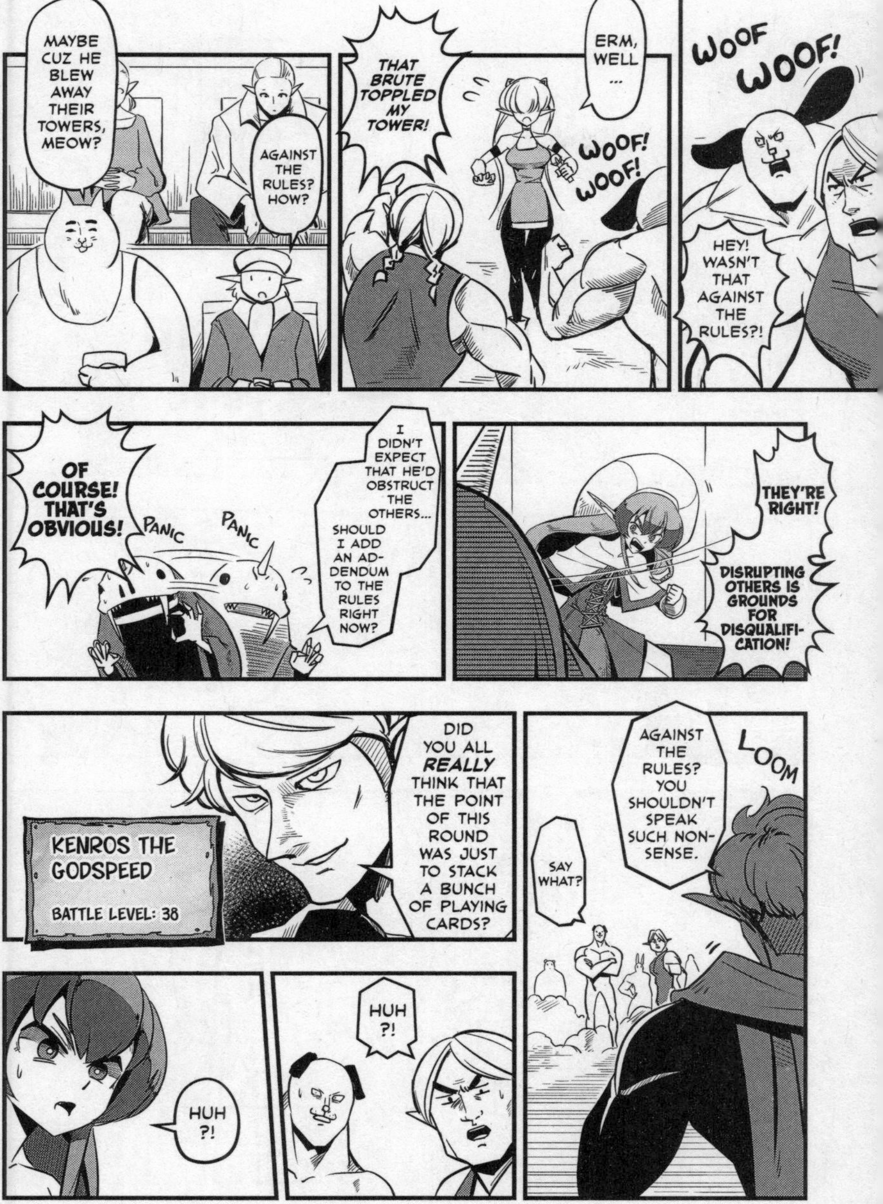
WOOF WOOF!
HEY! WASN'T THAT AGAINST THE RULES?!
ERM, WELL...
THAT BRUTE TOPPLED MY TOWER!
WOOF! WOOF!
AGAINST THE RULES? HOW?
MAYBE CUZ HE BLEW AWAY THEIR TOWERS, MEOW?
THEY'RE RIGHT!
DISRUPTING OTHERS IS GROUNDS FOR DISQUALIFICATION!
I DIDN'T EXPECT THAT HE'D OBSTRUCT THE OTHERS... SHOULD I ADD AN ADDENDUM TO THE RULES RIGHT NOW?
OF COURSE! THAT'S OBVIOUS!
PANIC
PANIC
LOOM
AGAINST THE RULES? YOU SHOULDN'T SPEAK SUCH NONSENSE.
SAY WHAT?
DID YOU ALL *REALLY* THINK THAT THE POINT OF THIS ROUND WAS JUST TO STACK A BUNCH OF PLAYING CARDS?
KENROS THE GODSPEED
BATTLE LEVEL: 38
HUH ?!
HUH ?!

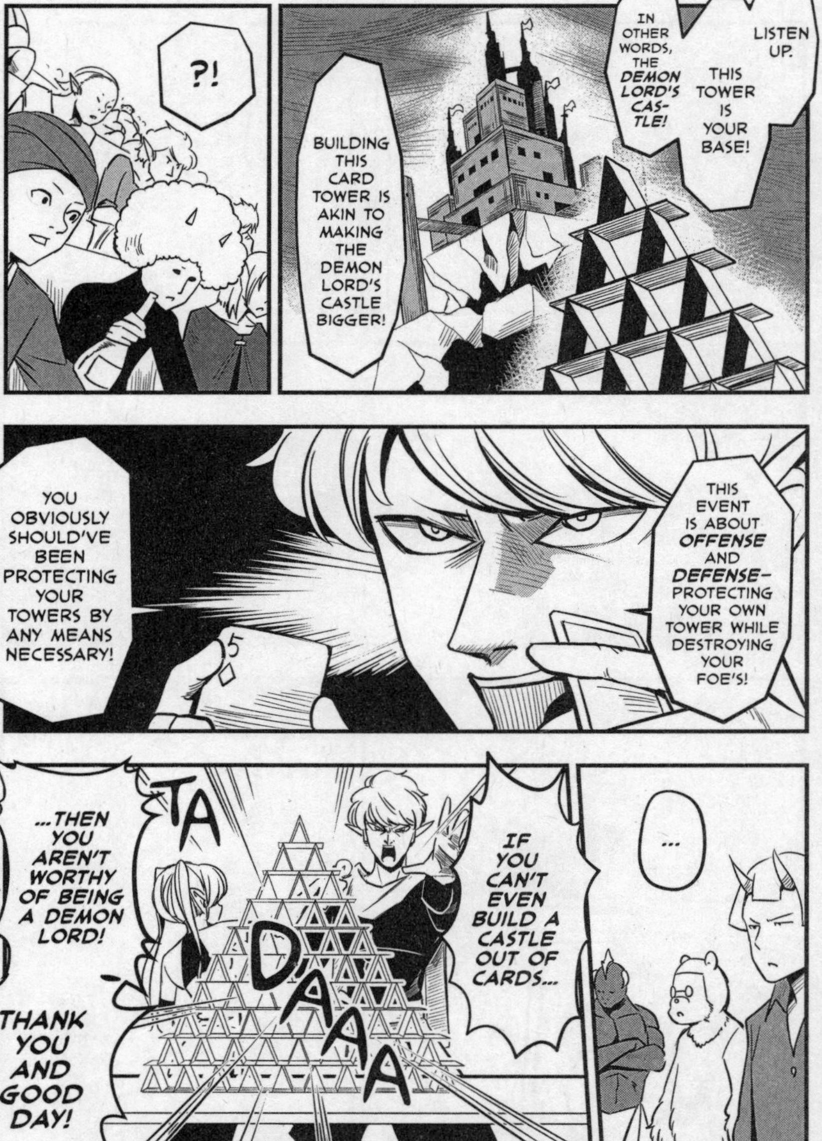
LISTEN UP. THIS TOWER IS YOUR BASE!
IN OTHER WORDS, THE DEMON LORD'S CAS-TLE!
BUILDING THIS CARD TOWER IS AKIN TO MAKING THE DEMON LORD'S CASTLE BIGGER!
?!
THIS EVENT IS ABOUT OFFENSE AND DEFENSE–PROTECTING YOUR OWN TOWER WHILE DESTROYING YOUR FOE'S!
YOU OBVIOUSLY SHOULD'VE BEEN PROTECTING YOUR TOWERS BY ANY MEANS NECESSARY!
...
IF YOU CAN'T EVEN BUILD A CASTLE OUT OF CARDS...
...THEN YOU AREN'T WORTHY OF BEING A DEMON LORD!
TADAAAA
THANK YOU AND GOOD DAY!

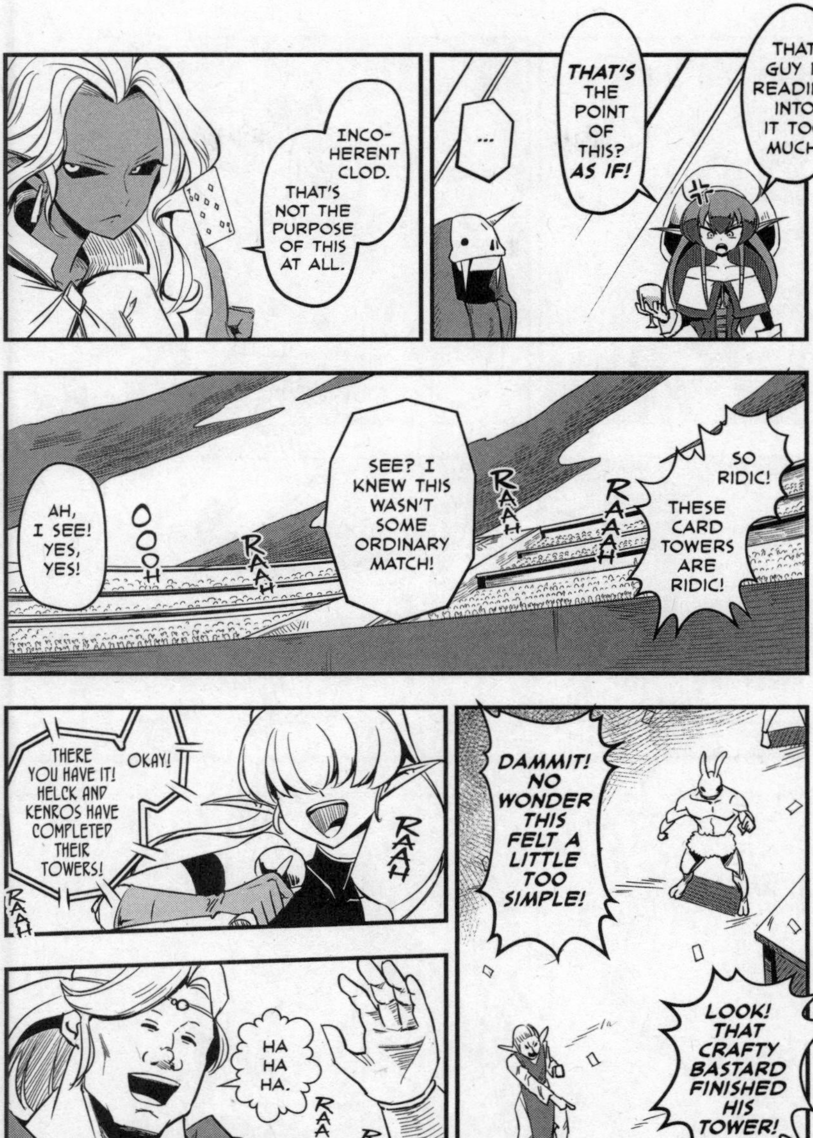
THAT GUY IS READING INTO IT TOO MUCH!
THAT'S THE POINT OF THIS? *AS IF!*
...
INCO-HERENT CLOD.
THAT'S NOT THE PURPOSE OF THIS AT ALL.
SO RIDIC!
THESE CARD TOWERS ARE RIDIC!
RAAAH
RAAH
SEE? I KNEW THIS WASN'T SOME ORDINARY MATCH!
RAAH
OOOH
AH, I SEE! YES, YES!
DAMMIT! NO WONDER THIS FELT A LITTLE TOO SIMPLE!
LOOK! THAT CRAFTY BASTARD FINISHED HIS TOWER!
RAAH
OKAY!
THERE YOU HAVE IT! HELCK AND KENROS HAVE COMPLETED THEIR TOWERS!
RAAH
HA HA HA.
RAAH
RAAH

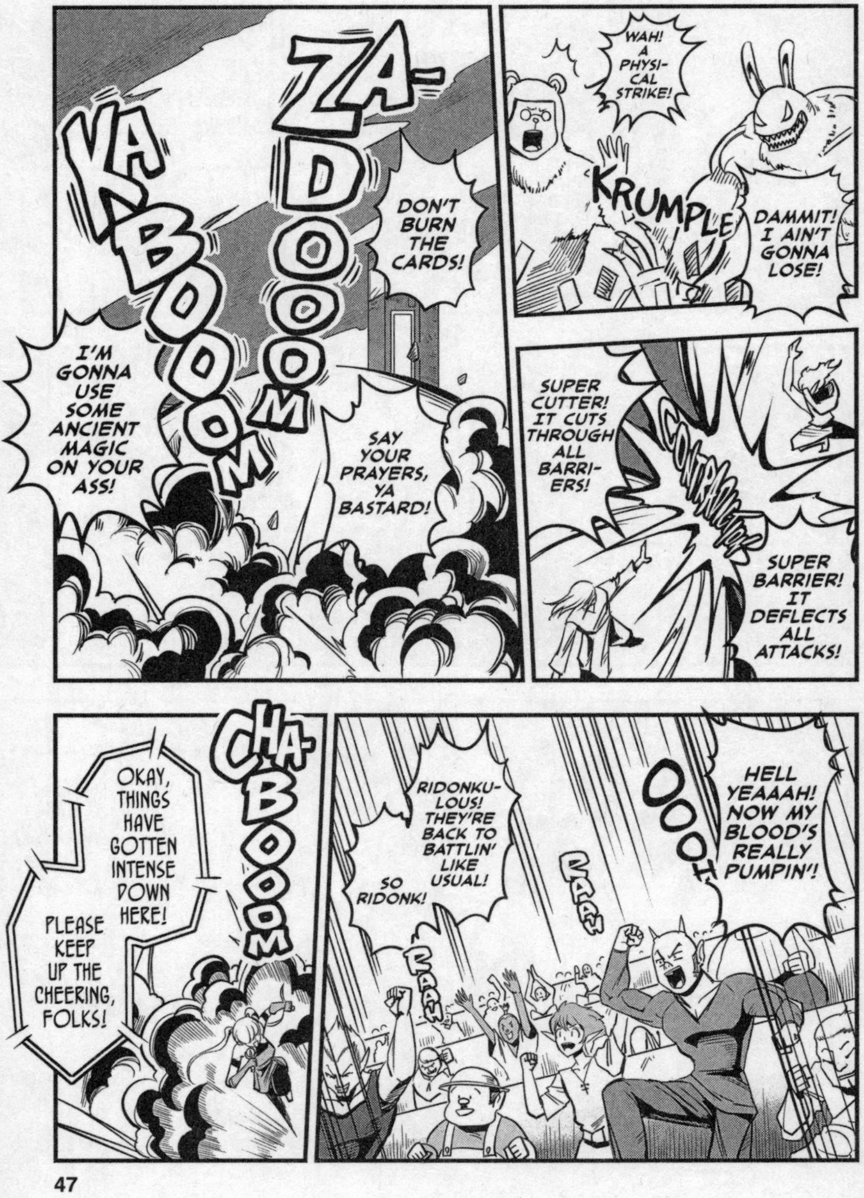
WAH! A PHYSICAL STRIKE!
KRUMPLE
DAMMIT! I AIN'T GONNA LOSE!
SUPER CUTTER! IT CUTS THROUGH ALL BARRIERS!
SUPER BARRIER! IT DEFLECTS ALL ATTACKS!
ZA-DOOOOM
DON'T BURN THE CARDS!
KA-BOOOOM
SAY YOUR PRAYERS, YA BASTARD!
I'M GONNA USE SOME ANCIENT MAGIC ON YOUR ASS!
HELL YEAAAH! NOW MY BLOOD'S REALLY PUMPIN'!
OOOOH
RIDONKULOUS! THEY'RE BACK TO BATTLIN' LIKE USUAL!
SO RIDONK!
RAAAH
RAAAH
CHA-BOOOOM
OKAY, THINGS HAVE GOTTEN INTENSE DOWN HERE!
PLEASE KEEP UP THE CHEERING, FOLKS!

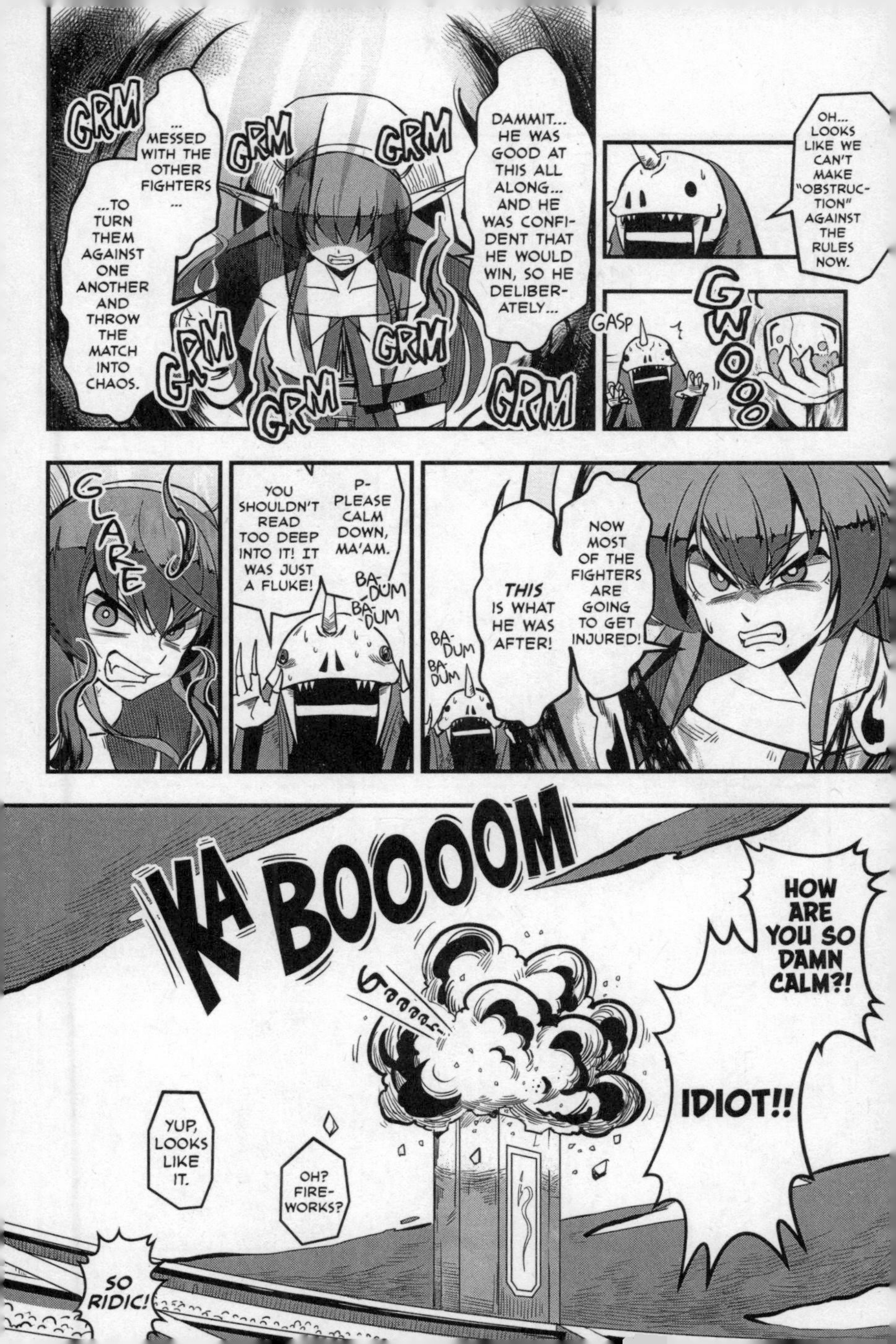
OH... LOOKS LIKE WE CAN'T MAKE "OBSTRUCTION" AGAINST THE RULES NOW.
GWOOO
GASP
DAMMIT... HE WAS GOOD AT THIS ALL ALONG... AND HE WAS CONFIDENT THAT HE WOULD WIN, SO HE DELIBERATELY...
GRM GRM GRM GRM GRM GRM GRM
... MESSED WITH THE OTHER FIGHTERS ...
...TO TURN THEM AGAINST ONE ANOTHER AND THROW THE MATCH INTO CHAOS.
NOW MOST OF THE FIGHTERS ARE GOING TO GET INJURED!
THIS IS WHAT HE WAS AFTER!
BA-DUM BA-DUM
P-PLEASE CALM DOWN, MA'AM.
YOU SHOULDN'T READ TOO DEEP INTO IT! IT WAS JUST A FLUKE!
BA-DUM BA-DUM
GLARE
HOW ARE YOU SO DAMN CALM?!
IDIOT!!
KA BOOOOM
OH? FIRE-WORKS?
YUP, LOOKS LIKE IT.
SO RIDIC!

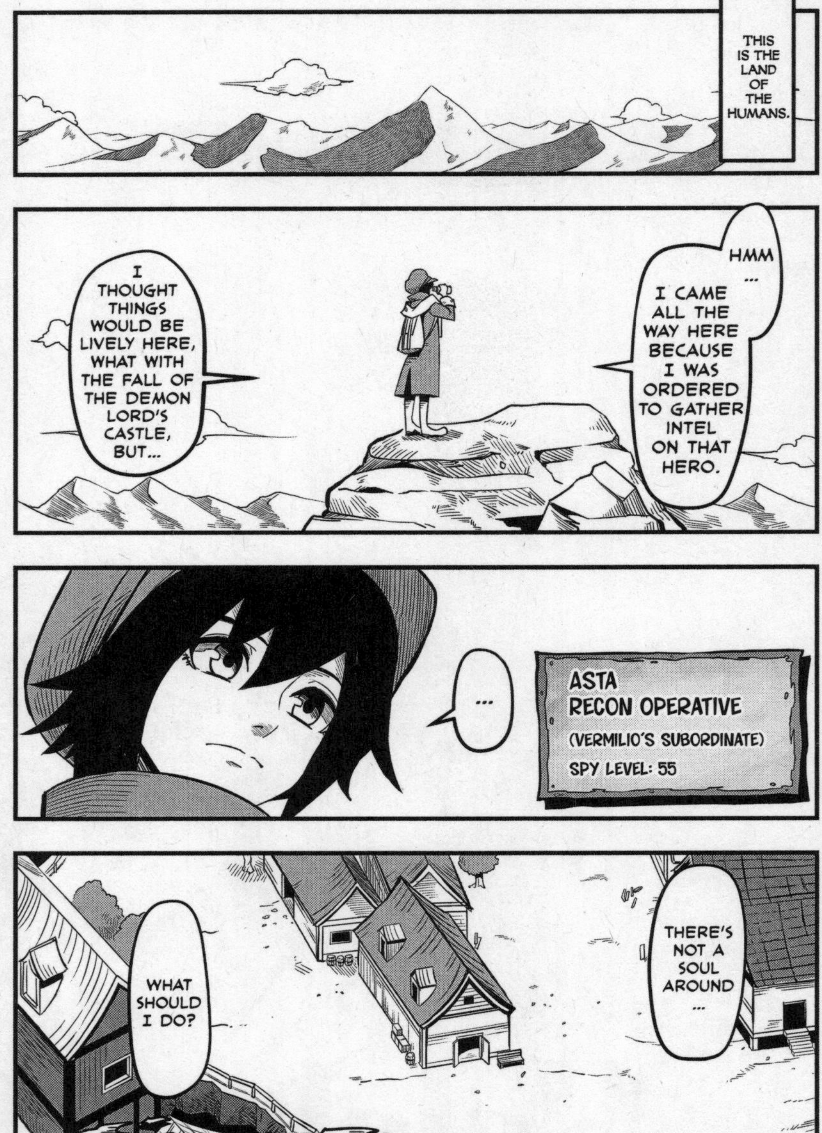
THIS IS THE LAND OF THE HUMANS.
HMM... I CAME ALL THE WAY HERE BECAUSE I WAS ORDERED TO GATHER INTEL ON THAT HERO.
I THOUGHT THINGS WOULD BE LIVELY HERE, WHAT WITH THE FALL OF THE DEMON LORD'S CASTLE, BUT...
ASTA RECON OPERATIVE (VERMILIO'S SUBORDINATE) SPY LEVEL: 55
...
THERE'S NOT A SOUL AROUND...
WHAT SHOULD I DO?
To be continued

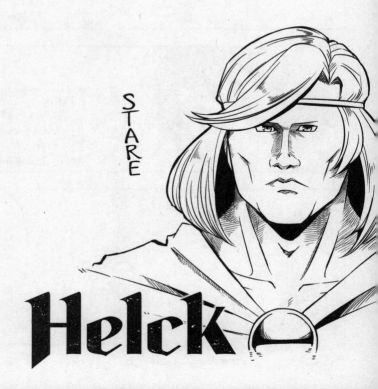

STARE

Helck

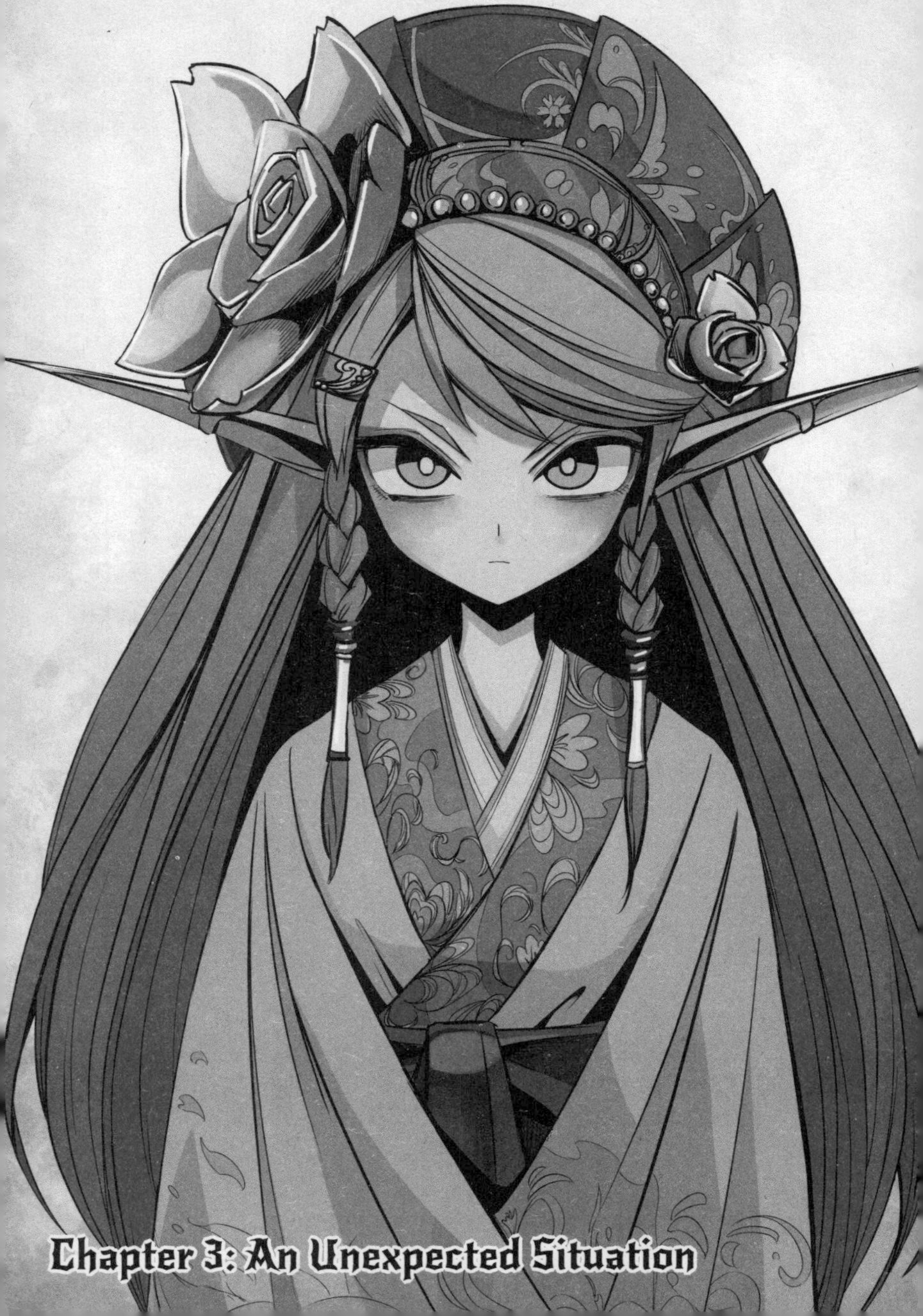

Chapter 3: An Unexpected Situation

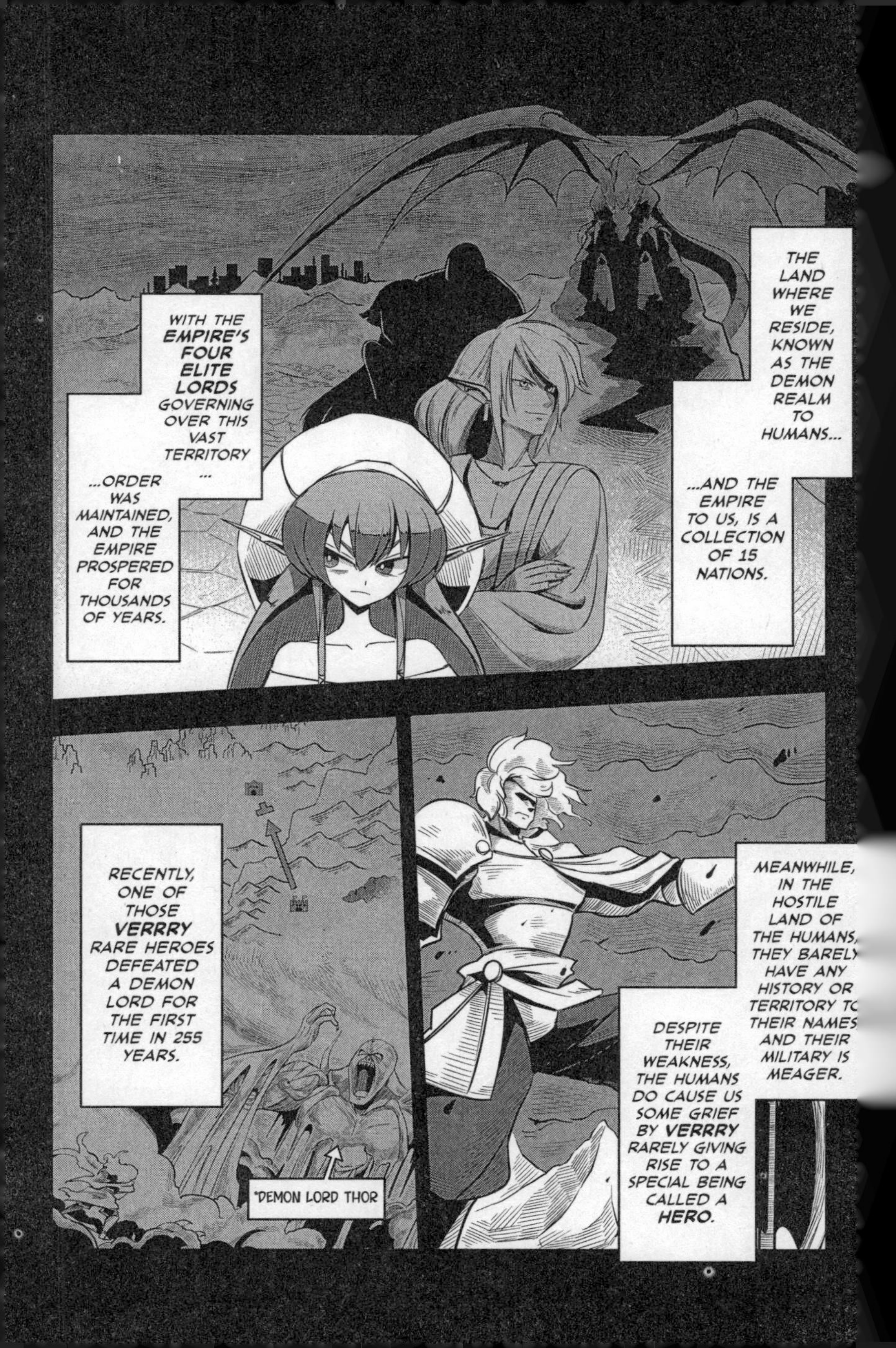
THE LAND WHERE WE RESIDE, KNOWN AS THE DEMON REALM TO HUMANS...
...AND THE EMPIRE TO US, IS A COLLECTION OF 15 NATIONS.
WITH THE EMPIRE'S FOUR ELITE LORDS GOVERNING OVER THIS VAST TERRITORY...
...ORDER WAS MAINTAINED, AND THE EMPIRE PROSPERED FOR THOUSANDS OF YEARS.
MEANWHILE, IN THE HOSTILE LAND OF THE HUMANS, THEY BARELY HAVE ANY HISTORY OR TERRITORY TO THEIR NAMES AND THEIR MILITARY IS MEAGER.
DESPITE THEIR WEAKNESS, THE HUMANS DO CAUSE US SOME GRIEF BY VERRRY RARELY GIVING RISE TO A SPECIAL BEING CALLED A HERO.
RECENTLY, ONE OF THOSE VERRRY RARE HEROES DEFEATED A DEMON LORD FOR THE FIRST TIME IN 255 YEARS.
*DEMON LORD THOR

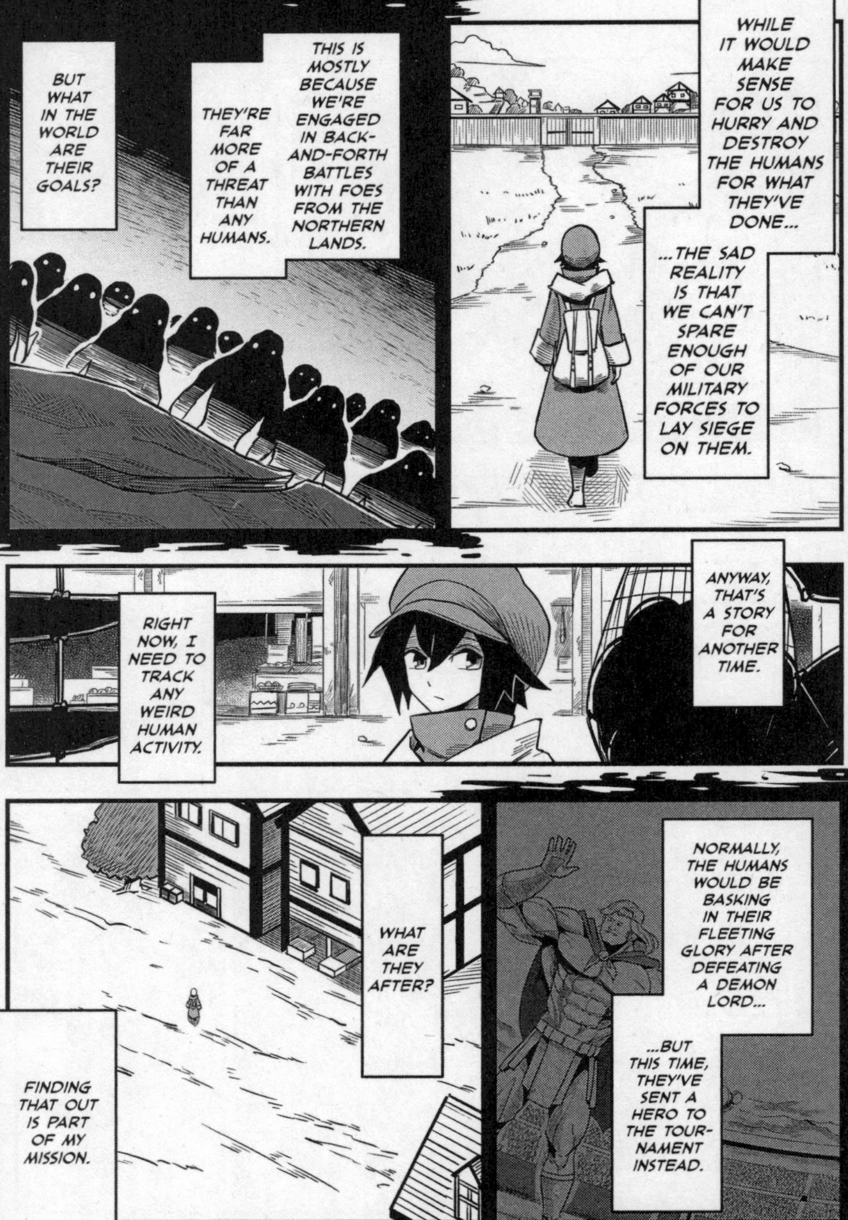
WHILE IT WOULD MAKE SENSE FOR US TO HURRY AND DESTROY THE HUMANS FOR WHAT THEY'VE DONE...
...THE SAD REALITY IS THAT WE CAN'T SPARE ENOUGH OF OUR MILITARY FORCES TO LAY SIEGE ON THEM.
THIS IS MOSTLY BECAUSE WE'RE ENGAGED IN BACK-AND-FORTH BATTLES WITH FOES FROM THE NORTHERN LANDS.
THEY'RE FAR MORE OF A THREAT THAN ANY HUMANS.
BUT WHAT IN THE WORLD ARE THEIR GOALS?
ANYWAY, THAT'S A STORY FOR ANOTHER TIME.
RIGHT NOW, I NEED TO TRACK ANY WEIRD HUMAN ACTIVITY.
NORMALLY, THE HUMANS WOULD BE BASKING IN THEIR FLEETING GLORY AFTER DEFEATING A DEMON LORD...
...BUT THIS TIME, THEY'VE SENT A HERO TO THE TOUR-NAMENT INSTEAD.
WHAT ARE THEY AFTER?
FINDING THAT OUT IS PART OF MY MISSION.

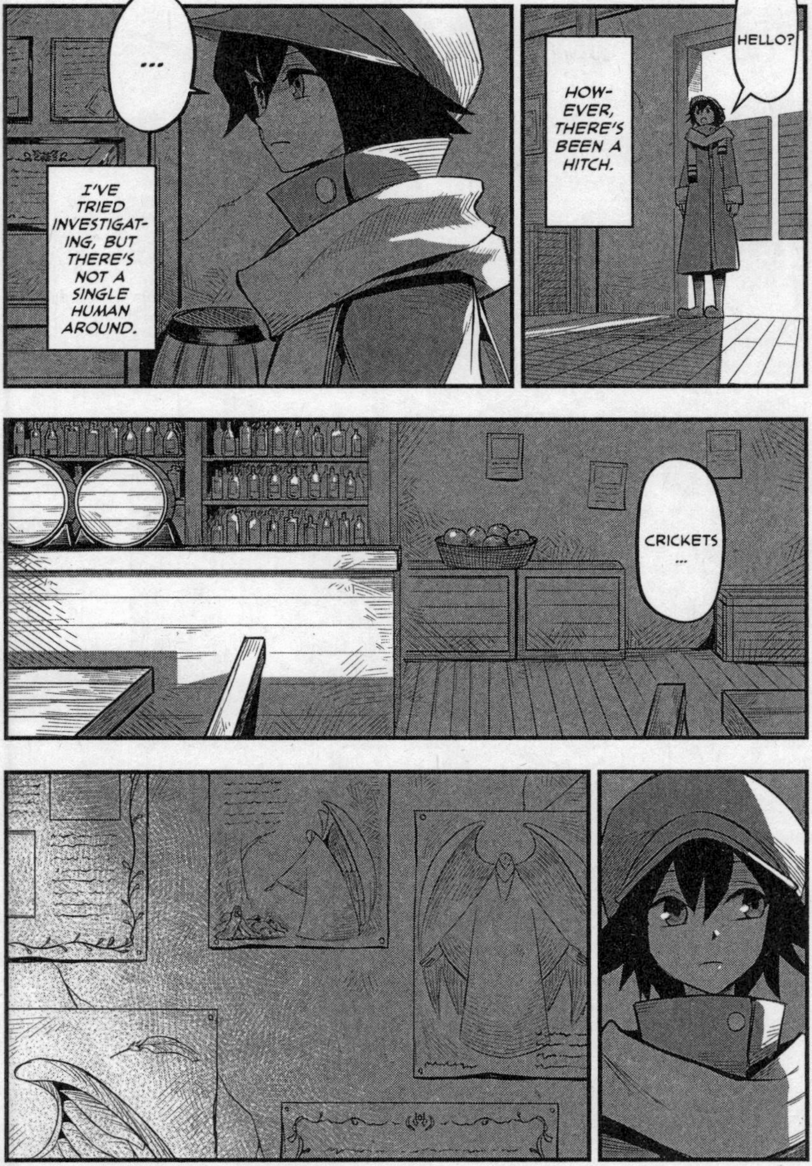
HELLO?
HOW-EVER, THERE'S BEEN A HITCH.
...
I'VE TRIED INVESTIGAT-ING, BUT THERE'S NOT A SINGLE HUMAN AROUND.
CRICKETS ...

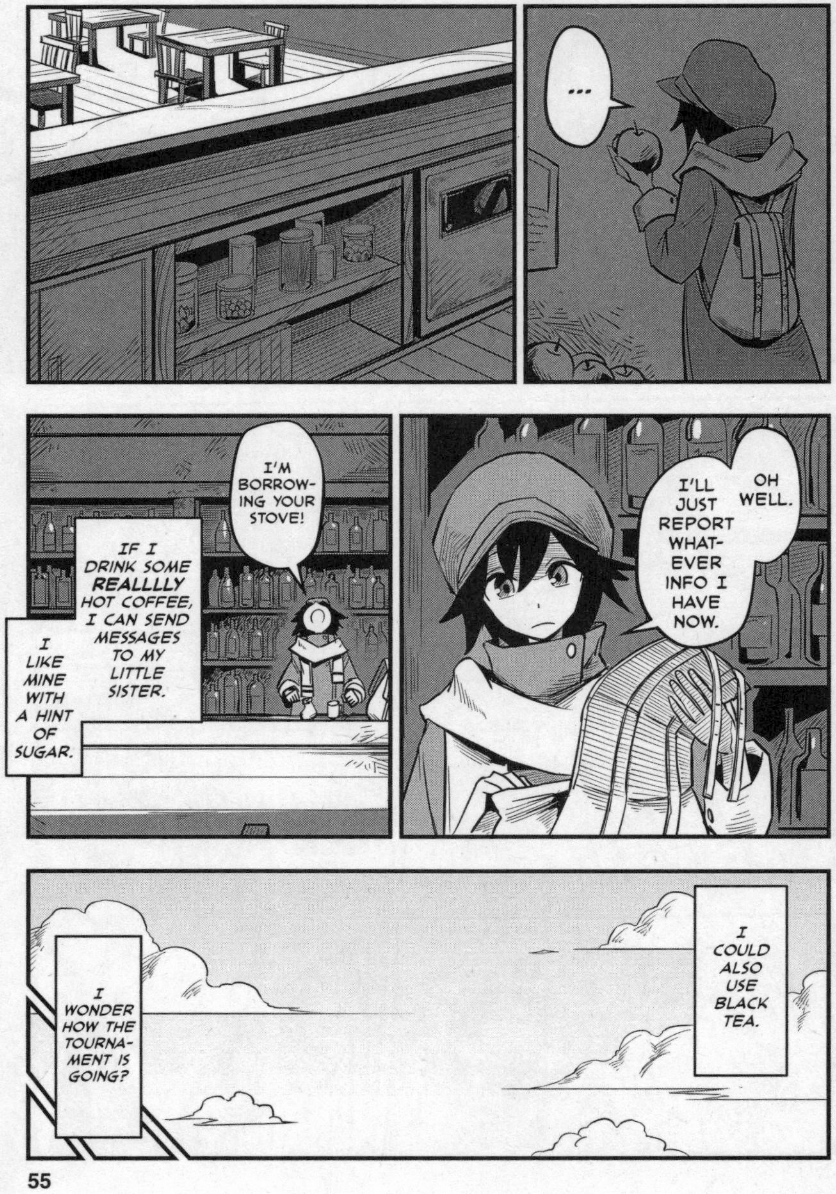
...
OH WELL.
I'LL JUST REPORT WHATEVER INFO I HAVE NOW.
I'M BORROWING YOUR STOVE!
IF I DRINK SOME REALLLLY HOT COFFEE, I CAN SEND MESSAGES TO MY LITTLE SISTER.
I LIKE MINE WITH A HINT OF SUGAR.
I COULD ALSO USE BLACK TEA.
I WONDER HOW THE TOURNAMENT IS GOING?

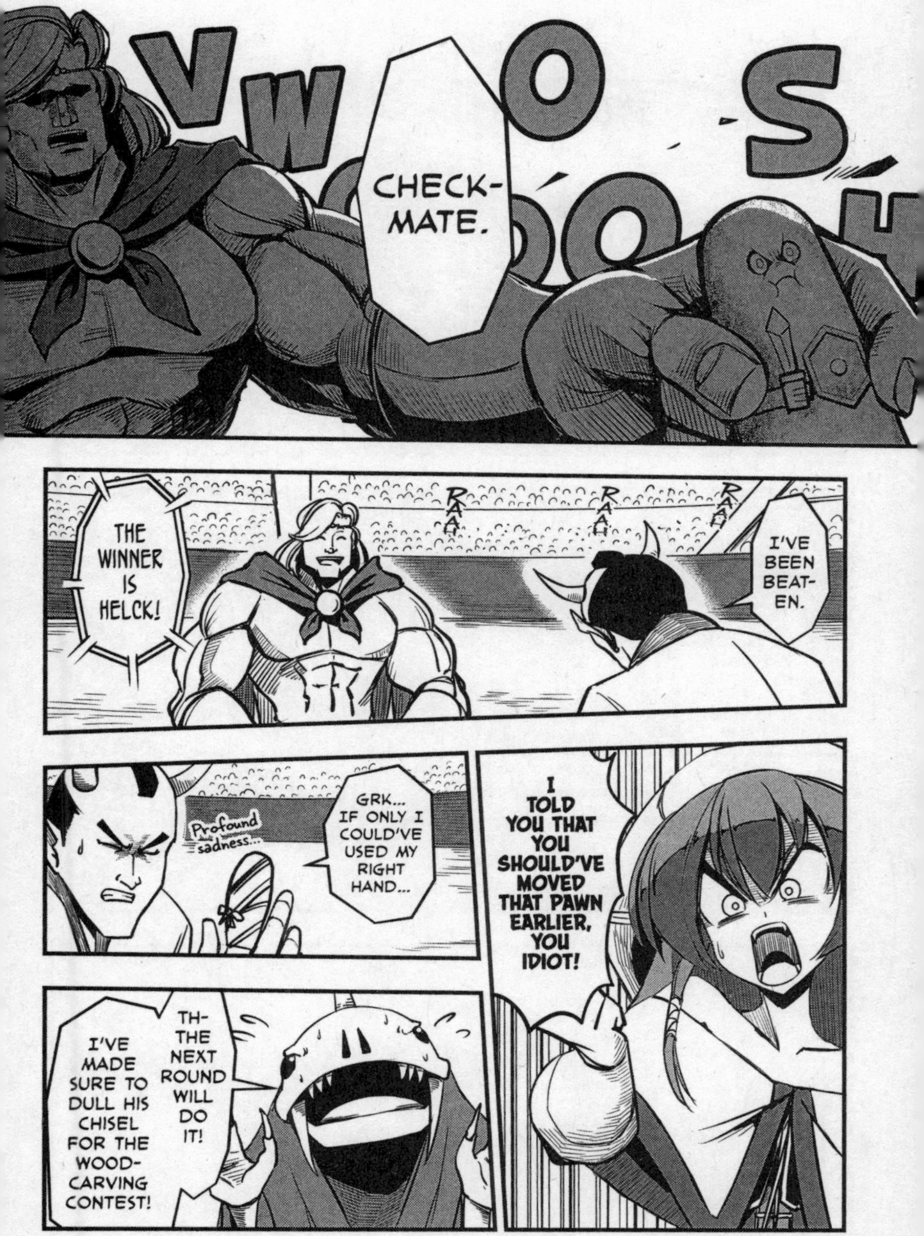
VWOOSH
CHECK-MATE.
RAA
RAA
RAA
I'VE BEEN BEAT-EN.
THE WINNER IS HELCK!
I TOLD YOU THAT YOU SHOULD'VE MOVED THAT PAWN EARLIER, YOU IDIOT!
Profound sadness...
GRK... IF ONLY I COULD'VE USED MY RIGHT HAND...
TH-THE NEXT ROUND WILL DO IT!
I'VE MADE SURE TO DULL HIS CHISEL FOR THE WOOD-CARVING CONTEST!

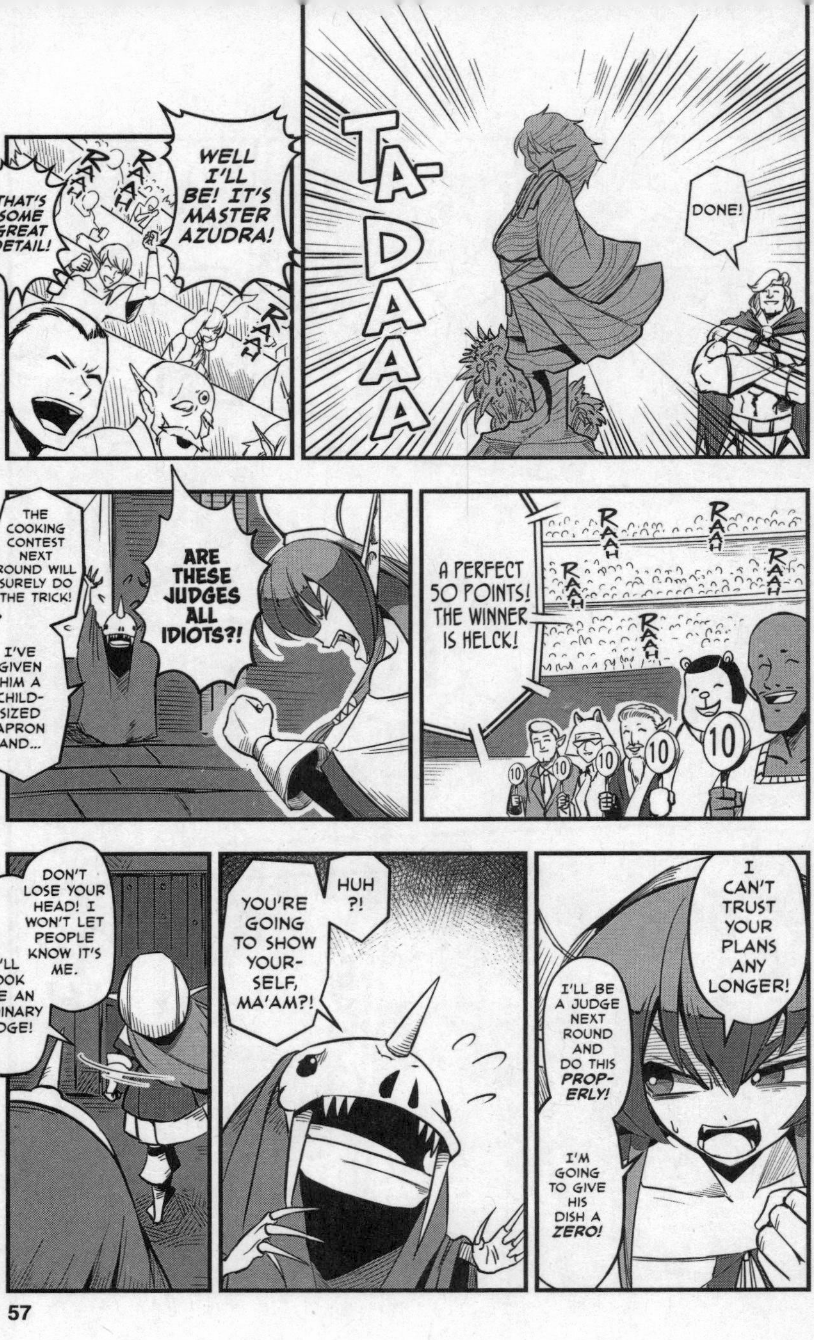

DONE!
TA-DAAA
WELL I'LL BE! IT'S MASTER AZUDRA!
THAT'S SOME GREAT DETAIL!
RAAH
RAAH
RAAH
A PERFECT 50 POINTS! THE WINNER IS HELCK!
RAAH
RAAH
RAAH
RAAH
RAAH
10
10
10
10
10
ARE THESE JUDGES ALL IDIOTS?!
THE COOKING CONTEST NEXT ROUND WILL SURELY DO THE TRICK!
I'VE GIVEN HIM A CHILD-SIZED APRON AND...
I CAN'T TRUST YOUR PLANS ANY LONGER!
I'LL BE A JUDGE NEXT ROUND AND DO THIS *PROPERLY!*
I'M GOING TO GIVE HIS DISH A *ZERO!*
HUH ?!
YOU'RE GOING TO SHOW YOURSELF, MA'AM?!
DON'T LOSE YOUR HEAD! I WON'T LET PEOPLE KNOW IT'S ME.
I'LL LOOK LIKE AN ORDINARY JUDGE!

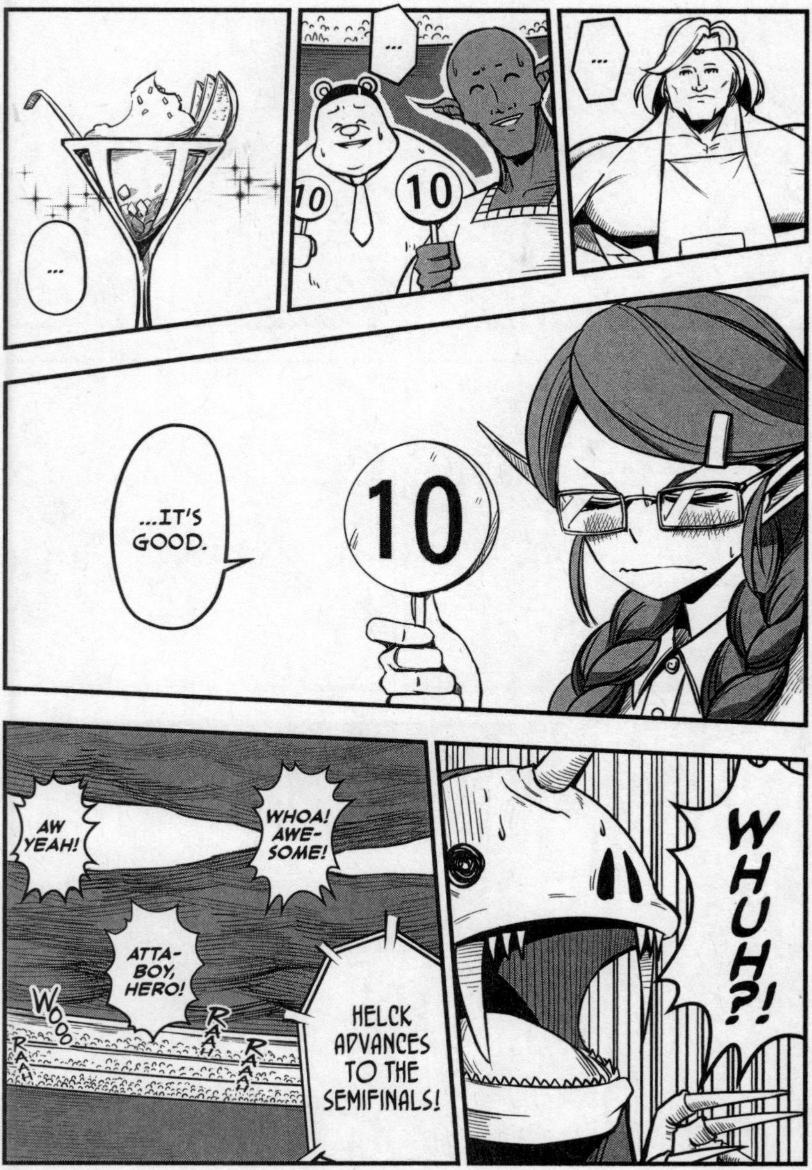
...
...
...
...IT'S GOOD.
WHUH?!
WHOA! AWE-SOME!
AW YEAH!
ATTA-BOY, HERO!
HELCK ADVANCES TO THE SEMIFINALS!
RAAAH
RAAH
WOOO
RAAH

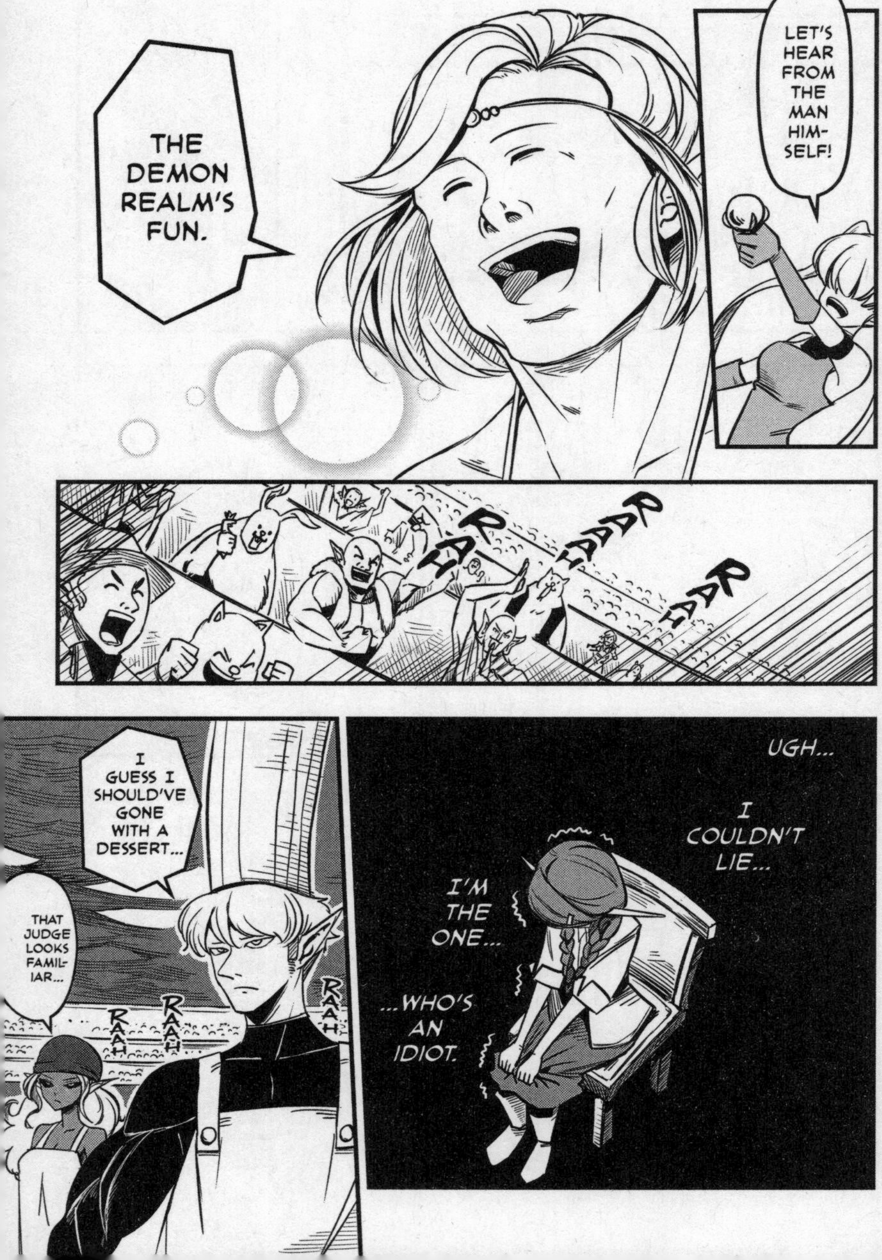
LET'S HEAR FROM THE MAN HIM-SELF!
THE DEMON REALM'S FUN.
RAAH
RAAH
RAAH
UGH...
I COULDN'T LIE...
I'M THE ONE...
...WHO'S AN IDIOT.
I GUESS I SHOULD'VE GONE WITH A DESSERT...
RAAH
RAAH
RAAH
THAT JUDGE LOOKS FAMIL-IAR...

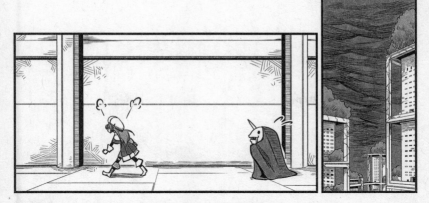

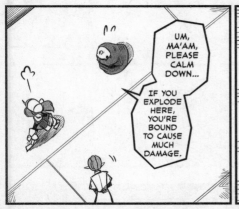

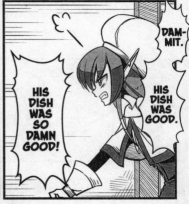

DAM-MIT.
HIS DISH WAS GOOD.
HIS DISH WAS SO DAMN GOOD!
UM, MA'AM, PLEASE CALM DOWN...
IF YOU EXPLODE HERE, YOU'RE BOUND TO CAUSE MUCH DAMAGE.
I KNOW!
OH, HELLO. KEEP UP THE GOOD WORK!

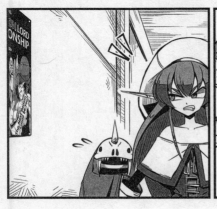

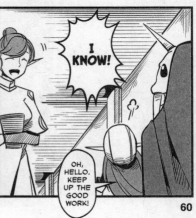

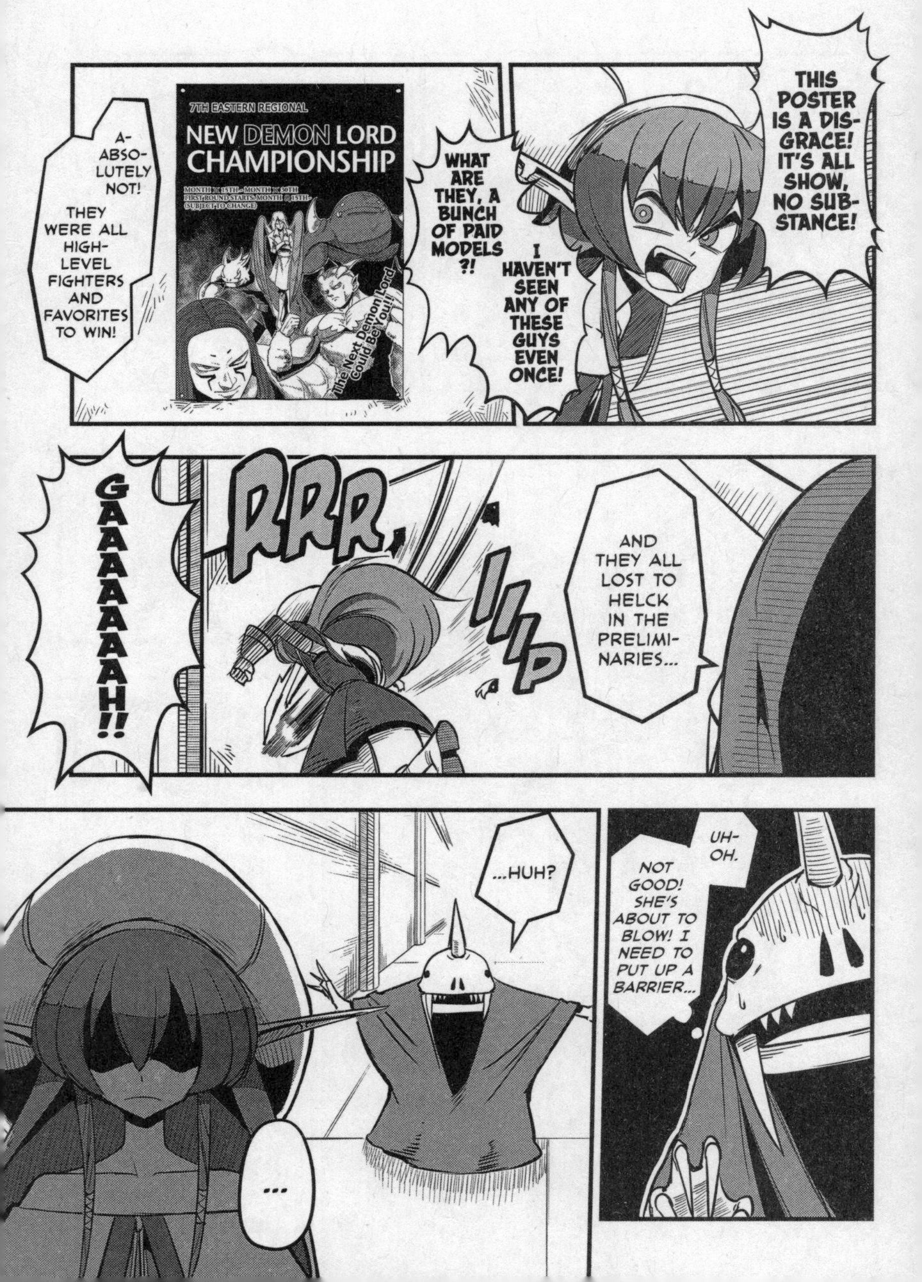
THIS POSTER IS A DISGRACE! IT'S ALL SHOW, NO SUBSTANCE!
WHAT ARE THEY, A BUNCH OF PAID MODELS?!
I HAVEN'T SEEN ANY OF THESE GUYS EVEN ONCE!
7TH EASTERN REGIONAL
NEW DEMON LORD CHAMPIONSHIP
(SUBJECT TO CHANGE)
The Next Demon Lord Could Be You!!
A-ABSOLUTELY NOT!
THEY WERE ALL HIGH-LEVEL FIGHTERS AND FAVORITES TO WIN!
AND THEY ALL LOST TO HELCK IN THE PRELIMINARIES...
RRRIIIP
GAAAAAAAAAH!!
UH-OH.
NOT GOOD! SHE'S ABOUT TO BLOW! I NEED TO PUT UP A BARRIER...
...HUH?
...

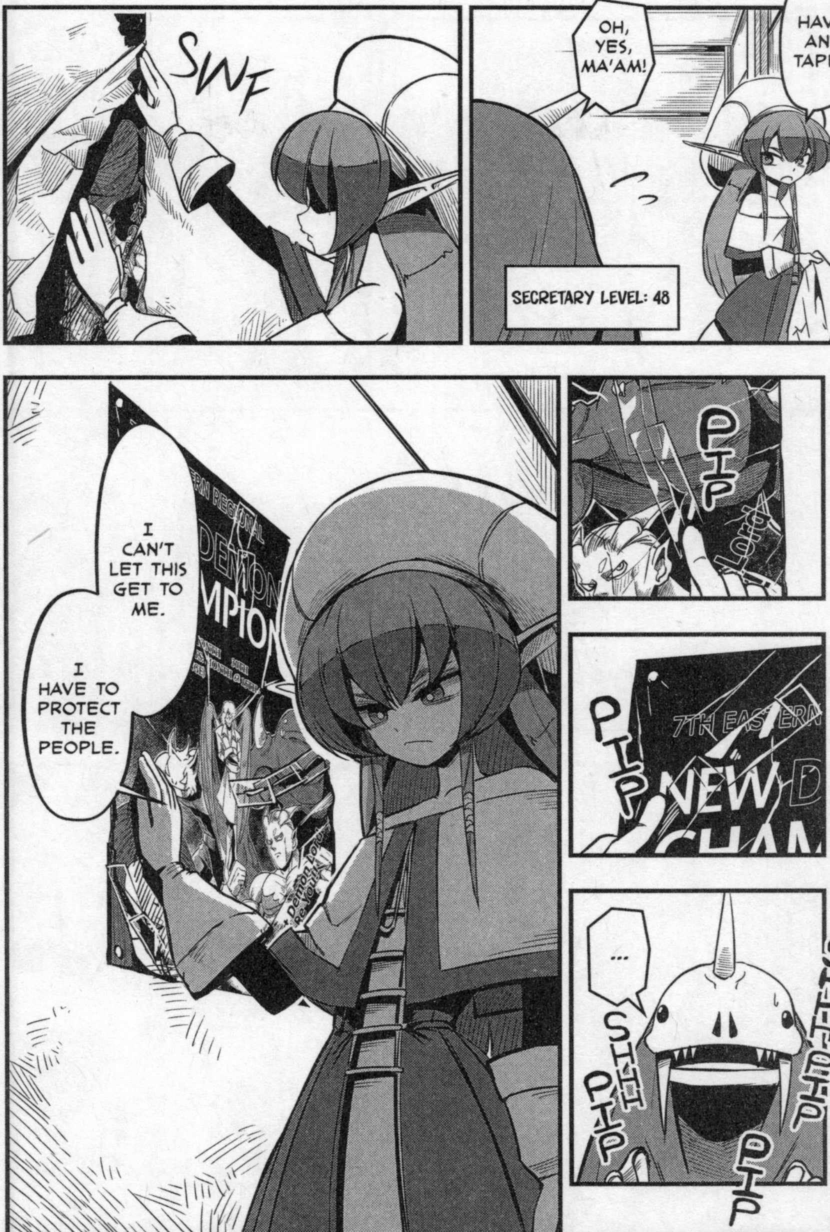

HAVE ANY TAPE?
OH, YES, MA'AM!
SECRETARY LEVEL: 48
SWF
PIP
PIP
PIP
PIP
7TH EASTERN
NEW D
CHAM
...
SHHH
PIP
SHHH
PIP
PIP
PIP
PIP
I CAN'T LET THIS GET TO ME.
I HAVE TO PROTECT THE PEOPLE.
DEMON
MPION

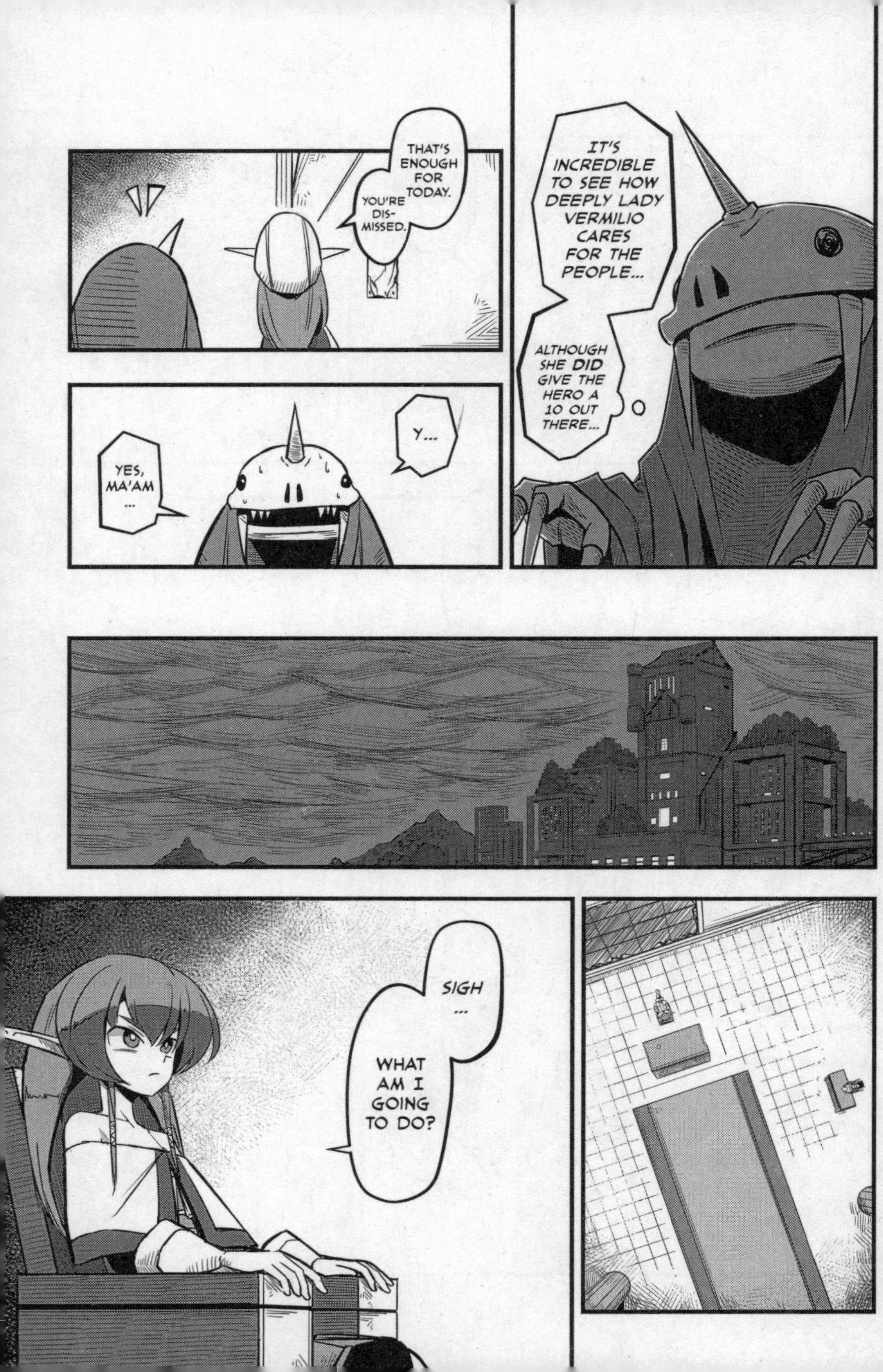
IT'S INCREDIBLE TO SEE HOW DEEPLY LADY VERMILIO CARES FOR THE PEOPLE...
ALTHOUGH SHE **DID** GIVE THE HERO A 10 OUT THERE...
THAT'S ENOUGH FOR TODAY.
YOU'RE DIS-MISSED.
Y...
YES, MA'AM ...
SIGH ...
WHAT AM I GOING TO DO?

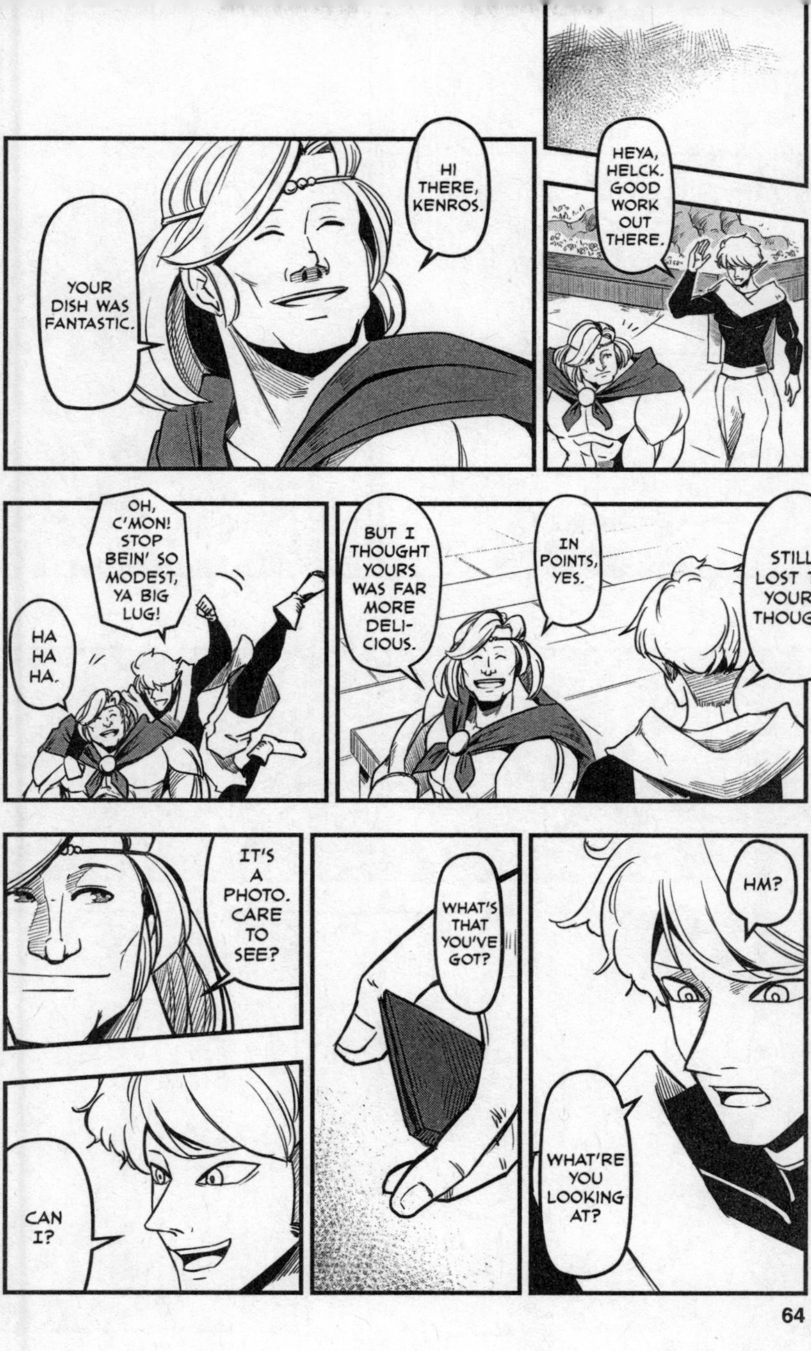
HEYA, HELCK. GOOD WORK OUT THERE.
HI THERE, KENROS.
YOUR DISH WAS FANTASTIC.
STILL LOST TO YOURS THOUGH.
IN POINTS, YES.
BUT I THOUGHT YOURS WAS FAR MORE DELI-CIOUS.
OH, C'MON! STOP BEIN' SO MODEST, YA BIG LUG!
HA HA HA.
HM?
WHAT'RE YOU LOOKING AT?
WHAT'S THAT YOU'VE GOT?
IT'S A PHOTO. CARE TO SEE?
CAN I?

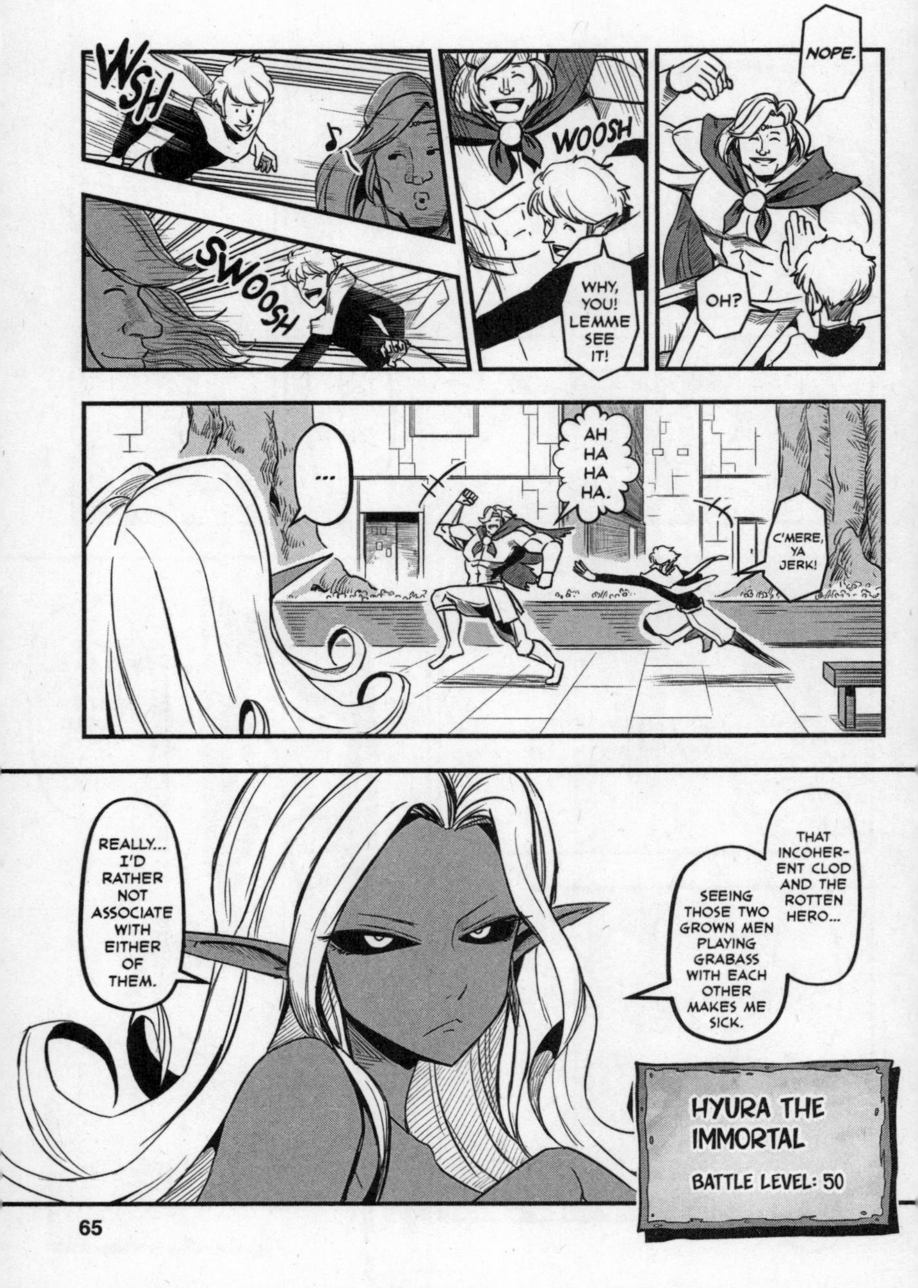
NOPE.
OH?
WOOSH
WHY, YOU! LEMME SEE IT!
WSH
♪
SWOOSH
C'MERE, YA JERK!
AH HA HA HA.
...
THAT INCOHER-ENT CLOD AND THE ROTTEN HERO...
SEEING THOSE TWO GROWN MEN PLAYING GRABASS WITH EACH OTHER MAKES ME SICK.
REALLY... I'D RATHER NOT ASSOCIATE WITH EITHER OF THEM.
HYURA THE IMMORTAL
BATTLE LEVEL: 50

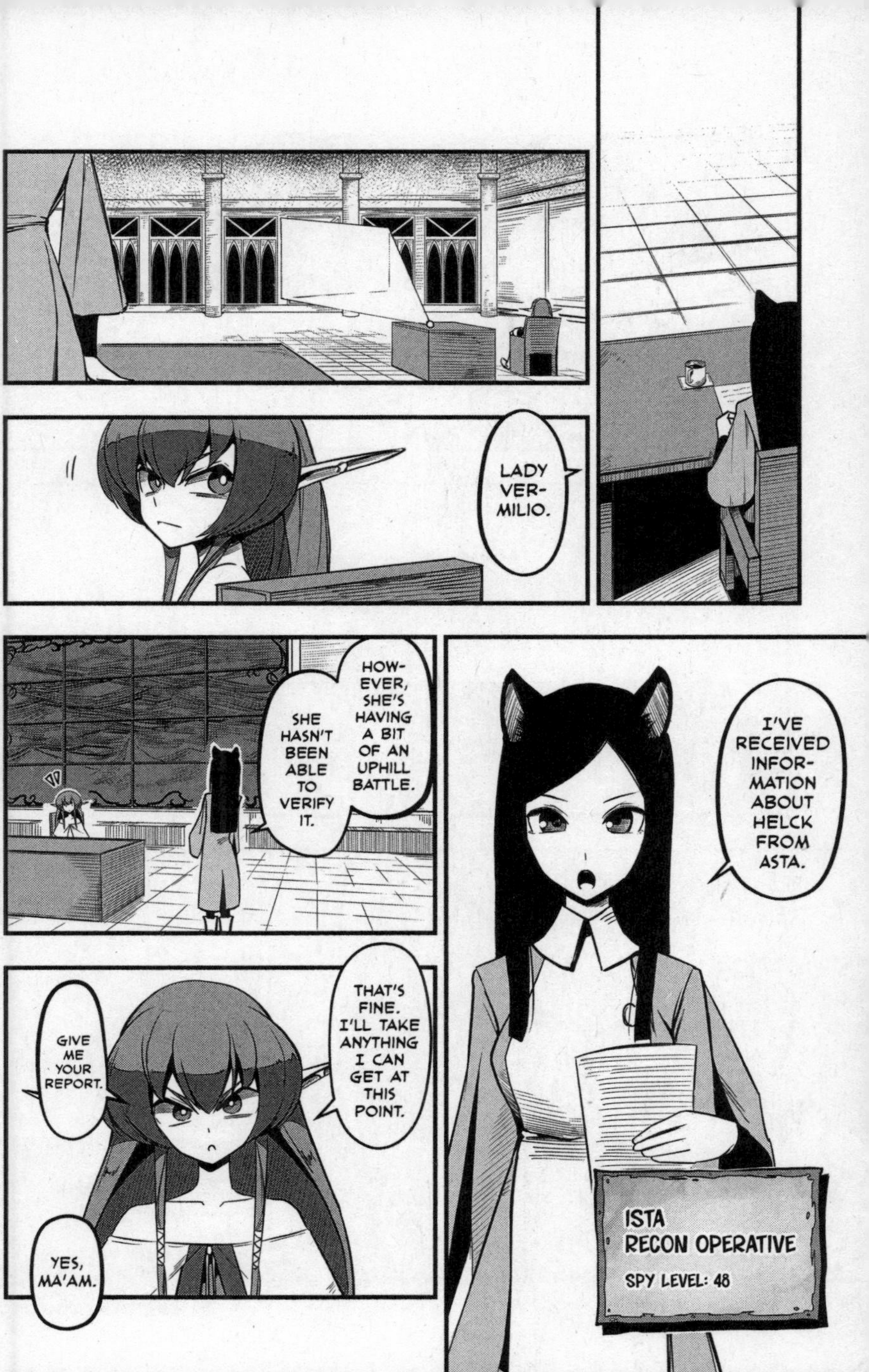
LADY VERMILIO.
I'VE RECEIVED INFORMATION ABOUT HELCK FROM ASTA.
ISTA RECON OPERATIVE
SPY LEVEL: 48
HOWEVER, SHE'S HAVING A BIT OF AN UPHILL BATTLE.
SHE HASN'T BEEN ABLE TO VERIFY IT.
THAT'S FINE. I'LL TAKE ANYTHING I CAN GET AT THIS POINT.
GIVE ME YOUR REPORT.
YES, MA'AM.

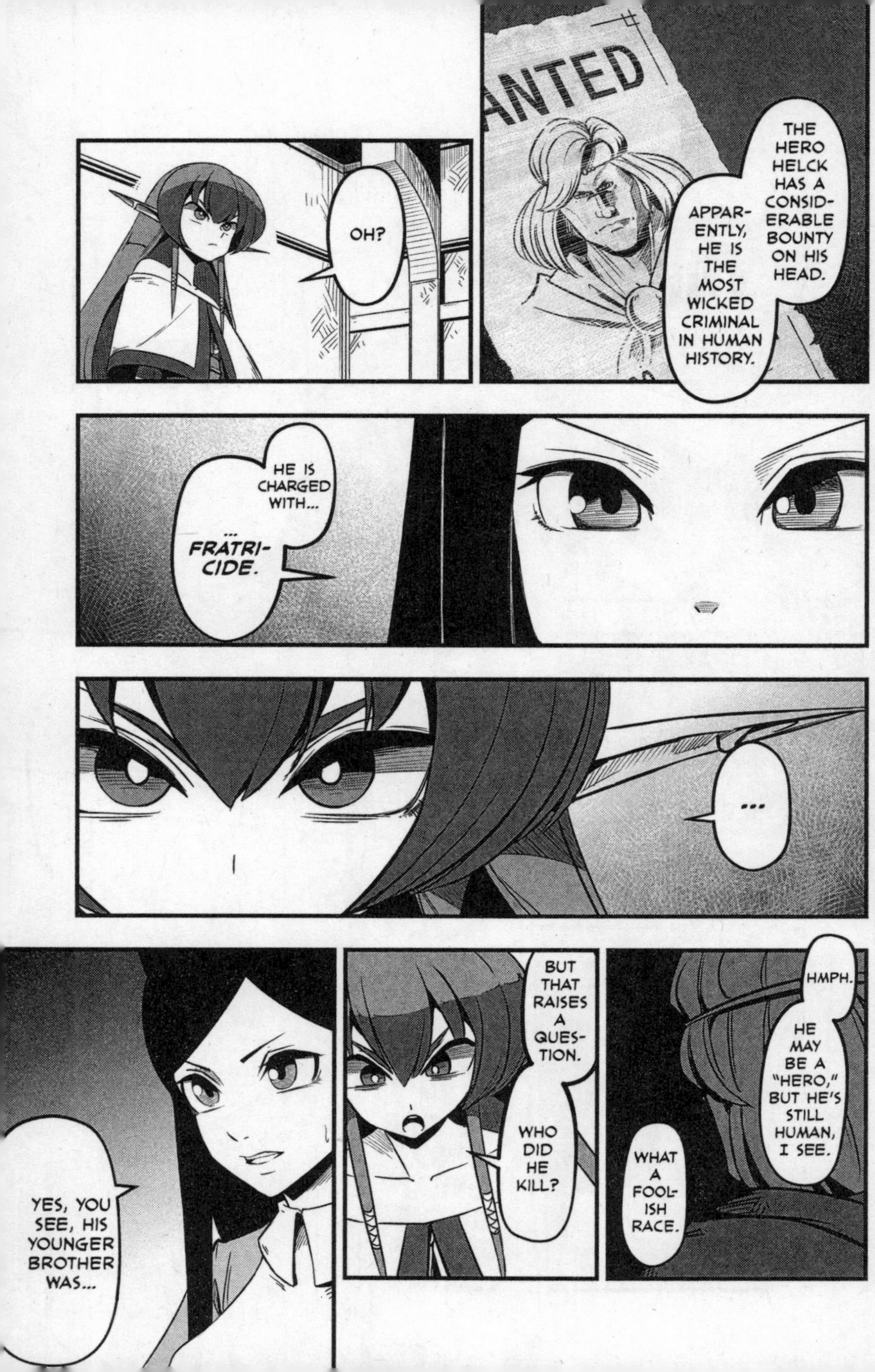

ANTED
THE HERO HELCK HAS A CONSIDERABLE BOUNTY ON HIS HEAD.
APPARENTLY, HE IS THE MOST WICKED CRIMINAL IN HUMAN HISTORY.
OH?
HE IS CHARGED WITH...
...FRATRICIDE.
...
HMPH.
HE MAY BE A "HERO," BUT HE'S STILL HUMAN, I SEE.
WHAT A FOOLISH RACE.
BUT THAT RAISES A QUESTION.
WHO DID HE KILL?
YES, YOU SEE, HIS YOUNGER BROTHER WAS...

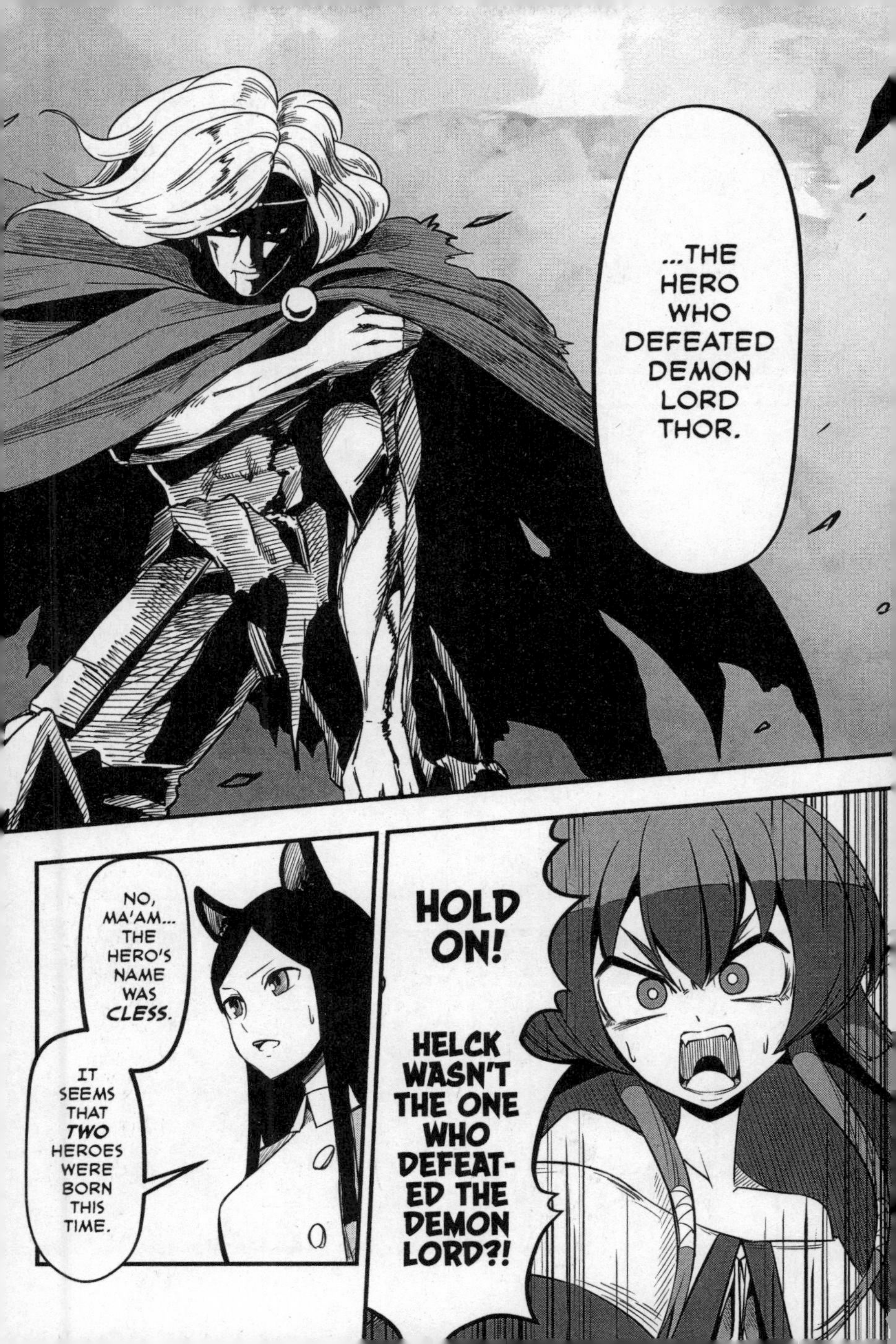
...THE HERO WHO DEFEATED DEMON LORD THOR.
HOLD ON!
HELCK WASN'T THE ONE WHO DEFEAT-ED THE DEMON LORD?!
NO, MA'AM... THE HERO'S NAME WAS CLESS.
IT SEEMS THAT TWO HEROES WERE BORN THIS TIME.

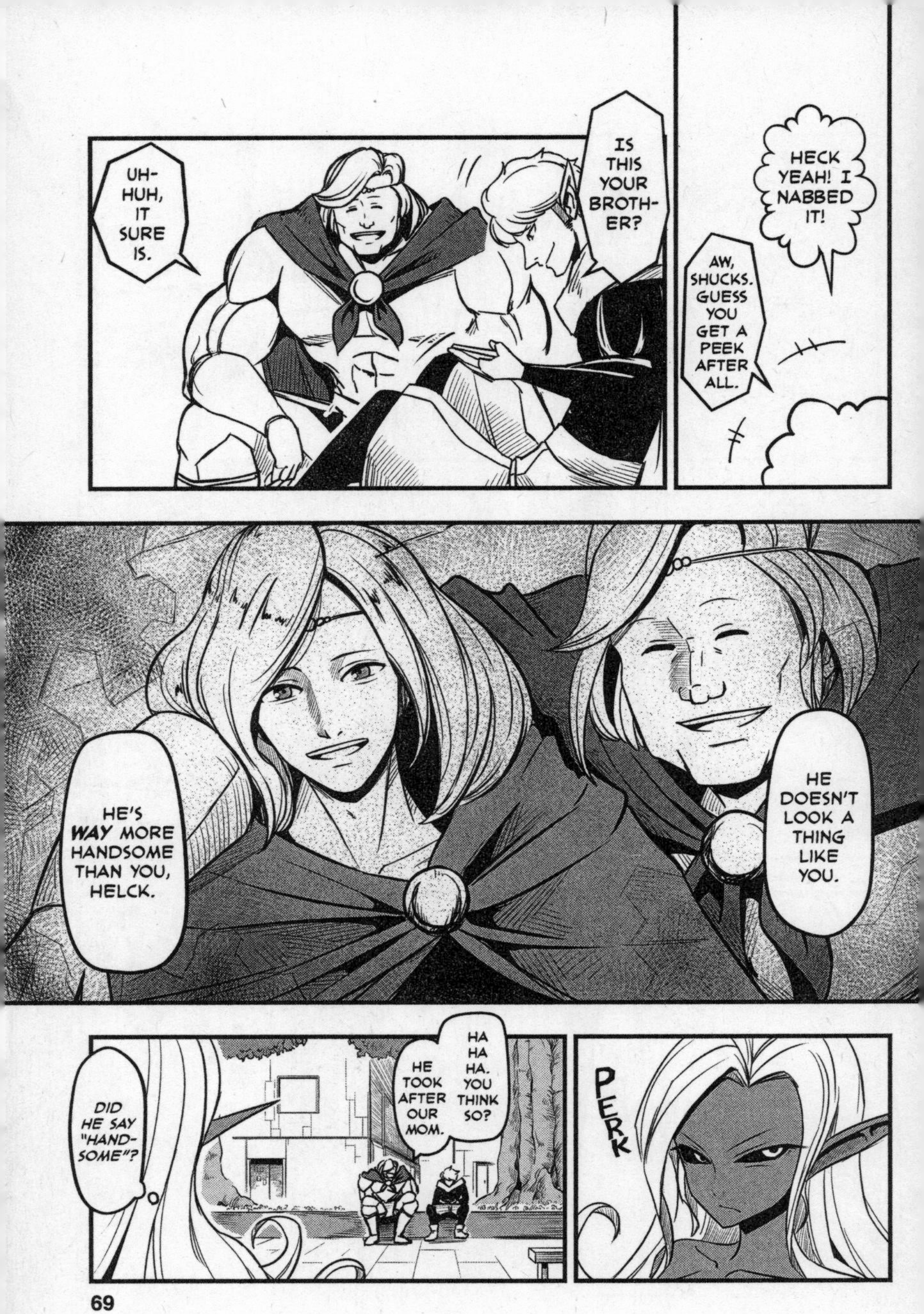
HECK YEAH! I NABBED IT!
AW, SHUCKS. GUESS YOU GET A PEEK AFTER ALL.
IS THIS YOUR BROTHER?
UH-HUH, IT SURE IS.
HE DOESN'T LOOK A THING LIKE YOU.
HE'S **WAY** MORE HANDSOME THAN YOU, HELCK.
PERK
HA HA HA. YOU THINK SO?
HE TOOK AFTER OUR MOM.
DID HE SAY "HANDSOME"?

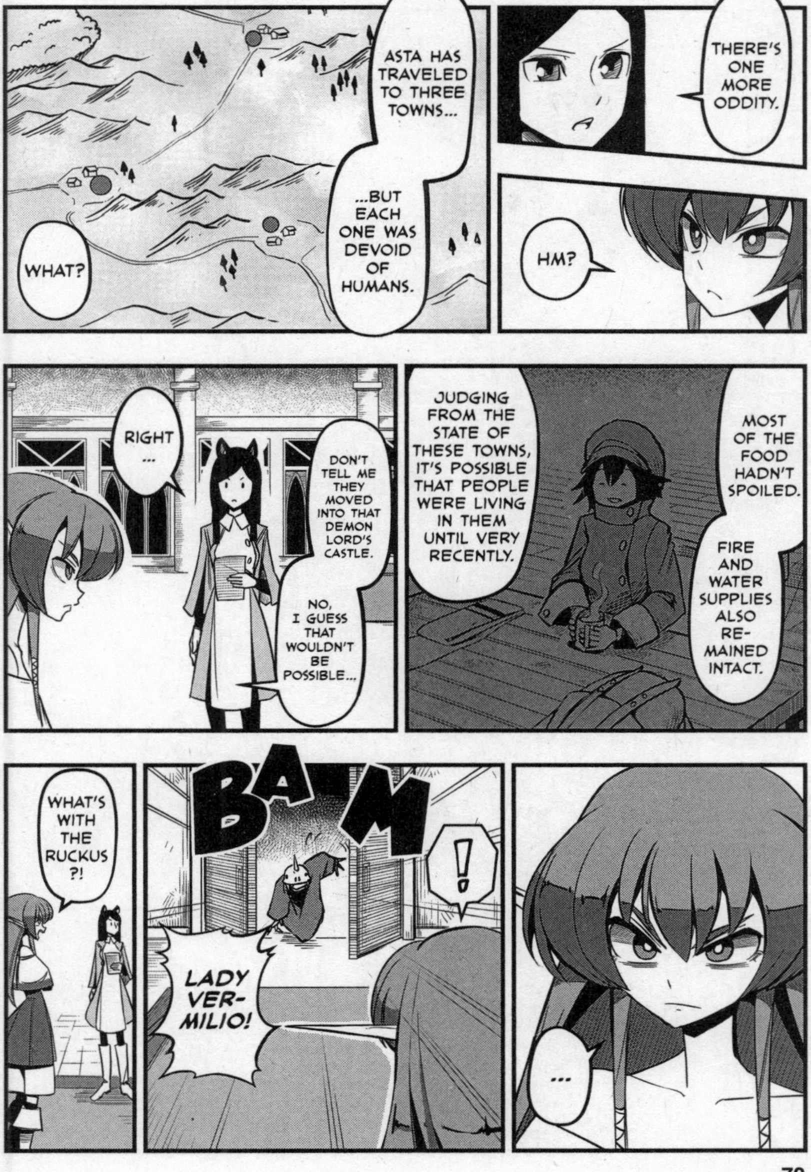
THERE'S ONE MORE ODDITY.
HM?
ASTA HAS TRAVELED TO THREE TOWNS...
...BUT EACH ONE WAS DEVOID OF HUMANS.
WHAT?
MOST OF THE FOOD HADN'T SPOILED.
FIRE AND WATER SUPPLIES ALSO RE-MAINED INTACT.
JUDGING FROM THE STATE OF THESE TOWNS, IT'S POSSIBLE THAT PEOPLE WERE LIVING IN THEM UNTIL VERY RECENTLY.
DON'T TELL ME THEY MOVED INTO THAT DEMON LORD'S CASTLE.
RIGHT ...
NO, I GUESS THAT WOULDN'T BE POSSIBLE...
...
BAM
!
LADY VER-MILIO!
WHAT'S WITH THE RUCKUS?!

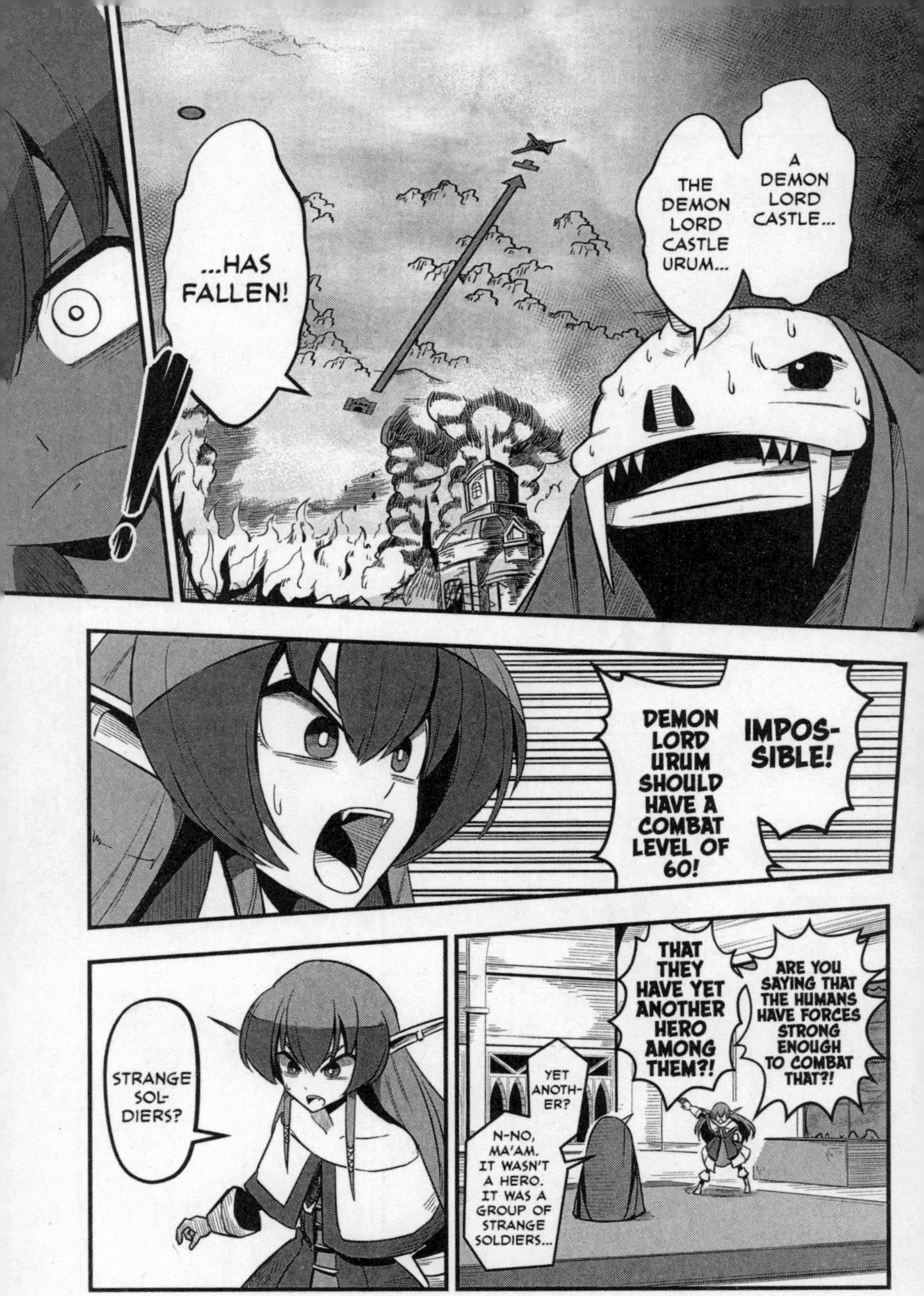
A DEMON LORD CASTLE...
THE DEMON LORD CASTLE URUM...
...HAS FALLEN!
IMPOSSIBLE!
DEMON LORD URUM SHOULD HAVE A COMBAT LEVEL OF 60!
ARE YOU SAYING THAT THE HUMANS HAVE FORCES STRONG ENOUGH TO COMBAT THAT?!
THAT THEY HAVE YET ANOTHER HERO AMONG THEM?!
YET ANOTHER?
N-NO, MA'AM. IT WASN'T A HERO. IT WAS A GROUP OF STRANGE SOLDIERS...
STRANGE SOLDIERS?

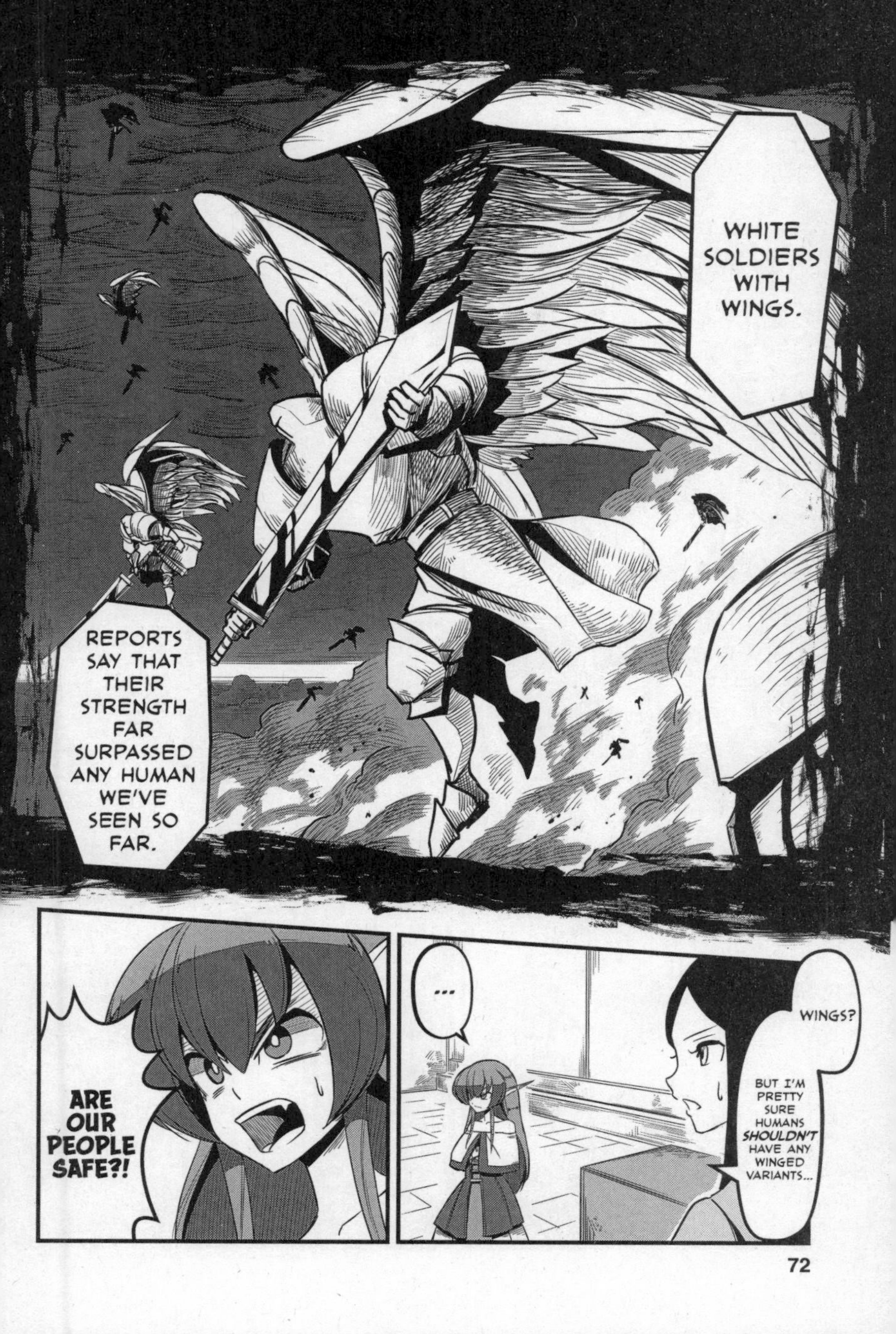
WHITE SOLDIERS WITH WINGS.
REPORTS SAY THAT THEIR STRENGTH FAR SURPASSED ANY HUMAN WE'VE SEEN SO FAR.
WINGS?
BUT I'M PRETTY SURE HUMANS SHOULDN'T HAVE ANY WINGED VARIANTS...
...
ARE OUR PEOPLE SAFE?!

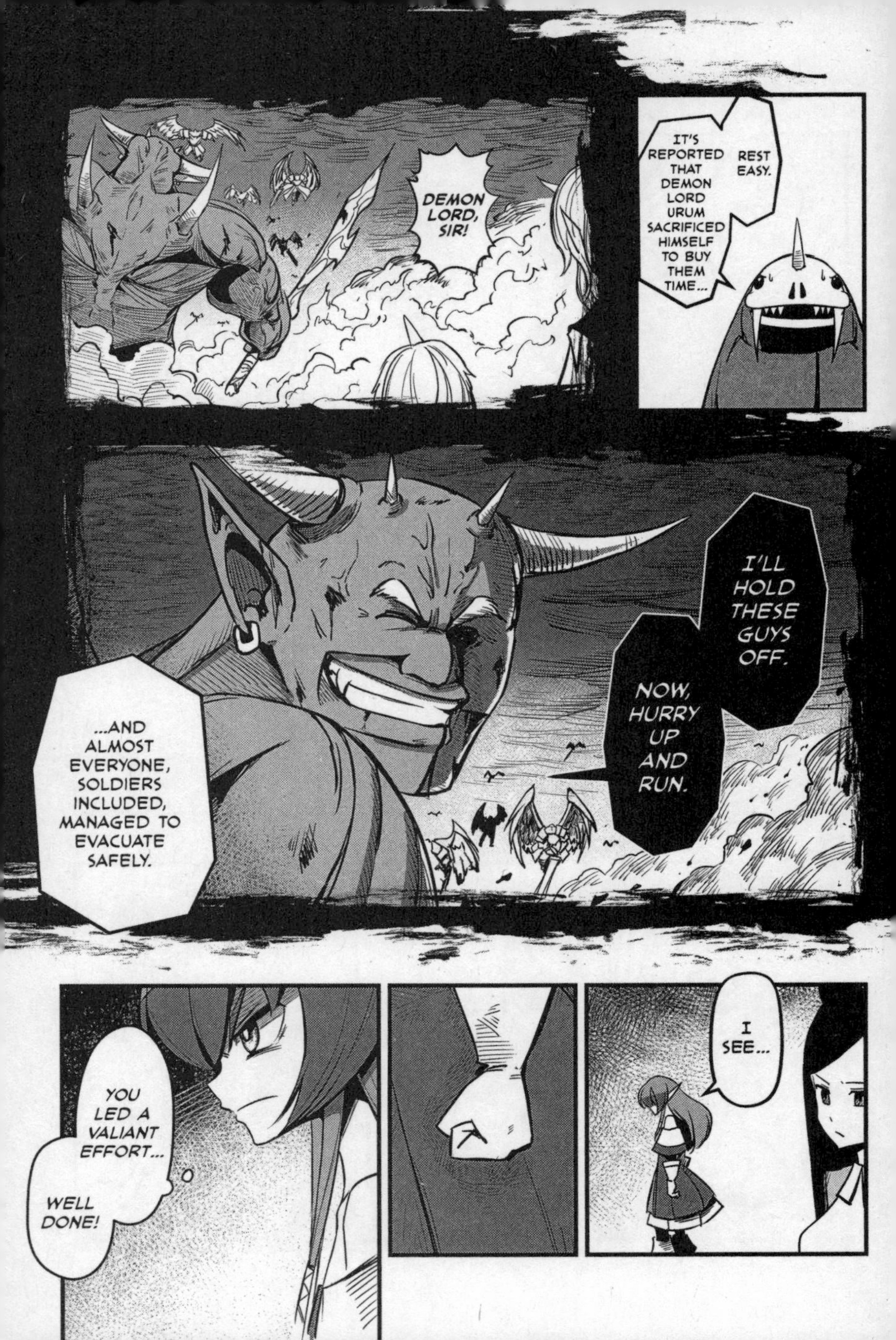
REST EASY.
IT'S REPORTED THAT DEMON LORD URUM SACRIFICED HIMSELF TO BUY THEM TIME...
DEMON LORD, SIR!
I'LL HOLD THESE GUYS OFF.
NOW, HURRY UP AND RUN.
...AND ALMOST EVERYONE, SOLDIERS INCLUDED, MANAGED TO EVACUATE SAFELY.
I SEE...
YOU LED A VALIANT EFFORT...
WELL DONE!

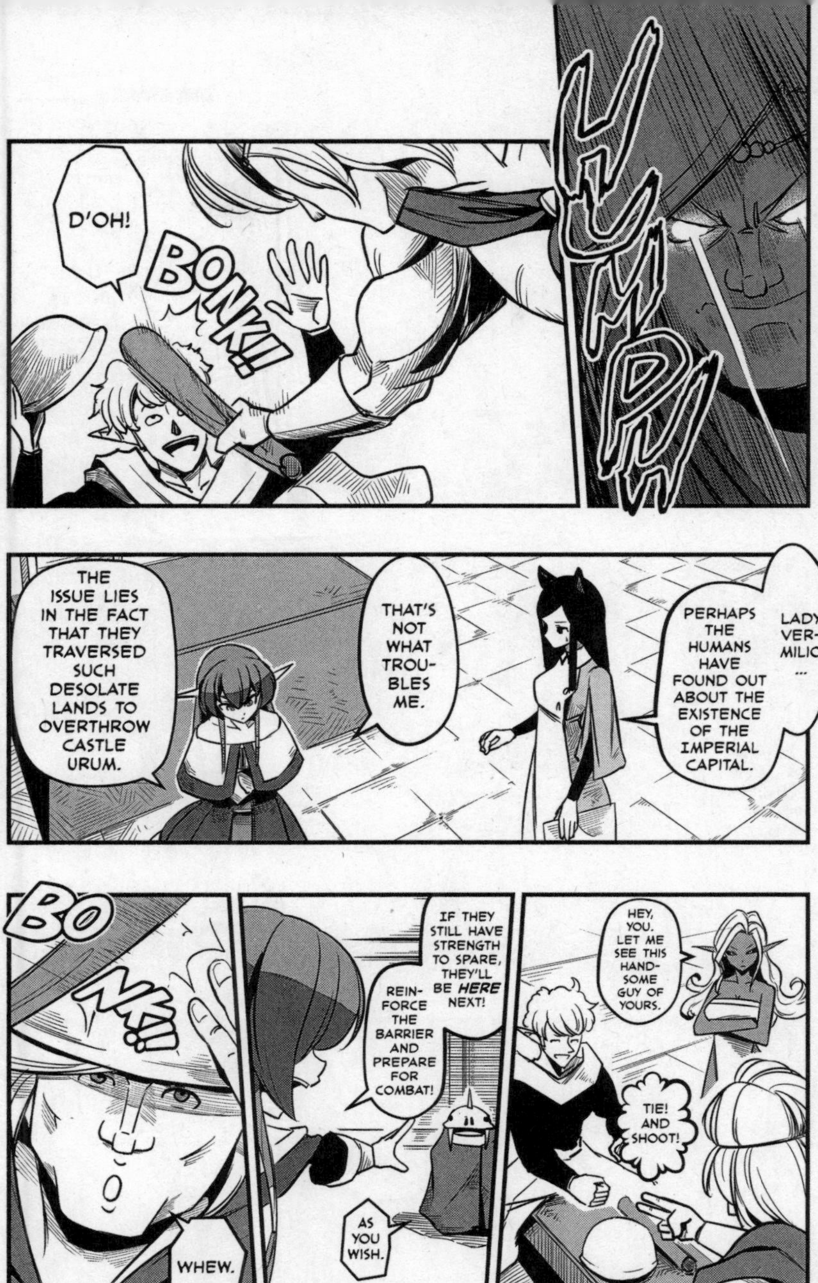
HUMPH
D'OH!
BONK!!
LADY VER-MILIO ...
PERHAPS THE HUMANS HAVE FOUND OUT ABOUT THE EXISTENCE OF THE IMPERIAL CAPITAL.
THAT'S NOT WHAT TROU-BLES ME.
THE ISSUE LIES IN THE FACT THAT THEY TRAVERSED SUCH DESOLATE LANDS TO OVERTHROW CASTLE URUM.
HEY, YOU. LET ME SEE THIS HAND-SOME GUY OF YOURS.
TIE! AND SHOOT!
IF THEY STILL HAVE STRENGTH TO SPARE, THEY'LL BE *HERE* NEXT!
REIN-FORCE THE BARRIER AND PREPARE FOR COMBAT!
AS YOU WISH.
BONK!!!
WHEW.

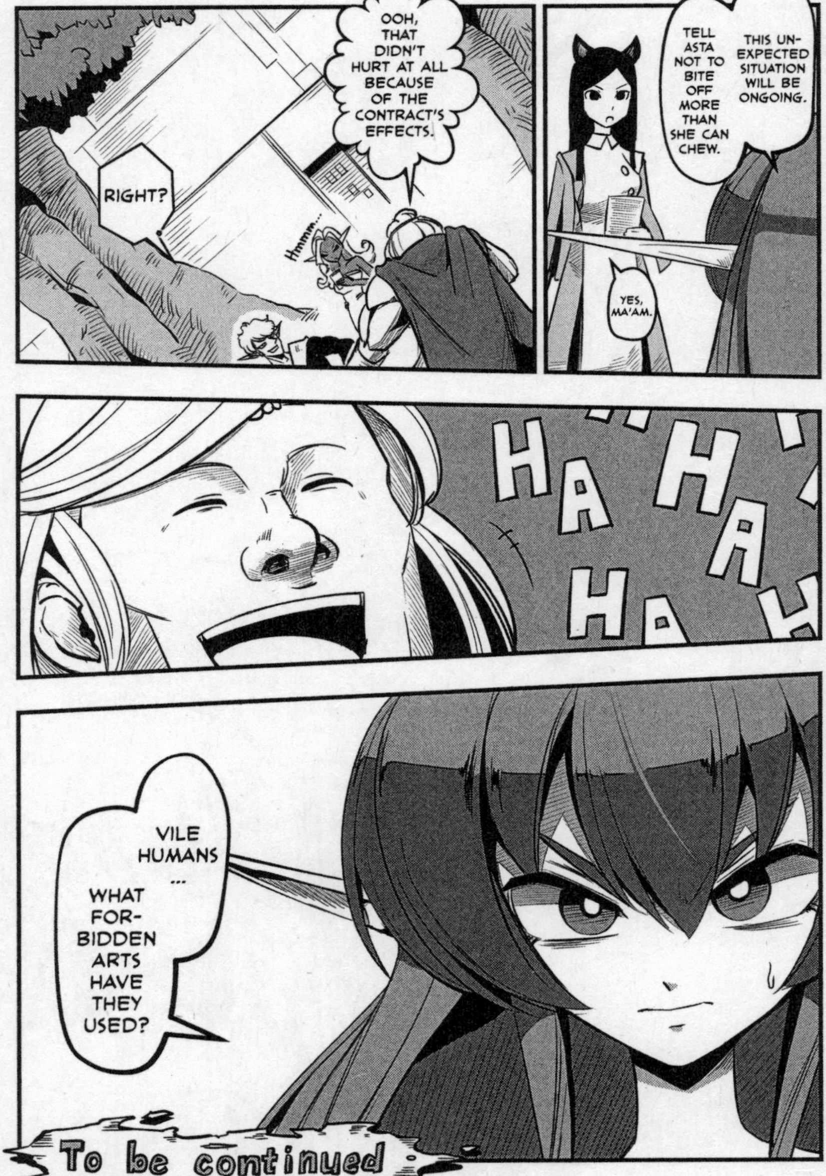
THIS UN-EXPECTED SITUATION WILL BE ONGOING.
TELL ASTA NOT TO BITE OFF MORE THAN SHE CAN CHEW.
YES, MA'AM.
OOH, THAT DIDN'T HURT AT ALL BECAUSE OF THE CONTRACT'S EFFECTS.
RIGHT?
Hmmm...
HA HA HA HA HA HA
VILE HUMANS ... WHAT FOR-BIDDEN ARTS HAVE THEY USED?
To be continued

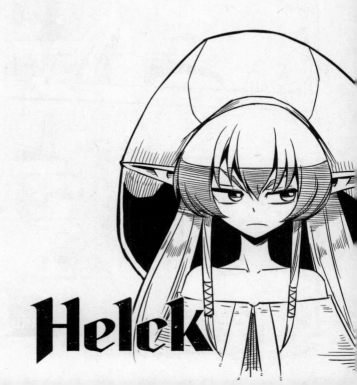

Helck

Helck

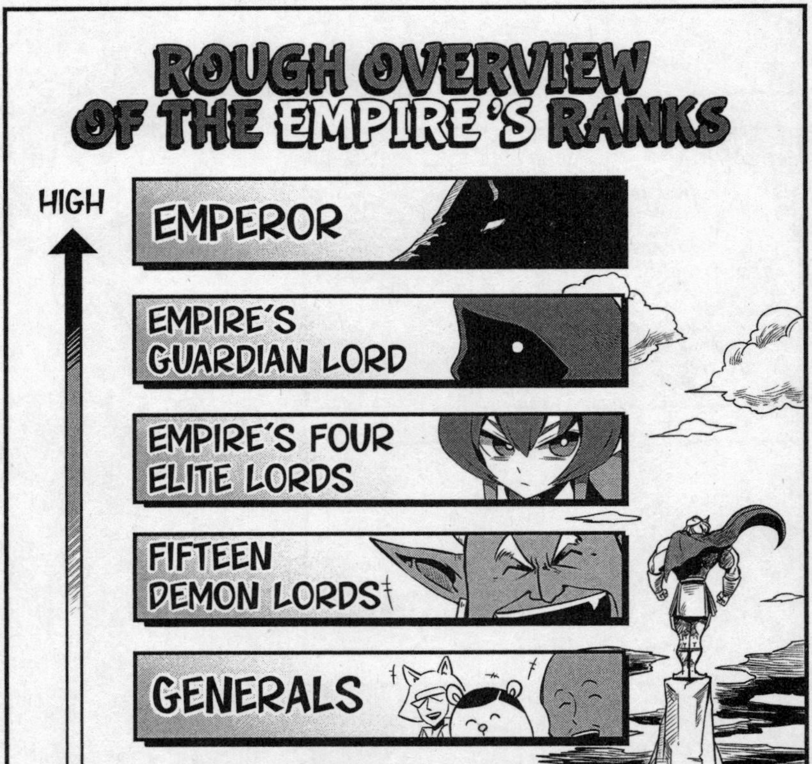

ROUGH OVERVIEW OF THE EMPIRE'S RANKS

HIGH

| EMPEROR |

| EMPIRE'S GUARDIAN LORD |

| EMPIRE'S FOUR ELITE LORDS |

| FIFTEEN DEMON LORDS‡ |

| GENERALS |

| OTHERS |

LOW

Chapter 4: The Racing Contest

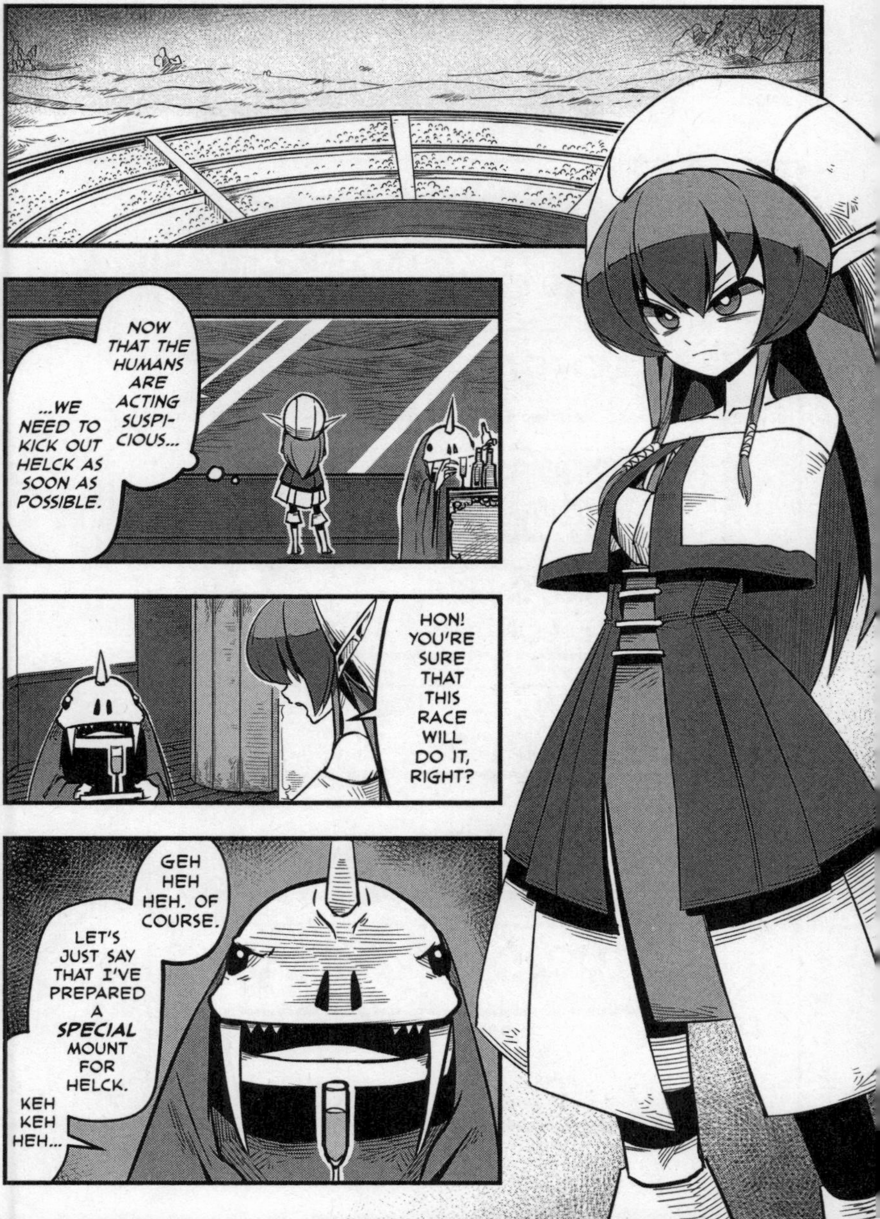
NOW THAT THE HUMANS ARE ACTING SUSPICIOUS...
...WE NEED TO KICK OUT HELCK AS SOON AS POSSIBLE.
HON! YOU'RE SURE THAT THIS RACE WILL DO IT, RIGHT?
GEH HEH HEH. OF COURSE.
LET'S JUST SAY THAT I'VE PREPARED A *SPECIAL* MOUNT FOR HELCK.
KEH KEH HEH...

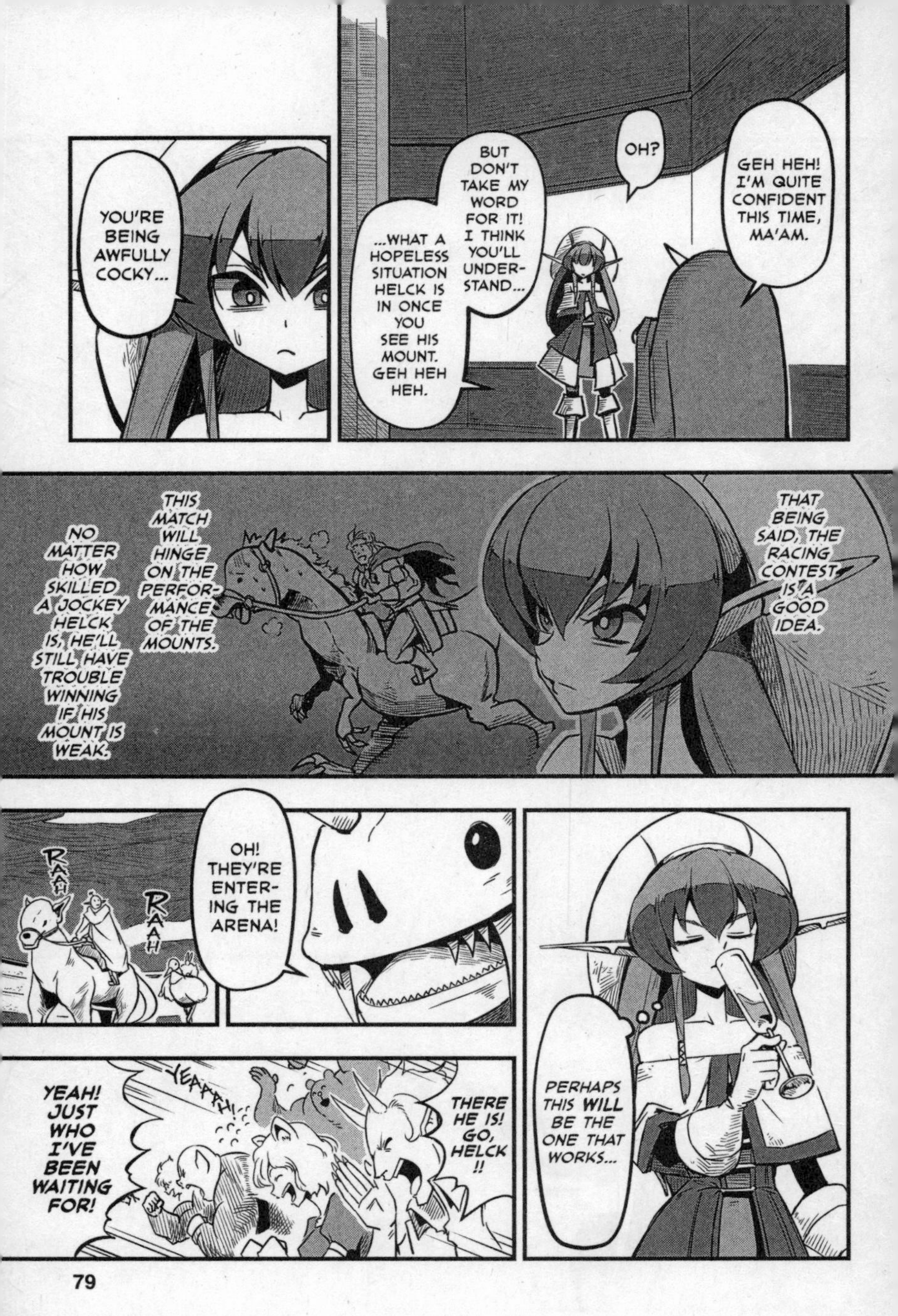
GEH HEH! I'M QUITE CONFIDENT THIS TIME, MA'AM.
OH?
BUT DON'T TAKE MY WORD FOR IT! I THINK YOU'LL UNDERSTAND...
...WHAT A HOPELESS SITUATION HELCK IS IN ONCE YOU SEE HIS MOUNT. GEH HEH HEH.
YOU'RE BEING AWFULLY COCKY...
THAT BEING SAID, THE RACING CONTEST IS A GOOD IDEA.
THIS MATCH WILL HINGE ON THE PERFORMANCE OF THE MOUNTS.
NO MATTER HOW SKILLED A JOCKEY HELCK IS, HE'LL STILL HAVE TROUBLE WINNING IF HIS MOUNT IS WEAK.
PERHAPS THIS **WILL** BE THE ONE THAT WORKS...
OH! THEY'RE ENTERING THE ARENA!
RAAH
RAAH
YEAAAH!!
THERE HE IS! GO, HELCK!!
YEAH! JUST WHO I'VE BEEN WAITING FOR!

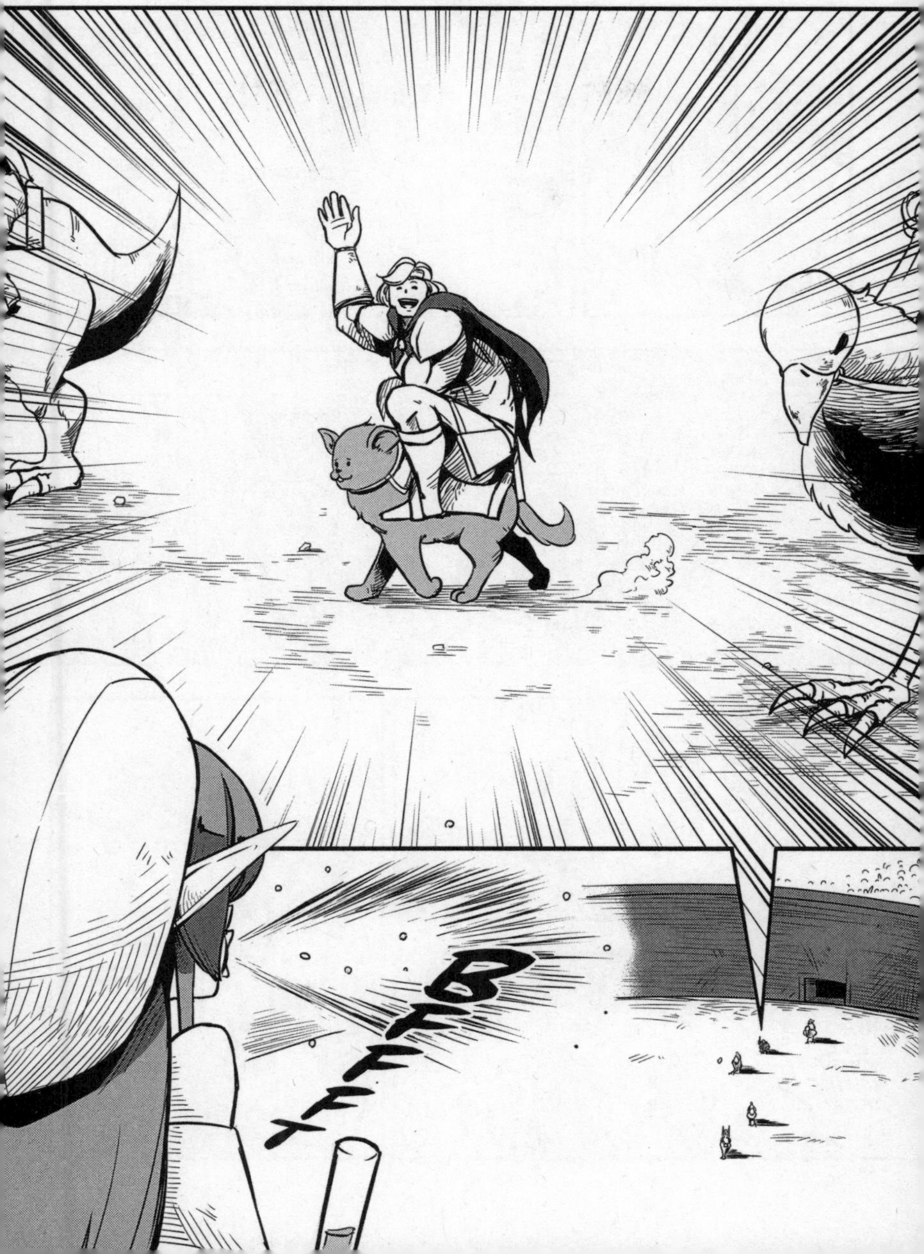
BFFFFT

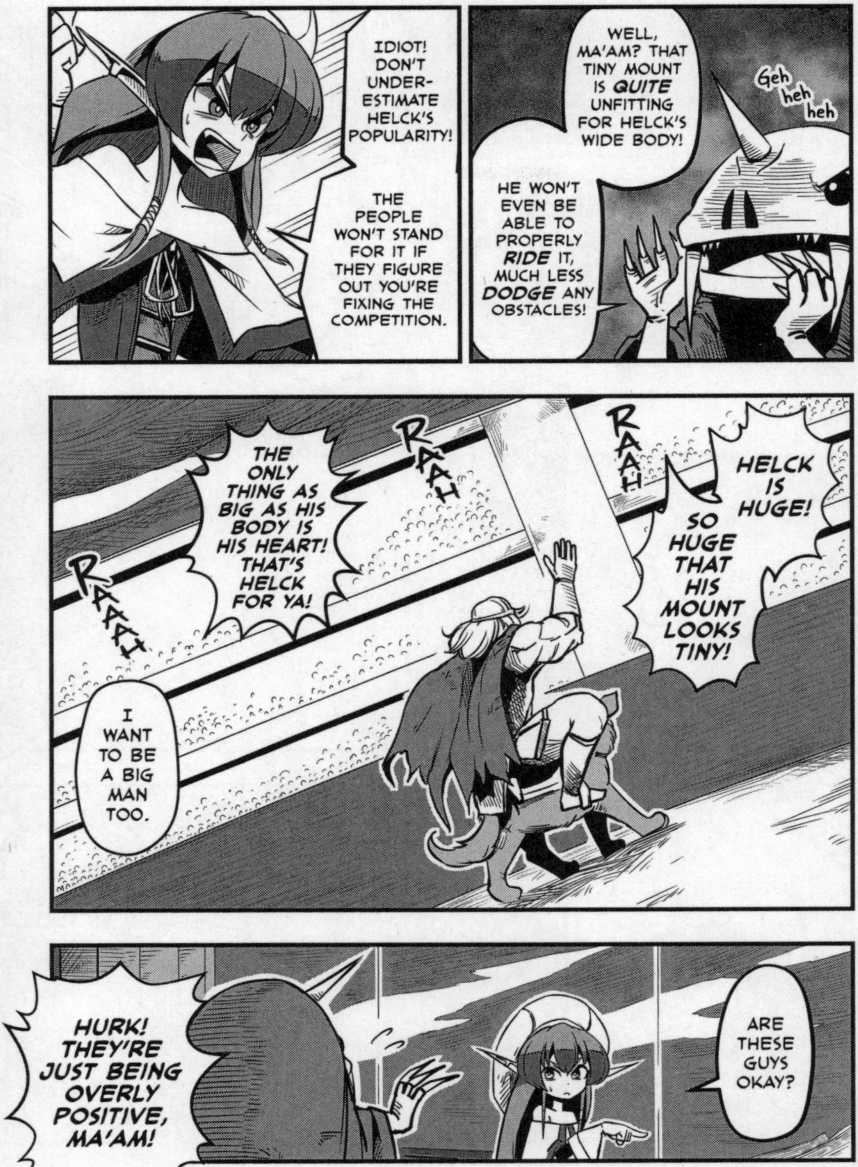
WELL, MA'AM? THAT TINY MOUNT IS QUITE UNFITTING FOR HELCK'S WIDE BODY!
Geh heh heh
HE WON'T EVEN BE ABLE TO PROPERLY RIDE IT, MUCH LESS DODGE ANY OBSTACLES!
IDIOT! DON'T UNDER-ESTIMATE HELCK'S POPULARITY!
THE PEOPLE WON'T STAND FOR IT IF THEY FIGURE OUT YOU'RE FIXING THE COMPETITION.
RAAH
HELCK IS HUGE!
SO HUGE THAT HIS MOUNT LOOKS TINY!
RAAH
THE ONLY THING AS BIG AS HIS BODY IS HIS HEART! THAT'S HELCK FOR YA!
RAAH
I WANT TO BE A BIG MAN TOO.
ARE THESE GUYS OKAY?
HURK! THEY'RE JUST BEING OVERLY POSITIVE, MA'AM!

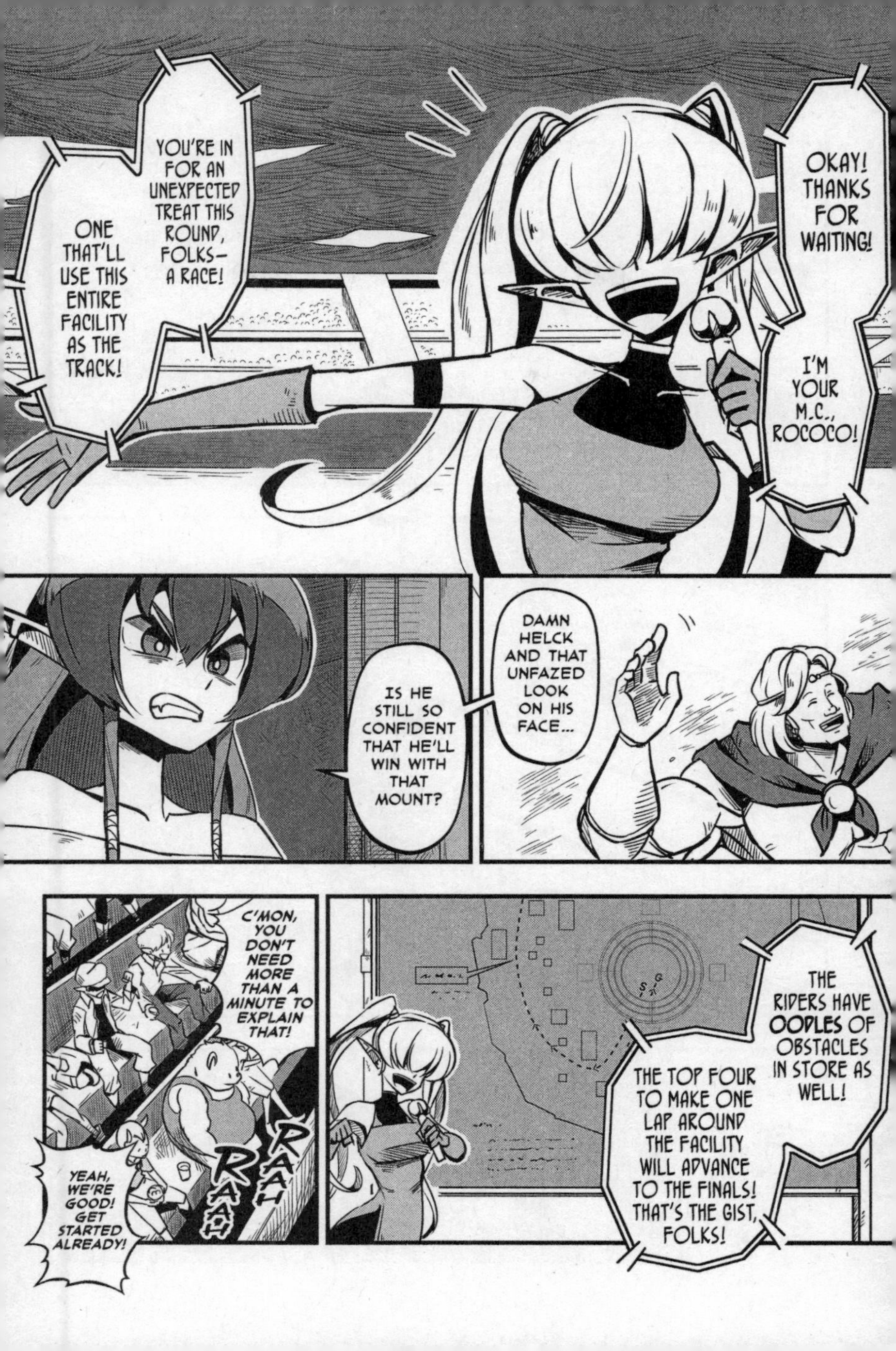
OKAY! THANKS FOR WAITING!
I'M YOUR M.C., ROCOCO!
YOU'RE IN FOR AN UNEXPECTED TREAT THIS ROUND, FOLKS— A RACE!
ONE THAT'LL USE THIS ENTIRE FACILITY AS THE TRACK!
DAMN HELCK AND THAT UNFAZED LOOK ON HIS FACE...
IS HE STILL SO CONFIDENT THAT HE'LL WIN WITH THAT MOUNT?
THE RIDERS HAVE OODLES OF OBSTACLES IN STORE AS WELL!
THE TOP FOUR TO MAKE ONE LAP AROUND THE FACILITY WILL ADVANCE TO THE FINALS! THAT'S THE GIST, FOLKS!
C'MON, YOU DON'T NEED MORE THAN A MINUTE TO EXPLAIN THAT!
RAAH
RAAH
YEAH, WE'RE GOOD! GET STARTED ALREADY!

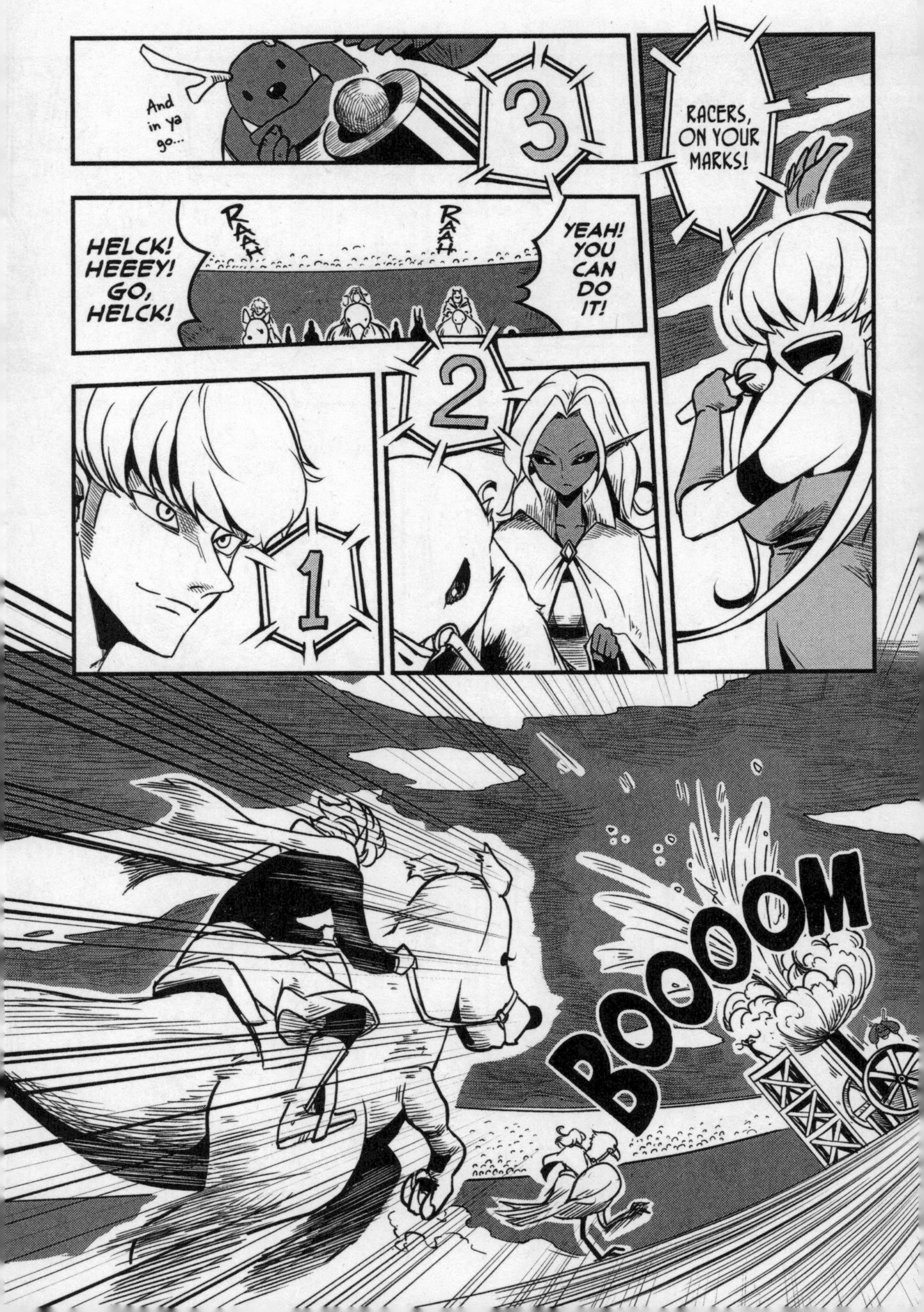
RACERS, ON YOUR MARKS!
3
And in ya go...
YEAH! YOU CAN DO IT!
RAAAH
RAAAH
HELCK! HEEEY! GO, HELCK!
2
1
BOOOOM

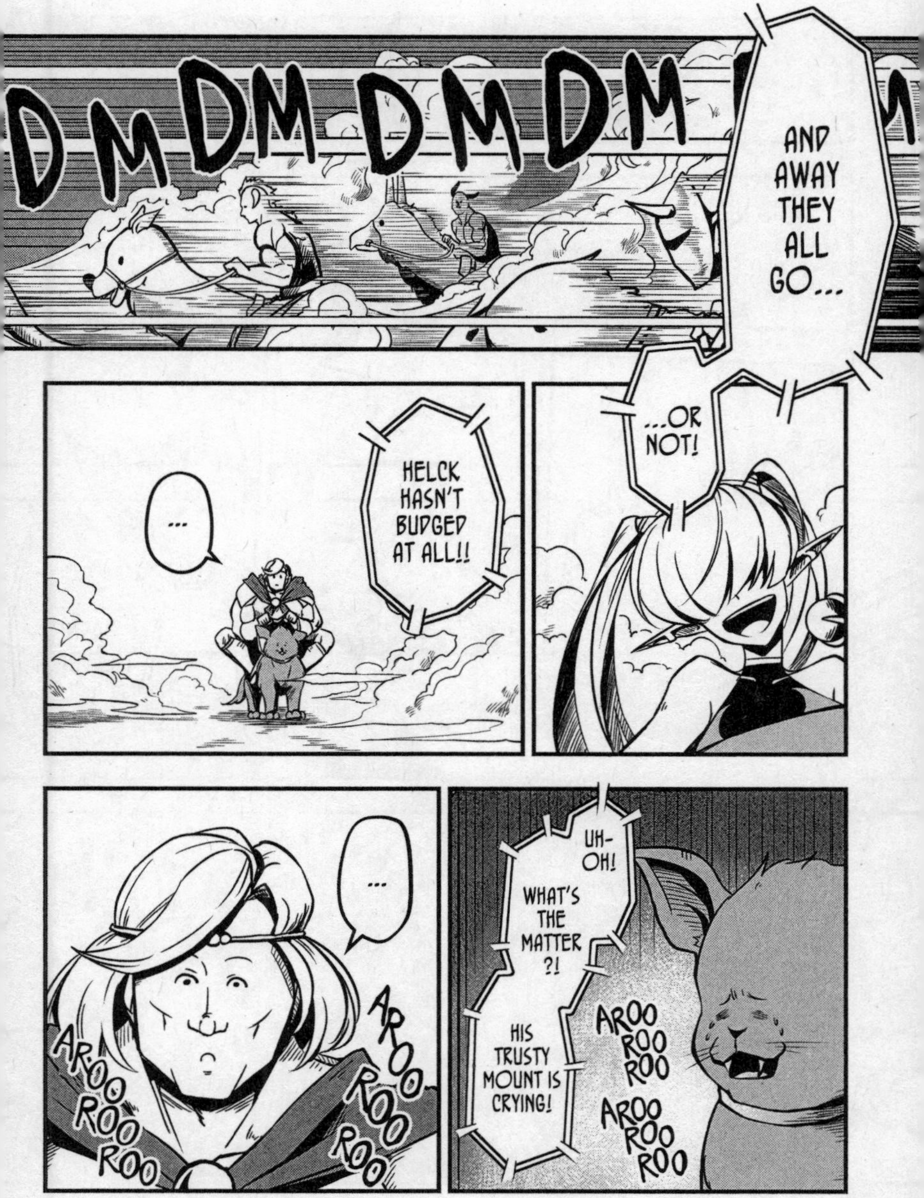
DMDMDMDMDM
AND AWAY THEY ALL GO...
...OR NOT!
HELCK HASN'T BUDGED AT ALL!!
...
UH-OH!
WHAT'S THE MATTER?!
HIS TRUSTY MOUNT IS CRYING!
AROO ROO ROO
AROO ROO ROO
...
AROO ROO ROO
AROO ROO ROO

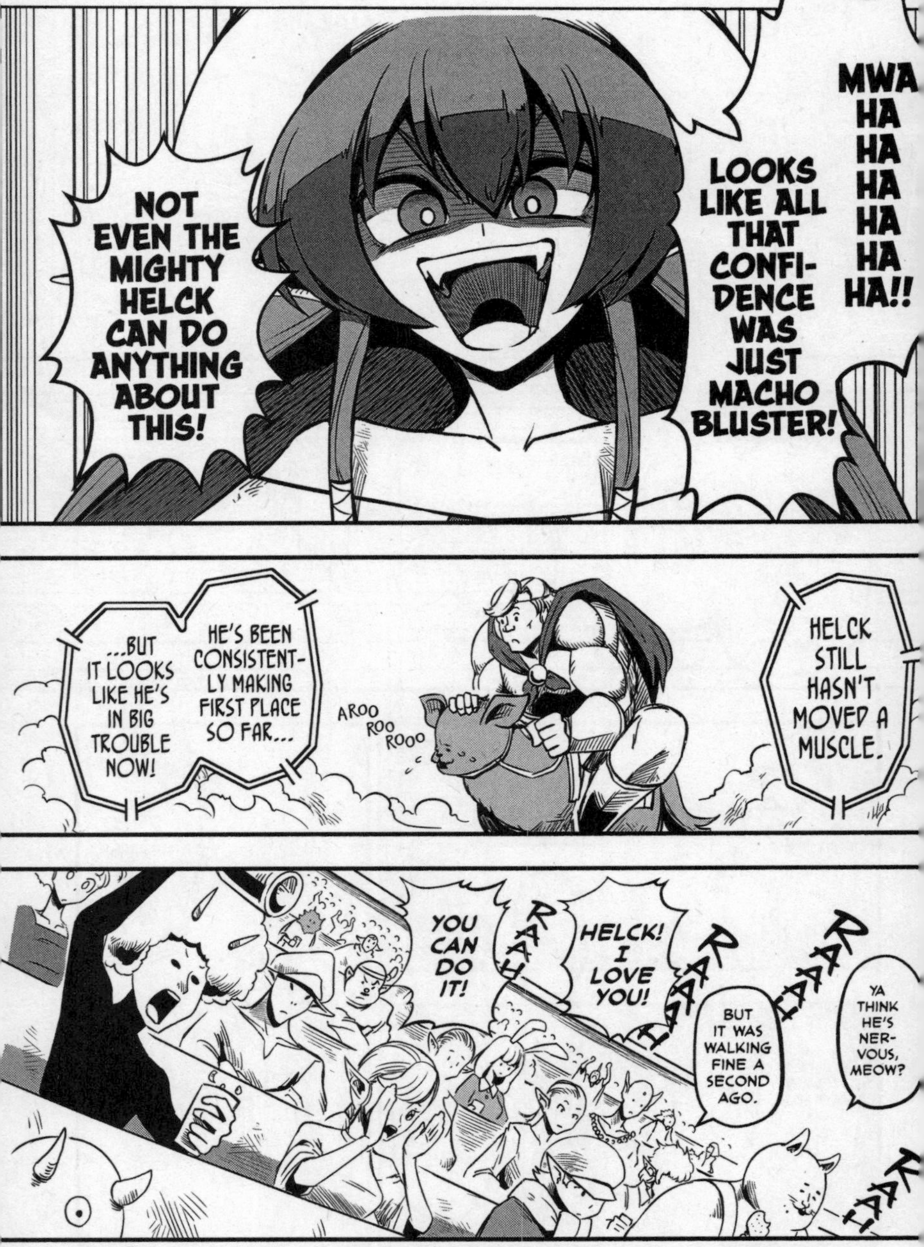
MWA HA HA HA HA HA HA!!
LOOKS LIKE ALL THAT CONFI-DENCE WAS JUST MACHO BLUSTER!
NOT EVEN THE MIGHTY HELCK CAN DO ANYTHING ABOUT THIS!
HELCK STILL HASN'T MOVED A MUSCLE.
AROO ROO ROOO
HE'S BEEN CONSISTENT-LY MAKING FIRST PLACE SO FAR...
...BUT IT LOOKS LIKE HE'S IN BIG TROUBLE NOW!
YA THINK HE'S NER-VOUS, MEOW?
RAAH
RAAAH
BUT IT WAS WALKING FINE A SECOND AGO.
RAAAH
HELCK! I LOVE YOU!
RAAH
YOU CAN DO IT!

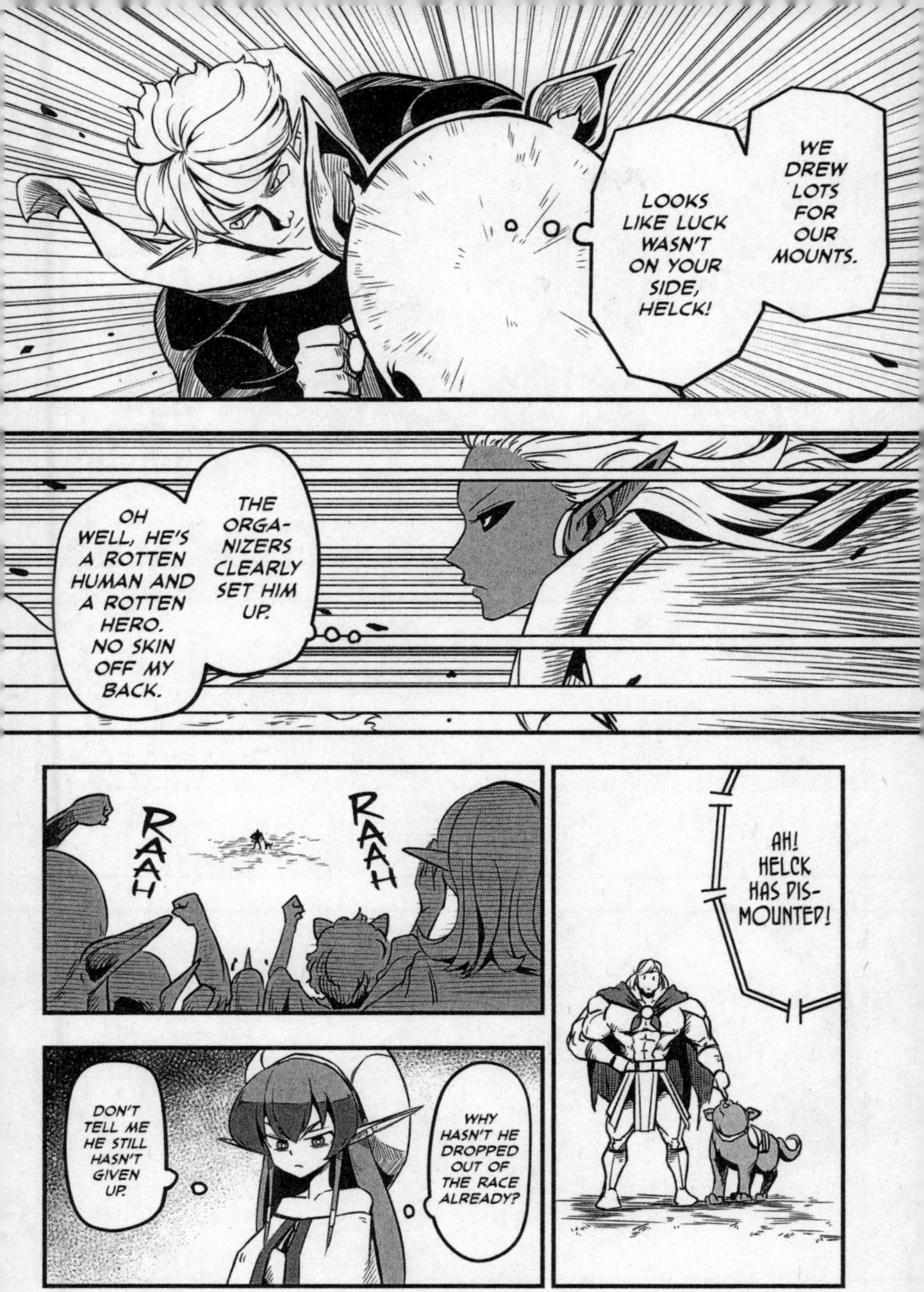
WE DREW LOTS FOR OUR MOUNTS.
LOOKS LIKE LUCK WASN'T ON YOUR SIDE, HELCK!
THE ORGA-NIZERS CLEARLY SET HIM UP.
OH WELL, HE'S A ROTTEN HUMAN AND A ROTTEN HERO. NO SKIN OFF MY BACK.
AH! HELCK HAS DIS-MOUNTED!
RAAH
RAAH
WHY HASN'T HE DROPPED OUT OF THE RACE ALREADY?
DON'T TELL ME HE STILL HASN'T GIVEN UP.

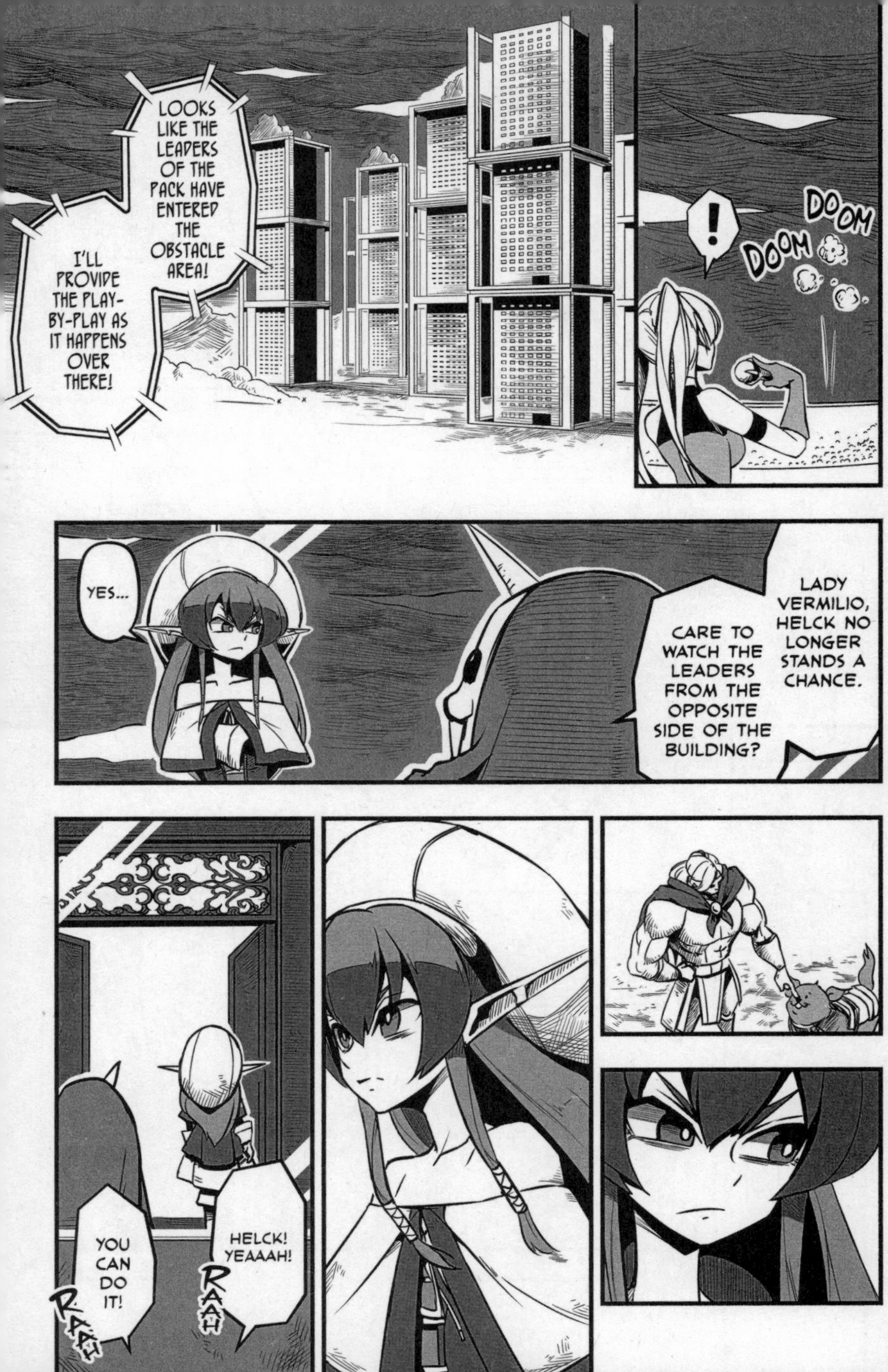
!
DOOM
DOOM
LOOKS LIKE THE LEADERS OF THE PACK HAVE ENTERED THE OBSTACLE AREA!
I'LL PROVIDE THE PLAY-BY-PLAY AS IT HAPPENS OVER THERE!
LADY VERMILIO, HELCK NO LONGER STANDS A CHANCE.
CARE TO WATCH THE LEADERS FROM THE OPPOSITE SIDE OF THE BUILDING?
YES...
HELCK! YEAAAH!
RAAAH
YOU CAN DO IT!
RAAAH

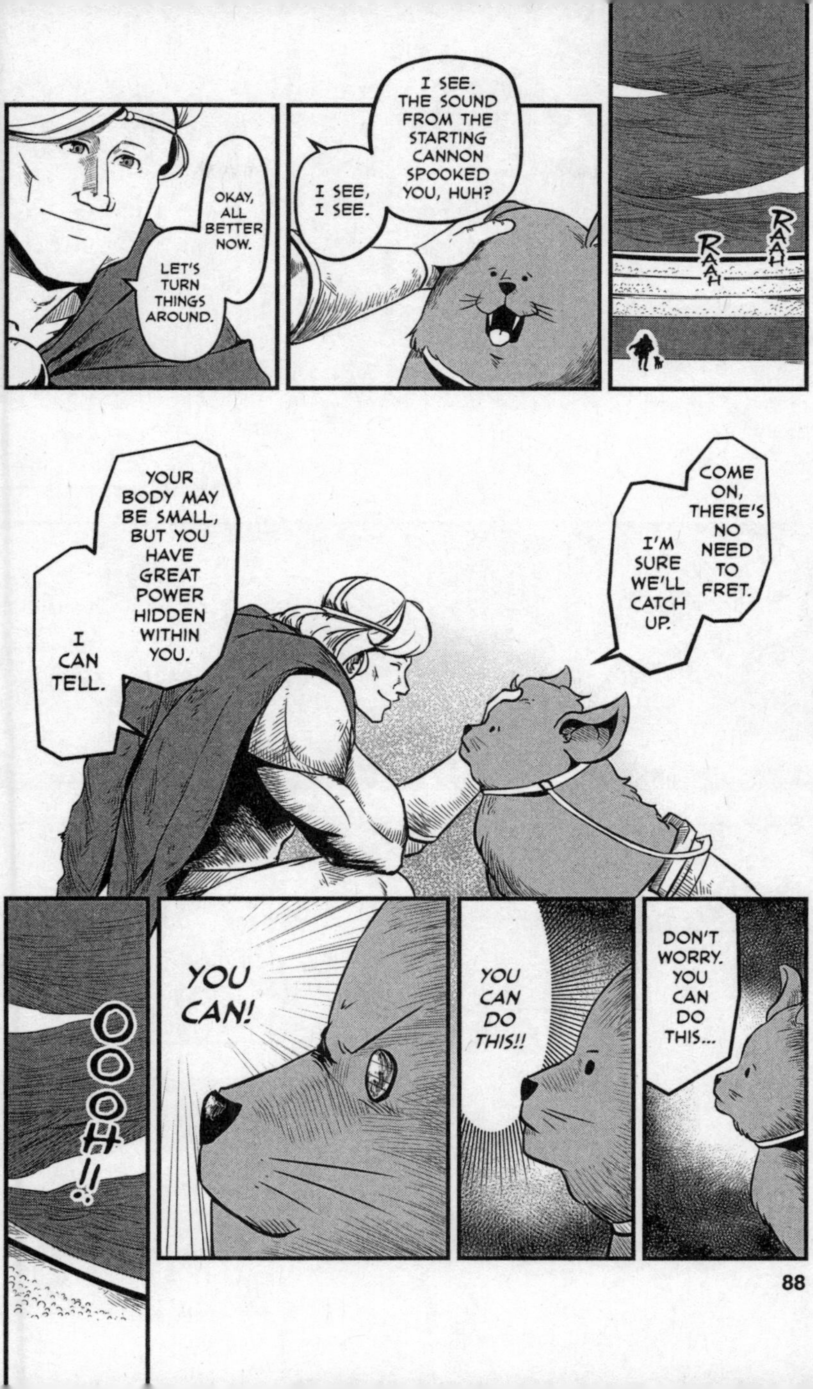
RAAH
RAAH
I SEE. THE SOUND FROM THE STARTING CANNON SPOOKED YOU, HUH?
I SEE, I SEE.
OKAY, ALL BETTER NOW.
LET'S TURN THINGS AROUND.
COME ON, THERE'S NO NEED TO FRET.
I'M SURE WE'LL CATCH UP.
YOUR BODY MAY BE SMALL, BUT YOU HAVE GREAT POWER HIDDEN WITHIN YOU.
I CAN TELL.
DON'T WORRY. YOU CAN DO THIS...
YOU CAN DO THIS!!
YOU CAN!
OOOOH!!

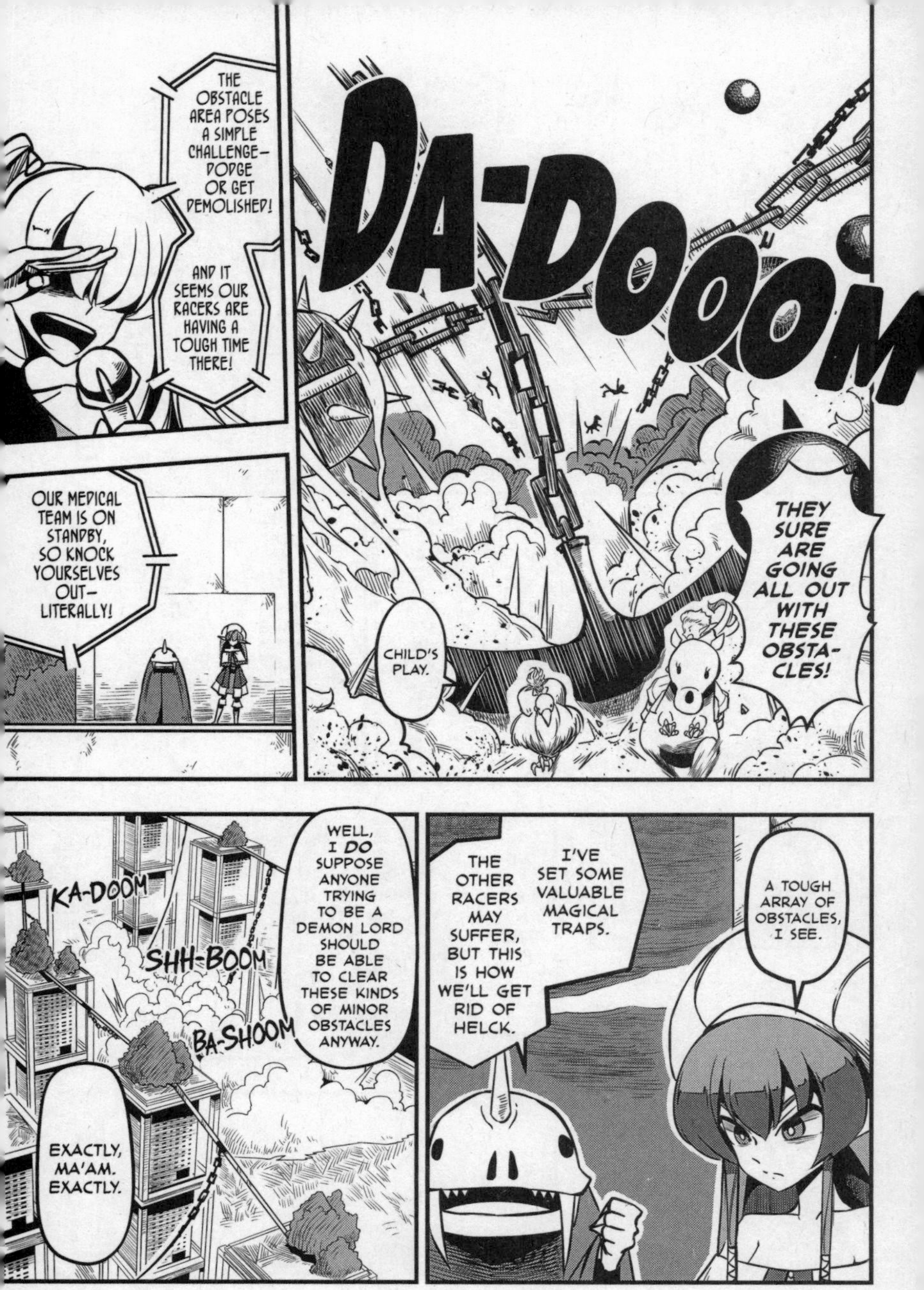
DA-DOOOM
THEY SURE ARE GOING ALL OUT WITH THESE OBSTACLES!
CHILD'S PLAY.
THE OBSTACLE AREA POSES A SIMPLE CHALLENGE—DODGE OR GET DEMOLISHED!
AND IT SEEMS OUR RACERS ARE HAVING A TOUGH TIME THERE!
OUR MEDICAL TEAM IS ON STANDBY, SO KNOCK YOURSELVES OUT—LITERALLY!
A TOUGH ARRAY OF OBSTACLES, I SEE.
I'VE SET SOME VALUABLE MAGICAL TRAPS.
THE OTHER RACERS MAY SUFFER, BUT THIS IS HOW WE'LL GET RID OF HELCK.
WELL, I *DO* SUPPOSE ANYONE TRYING TO BE A DEMON LORD SHOULD BE ABLE TO CLEAR THESE KINDS OF MINOR OBSTACLES ANYWAY.
KA-DOOM
SHH-BOOM
BA-SHOOM
EXACTLY, MA'AM. EXACTLY.

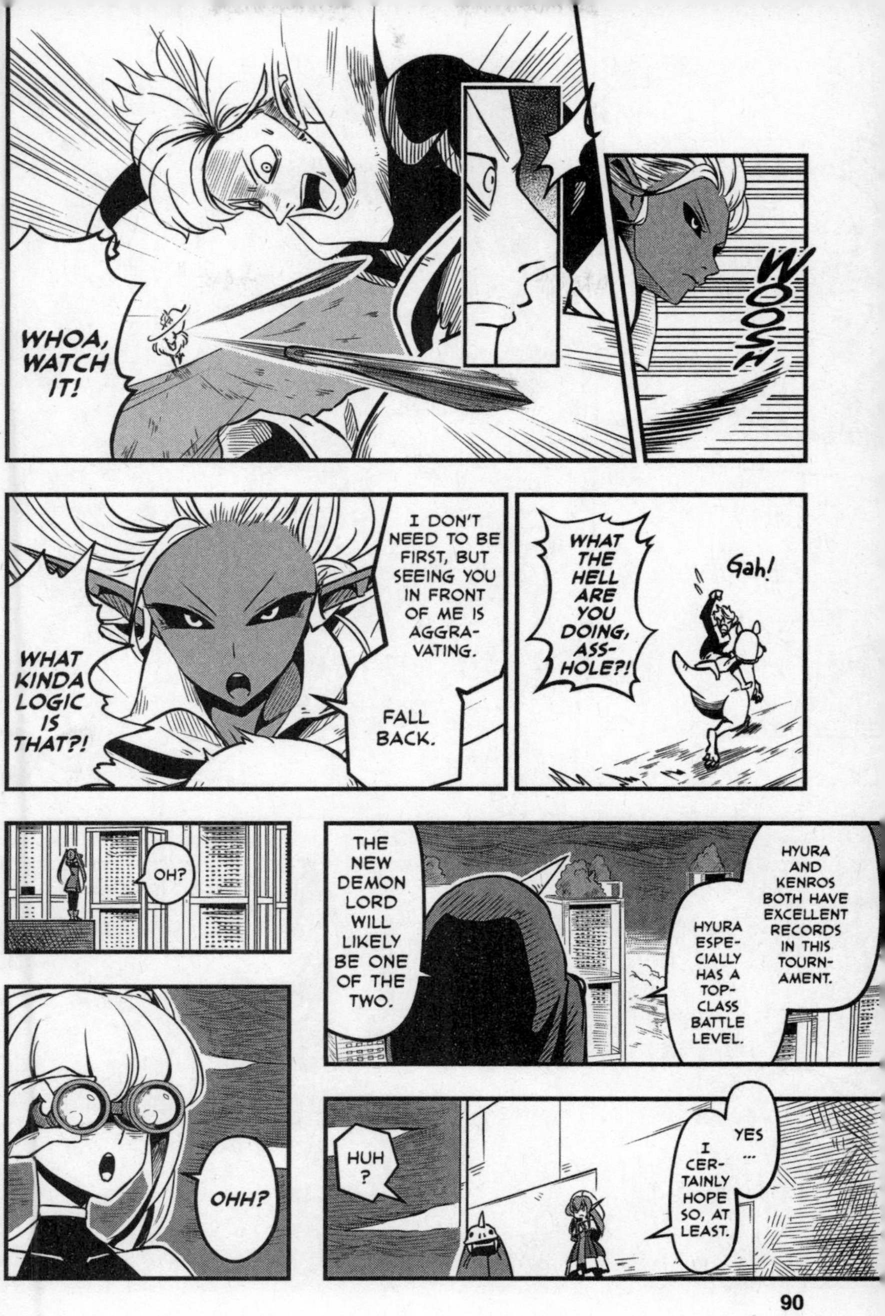
WOOSH
WHOA, WATCH IT!
Gah!
WHAT THE HELL ARE YOU DOING, ASS-HOLE?!
I DON'T NEED TO BE FIRST, BUT SEEING YOU IN FRONT OF ME IS AGGRA-VATING.
FALL BACK.
WHAT KINDA LOGIC IS THAT?!
HYURA AND KENROS BOTH HAVE EXCELLENT RECORDS IN THIS TOURN-AMENT.
HYURA ESPE-CIALLY HAS A TOP-CLASS BATTLE LEVEL.
THE NEW DEMON LORD WILL LIKELY BE ONE OF THE TWO.
OH?
YES ... I CER-TAINLY HOPE SO, AT LEAST.
HUH?
OHH?

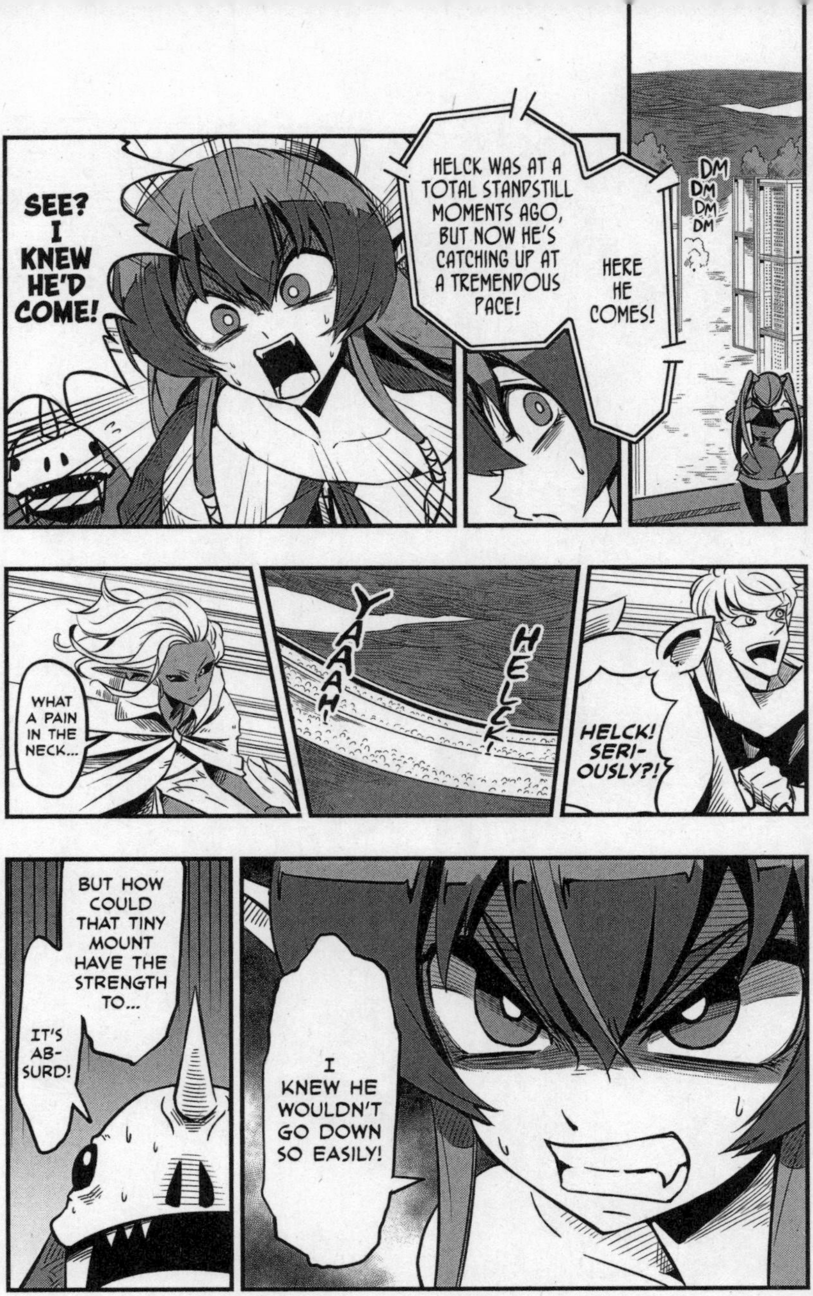
DM DM DM DM
HERE HE COMES!
HELCK WAS AT A TOTAL STANDSTILL MOMENTS AGO, BUT NOW HE'S CATCHING UP AT A TREMENDOUS PACE!
SEE? I KNEW HE'D COME!
HELCK! SERI-OUSLY?!
HELCK!
YAAAH!
WHAT A PAIN IN THE NECK...
I KNEW HE WOULDN'T GO DOWN SO EASILY!
BUT HOW COULD THAT TINY MOUNT HAVE THE STRENGTH TO...
IT'S AB-SURD!

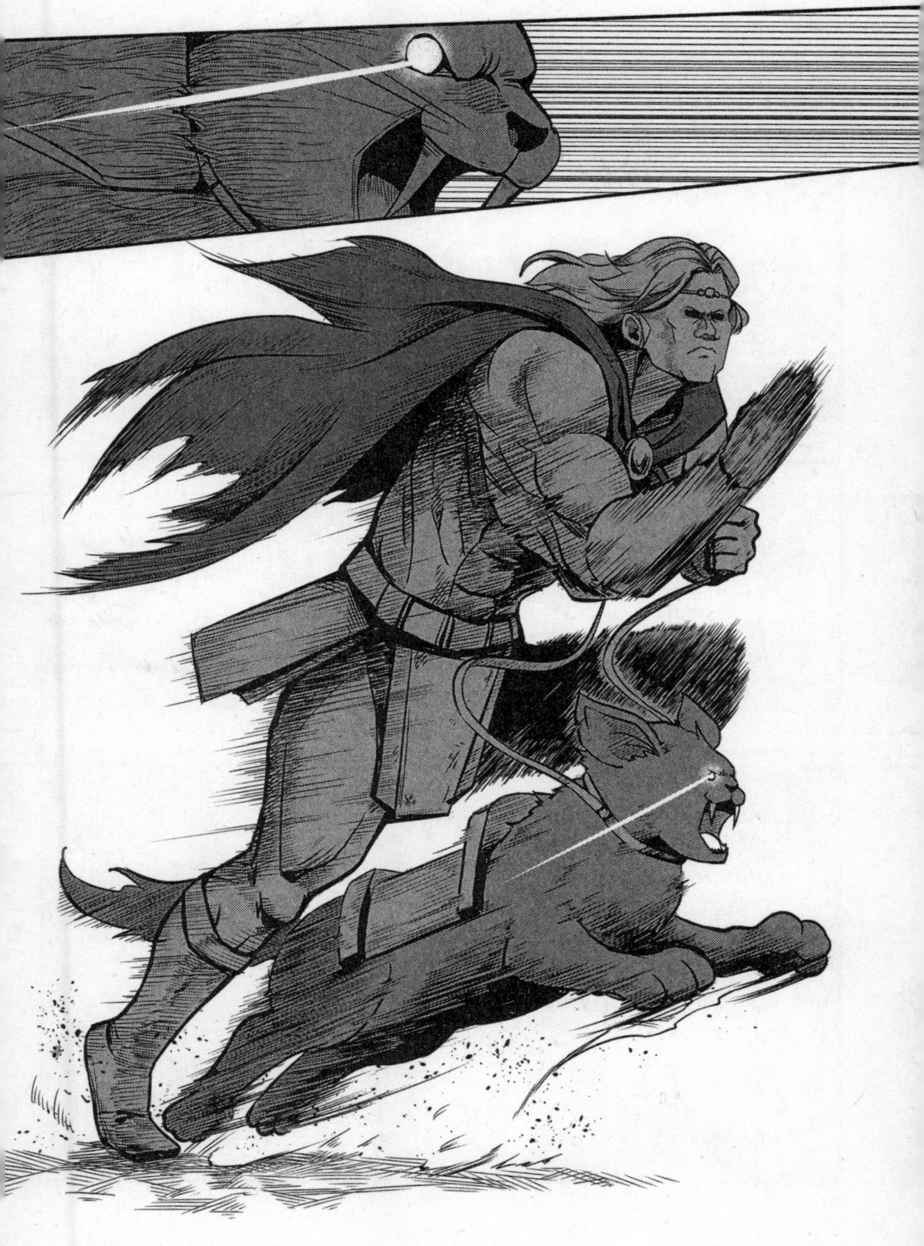

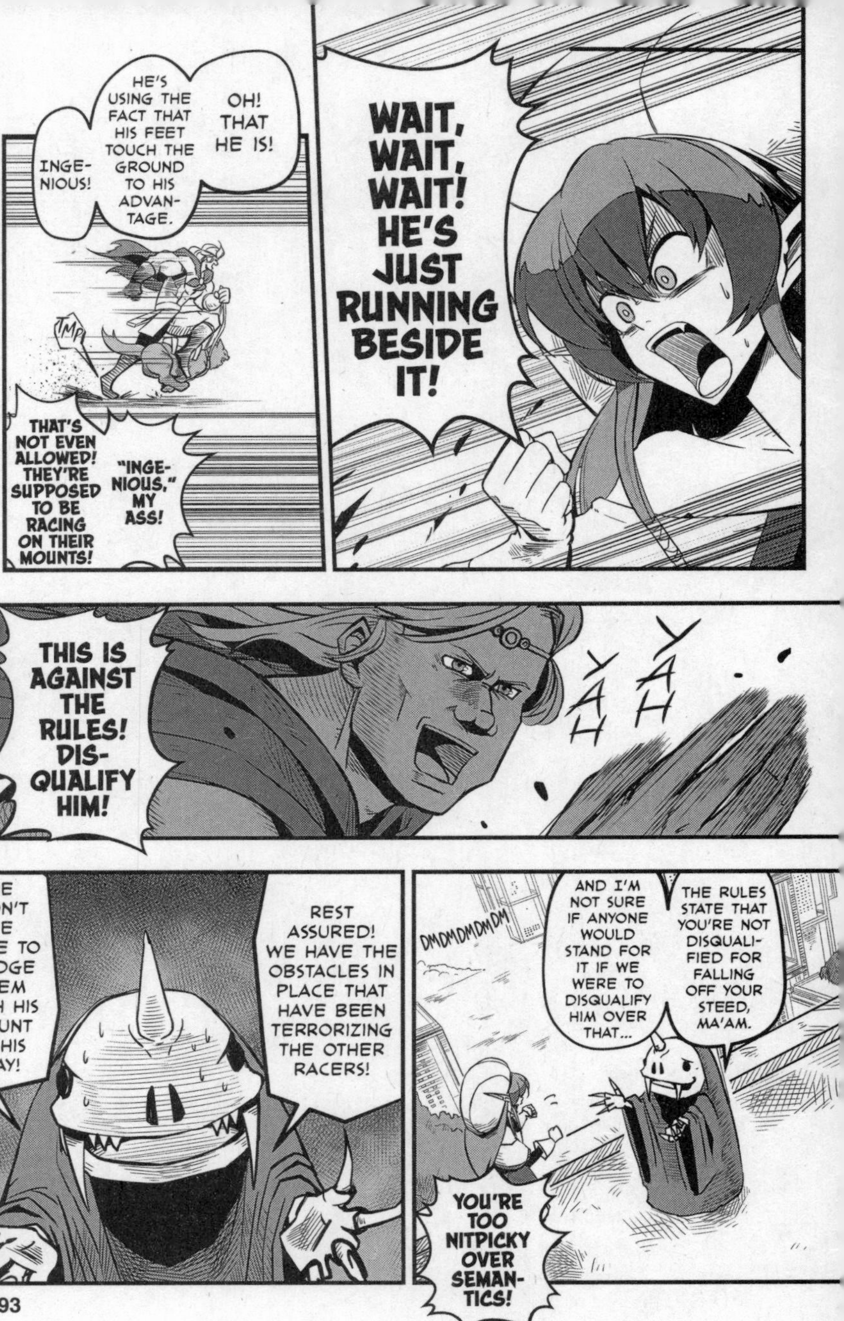
WAIT, WAIT, WAIT! HE'S JUST RUNNING BESIDE IT!
OH! THAT HE IS!
HE'S USING THE FACT THAT HIS FEET TOUCH THE GROUND TO HIS ADVANTAGE.
INGENIOUS!
TMP
"INGENIOUS," MY ASS!
THAT'S NOT EVEN ALLOWED! THEY'RE SUPPOSED TO BE RACING ON THEIR MOUNTS!
YAH
YAH
THIS IS AGAINST THE RULES! DISQUALIFY HIM!
THE RULES STATE THAT YOU'RE NOT DISQUALIFIED FOR FALLING OFF YOUR STEED, MA'AM.
AND I'M NOT SURE IF ANYONE WOULD STAND FOR IT IF WE WERE TO DISQUALIFY HIM OVER THAT...
DMDMDMDMDM
YOU'RE TOO NITPICKY OVER SEMANTICS!
REST ASSURED! WE HAVE THE OBSTACLES IN PLACE THAT HAVE BEEN TERRORIZING THE OTHER RACERS!
HE WON'T BE ABLE TO DODGE THEM WITH HIS MOUNT IN HIS WAY!

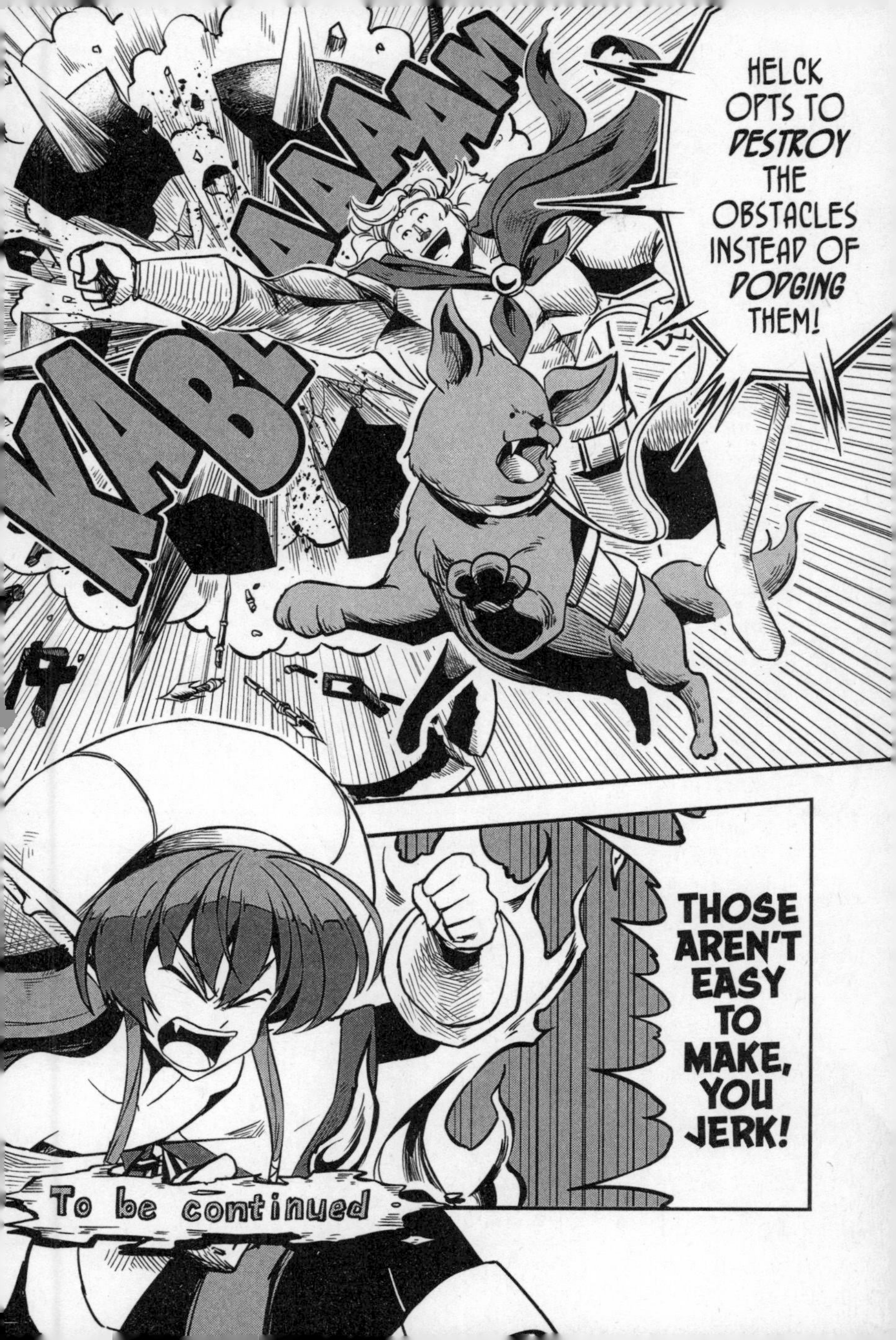
KABLAAAM
HELCK OPTS TO DESTROY THE OBSTACLES INSTEAD OF DODGING THEM!
THOSE AREN'T EASY TO MAKE, YOU JERK!
To be continued

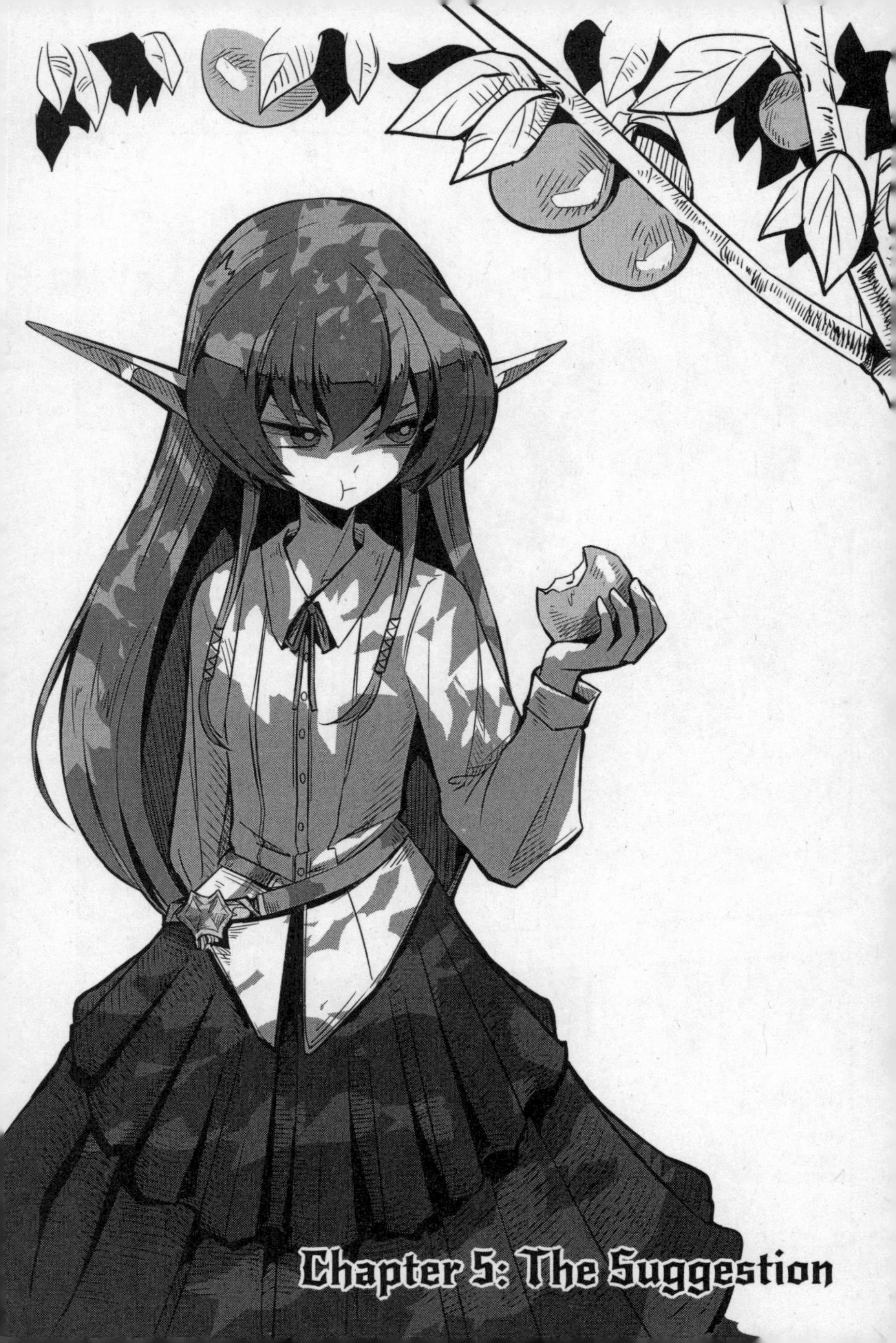

Chapter 5: The Suggestion

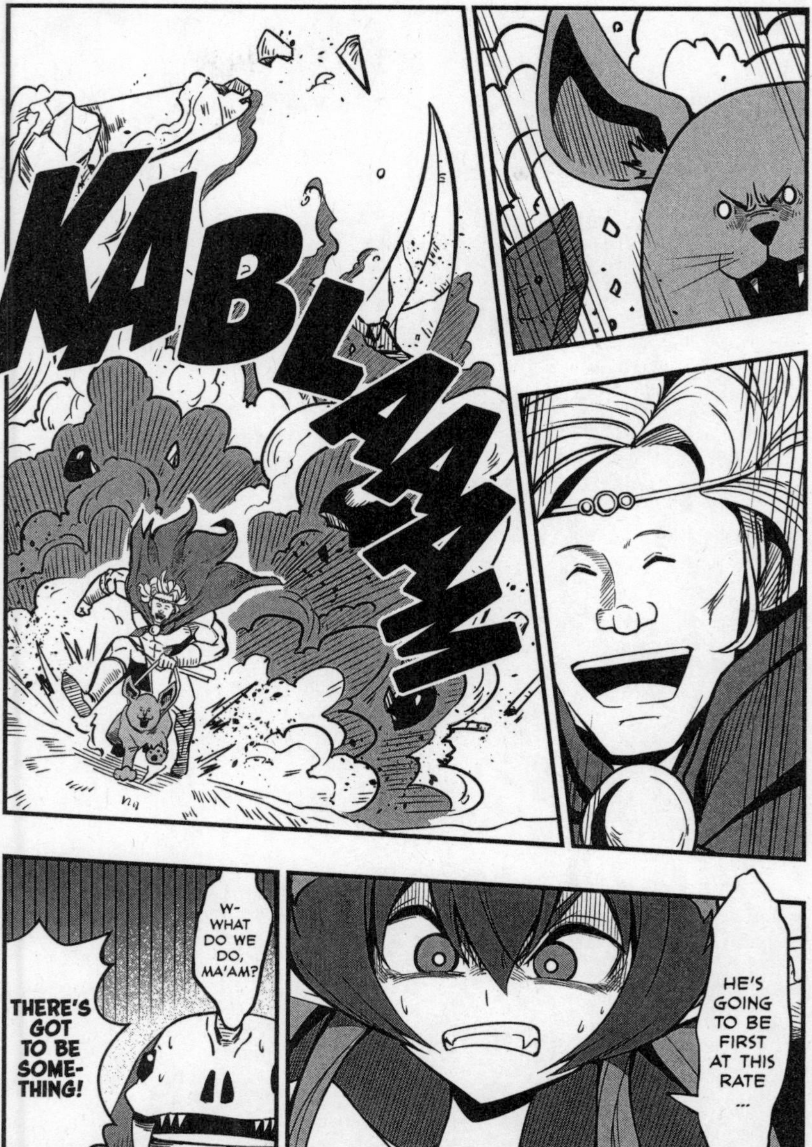
KABLAAAM!
HE'S GOING TO BE FIRST AT THIS RATE ...
W-WHAT DO WE DO, MA'AM?
THERE'S GOT TO BE SOME-THING!

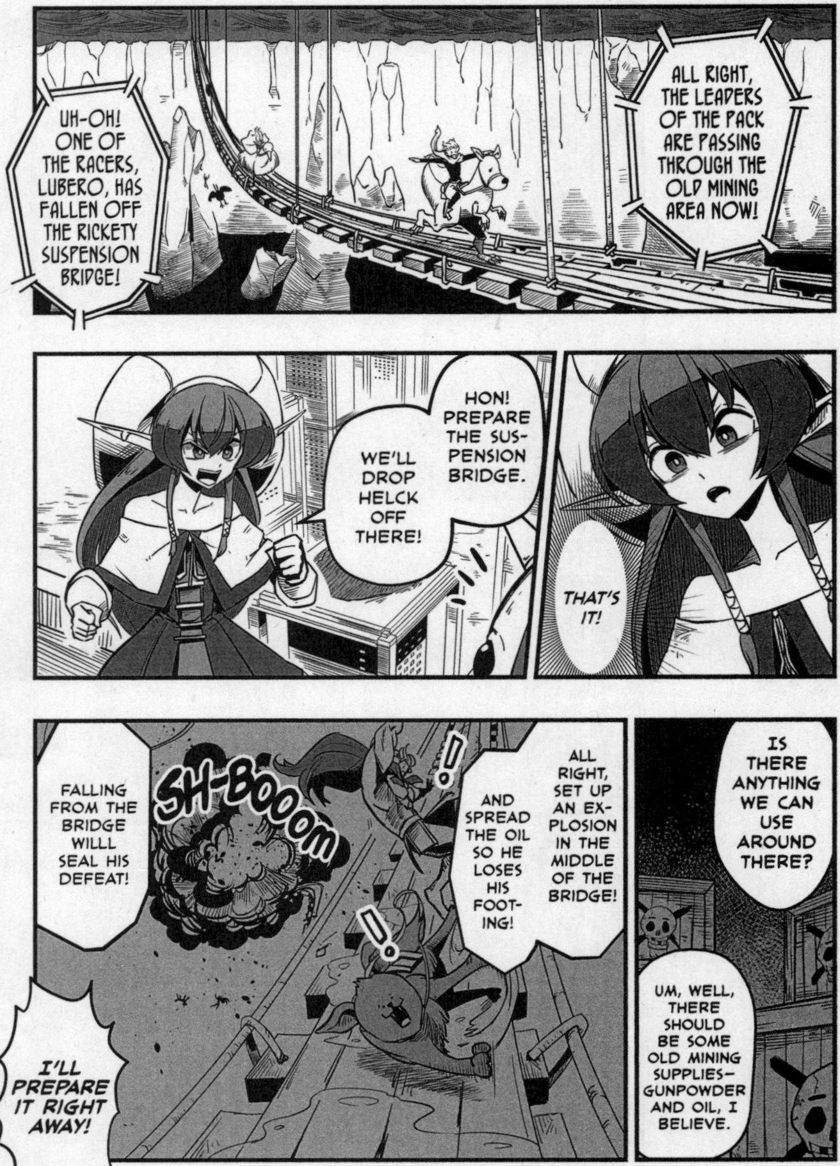
ALL RIGHT, THE LEADERS OF THE PACK ARE PASSING THROUGH THE OLD MINING AREA NOW!
UH-OH! ONE OF THE RACERS, LUBERO, HAS FALLEN OFF THE RICKETY SUSPENSION BRIDGE!
THAT'S IT!
HON! PREPARE THE SUS-PENSION BRIDGE.
WE'LL DROP HELCK OFF THERE!
IS THERE ANYTHING WE CAN USE AROUND THERE?
UM, WELL, THERE SHOULD BE SOME OLD MINING SUPPLIES—GUNPOWDER AND OIL, I BELIEVE.
ALL RIGHT, SET UP AN EX-PLOSION IN THE MIDDLE OF THE BRIDGE!
AND SPREAD THE OIL SO HE LOSES HIS FOOT-ING!
SH-BOOOM
FALLING FROM THE BRIDGE WILLL SEAL HIS DEFEAT!
I'LL PREPARE IT RIGHT AWAY!

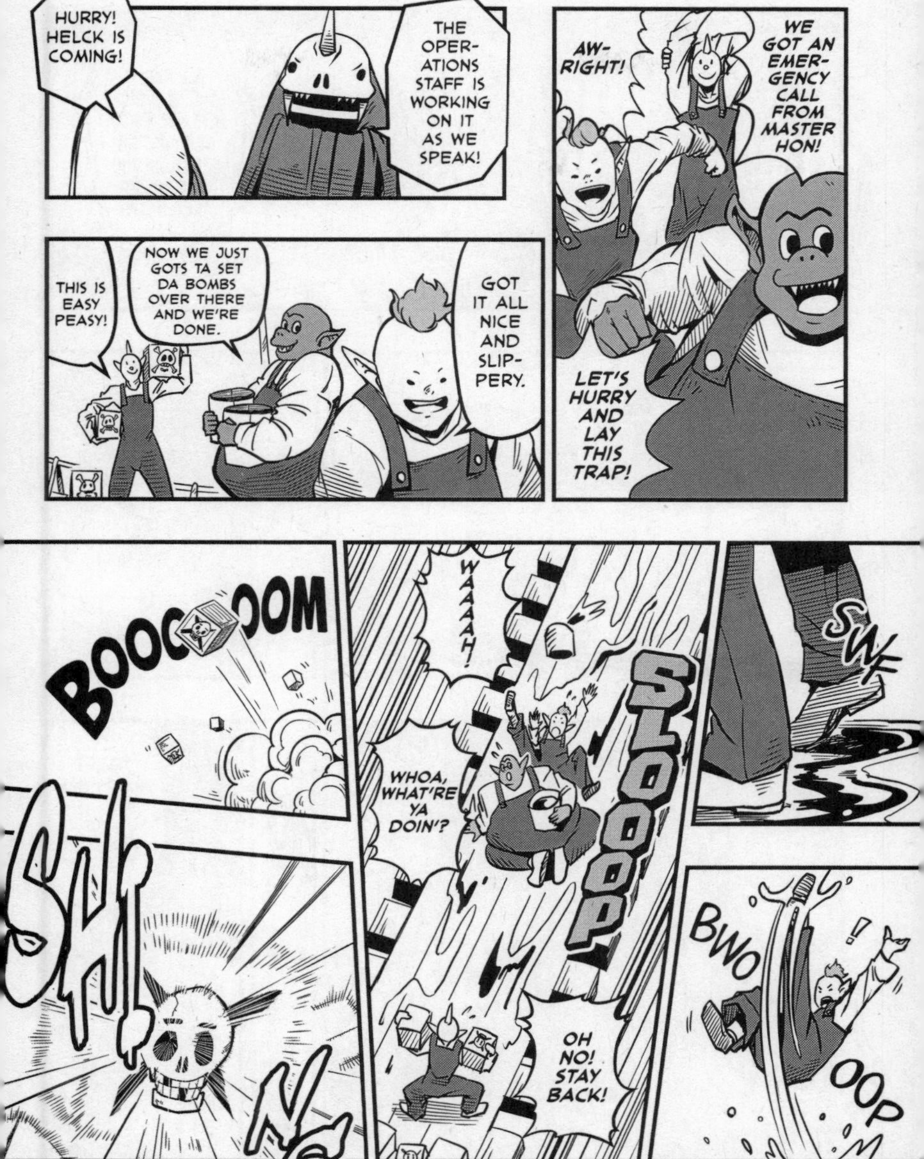
WE GOT AN EMERGENCY CALL FROM MASTER HON!
AW-RIGHT!
LET'S HURRY AND LAY THIS TRAP!
THE OPERATIONS STAFF IS WORKING ON IT AS WE SPEAK!
HURRY! HELCK IS COMING!
GOT IT ALL NICE AND SLIPPERY.
NOW WE JUST GOTS TA SET DA BOMBS OVER THERE AND WE'RE DONE.
THIS IS EASY PEASY!
SWF
BWOOOP
!
WAAAAH!
SLOOOOP
WHOA, WHAT'RE YA DOIN'?
OH NO! STAY BACK!
BOOOOM
SHING

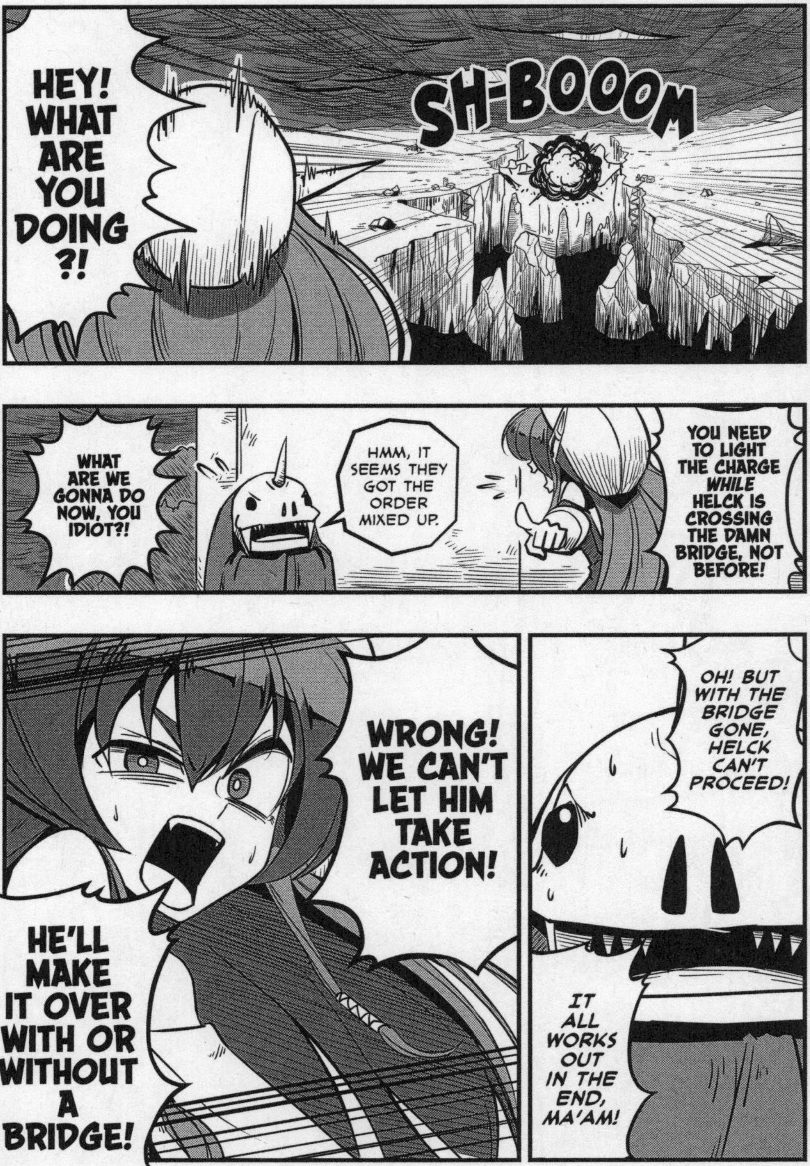
SH-BOOOM
HEY! WHAT ARE YOU DOING?!
YOU NEED TO LIGHT THE CHARGE WHILE HELCK IS CROSSING THE DAMN BRIDGE, NOT BEFORE!
HMM, IT SEEMS THEY GOT THE ORDER MIXED UP.
WHAT ARE WE GONNA DO NOW, YOU IDIOT?!
OH! BUT WITH THE BRIDGE GONE, HELCK CAN'T PROCEED!
IT ALL WORKS OUT IN THE END, MA'AM!
WRONG! WE CAN'T LET HIM TAKE ACTION!
HE'LL MAKE IT OVER WITH OR WITHOUT A BRIDGE!

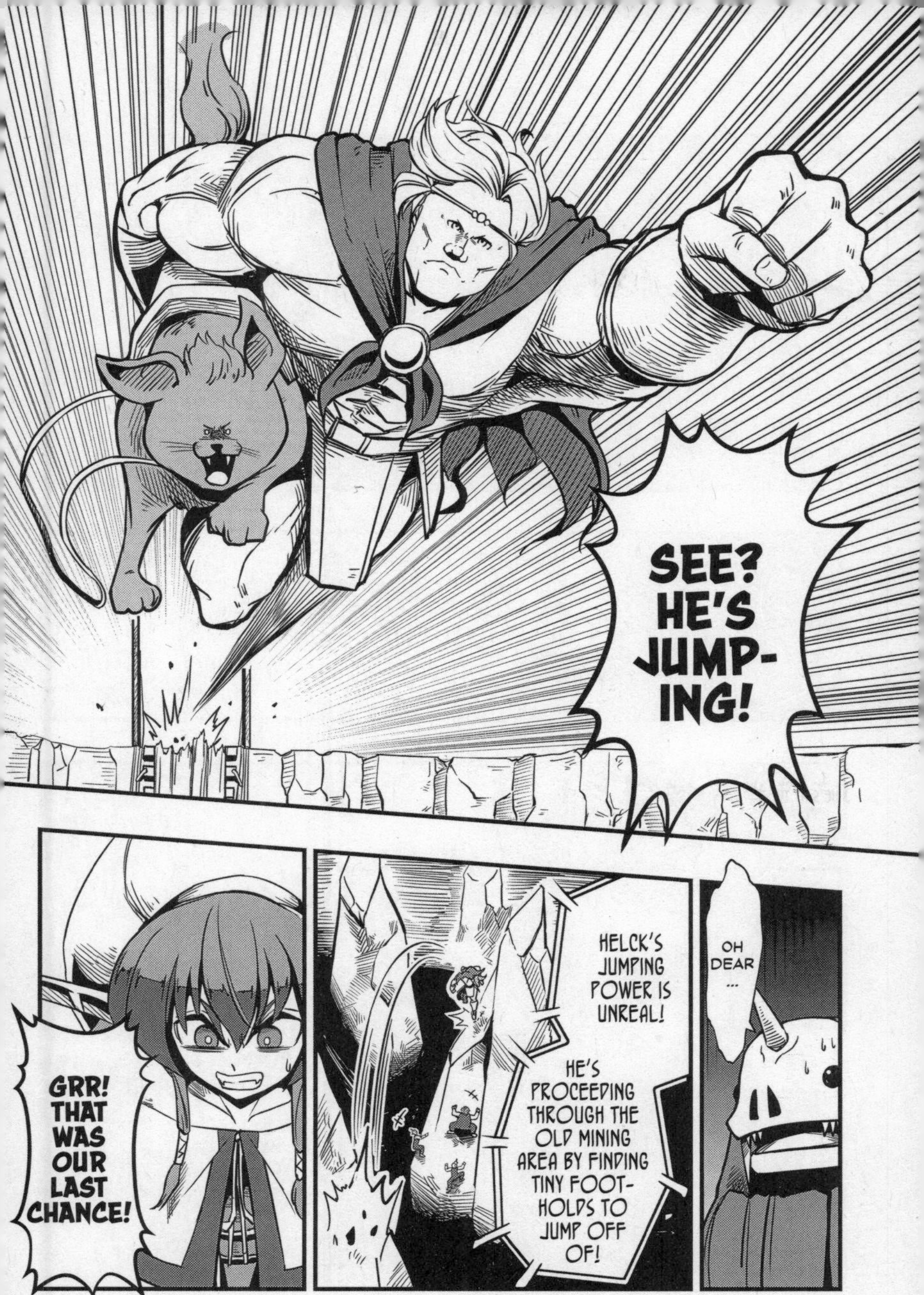
SEE? HE'S JUMP-ING!
OH DEAR ...
HELCK'S JUMPING POWER IS UNREAL!
HE'S PROCEEDING THROUGH THE OLD MINING AREA BY FINDING TINY FOOT-HOLDS TO JUMP OFF OF!
GRR! THAT WAS OUR LAST CHANCE!

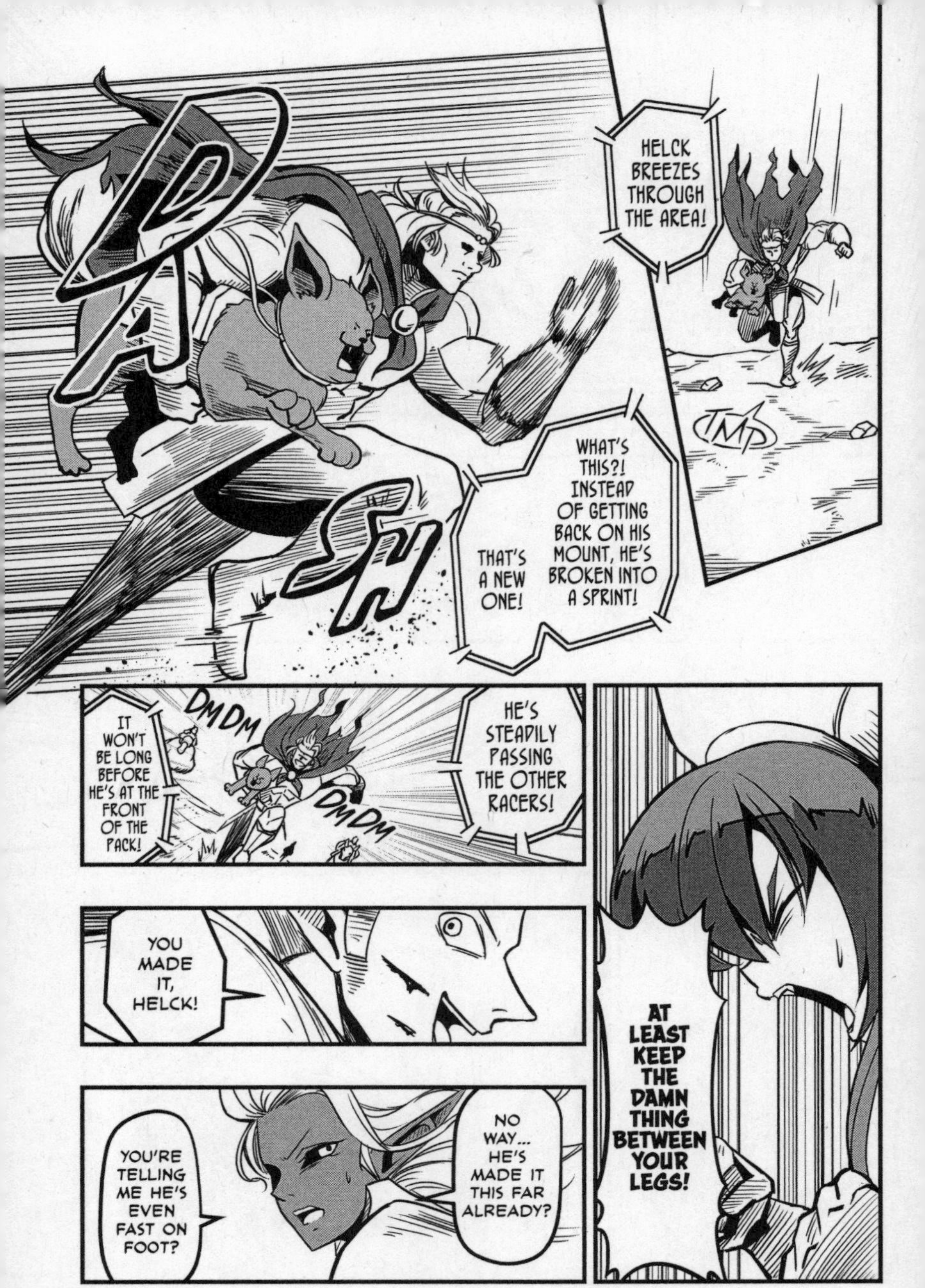

HELCK BREEZES THROUGH THE AREA!
TMP
WHAT'S THIS?! INSTEAD OF GETTING BACK ON HIS MOUNT, HE'S BROKEN INTO A SPRINT!
THAT'S A NEW ONE!
DA
SH
AT LEAST KEEP THE DAMN THING BETWEEN YOUR LEGS!
HE'S STEADILY PASSING THE OTHER RACERS!
DMDM
DMDM
IT WON'T BE LONG BEFORE HE'S AT THE FRONT OF THE PACK!
YOU MADE IT, HELCK!
NO WAY... HE'S MADE IT THIS FAR ALREADY?
YOU'RE TELLING ME HE'S EVEN FAST ON FOOT?

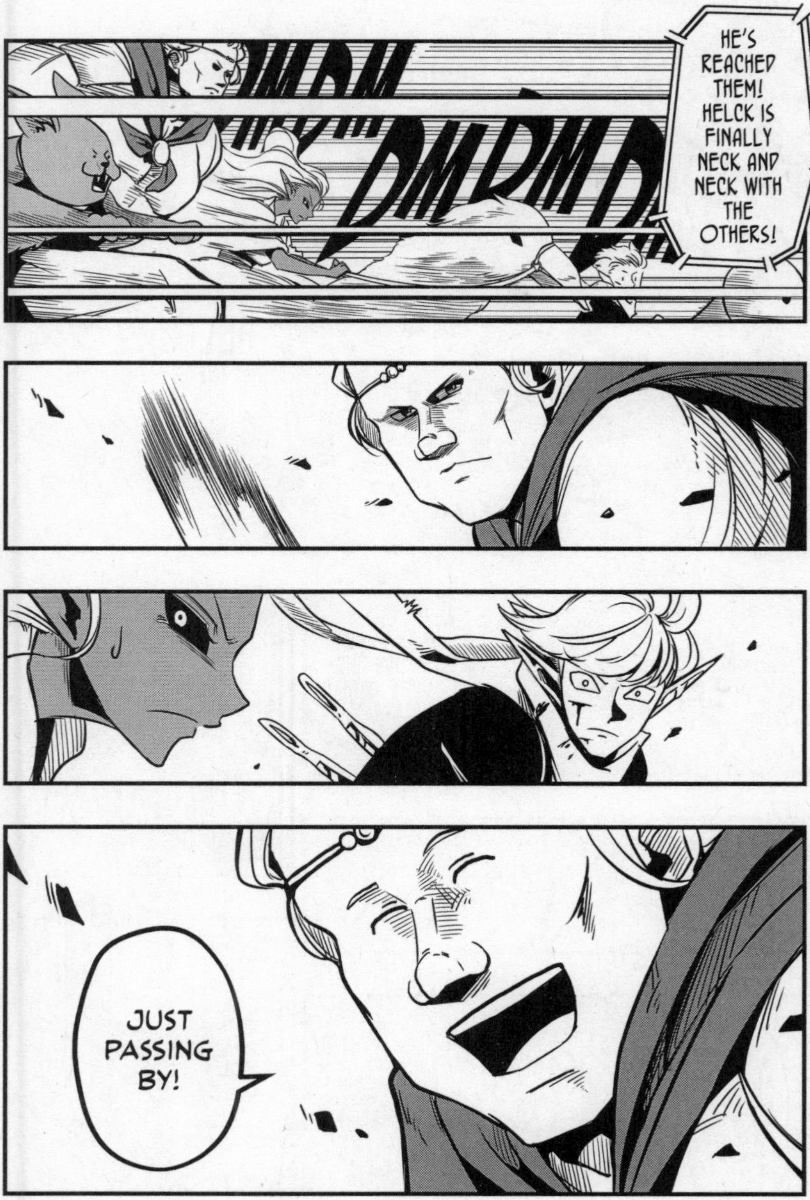

HE'S REACHED THEM! HELCK IS FINALLY NECK AND NECK WITH THE OTHERS!
DMDM DMDM
JUST PASSING BY!

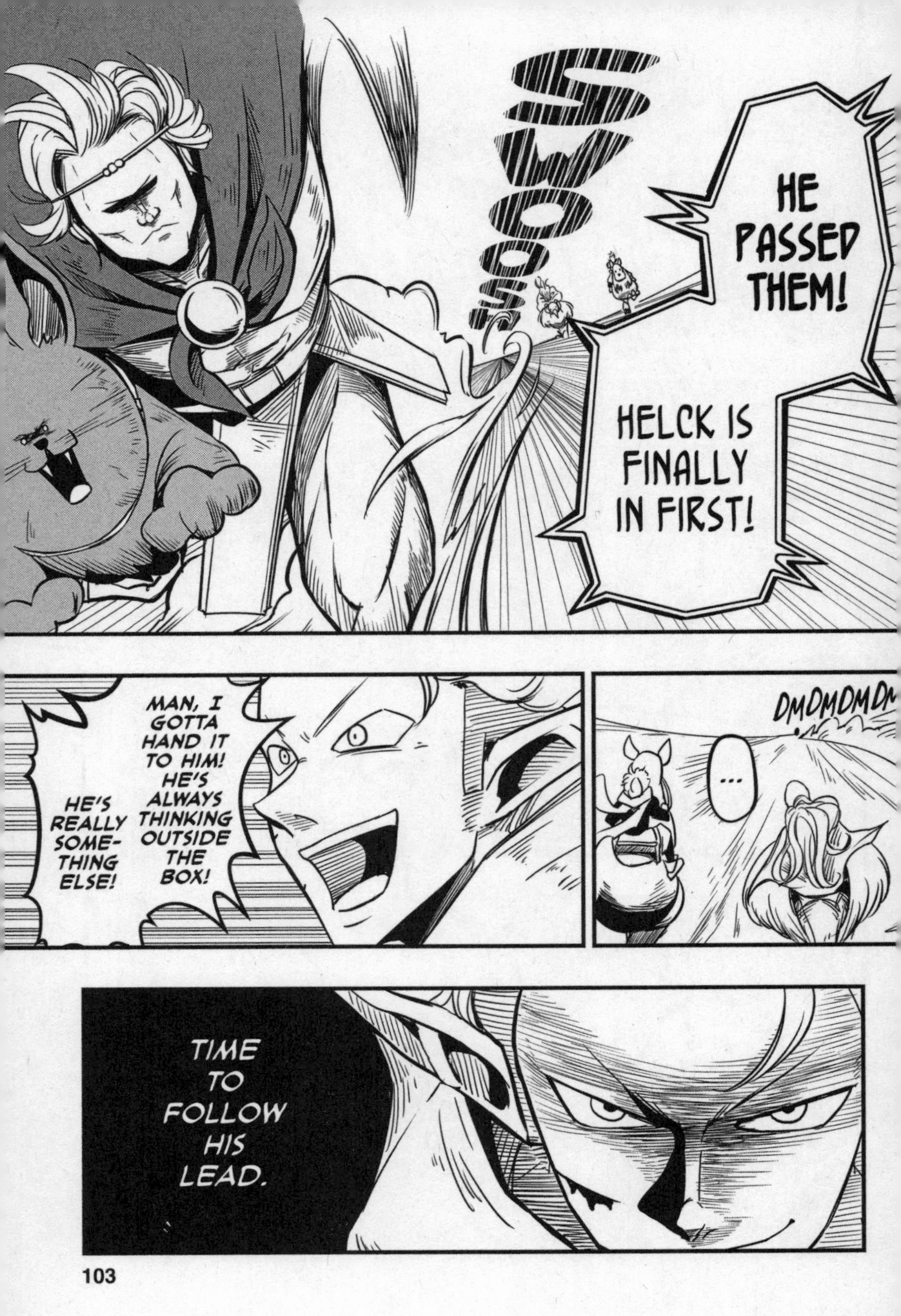
SWOOSH
HE PASSED THEM!
HELCK IS FINALLY IN FIRST!
DMDMDMDM
...
MAN, I GOTTA HAND IT TO HIM! HE'S ALWAYS THINKING OUTSIDE THE BOX!
HE'S REALLY SOMETHING ELSE!
TIME TO FOLLOW HIS LEAD.

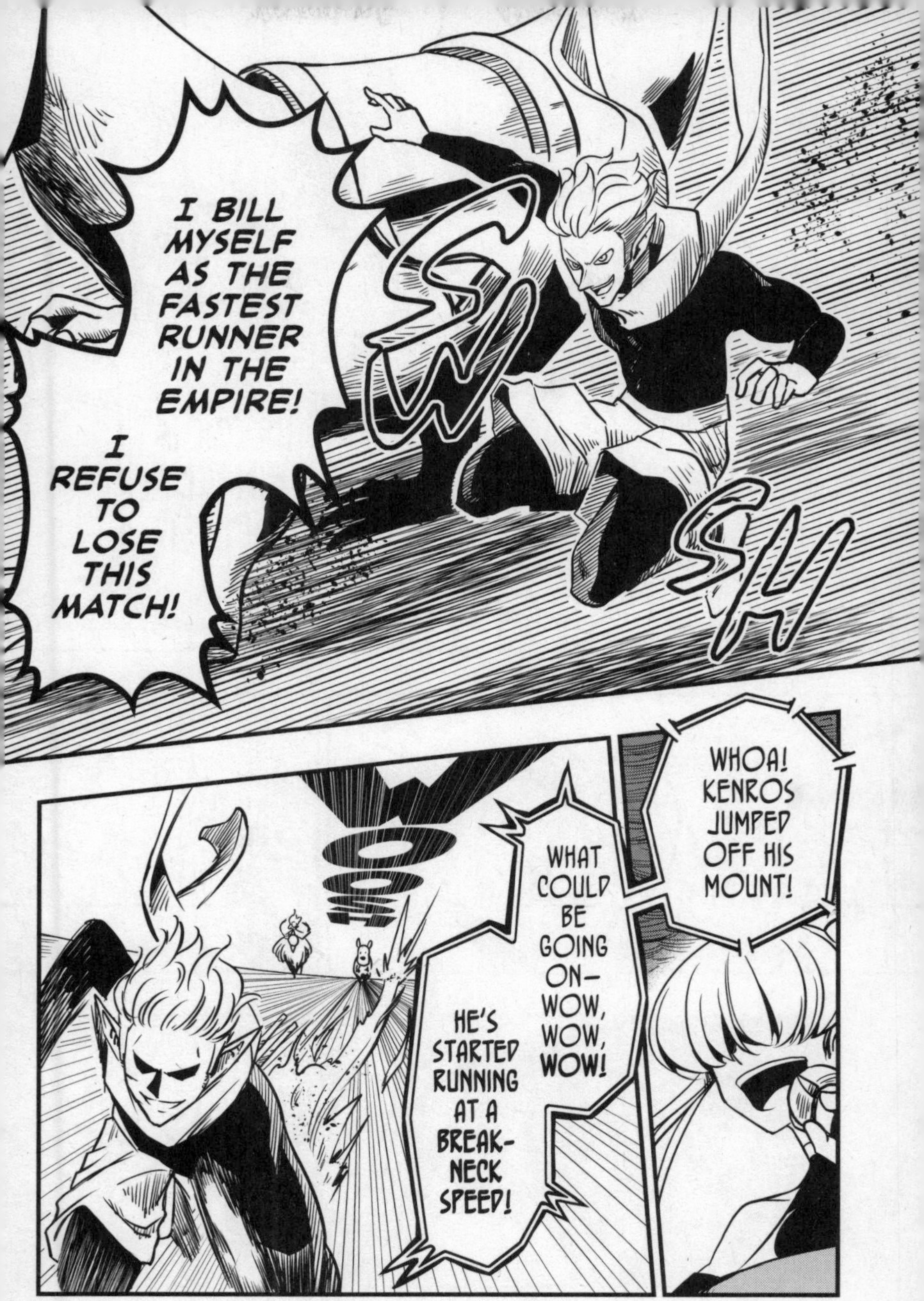
I BILL MYSELF AS THE FASTEST RUNNER IN THE EMPIRE!
I REFUSE TO LOSE THIS MATCH!
SH
SH
WHOA! KENROS JUMPED OFF HIS MOUNT!
WHAT COULD BE GOING ON—WOW, WOW, WOW!
HE'S STARTED RUNNING AT A BREAK-NECK SPEED!

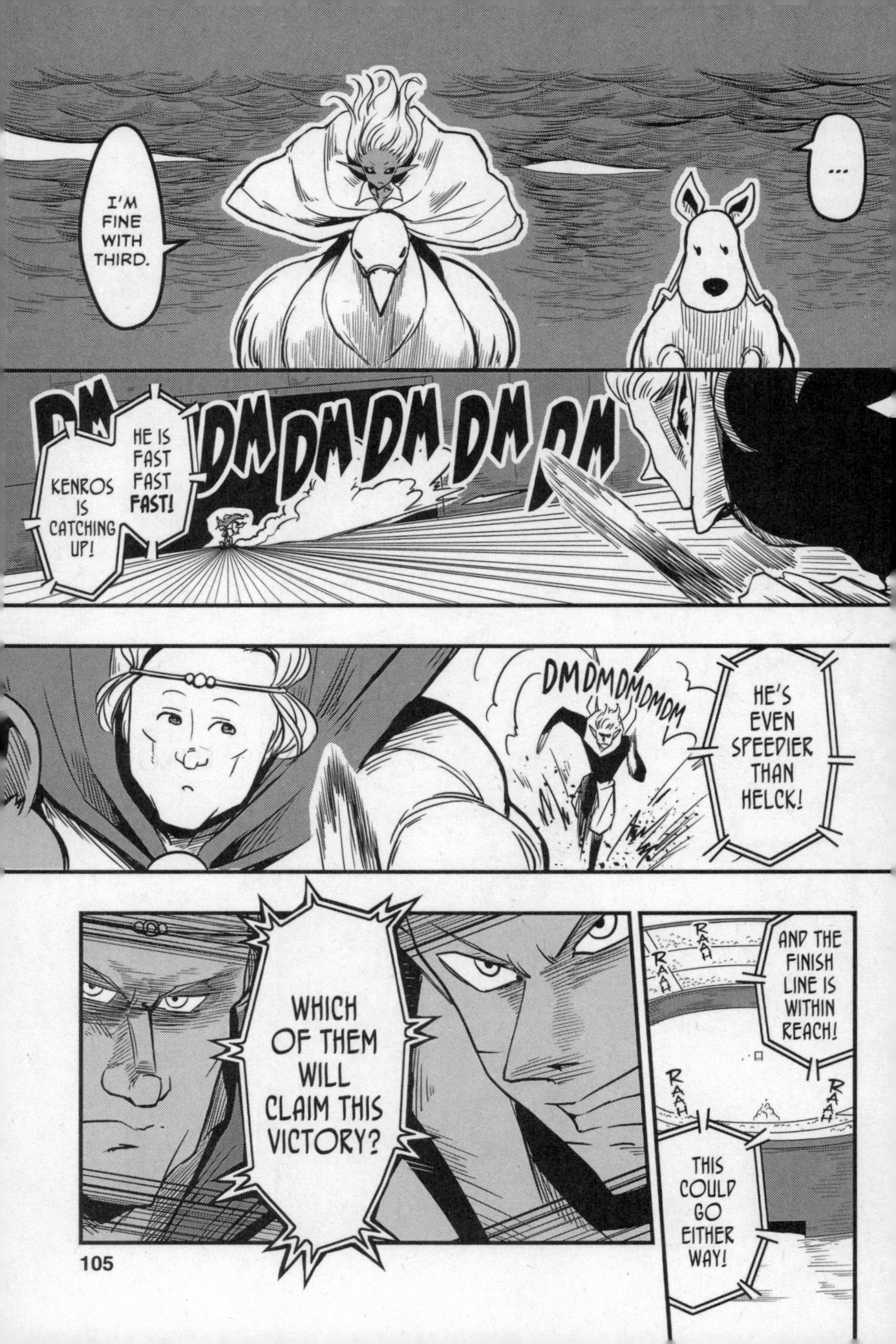
...
I'M FINE WITH THIRD.
DM DM DM DM DM DM DM
HE IS FAST FAST FAST!
KENROS IS CATCHING UP!
DMDMDMDMDM
HE'S EVEN SPEEDIER THAN HELCK!
RAAH RAAH
AND THE FINISH LINE IS WITHIN REACH!
RAAH RAAH
THIS COULD GO EITHER WAY!
WHICH OF THEM WILL CLAIM THIS VICTORY?

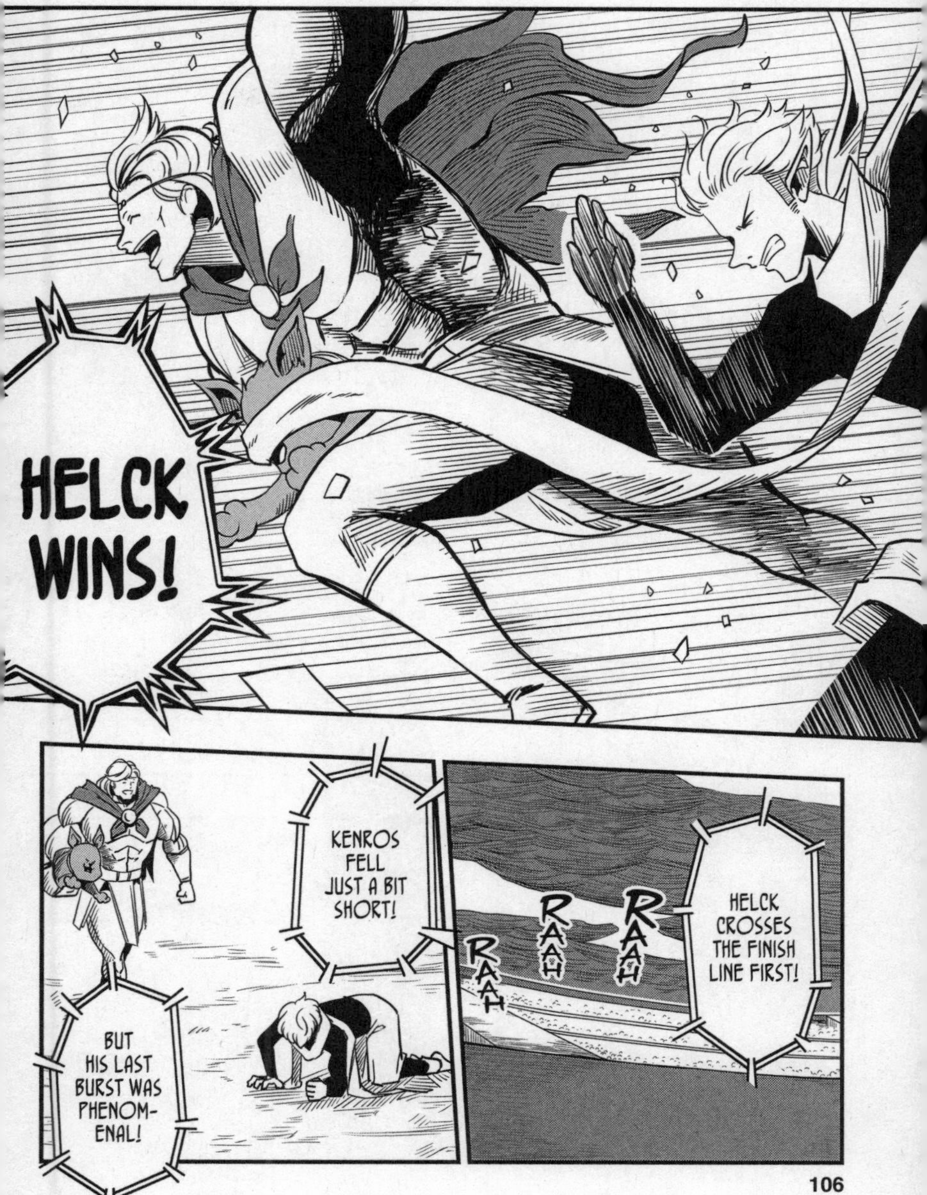
HELCK WINS!
HELCK CROSSES THE FINISH LINE FIRST!
RAAH RAAH RAAH
KENROS FELL JUST A BIT SHORT!
BUT HIS LAST BURST WAS PHENOM-ENAL!

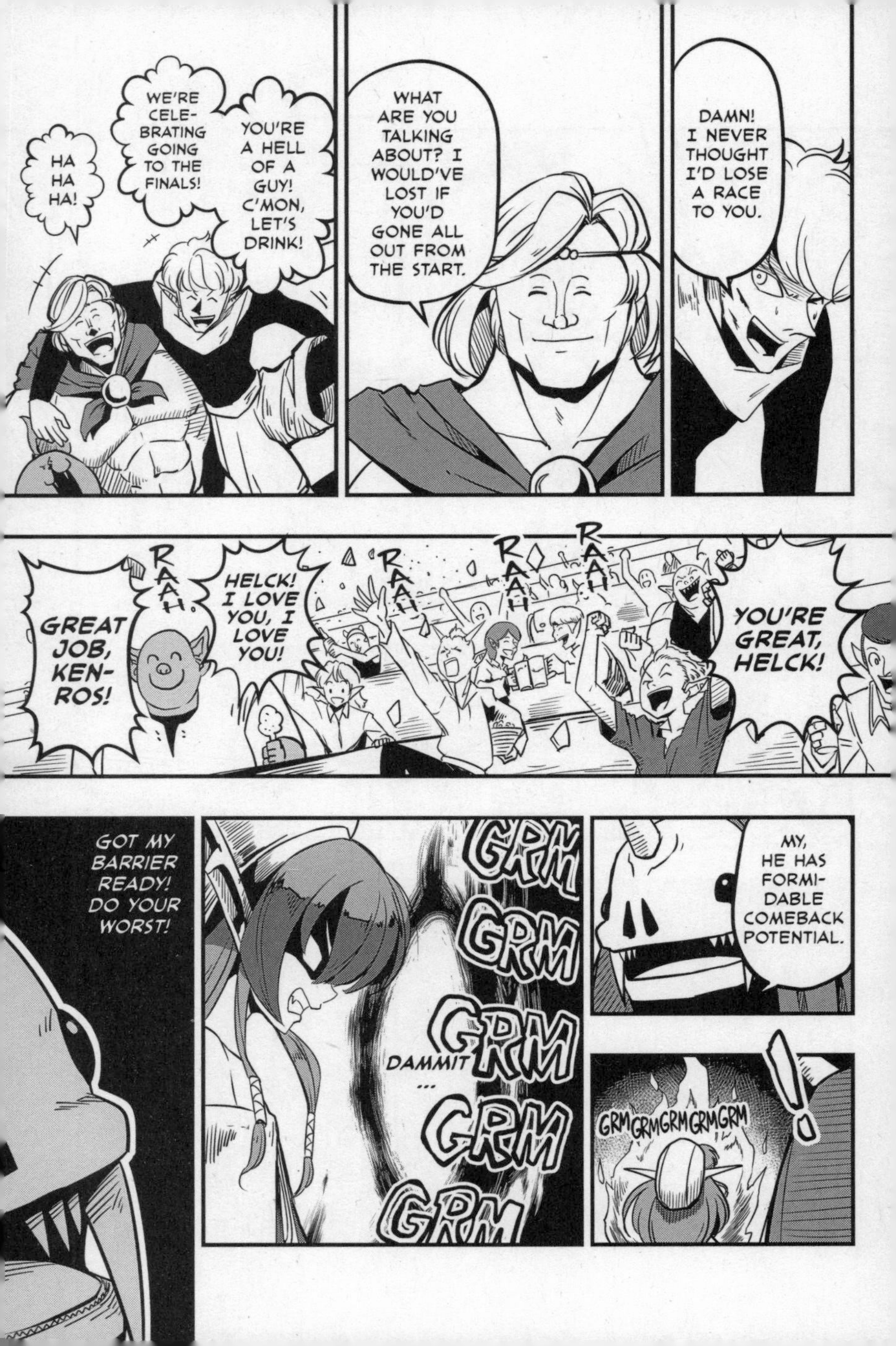
DAMN! I NEVER THOUGHT I'D LOSE A RACE TO YOU.
WHAT ARE YOU TALKING ABOUT? I WOULD'VE LOST IF YOU'D GONE ALL OUT FROM THE START.
YOU'RE A HELL OF A GUY! C'MON, LET'S DRINK!
WE'RE CELE-BRATING GOING TO THE FINALS!
HA HA HA!
YOU'RE GREAT, HELCK!
RAAH
RAAH
RAAH
HELCK! I LOVE YOU, I LOVE YOU!
RAAH
GREAT JOB, KEN-ROS!
MY, HE HAS FORMI-DABLE COMEBACK POTENTIAL.
!
GRMGRMGRMGRMGRM
GRM
GRM
GRM
DAMMIT ...
GRM
GRM
GOT MY BARRIER READY! DO YOUR WORST!

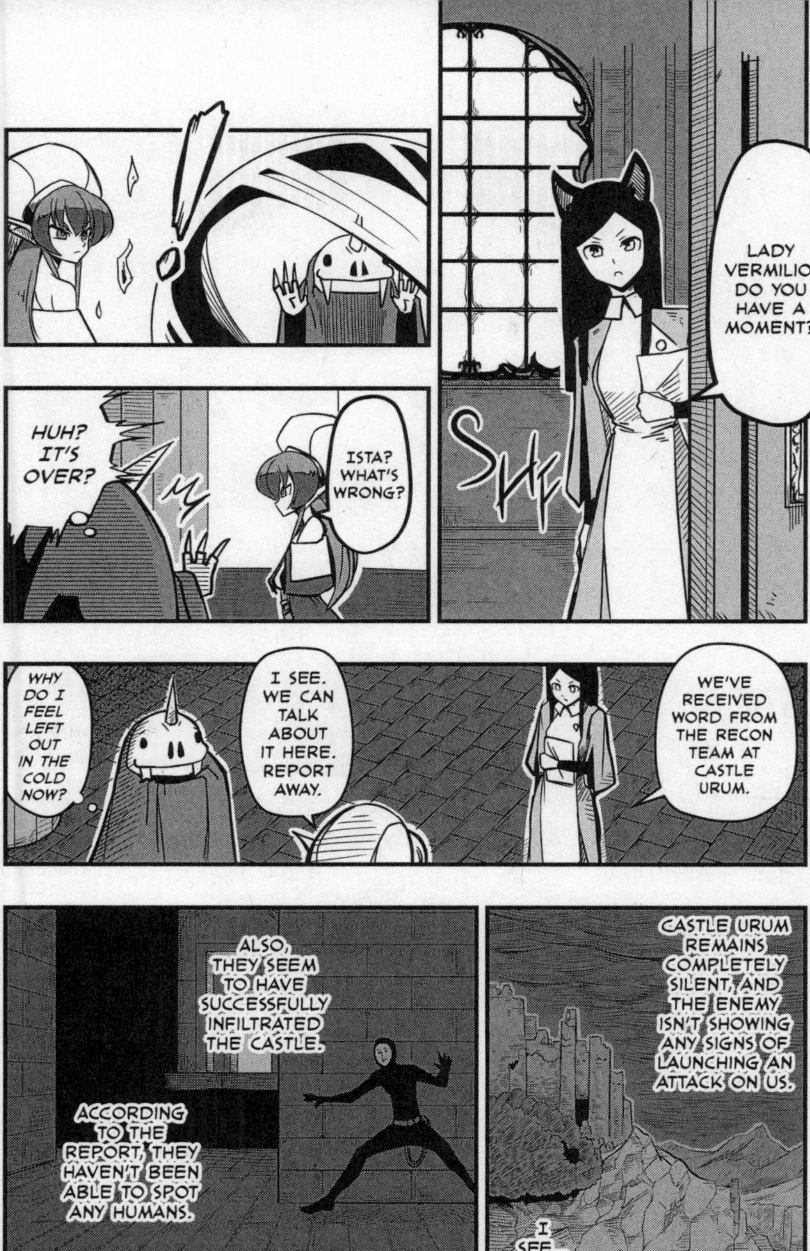
LADY VERMILIO, DO YOU HAVE A MOMENT?
SHF
ISTA? WHAT'S WRONG?
HUH? IT'S OVER?
WE'VE RECEIVED WORD FROM THE RECON TEAM AT CASTLE URUM.
I SEE. WE CAN TALK ABOUT IT HERE. REPORT AWAY.
WHY DO I FEEL LEFT OUT IN THE COLD NOW?
CASTLE URUM REMAINS COMPLETELY SILENT, AND THE ENEMY ISN'T SHOWING ANY SIGNS OF LAUNCHING AN ATTACK ON US.
I SEE...
ALSO, THEY SEEM TO HAVE SUCCESSFULLY INFILTRATED THE CASTLE.
ACCORDING TO THE REPORT, THEY HAVEN'T BEEN ABLE TO SPOT ANY HUMANS.

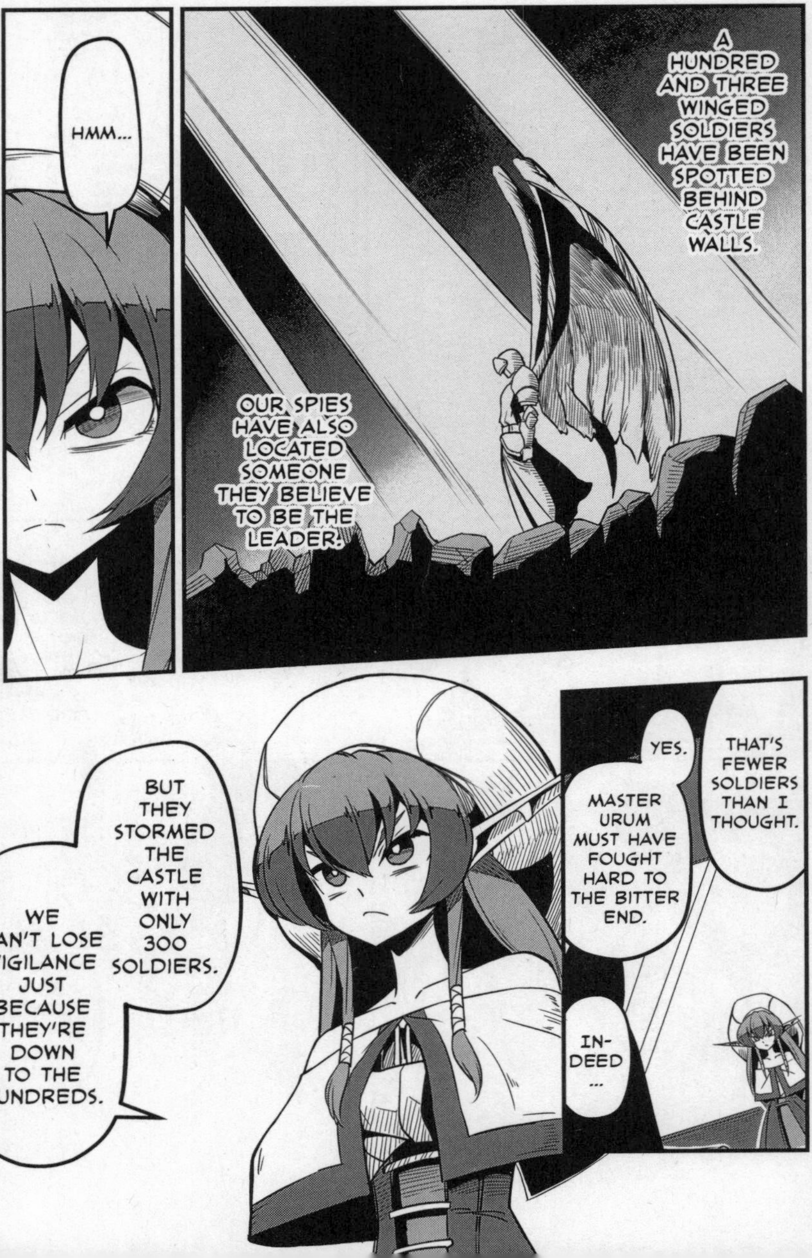
A HUNDRED AND THREE WINGED SOLDIERS HAVE BEEN SPOTTED BEHIND CASTLE WALLS.
OUR SPIES HAVE ALSO LOCATED SOMEONE THEY BELIEVE TO BE THE LEADER.
HMM...
THAT'S FEWER SOLDIERS THAN I THOUGHT.
YES.
MASTER URUM MUST HAVE FOUGHT HARD TO THE BITTER END.
IN-DEED...
BUT THEY STORMED THE CASTLE WITH ONLY 300 SOLDIERS.
WE CAN'T LOSE VIGILANCE JUST BECAUSE THEY'RE DOWN TO THE HUNDREDS.

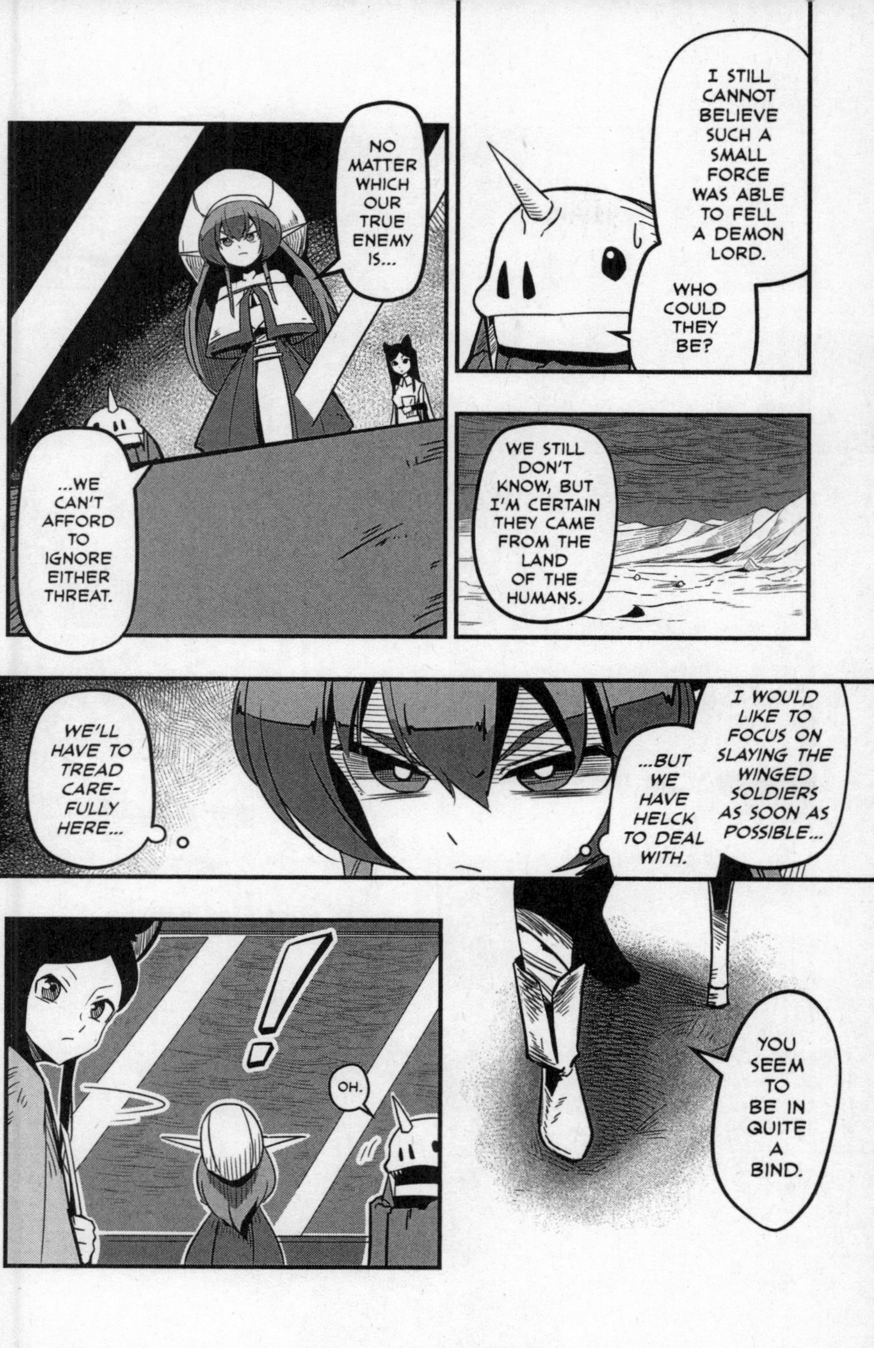

I STILL CANNOT BELIEVE SUCH A SMALL FORCE WAS ABLE TO FELL A DEMON LORD.
WHO COULD THEY BE?
WE STILL DON'T KNOW, BUT I'M CERTAIN THEY CAME FROM THE LAND OF THE HUMANS.
NO MATTER WHICH OUR TRUE ENEMY IS...
...WE CAN'T AFFORD TO IGNORE EITHER THREAT.
I WOULD LIKE TO FOCUS ON SLAYING THE WINGED SOLDIERS AS SOON AS POSSIBLE...
...BUT WE HAVE HELCK TO DEAL WITH.
WE'LL HAVE TO TREAD CARE-FULLY HERE...
YOU SEEM TO BE IN QUITE A BIND.
!
OH.

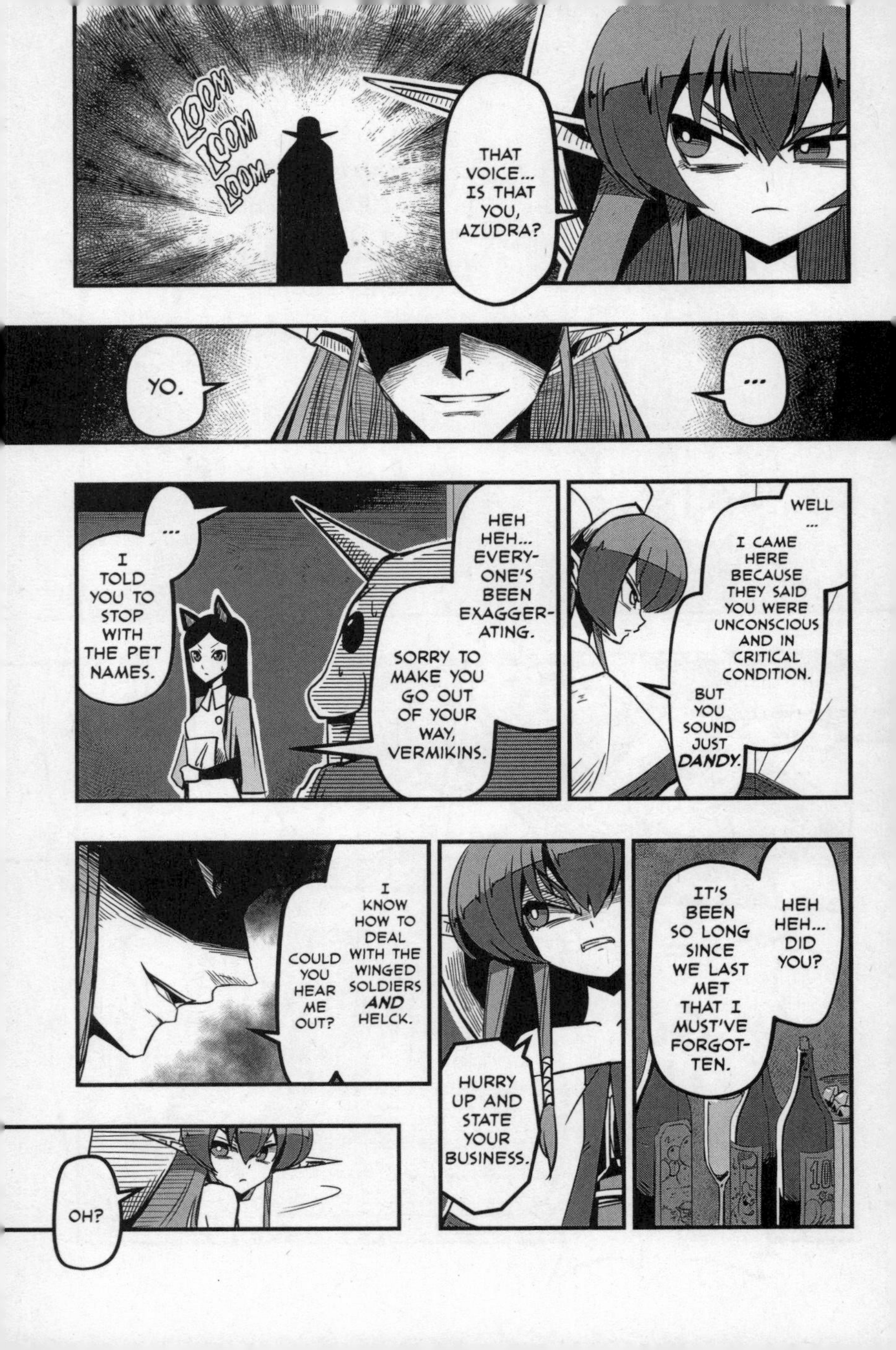
THAT VOICE... IS THAT YOU, AZUDRA?
LOOM LOOM LOOM...
...
YO.
WELL... I CAME HERE BECAUSE THEY SAID YOU WERE UNCONSCIOUS AND IN CRITICAL CONDITION.
BUT YOU SOUND JUST *DANDY*.
HEH HEH... EVERYONE'S BEEN EXAGGERATING.
SORRY TO MAKE YOU GO OUT OF YOUR WAY, VERMIKINS.
...
I TOLD YOU TO STOP WITH THE PET NAMES.
HEH HEH... DID YOU?
IT'S BEEN SO LONG SINCE WE LAST MET THAT I MUST'VE FORGOTTEN.
HURRY UP AND STATE YOUR BUSINESS.
I KNOW HOW TO DEAL WITH THE WINGED SOLDIERS *AND* HELCK.
COULD YOU HEAR ME OUT?
OH?

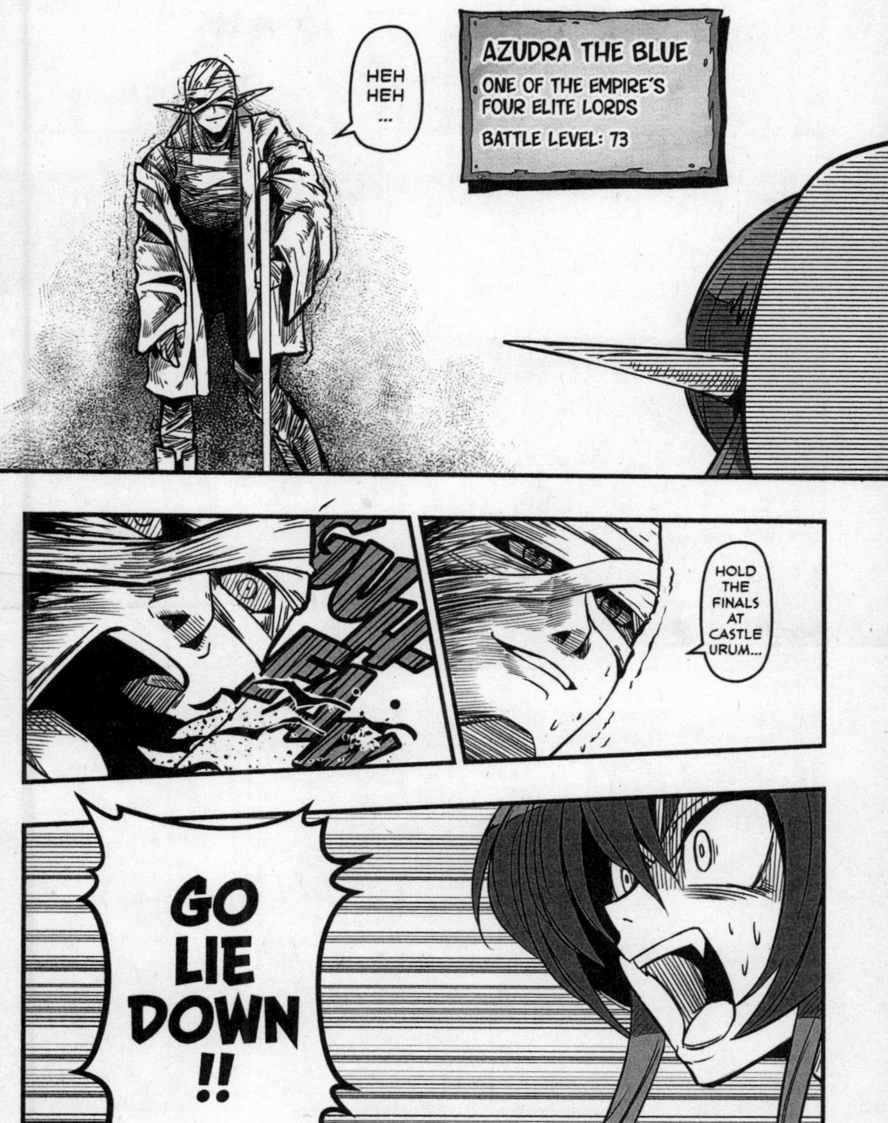
AZUDRA THE BLUE
ONE OF THE EMPIRE'S FOUR ELITE LORDS
BATTLE LEVEL: 73
HEH HEH ...
HOLD THE FINALS AT CASTLE URUM...
GO LIE DOWN !!

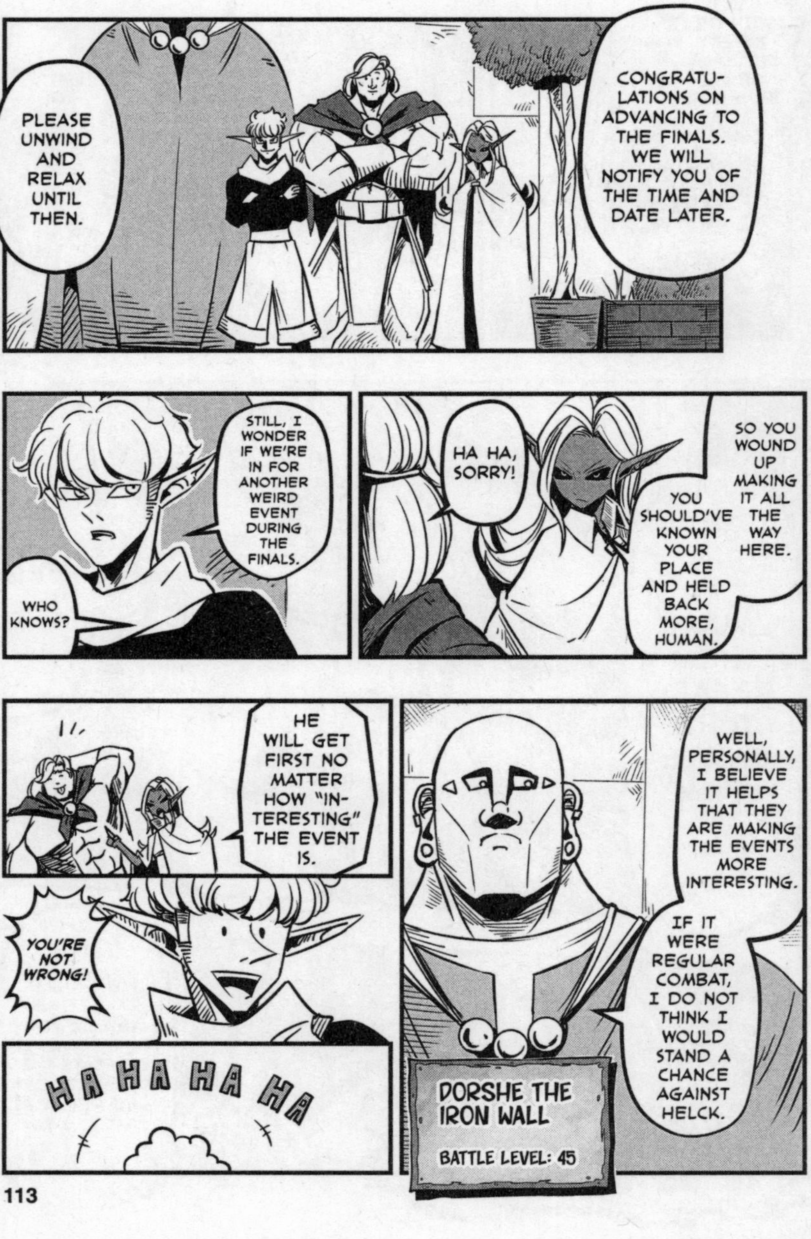
CONGRATULATIONS ON ADVANCING TO THE FINALS. WE WILL NOTIFY YOU OF THE TIME AND DATE LATER.
PLEASE UNWIND AND RELAX UNTIL THEN.
SO YOU WOUND UP MAKING IT ALL THE WAY HERE.
YOU SHOULD'VE KNOWN YOUR PLACE AND HELD BACK MORE, HUMAN.
HA HA, SORRY!
STILL, I WONDER IF WE'RE IN FOR ANOTHER WEIRD EVENT DURING THE FINALS.
WHO KNOWS?
WELL, PERSONALLY, I BELIEVE IT HELPS THAT THEY ARE MAKING THE EVENTS MORE INTERESTING.
IF IT WERE REGULAR COMBAT, I DO NOT THINK I WOULD STAND A CHANCE AGAINST HELCK.
DORSHE THE IRON WALL
BATTLE LEVEL: 45
HE WILL GET FIRST NO MATTER HOW "INTERESTING" THE EVENT IS.
YOU'RE NOT WRONG!
HA HA HA HA HA

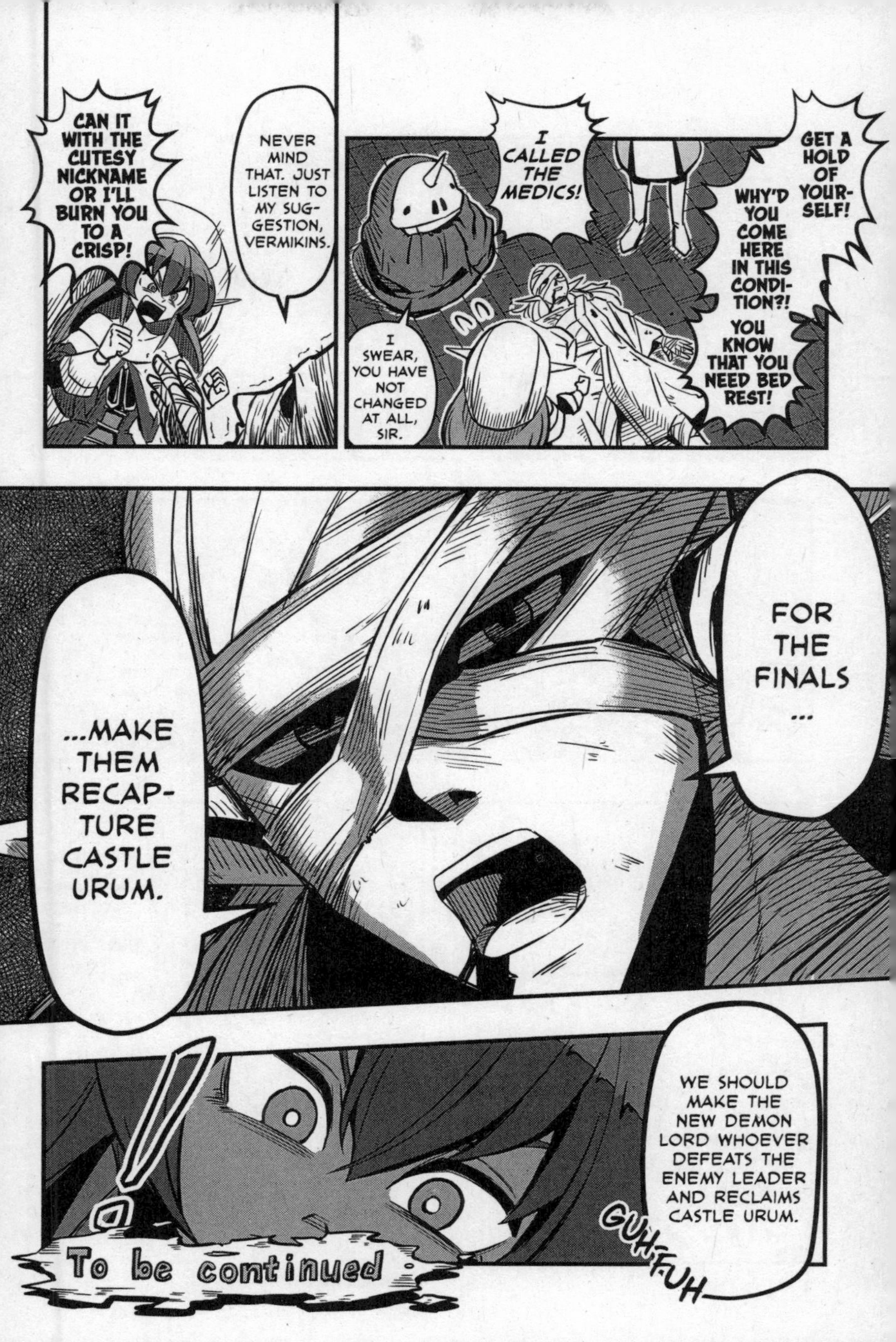
GET A HOLD OF YOURSELF!
WHY'D YOU COME HERE IN THIS CONDITION?!
YOU KNOW THAT YOU NEED BED REST!
I CALLED THE MEDICS!
I SWEAR, YOU HAVE NOT CHANGED AT ALL, SIR.
NEVER MIND THAT. JUST LISTEN TO MY SUGGESTION, VERMIKINS.
CAN IT WITH THE CUTESY NICKNAME OR I'LL BURN YOU TO A CRISP!
FOR THE FINALS...
...MAKE THEM RECAPTURE CASTLE URUM.
WE SHOULD MAKE THE NEW DEMON LORD WHOEVER DEFEATS THE ENEMY LEADER AND RECLAIMS CASTLE URUM.
GUH-FUH
!
To be continued

Chapter 6: Anne from Operations

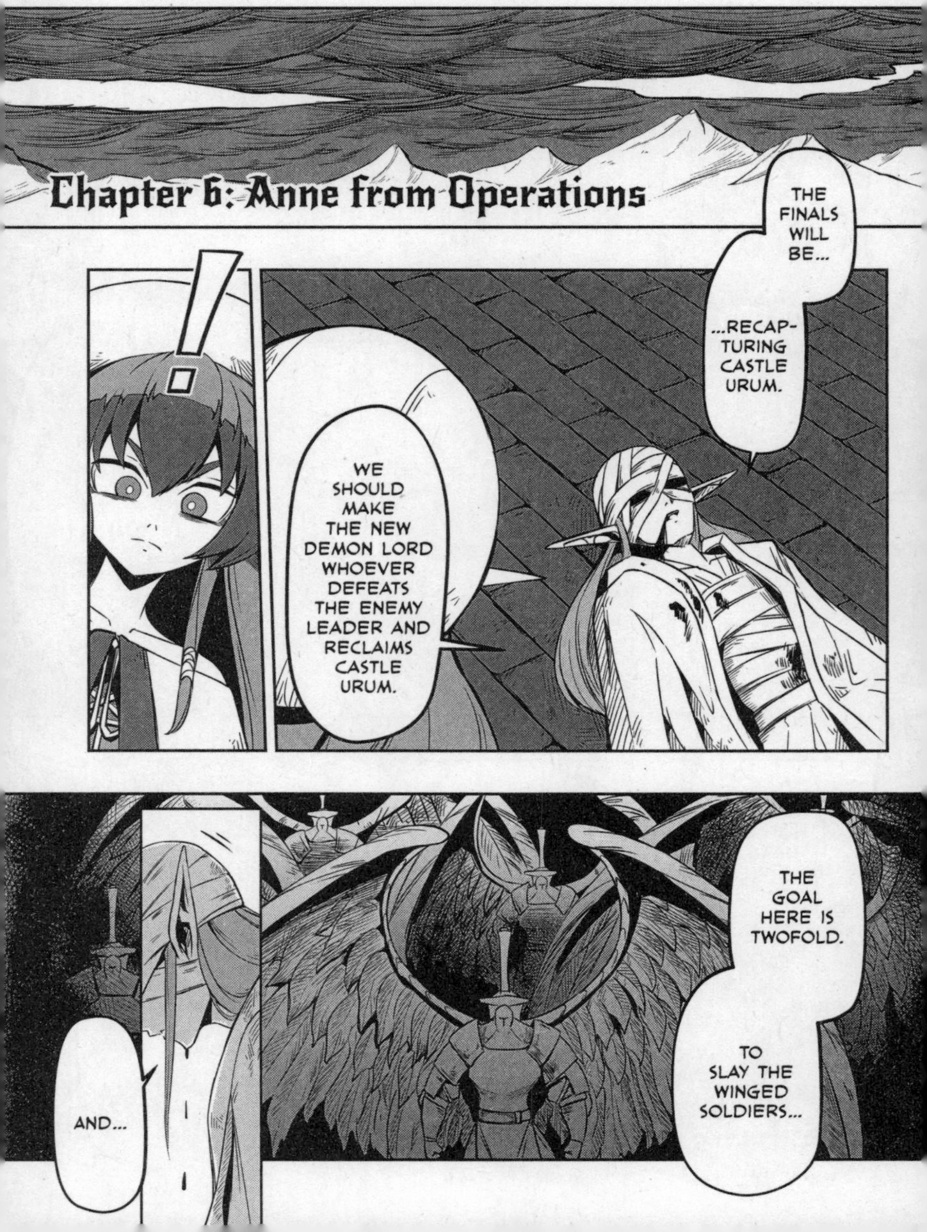
THE FINALS WILL BE...
...RECAPTURING CASTLE URUM.
WE SHOULD MAKE THE NEW DEMON LORD WHOEVER DEFEATS THE ENEMY LEADER AND RECLAIMS CASTLE URUM.
!
THE GOAL HERE IS TWOFOLD.
TO SLAY THE WINGED SOLDIERS...
AND...

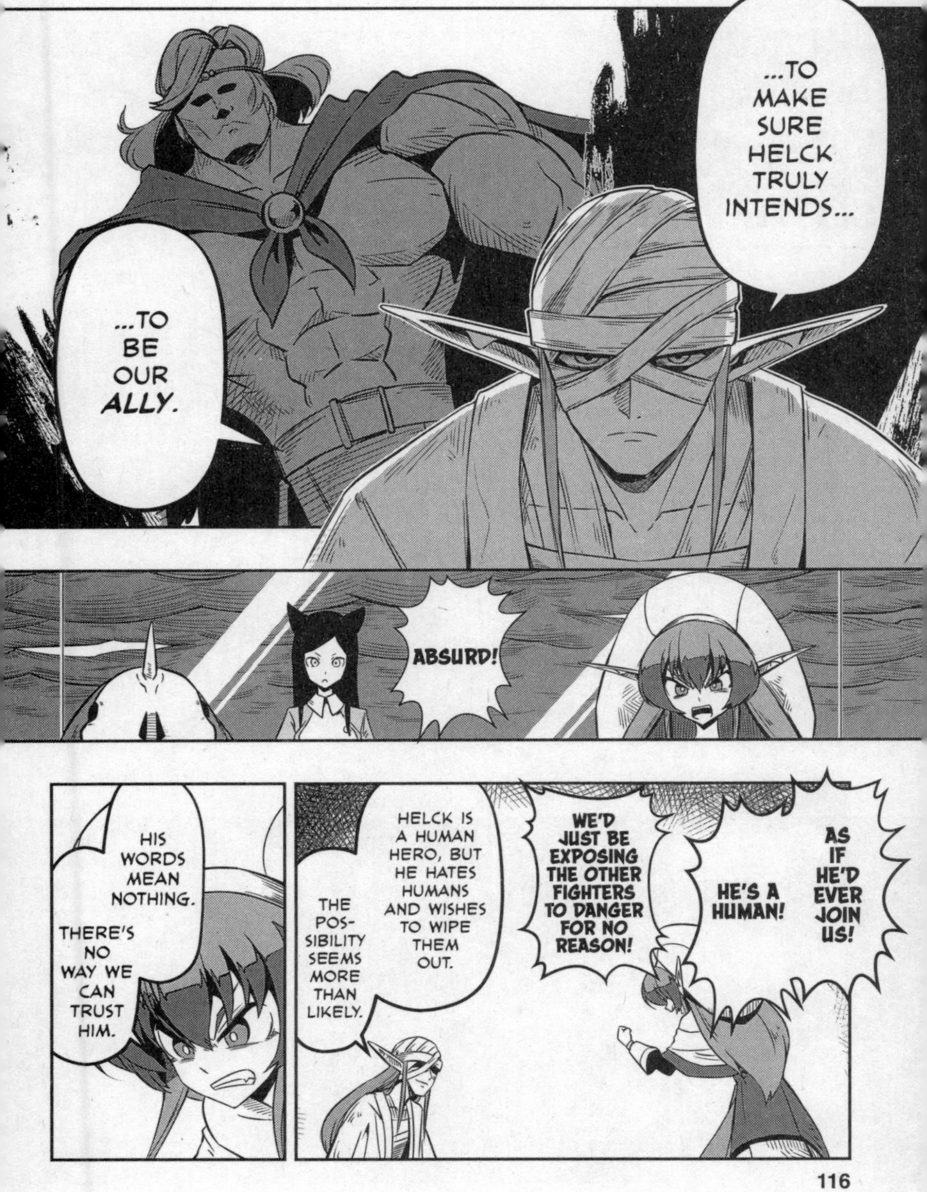
...TO MAKE SURE HELCK TRULY INTENDS...
...TO BE OUR *ALLY*.
ABSURD!
AS IF HE'D EVER JOIN US!
HE'S A HUMAN!
WE'D JUST BE EXPOSING THE OTHER FIGHTERS TO DANGER FOR NO REASON!
HELCK IS A HUMAN HERO, BUT HE HATES HUMANS AND WISHES TO WIPE THEM OUT.
THE POSSIBILITY SEEMS MORE THAN LIKELY.
HIS WORDS MEAN NOTHING.
THERE'S NO WAY WE CAN TRUST HIM.

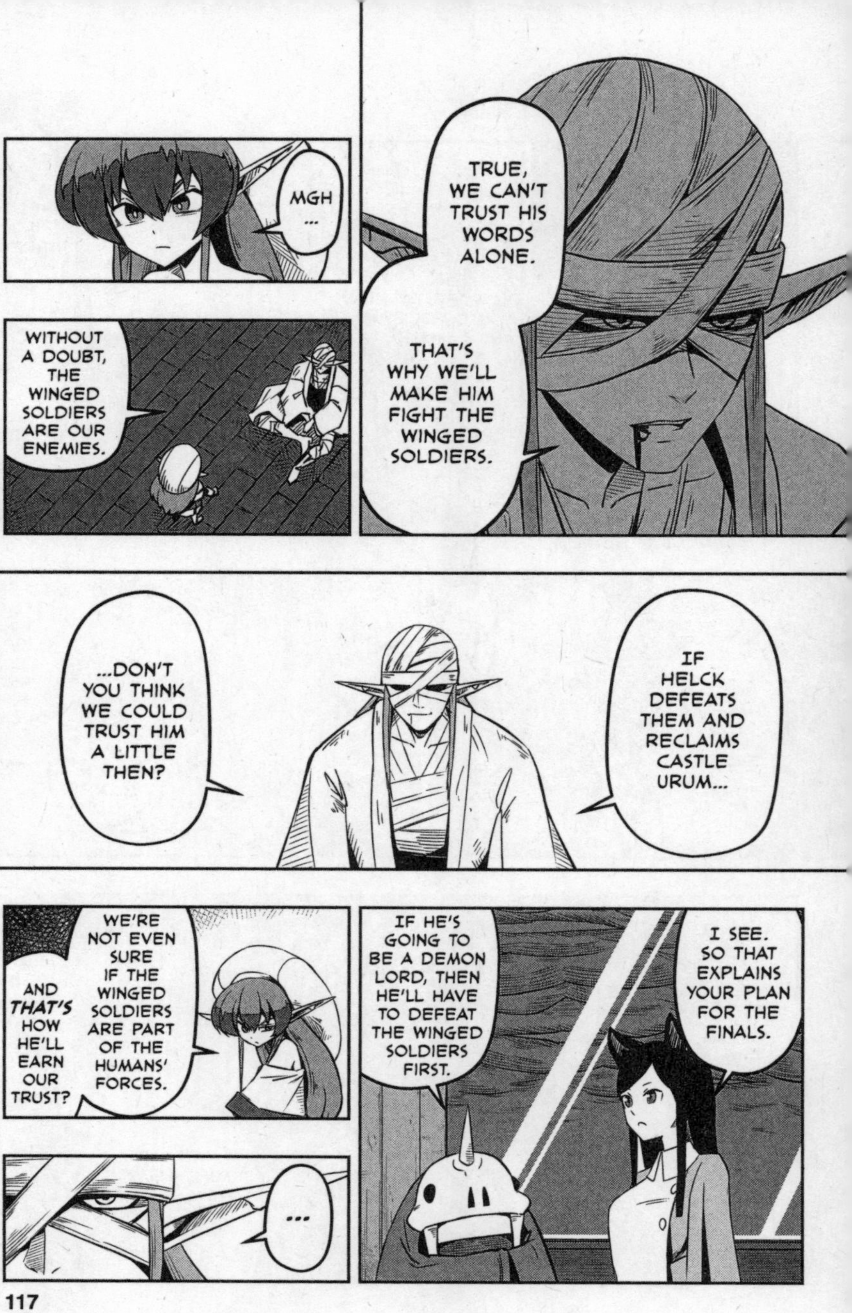
TRUE, WE CAN'T TRUST HIS WORDS ALONE.
THAT'S WHY WE'LL MAKE HIM FIGHT THE WINGED SOLDIERS.
MGH ...
WITHOUT A DOUBT, THE WINGED SOLDIERS ARE OUR ENEMIES.
IF HELCK DEFEATS THEM AND RECLAIMS CASTLE URUM...
...DON'T YOU THINK WE COULD TRUST HIM A LITTLE THEN?
I SEE. SO THAT EXPLAINS YOUR PLAN FOR THE FINALS.
IF HE'S GOING TO BE A DEMON LORD, THEN HE'LL HAVE TO DEFEAT THE WINGED SOLDIERS FIRST.
WE'RE NOT EVEN SURE IF THE WINGED SOLDIERS ARE PART OF THE HUMANS' FORCES.
AND *THAT'S* HOW HE'LL EARN OUR TRUST?
...

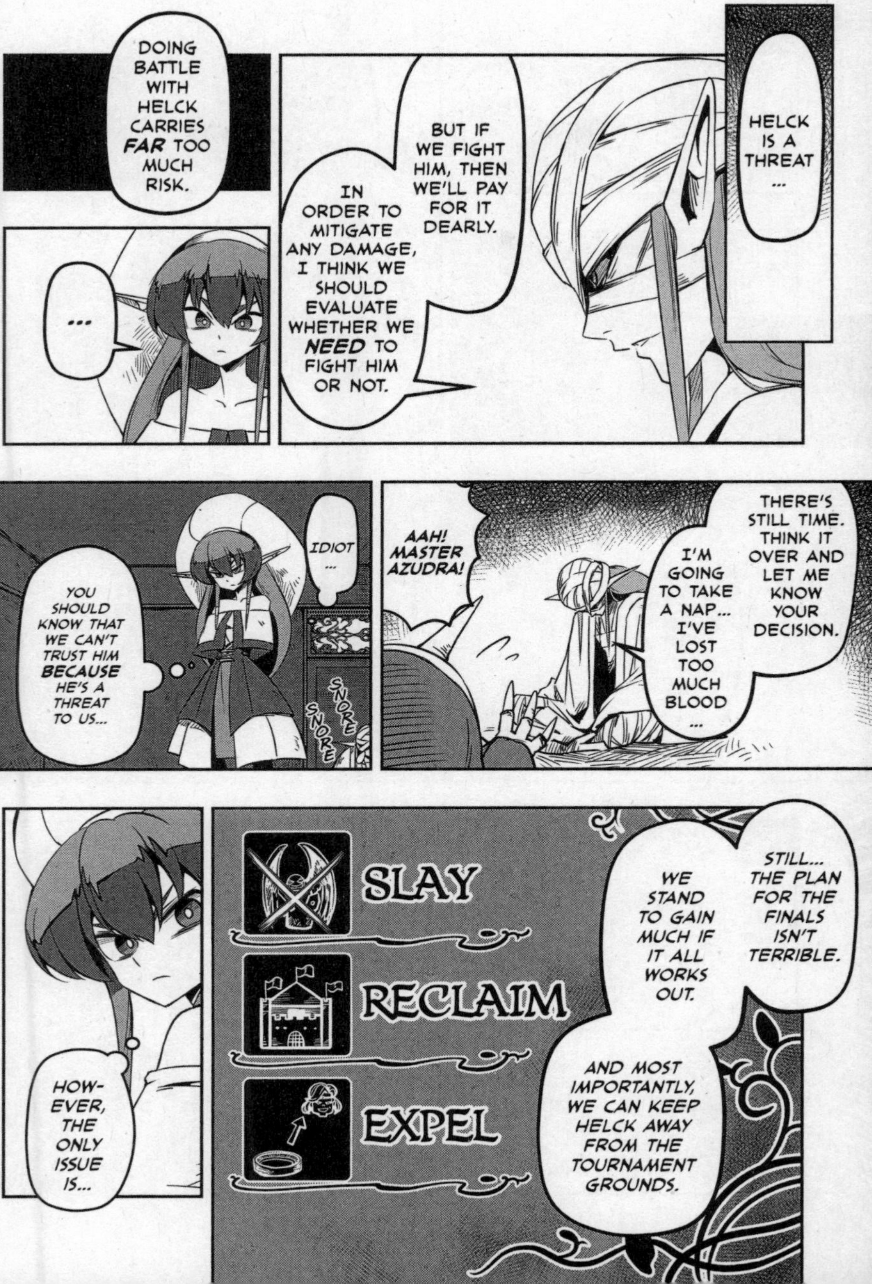
HELCK IS A THREAT ...
BUT IF WE FIGHT HIM, THEN WE'LL PAY FOR IT DEARLY.
IN ORDER TO MITIGATE ANY DAMAGE, I THINK WE SHOULD EVALUATE WHETHER WE **NEED** TO FIGHT HIM OR NOT.
DOING BATTLE WITH HELCK CARRIES **FAR** TOO MUCH RISK.
...
THERE'S STILL TIME. THINK IT OVER AND LET ME KNOW YOUR DECISION.
I'M GOING TO TAKE A NAP... I'VE LOST TOO MUCH BLOOD ...
AAH! MASTER AZUDRA!
IDIOT ...
YOU SHOULD KNOW THAT WE CAN'T TRUST HIM **BECAUSE** HE'S A THREAT TO US...
SNORE
SNORE
STILL... THE PLAN FOR THE FINALS ISN'T TERRIBLE.
WE STAND TO GAIN MUCH IF IT ALL WORKS OUT.
SLAY
RECLAIM
EXPEL
AND MOST IMPORTANTLY, WE CAN KEEP HELCK AWAY FROM THE TOURNAMENT GROUNDS.
HOW-EVER, THE ONLY ISSUE IS...

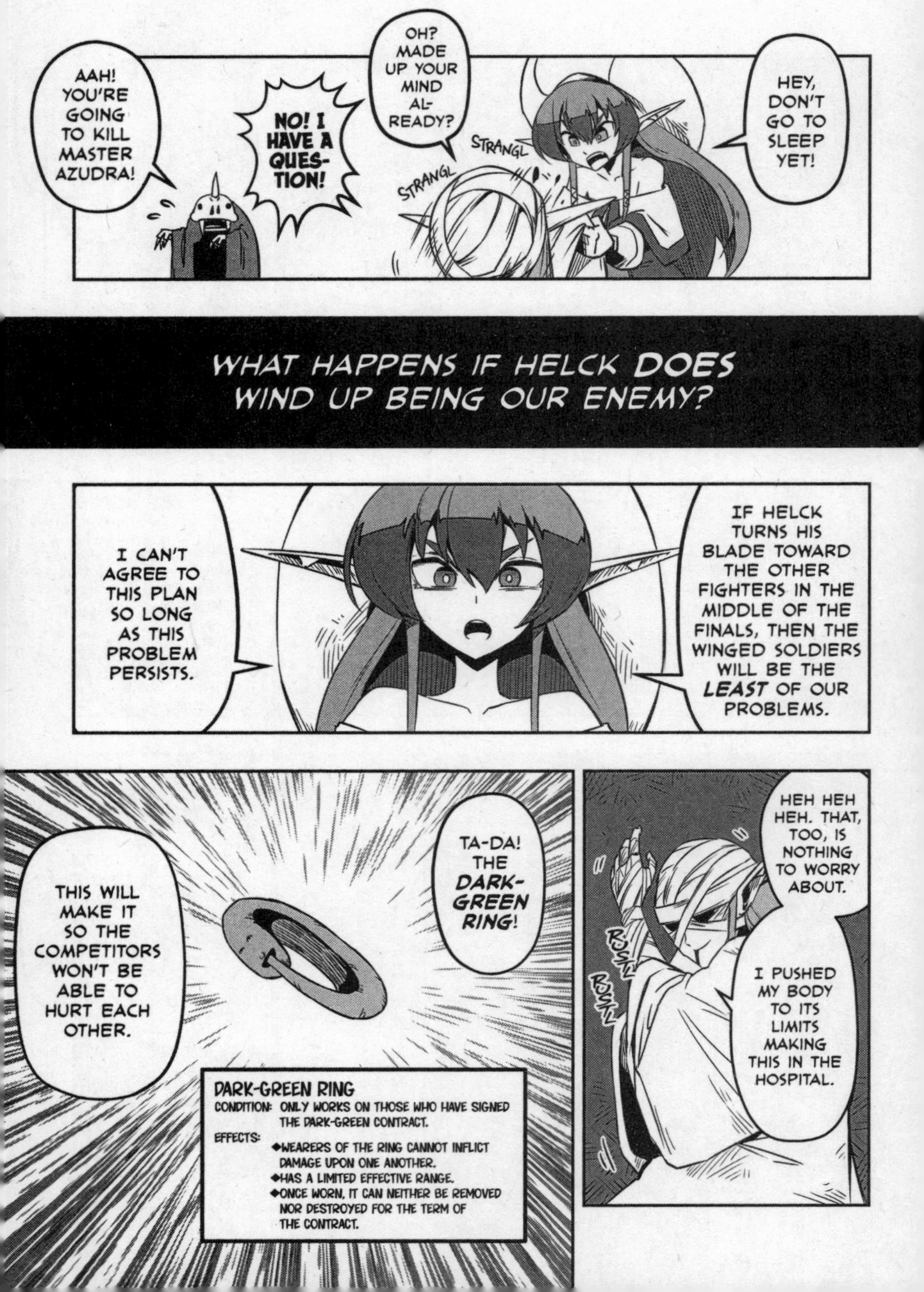
HEY, DON'T GO TO SLEEP YET!
STRANGL
STRANGL
OH? MADE UP YOUR MIND AL-READY?
NO! I HAVE A QUES-TION!
AAH! YOU'RE GOING TO KILL MASTER AZUDRA!
WHAT HAPPENS IF HELCK DOES WIND UP BEING OUR ENEMY?
IF HELCK TURNS HIS BLADE TOWARD THE OTHER FIGHTERS IN THE MIDDLE OF THE FINALS, THEN THE WINGED SOLDIERS WILL BE THE LEAST OF OUR PROBLEMS.
I CAN'T AGREE TO THIS PLAN SO LONG AS THIS PROBLEM PERSISTS.
HEH HEH HEH. THAT, TOO, IS NOTHING TO WORRY ABOUT.
I PUSHED MY BODY TO ITS LIMITS MAKING THIS IN THE HOSPITAL.
TA-DA! THE DARK-GREEN RING!
THIS WILL MAKE IT SO THE COMPETITORS WON'T BE ABLE TO HURT EACH OTHER.
DARK-GREEN RING
CONDITION: ONLY WORKS ON THOSE WHO HAVE SIGNED THE DARK-GREEN CONTRACT.
EFFECTS:
◆WEARERS OF THE RING CANNOT INFLICT DAMAGE UPON ONE ANOTHER.
◆HAS A LIMITED EFFECTIVE RANGE.
◆ONCE WORN, IT CAN NEITHER BE REMOVED NOR DESTROYED FOR THE TERM OF THE CONTRACT.

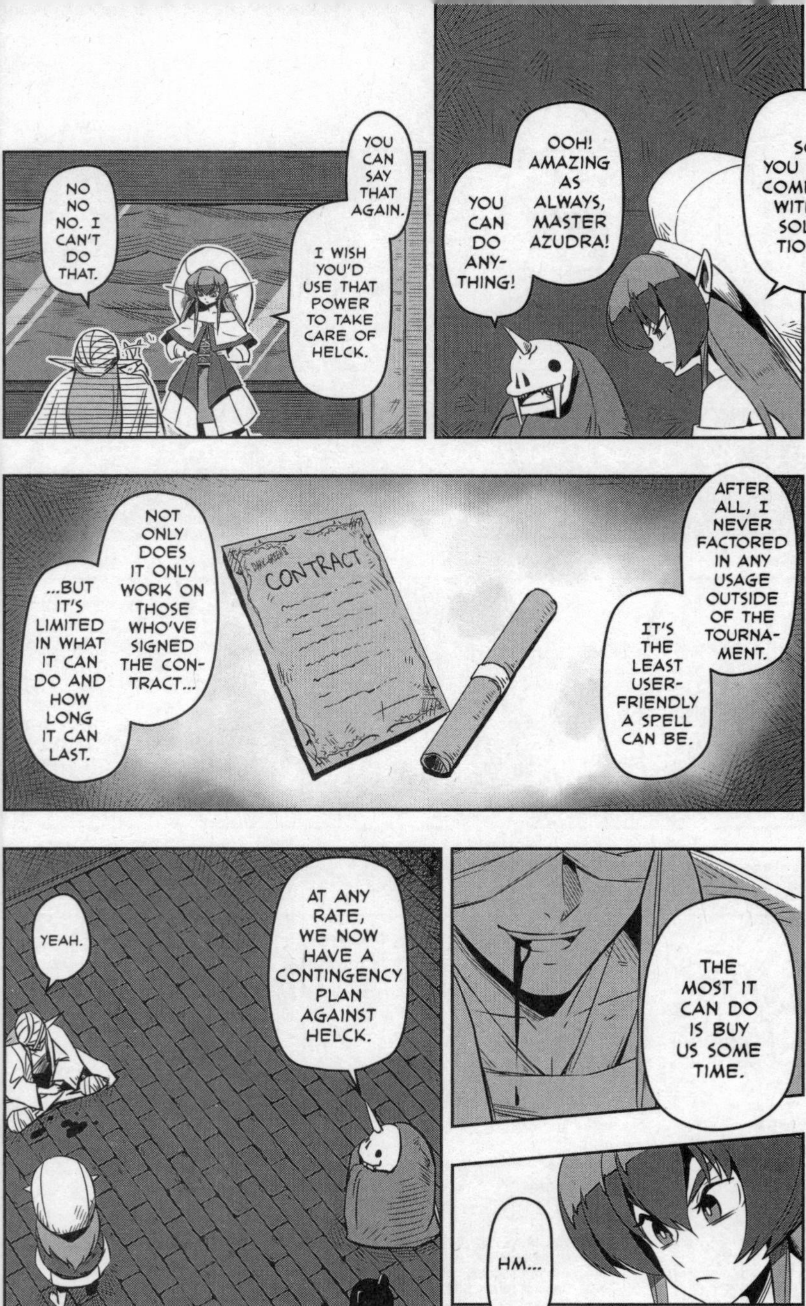
SO YOU *DID* COME UP WITH A SOLUTION...
OOH! AMAZING AS ALWAYS, MASTER AZUDRA!
YOU CAN DO ANYTHING!
YOU CAN SAY THAT AGAIN.
I WISH YOU'D USE THAT POWER TO TAKE CARE OF HELCK.
NO NO NO. I CAN'T DO THAT.
AFTER ALL, I NEVER FACTORED IN ANY USAGE OUTSIDE OF THE TOURNAMENT.
IT'S THE LEAST USER-FRIENDLY A SPELL CAN BE.
CONTRACT
NOT ONLY DOES IT ONLY WORK ON THOSE WHO'VE SIGNED THE CONTRACT...
...BUT IT'S LIMITED IN WHAT IT CAN DO AND HOW LONG IT CAN LAST.
THE MOST IT CAN DO IS BUY US SOME TIME.
HM...
AT ANY RATE, WE NOW HAVE A CONTINGENCY PLAN AGAINST HELCK.
YEAH.

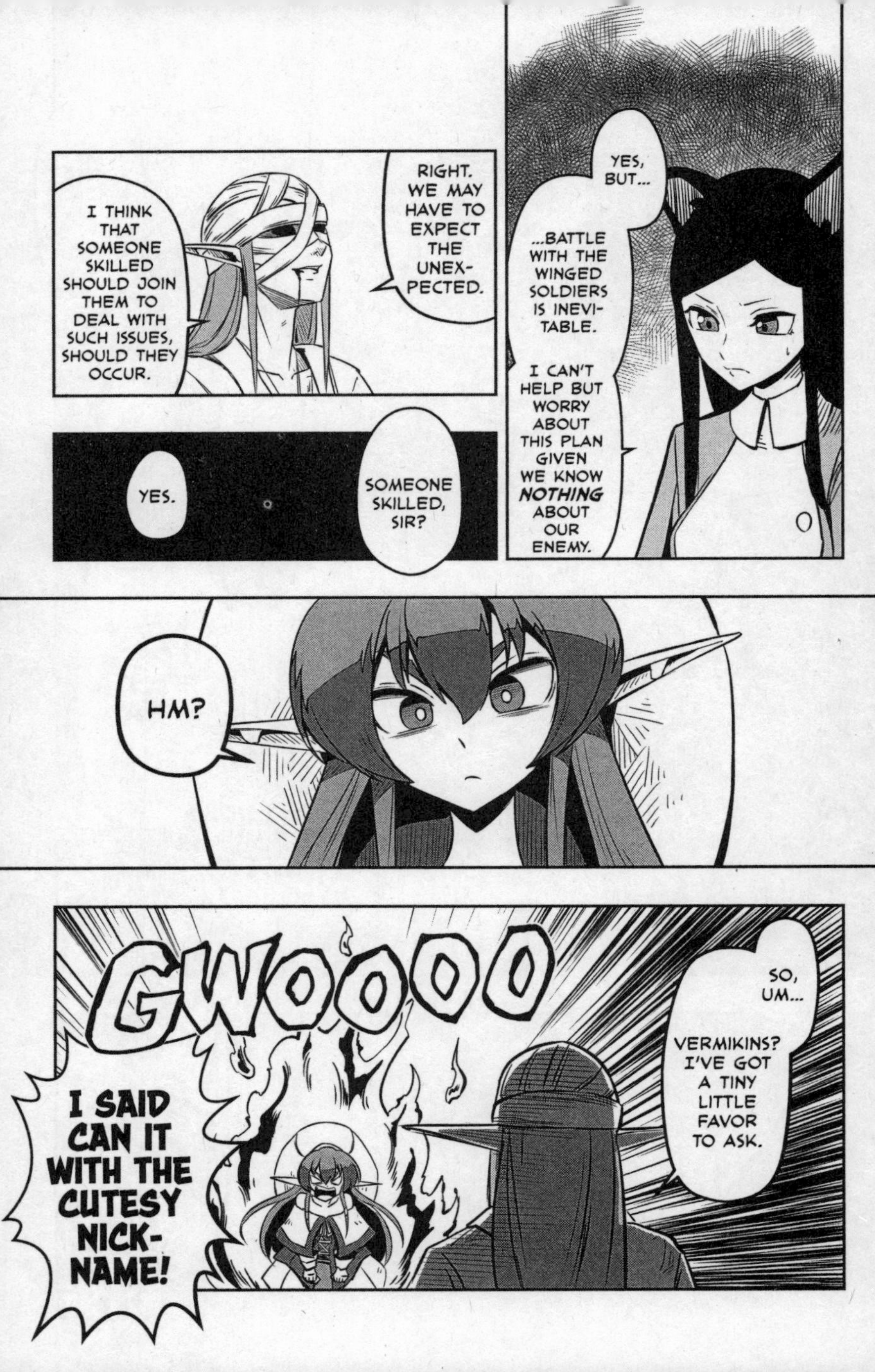
YES, BUT...
...BATTLE WITH THE WINGED SOLDIERS IS INEVITABLE.
I CAN'T HELP BUT WORRY ABOUT THIS PLAN GIVEN WE KNOW *NOTHING* ABOUT OUR ENEMY.
RIGHT. WE MAY HAVE TO EXPECT THE UNEXPECTED.
I THINK THAT SOMEONE SKILLED SHOULD JOIN THEM TO DEAL WITH SUCH ISSUES, SHOULD THEY OCCUR.
SOMEONE SKILLED, SIR?
YES.
HM?
SO, UM...
VERMIKINS? I'VE GOT A TINY LITTLE FAVOR TO ASK.
GWOOOO
I SAID CAN IT WITH THE CUTESY NICK-NAME!

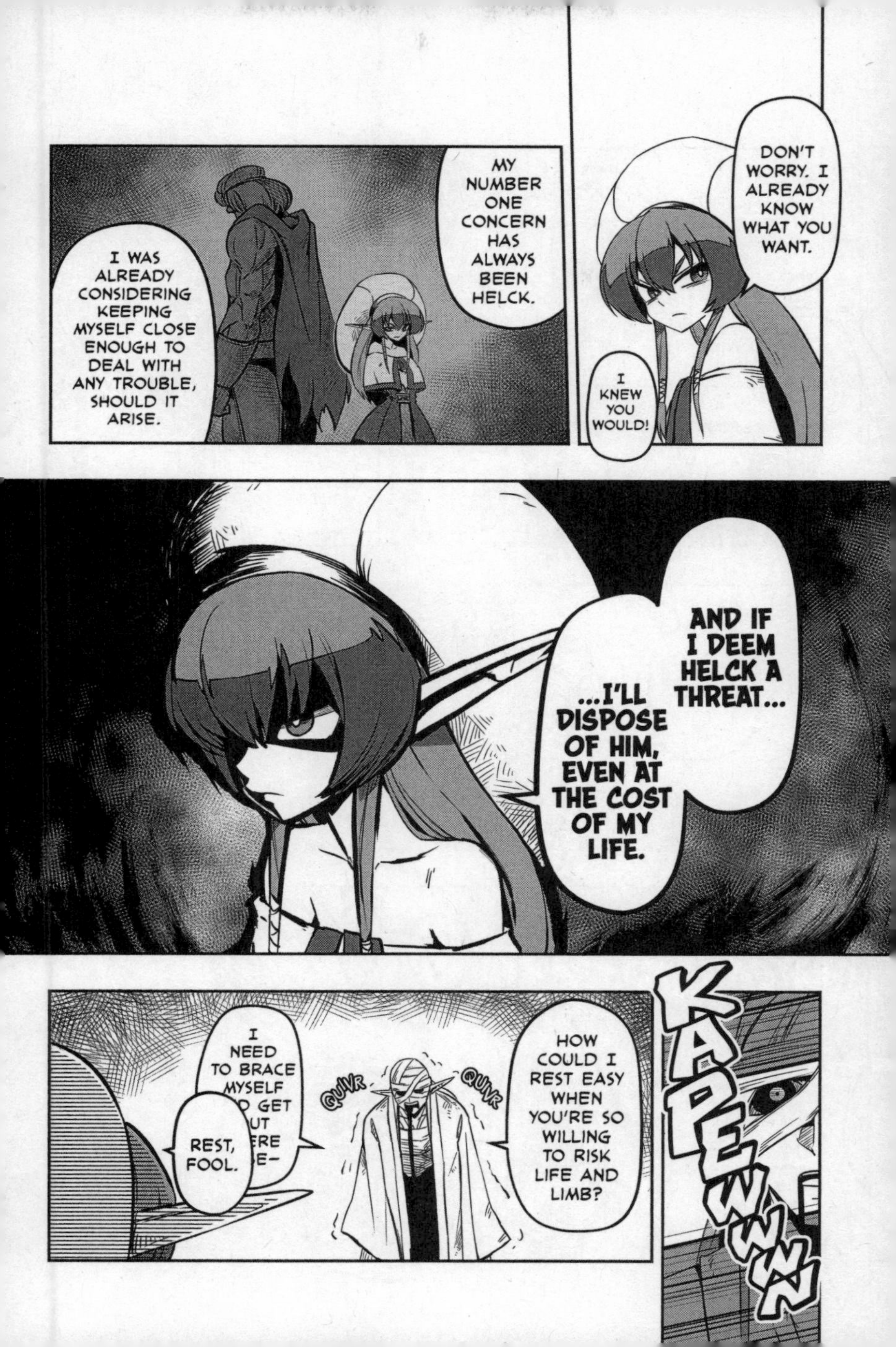
DON'T WORRY. I ALREADY KNOW WHAT YOU WANT.
I KNEW YOU WOULD!
MY NUMBER ONE CONCERN HAS ALWAYS BEEN HELCK.
I WAS ALREADY CONSIDERING KEEPING MYSELF CLOSE ENOUGH TO DEAL WITH ANY TROUBLE, SHOULD IT ARISE.
AND IF I DEEM HELCK A THREAT...
...I'LL DISPOSE OF HIM, EVEN AT THE COST OF MY LIFE.
KAPEWWWN
HOW COULD I REST EASY WHEN YOU'RE SO WILLING TO RISK LIFE AND LIMB?
QUIVR
QUIVR
I NEED TO BRACE MYSELF D GET UT ERE E–
REST, FOOL.

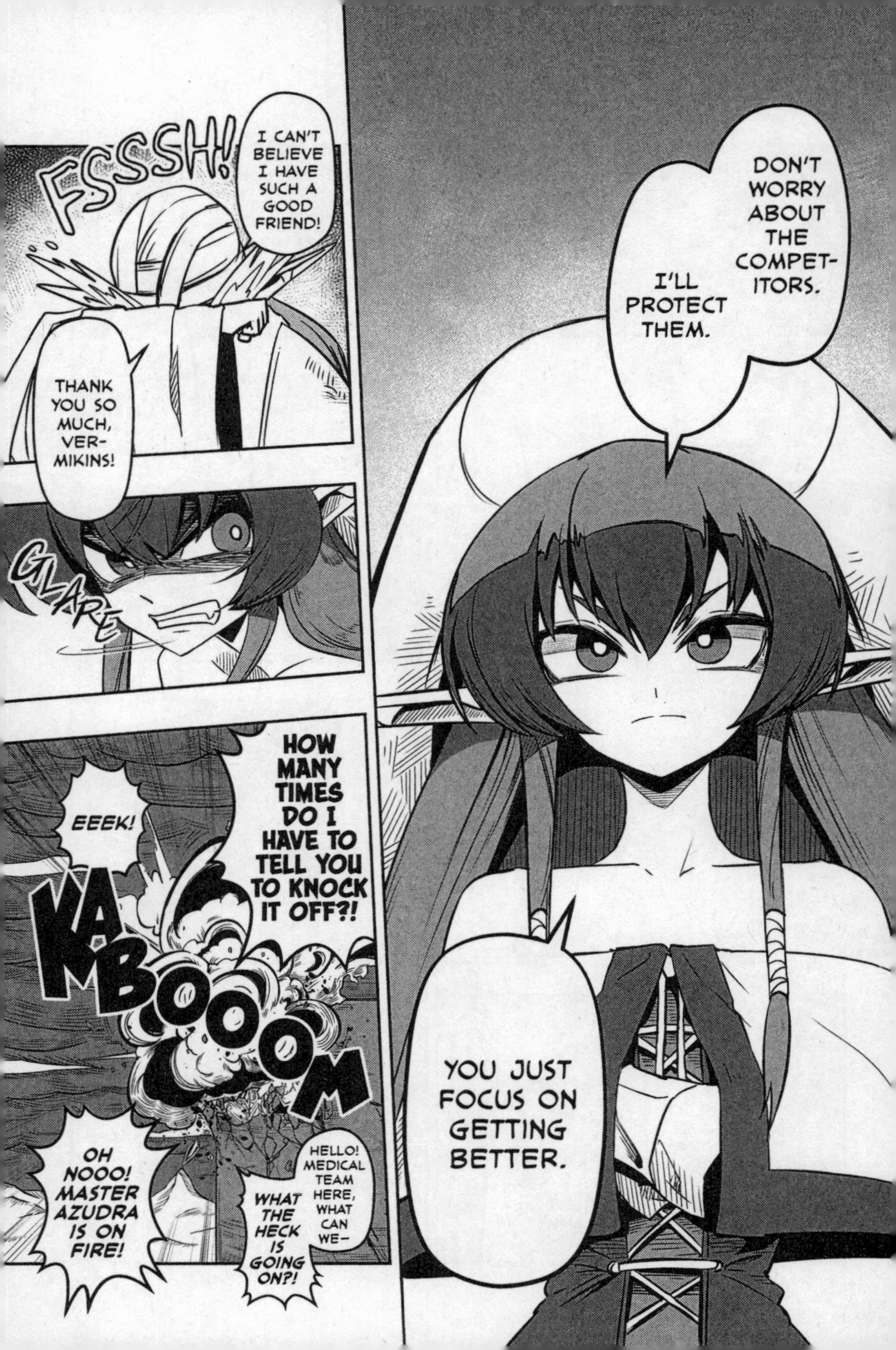
DON'T WORRY ABOUT THE COMPETITORS.
I'LL PROTECT THEM.
YOU JUST FOCUS ON GETTING BETTER.
FSSSH!
I CAN'T BELIEVE I HAVE SUCH A GOOD FRIEND!
THANK YOU SO MUCH, VERMIKINS!
GLARE
HOW MANY TIMES DO I HAVE TO TELL YOU TO KNOCK IT OFF?!
EEEK!
KABOOOOM
HELLO! MEDICAL TEAM HERE, WHAT CAN WE—
WHAT THE HECK IS GOING ON?!
OH NOOO! MASTER AZUDRA IS ON FIRE!

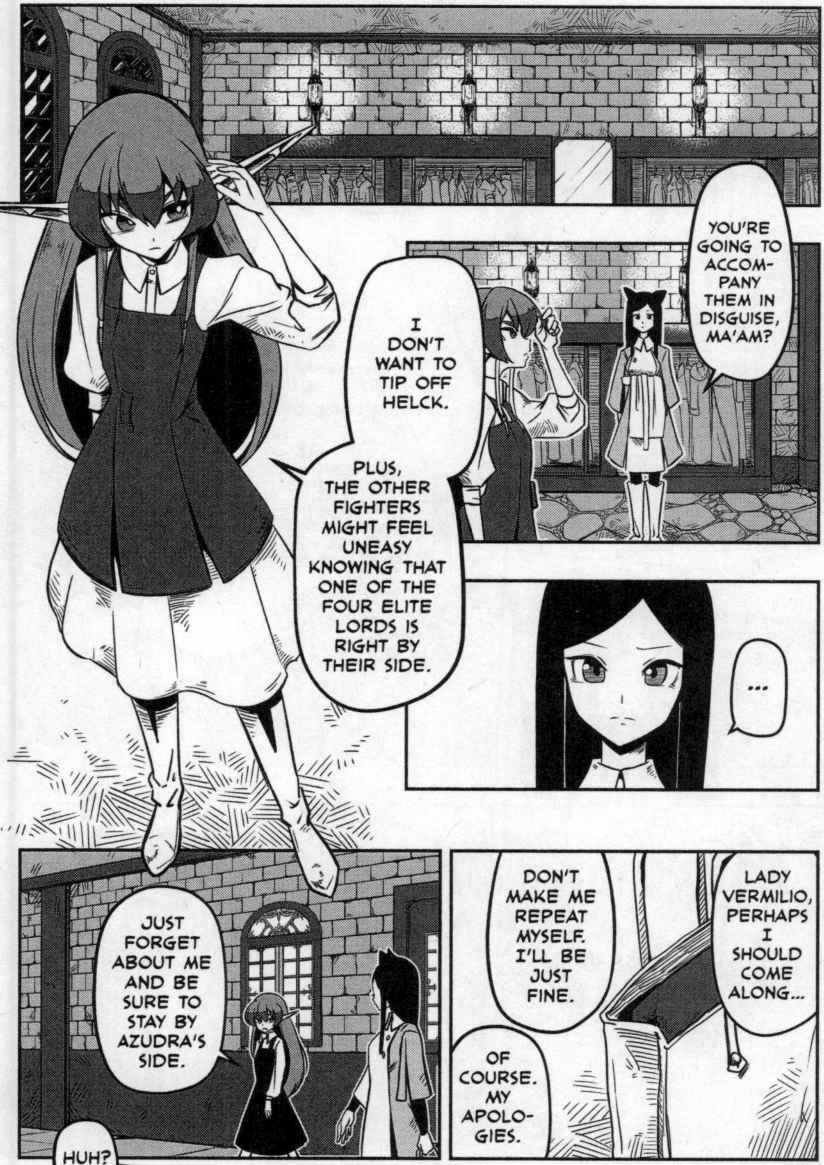
YOU'RE GOING TO ACCOMPANY THEM IN DISGUISE, MA'AM?
I DON'T WANT TO TIP OFF HELCK.
PLUS, THE OTHER FIGHTERS MIGHT FEEL UNEASY KNOWING THAT ONE OF THE FOUR ELITE LORDS IS RIGHT BY THEIR SIDE.
...
LADY VERMILIO, PERHAPS I SHOULD COME ALONG...
DON'T MAKE ME REPEAT MYSELF. I'LL BE JUST FINE.
OF COURSE. MY APOLOGIES.
JUST FORGET ABOUT ME AND BE SURE TO STAY BY AZUDRA'S SIDE.
HUH?

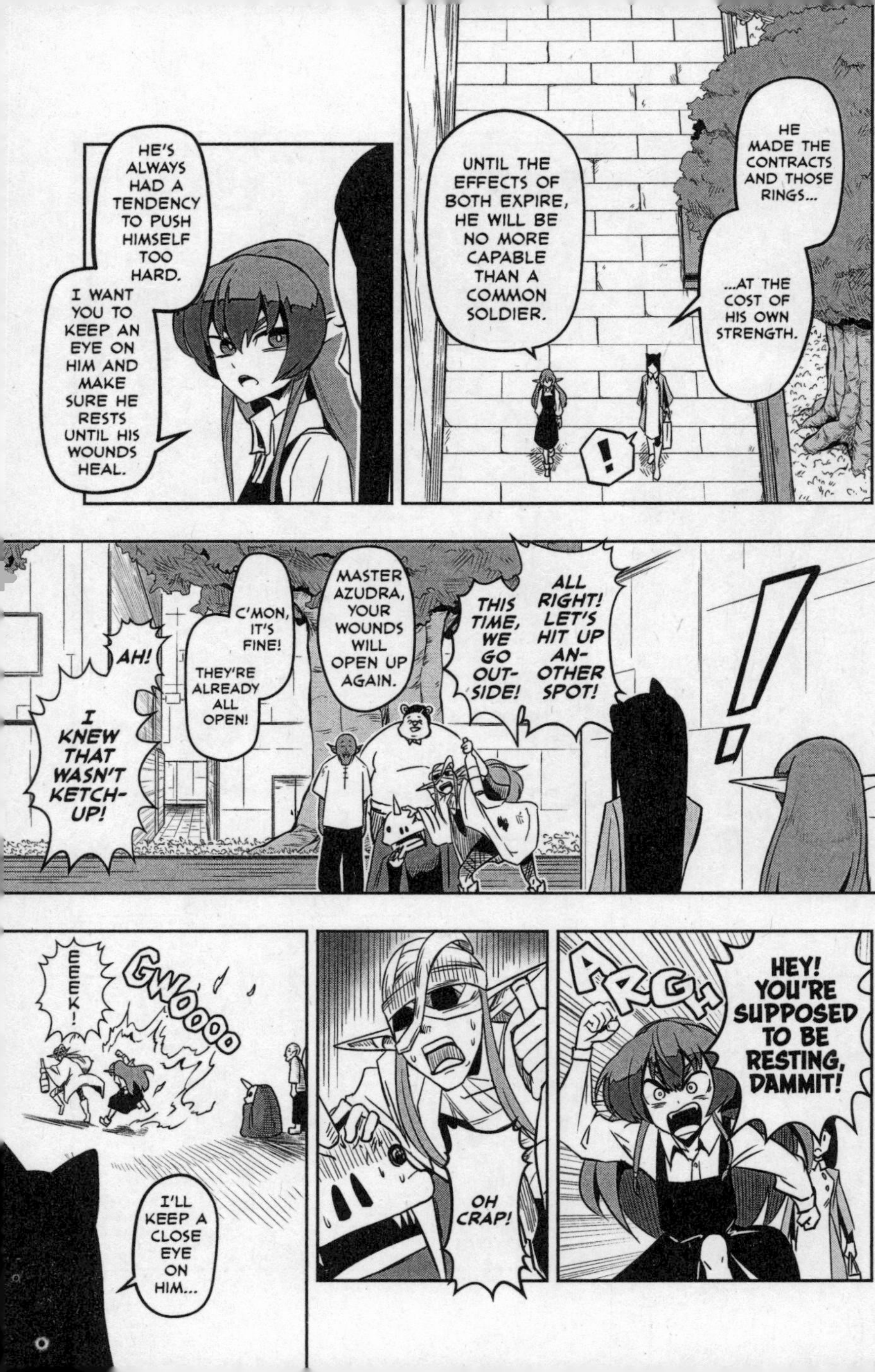
HE MADE THE CONTRACTS AND THOSE RINGS...
...AT THE COST OF HIS OWN STRENGTH.
UNTIL THE EFFECTS OF BOTH EXPIRE, HE WILL BE NO MORE CAPABLE THAN A COMMON SOLDIER.
!
HE'S ALWAYS HAD A TENDENCY TO PUSH HIMSELF TOO HARD.
I WANT YOU TO KEEP AN EYE ON HIM AND MAKE SURE HE RESTS UNTIL HIS WOUNDS HEAL.
!
ALL RIGHT! LET'S HIT UP AN-OTHER SPOT!
THIS TIME, WE GO OUT-SIDE!
MASTER AZUDRA, YOUR WOUNDS WILL OPEN UP AGAIN.
C'MON, IT'S FINE!
THEY'RE ALREADY ALL OPEN!
AH!
I KNEW THAT WASN'T KETCH-UP!
ARGH
HEY! YOU'RE SUPPOSED TO BE RESTING, DAMMIT!
OH CRAP!
EEEK!
GWOOOO
I'LL KEEP A CLOSE EYE ON HIM...

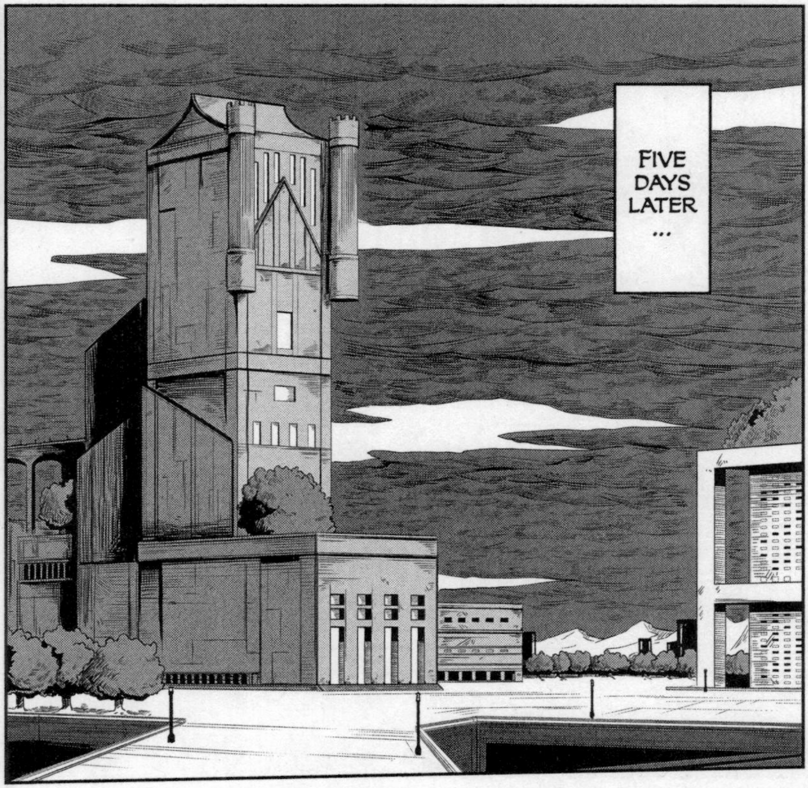
FIVE DAYS LATER ...
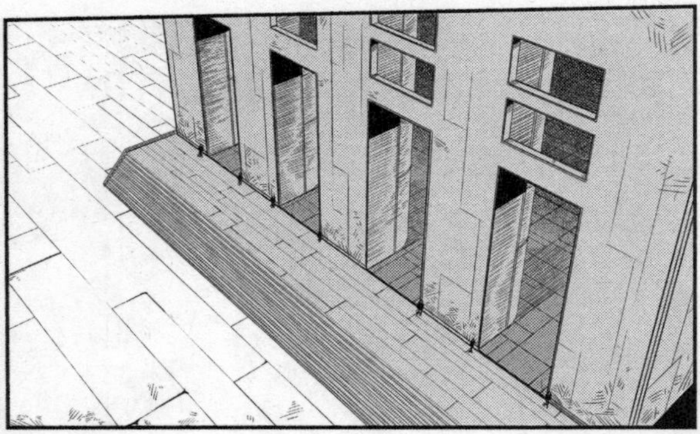
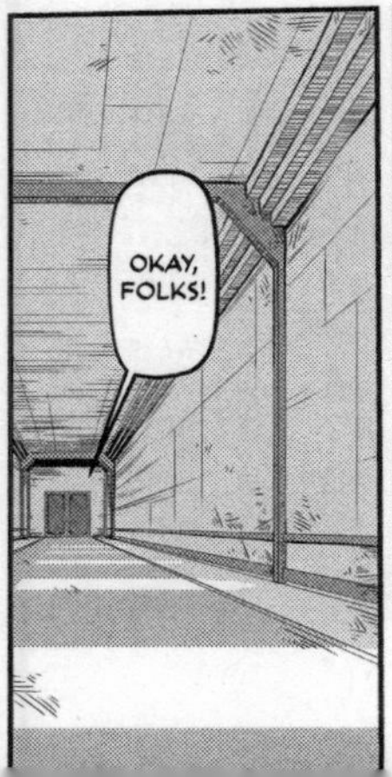
OKAY, FOLKS!

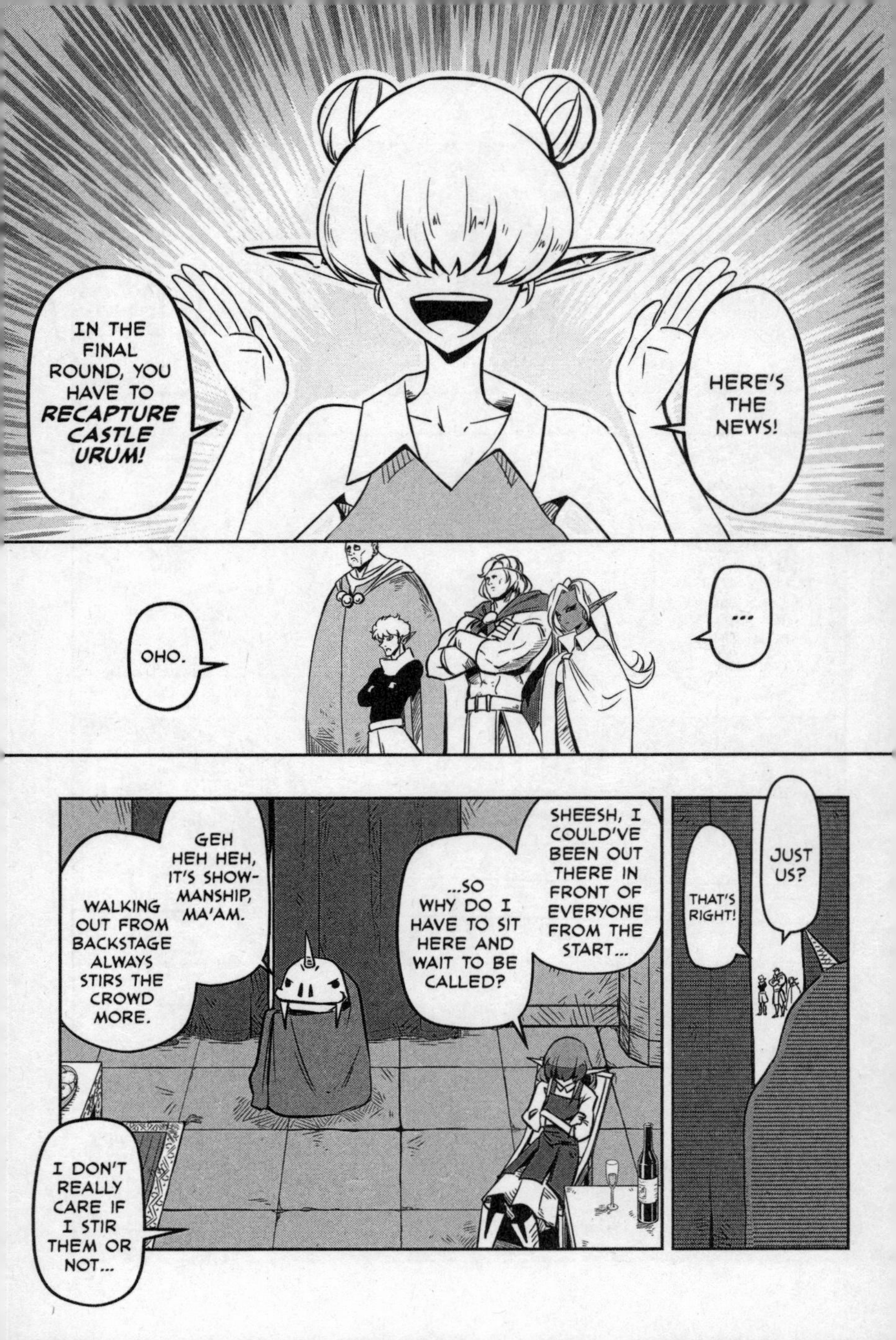
HERE'S THE NEWS!
IN THE FINAL ROUND, YOU HAVE TO *RECAPTURE CASTLE URUM!*
...
OHO.
JUST US?
THAT'S RIGHT!
SHEESH, I COULD'VE BEEN OUT THERE IN FRONT OF EVERYONE FROM THE START...
...SO WHY DO I HAVE TO SIT HERE AND WAIT TO BE CALLED?
GEH HEH HEH, IT'S SHOWMANSHIP, MA'AM.
WALKING OUT FROM BACKSTAGE ALWAYS STIRS THE CROWD MORE.
I DON'T REALLY CARE IF I STIR THEM OR NOT...

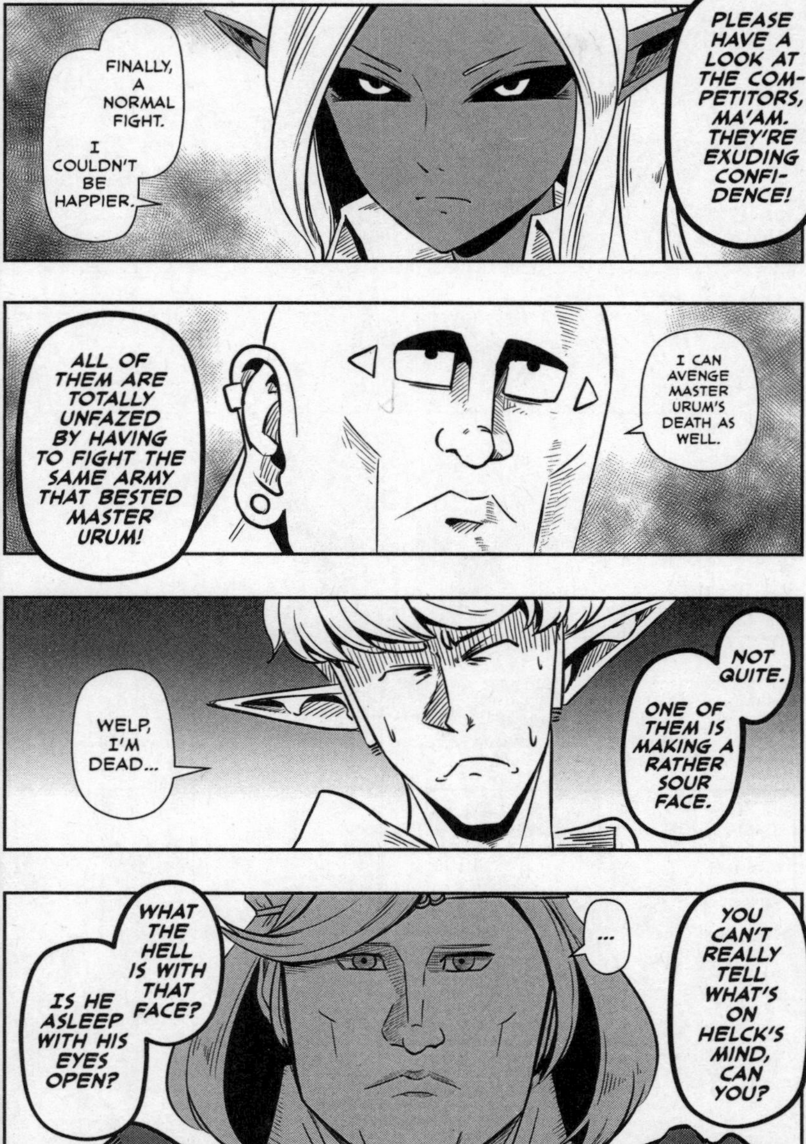
PLEASE HAVE A LOOK AT THE COMPETITORS, MA'AM. THEY'RE EXUDING CONFIDENCE!
FINALLY, A NORMAL FIGHT.
I COULDN'T BE HAPPIER.
ALL OF THEM ARE TOTALLY UNFAZED BY HAVING TO FIGHT THE SAME ARMY THAT BESTED MASTER URUM!
I CAN AVENGE MASTER URUM'S DEATH AS WELL.
NOT QUITE.
ONE OF THEM IS MAKING A RATHER SOUR FACE.
WELP, I'M DEAD...
YOU CAN'T REALLY TELL WHAT'S ON HELCK'S MIND, CAN YOU?
...
WHAT THE HELL IS WITH THAT FACE?
IS HE ASLEEP WITH HIS EYES OPEN?

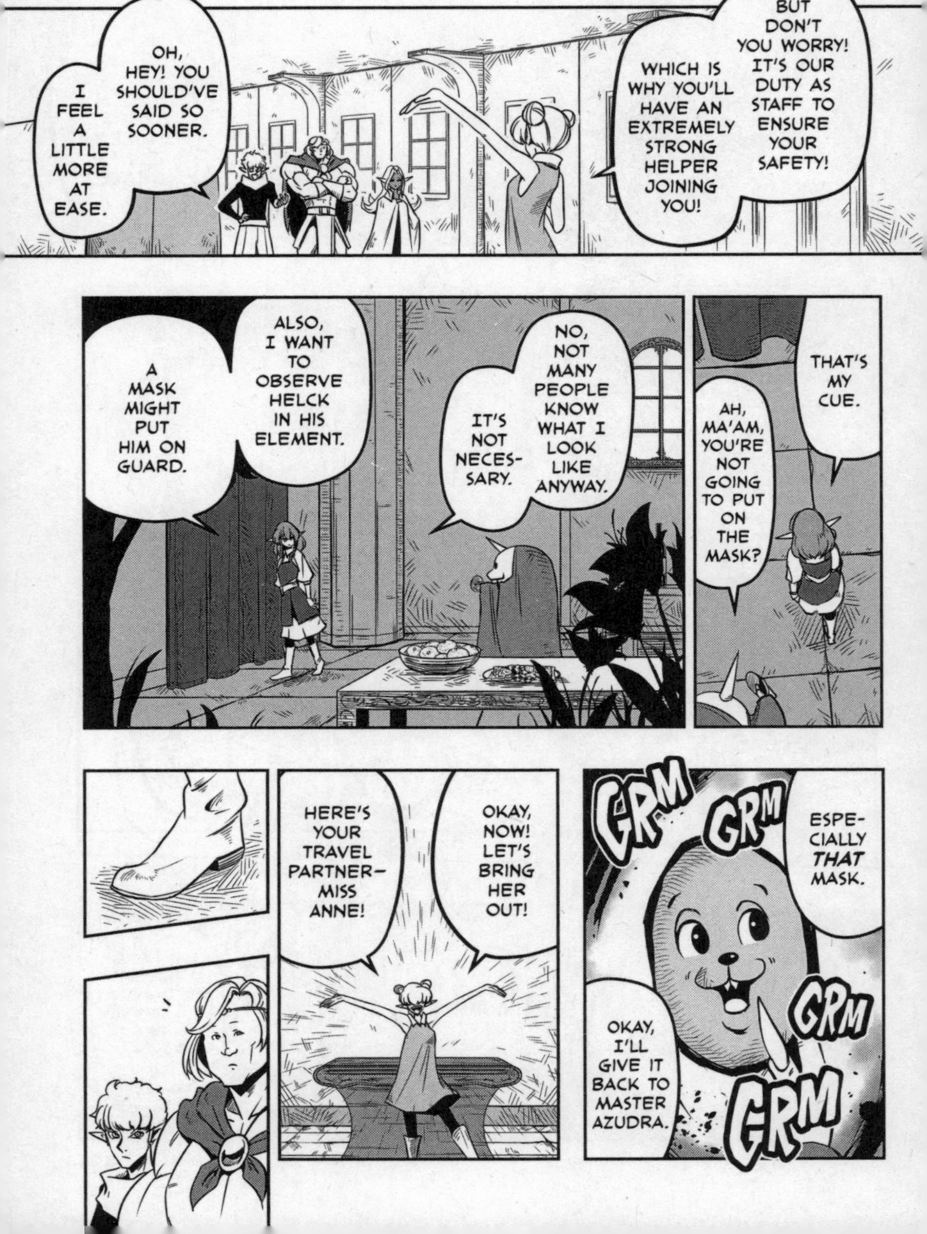
BUT DON'T YOU WORRY! IT'S OUR DUTY AS STAFF TO ENSURE YOUR SAFETY!
WHICH IS WHY YOU'LL HAVE AN EXTREMELY STRONG HELPER JOINING YOU!
OH, HEY! YOU SHOULD'VE SAID SO SOONER.
I FEEL A LITTLE MORE AT EASE.
THAT'S MY CUE.
AH, MA'AM, YOU'RE NOT GOING TO PUT ON THE MASK?
NO, NOT MANY PEOPLE KNOW WHAT I LOOK LIKE ANYWAY.
IT'S NOT NECES-SARY.
ALSO, I WANT TO OBSERVE HELCK IN HIS ELEMENT.
A MASK MIGHT PUT HIM ON GUARD.
GRM
GRM
ESPE-CIALLY *THAT* MASK.
GRM
GRM
OKAY, I'LL GIVE IT BACK TO MASTER AZUDRA.
OKAY, NOW! LET'S BRING HER OUT!
HERE'S YOUR TRAVEL PARTNER—MISS ANNE!

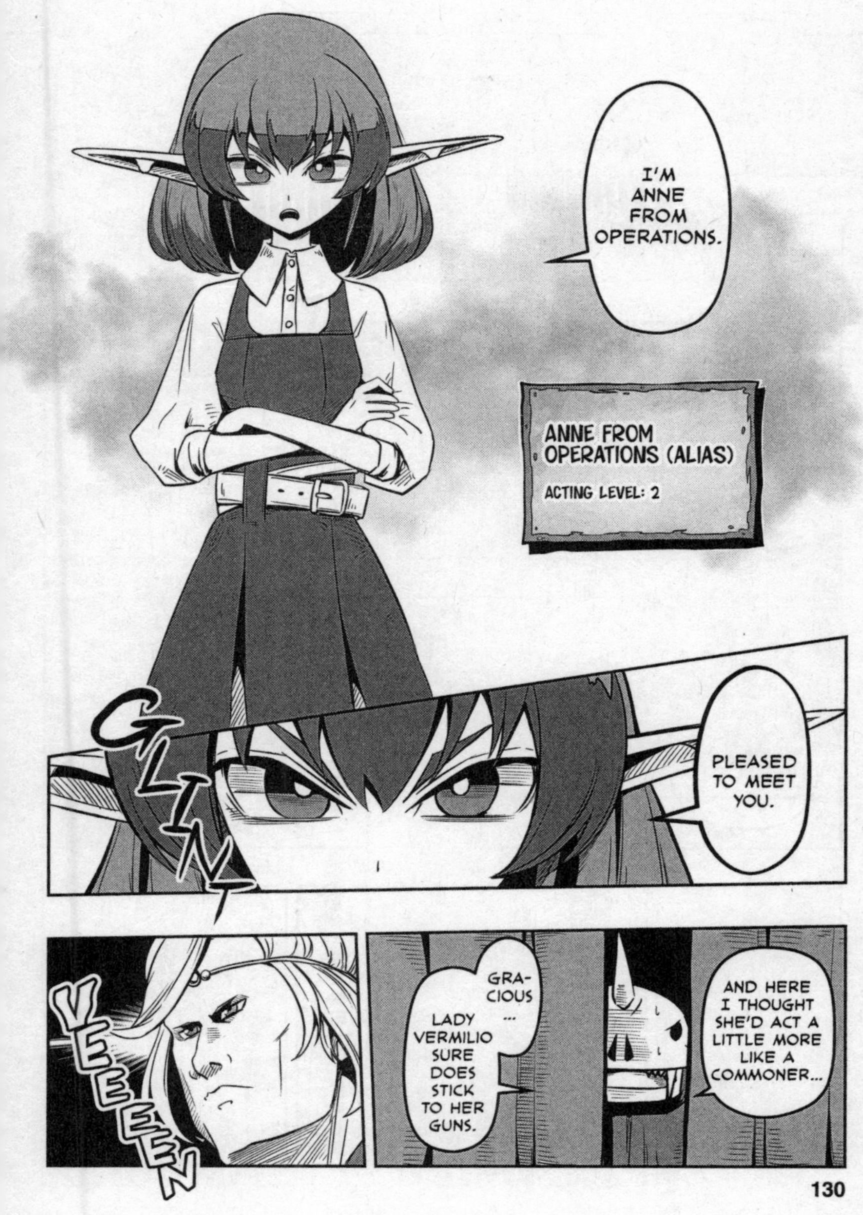
I'M ANNE FROM OPERATIONS.
ANNE FROM OPERATIONS (ALIAS)
ACTING LEVEL: 2
PLEASED TO MEET YOU.
GLINT
AND HERE I THOUGHT SHE'D ACT A LITTLE MORE LIKE A COMMONER...
GRA-CIOUS ... LADY VERMILIO SURE DOES STICK TO HER GUNS.
VEEEEEN

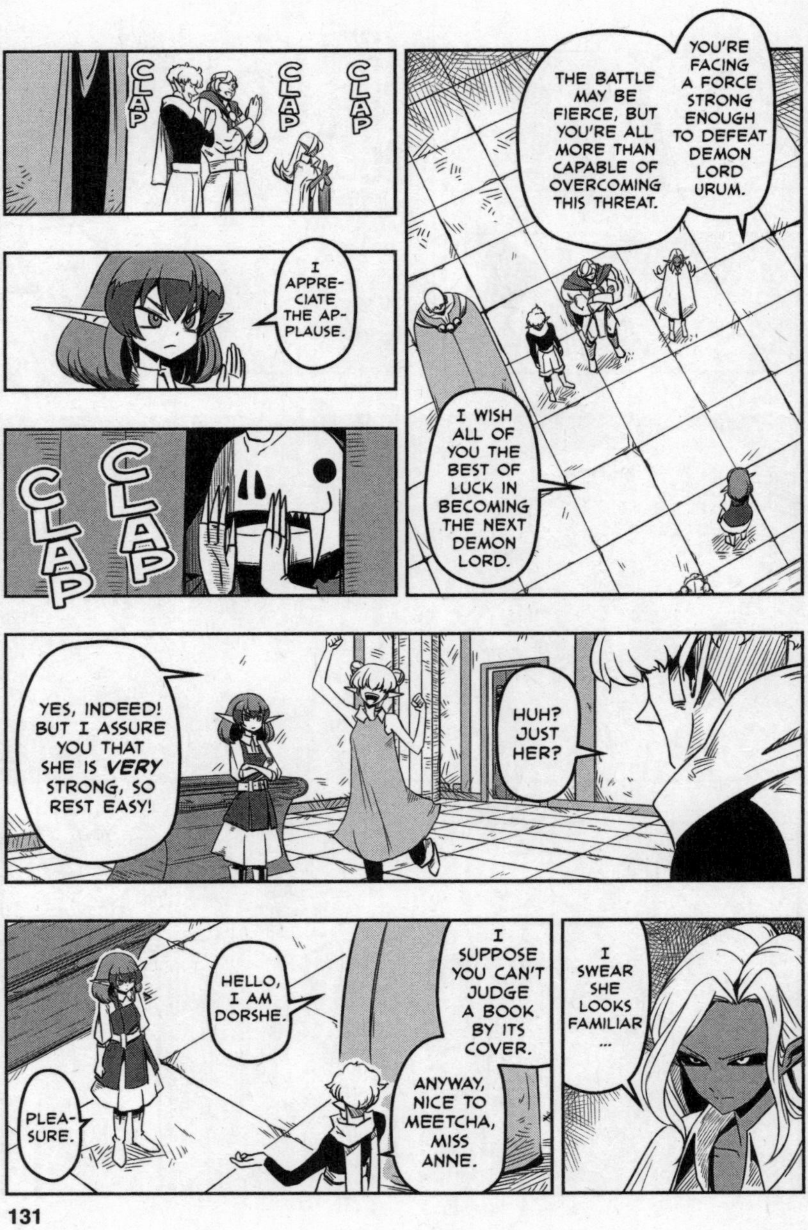
YOU'RE FACING A FORCE STRONG ENOUGH TO DEFEAT DEMON LORD URUM.
THE BATTLE MAY BE FIERCE, BUT YOU'RE ALL MORE THAN CAPABLE OF OVERCOMING THIS THREAT.
I WISH ALL OF YOU THE BEST OF LUCK IN BECOMING THE NEXT DEMON LORD.
CLAP
CLAP
CLAP
I APPRECIATE THE APPLAUSE.
CLAP
CLAP
HUH? JUST HER?
YES, INDEED! BUT I ASSURE YOU THAT SHE IS *VERY* STRONG, SO REST EASY!
I SWEAR SHE LOOKS FAMILIAR ...
I SUPPOSE YOU CAN'T JUDGE A BOOK BY ITS COVER.
ANYWAY, NICE TO MEETCHA, MISS ANNE.
HELLO, I AM DORSHE.
PLEASURE.

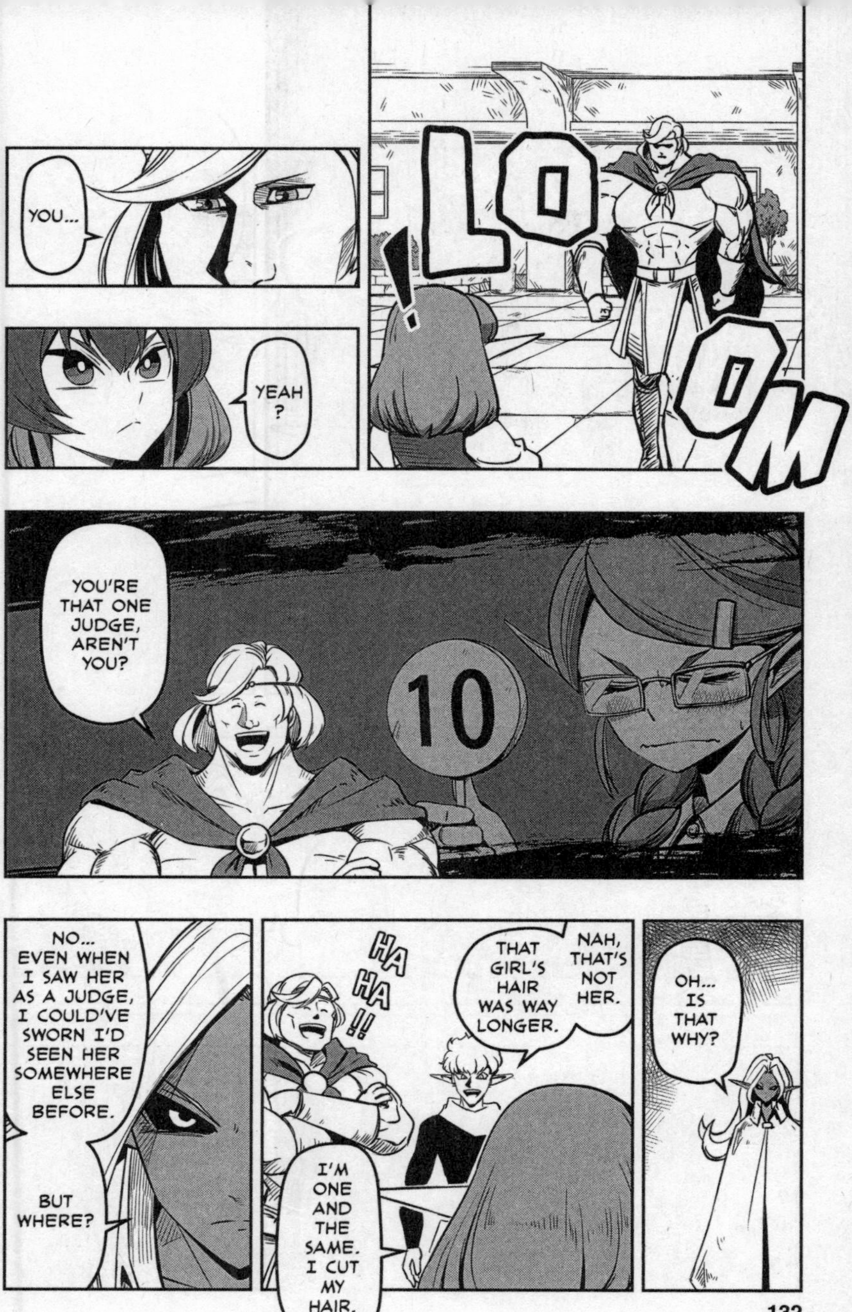
!
LOOM
YOU...
YEAH?
YOU'RE THAT ONE JUDGE, AREN'T YOU?
10
OH... IS THAT WHY?
NAH, THAT'S NOT HER.
THAT GIRL'S HAIR WAS WAY LONGER.
HA HA!!
I'M ONE AND THE SAME. I CUT MY HAIR.
NO... EVEN WHEN I SAW HER AS A JUDGE, I COULD'VE SWORN I'D SEEN HER SOMEWHERE ELSE BEFORE.
BUT WHERE?

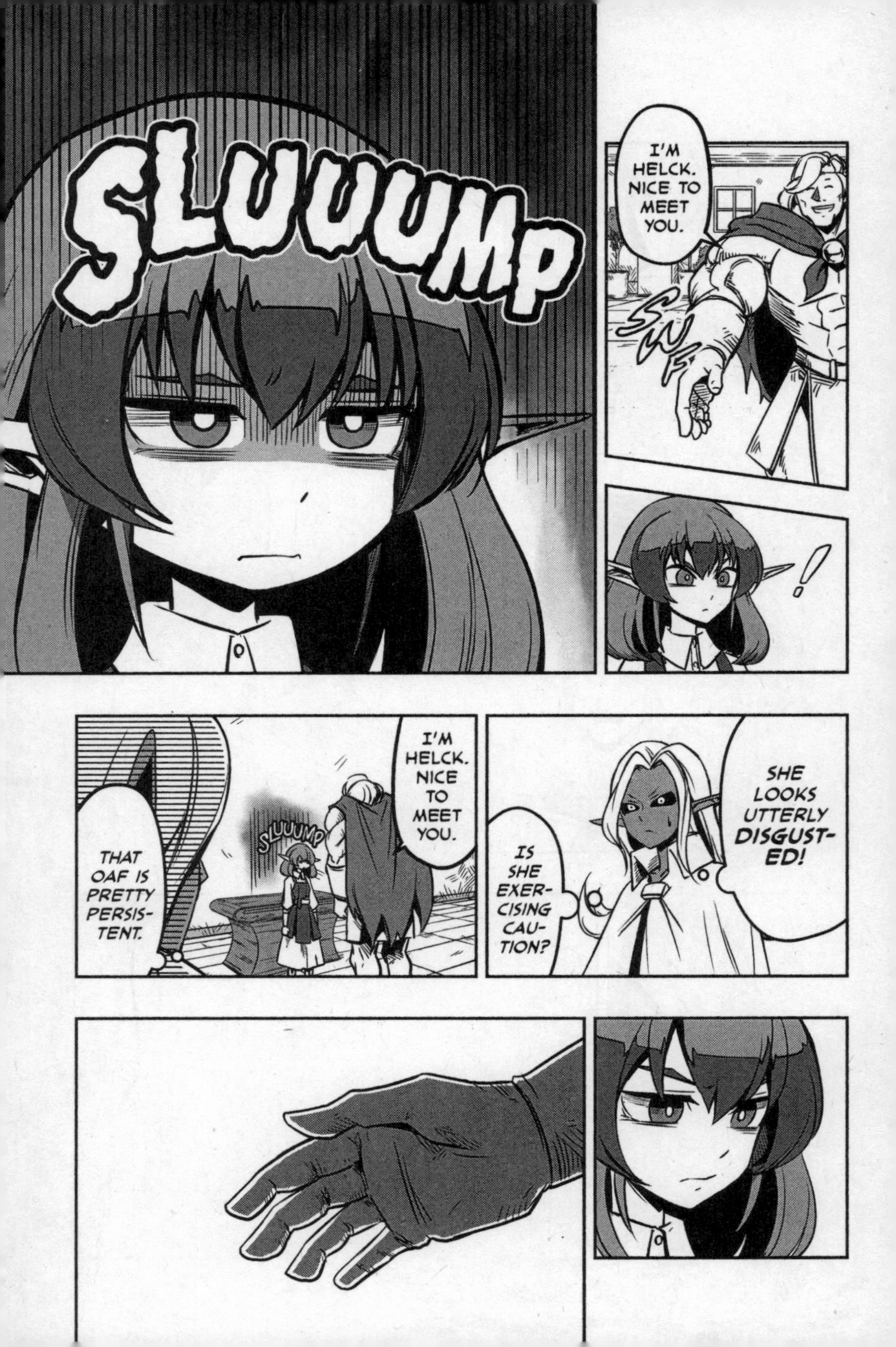

I'M HELCK. NICE TO MEET YOU.
!
SLUUUMP
SHE LOOKS UTTERLY DISGUSTED!
IS SHE EXERCISING CAUTION?
I'M HELCK. NICE TO MEET YOU.
SLUUUMP
THAT OAF IS PRETTY PERSISTENT.

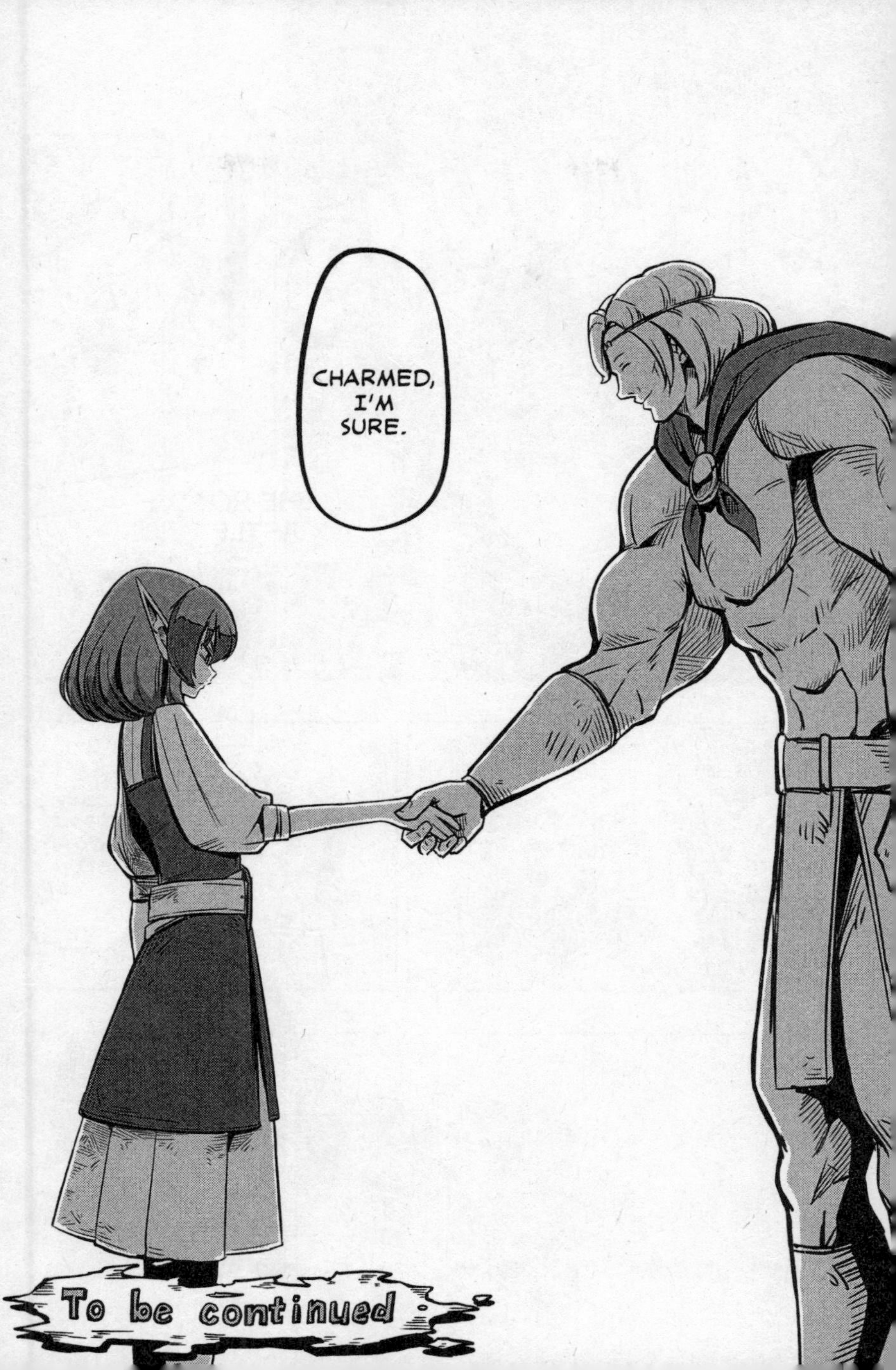
CHARMED, I'M SURE.
To be continued

Helck

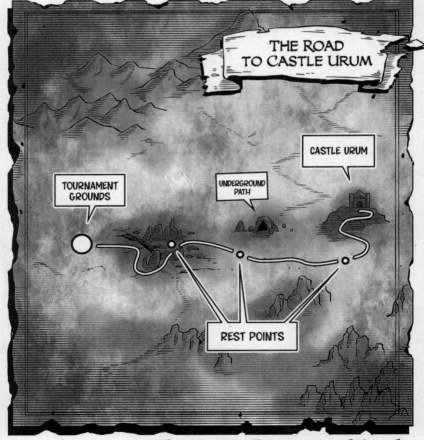

THE ROAD
TO CASTLE URUM

CASTLE URUM

TOURNAMENT
GROUNDS

UNDERGROUND
PATH

REST POINTS

Chapter 7: Devastated Lands

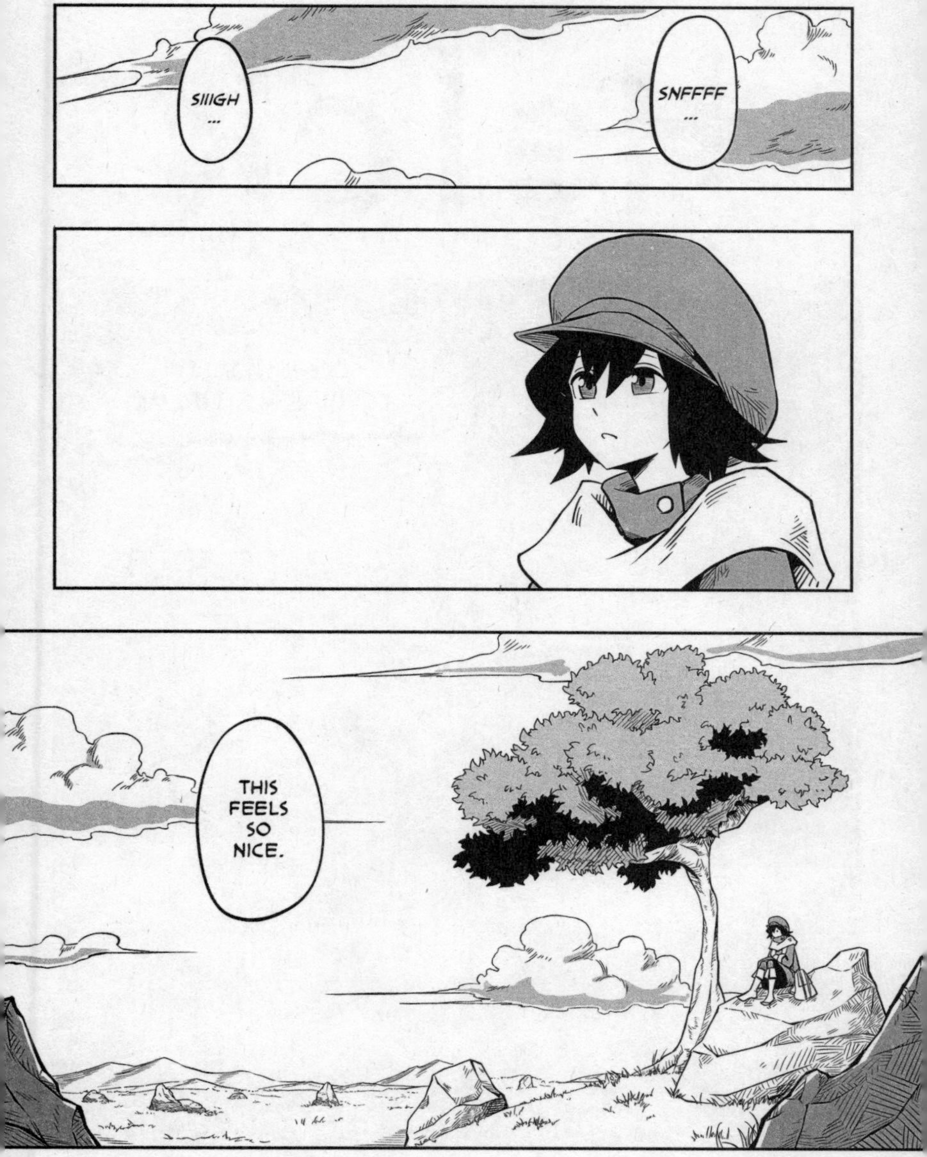
SNFFFF ...
SIIIGH ...
THIS FEELS SO NICE.

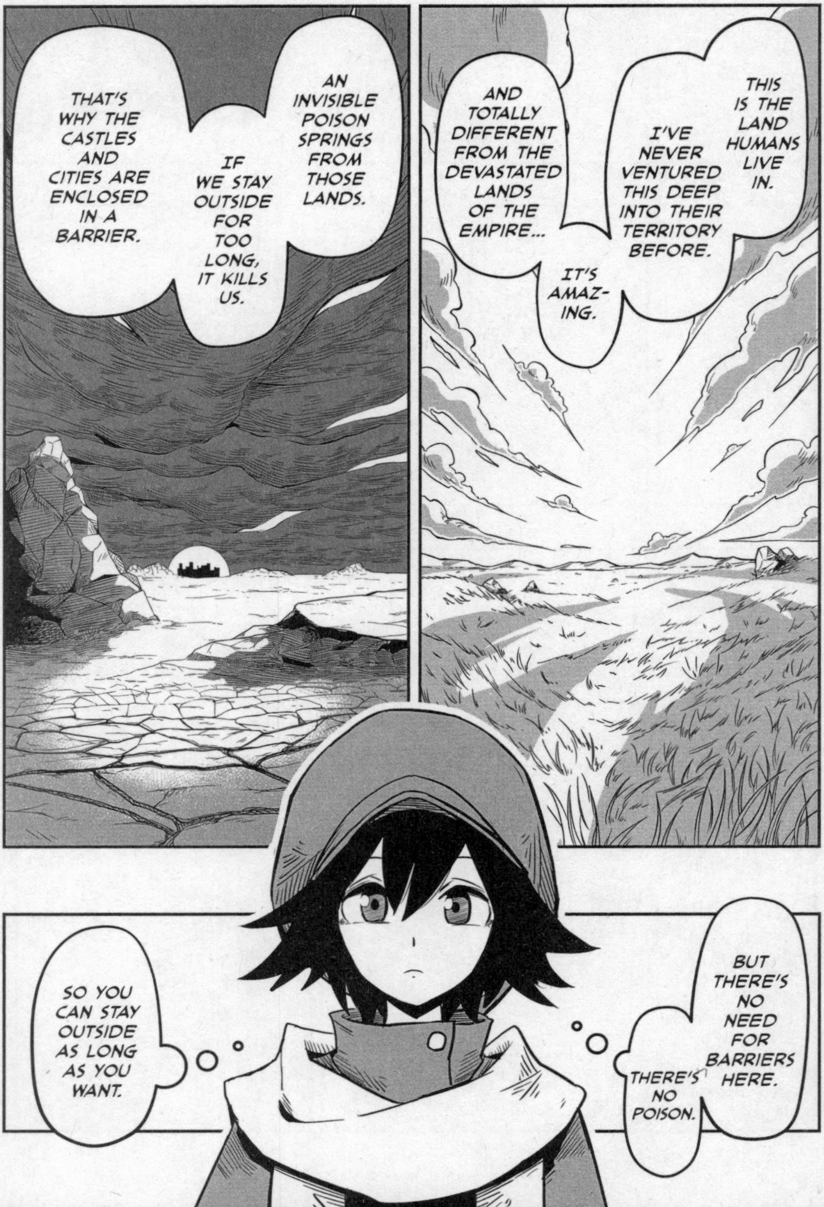
THIS IS THE LAND HUMANS LIVE IN.
I'VE NEVER VENTURED THIS DEEP INTO THEIR TERRITORY BEFORE.
AND TOTALLY DIFFERENT FROM THE DEVASTATED LANDS OF THE EMPIRE...
IT'S AMAZ-ING.
AN INVISIBLE POISON SPRINGS FROM THOSE LANDS.
IF WE STAY OUTSIDE FOR TOO LONG, IT KILLS US.
THAT'S WHY THE CASTLES AND CITIES ARE ENCLOSED IN A BARRIER.
BUT THERE'S NO NEED FOR BARRIERS HERE.
THERE'S NO POISON.
SO YOU CAN STAY OUTSIDE AS LONG AS YOU WANT.

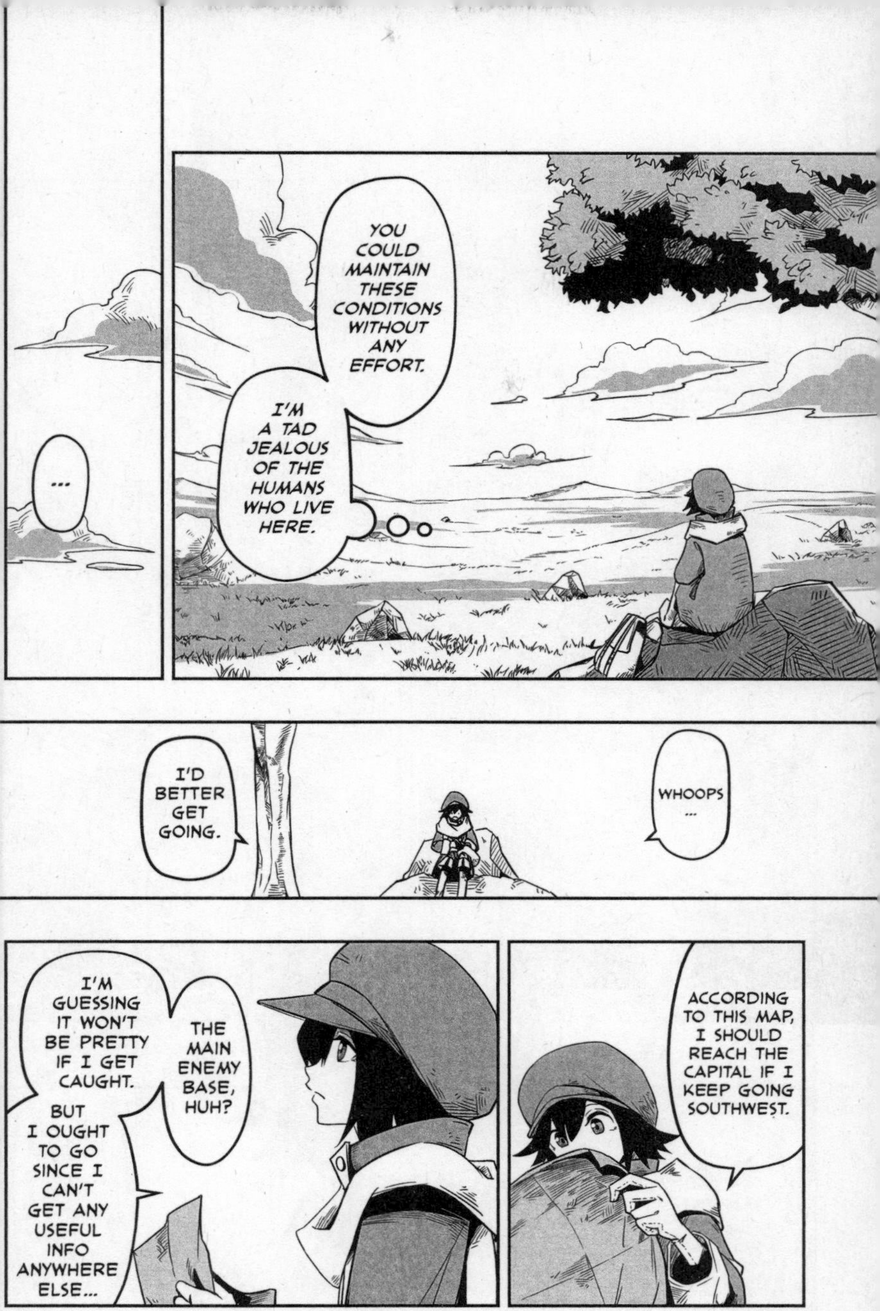
YOU COULD MAINTAIN THESE CONDITIONS WITHOUT ANY EFFORT.
I'M A TAD JEALOUS OF THE HUMANS WHO LIVE HERE.
...
WHOOPS ...
I'D BETTER GET GOING.
ACCORDING TO THIS MAP, I SHOULD REACH THE CAPITAL IF I KEEP GOING SOUTHWEST.
THE MAIN ENEMY BASE, HUH?
I'M GUESSING IT WON'T BE PRETTY IF I GET CAUGHT.
BUT I OUGHT TO GO SINCE I CAN'T GET ANY USEFUL INFO ANYWHERE ELSE...

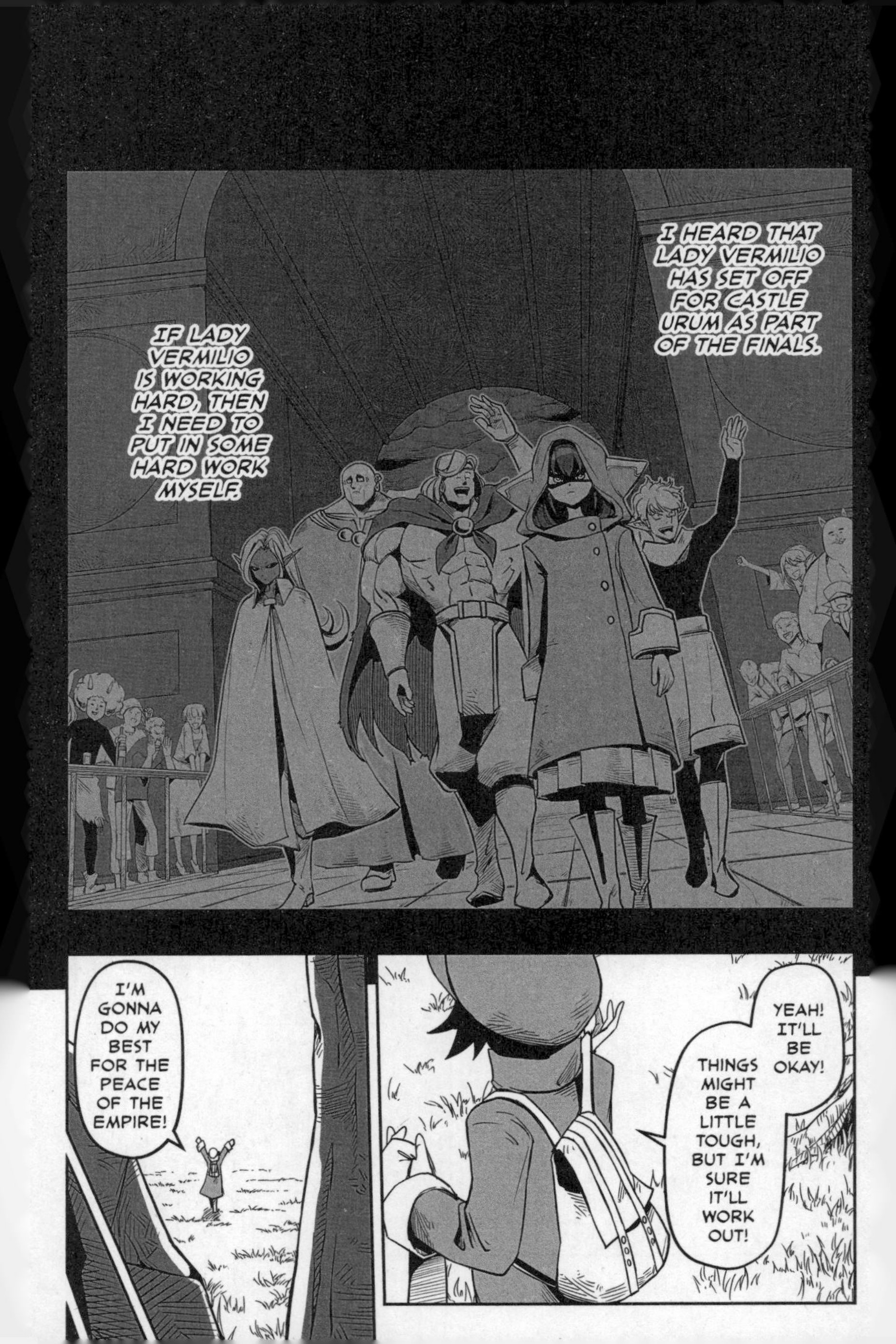
I HEARD THAT LADY VERMILIO HAS SET OFF FOR CASTLE URUM AS PART OF THE FINALS.
IF LADY VERMILIO IS WORKING HARD, THEN I NEED TO PUT IN SOME HARD WORK MYSELF.
YEAH! IT'LL BE OKAY!
THINGS MIGHT BE A LITTLE TOUGH, BUT I'M SURE IT'LL WORK OUT!
I'M GONNA DO MY BEST FOR THE PEACE OF THE EMPIRE!

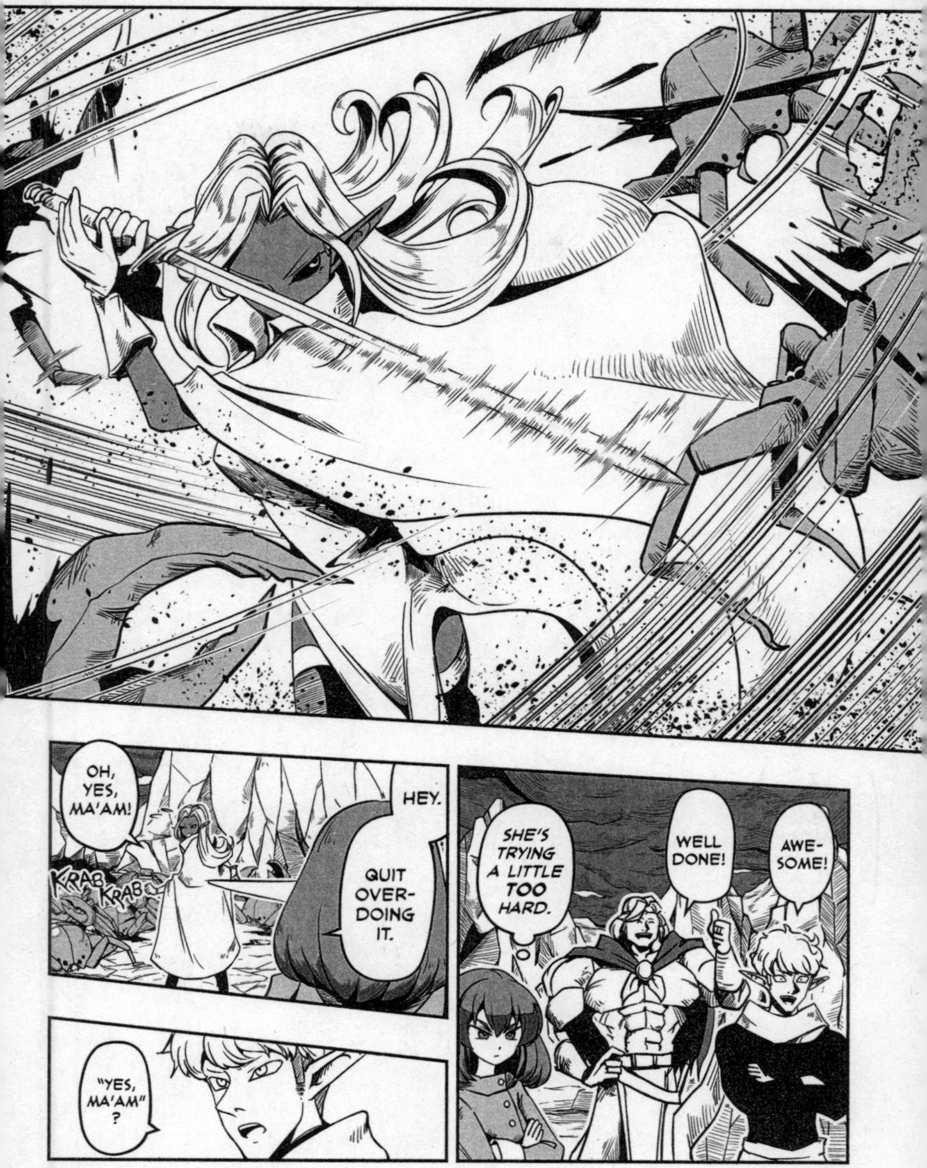
AWE-SOME!
WELL DONE!
SHE'S TRYING A LITTLE TOO HARD.
HEY.
QUIT OVER-DOING IT.
OH, YES, MA'AM!
KRAB KRAB
"YES, MA'AM"?

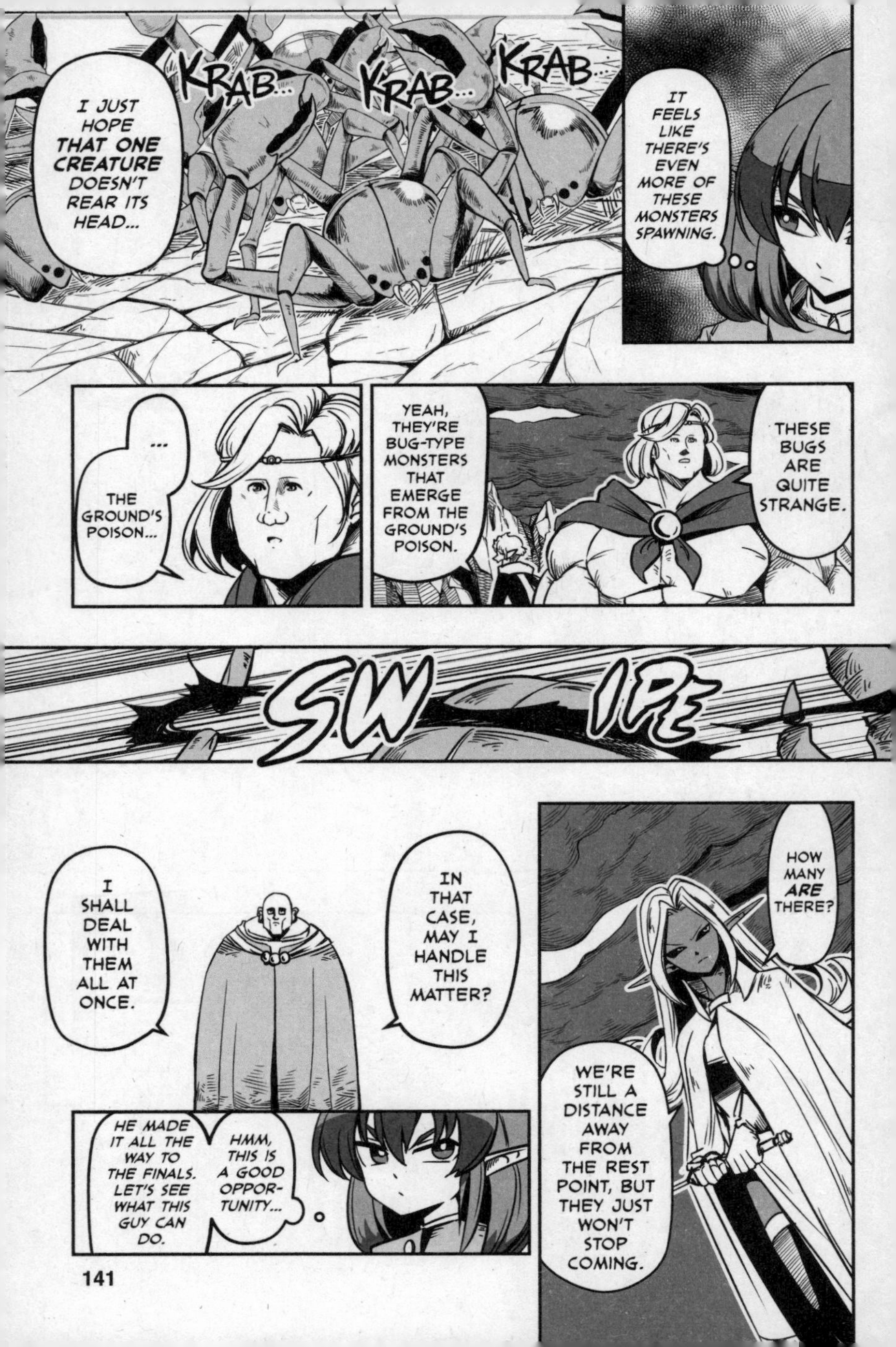
IT FEELS LIKE THERE'S EVEN MORE OF THESE MONSTERS SPAWNING.
KRAB... KRAB... KRAB...
I JUST HOPE THAT ONE CREATURE DOESN'T REAR ITS HEAD...
THESE BUGS ARE QUITE STRANGE.
YEAH, THEY'RE BUG-TYPE MONSTERS THAT EMERGE FROM THE GROUND'S POISON.
... THE GROUND'S POISON...
SWIPE
HOW MANY ARE THERE?
WE'RE STILL A DISTANCE AWAY FROM THE REST POINT, BUT THEY JUST WON'T STOP COMING.
IN THAT CASE, MAY I HANDLE THIS MATTER?
I SHALL DEAL WITH THEM ALL AT ONCE.
HMM, THIS IS A GOOD OPPORTUNITY...
HE MADE IT ALL THE WAY TO THE FINALS. LET'S SEE WHAT THIS GUY CAN DO.

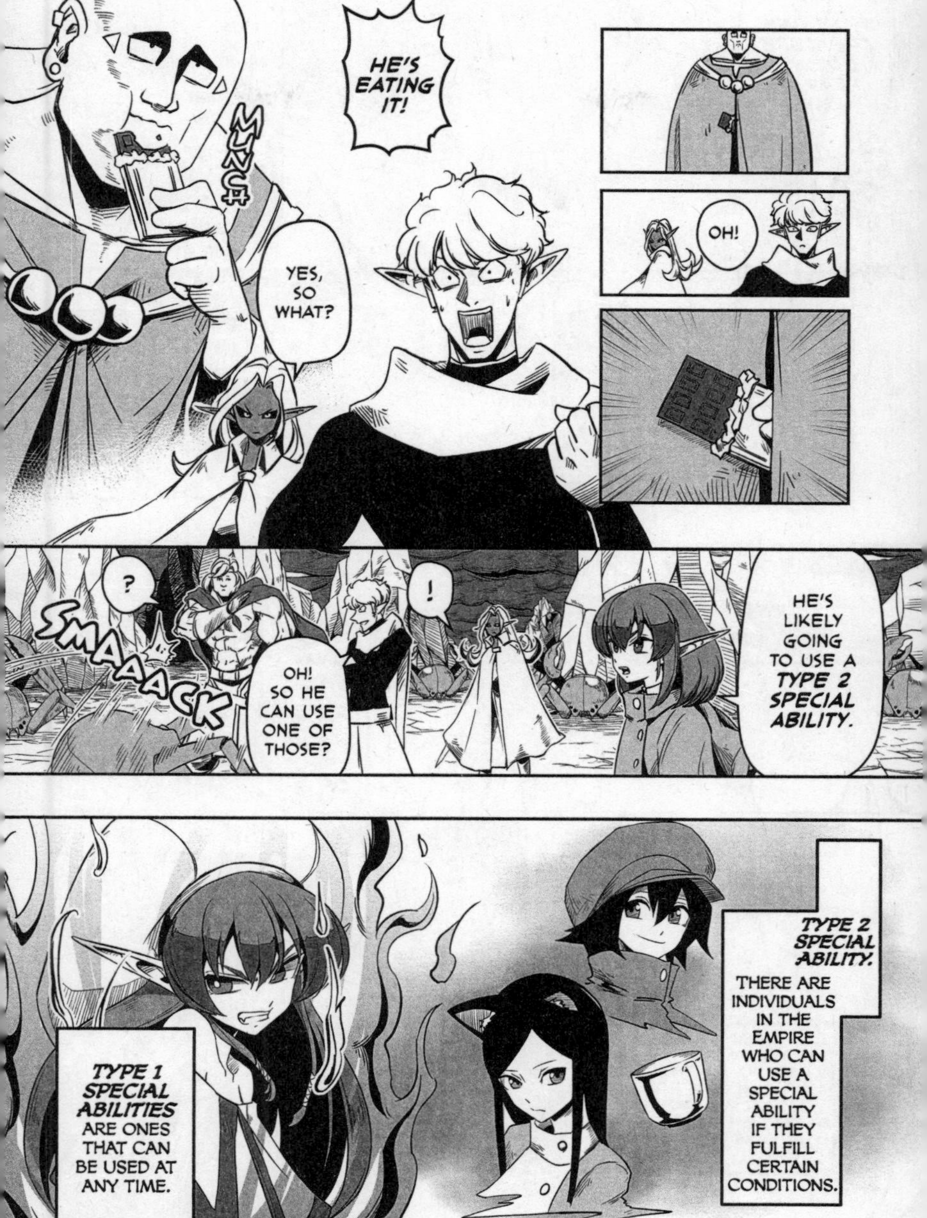
OH!
HE'S EATING IT!
MUNCH
YES, SO WHAT?
HE'S LIKELY GOING TO USE A TYPE 2 SPECIAL ABILITY.
!
OH! SO HE CAN USE ONE OF THOSE?
?
SMAAACK
TYPE 2 SPECIAL ABILITY. THERE ARE INDIVIDUALS IN THE EMPIRE WHO CAN USE A SPECIAL ABILITY IF THEY FULFILL CERTAIN CONDITIONS.
TYPE 1 SPECIAL ABILITIES ARE ONES THAT CAN BE USED AT ANY TIME.

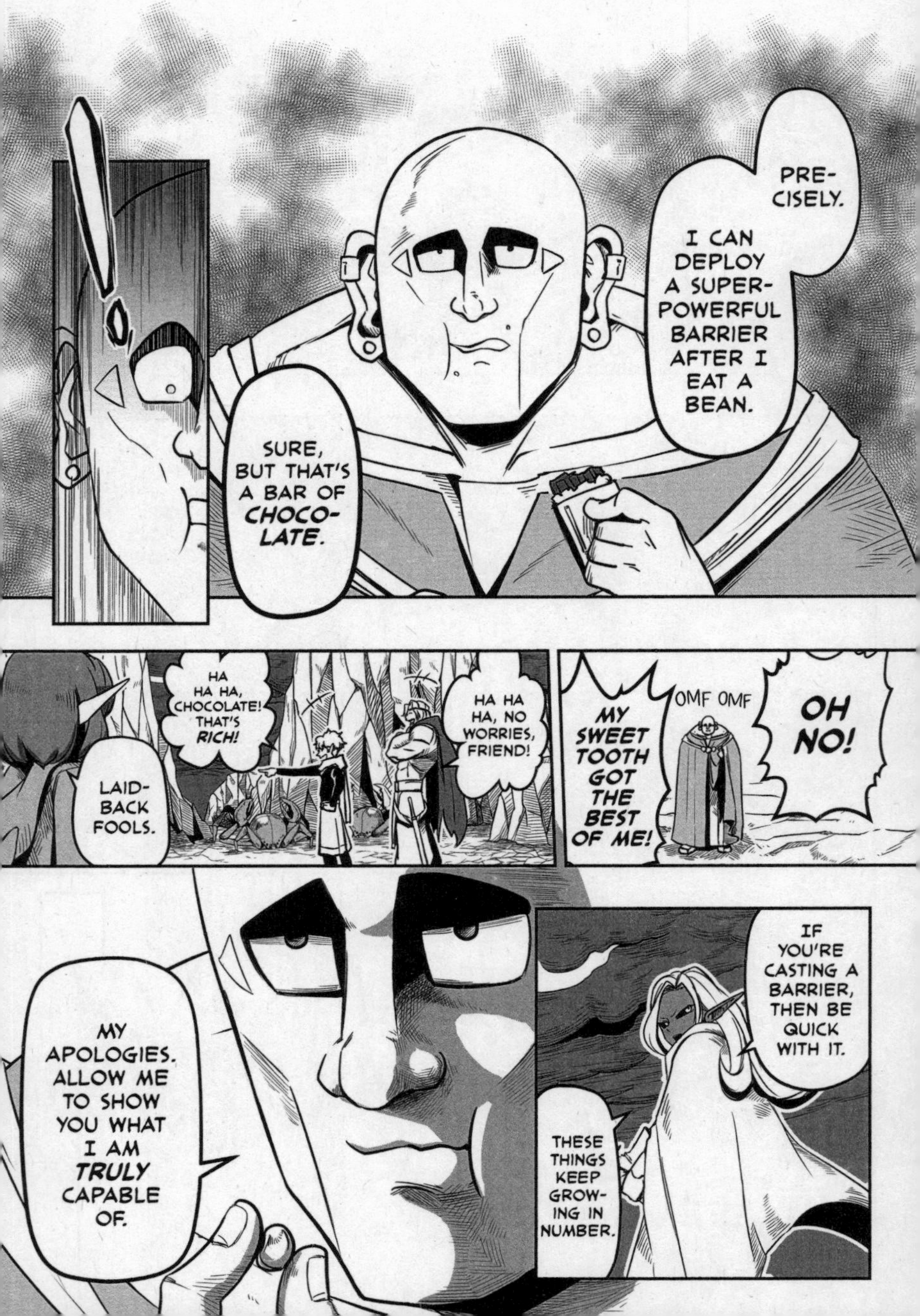
PRE-CISELY.
I CAN DEPLOY A SUPER-POWERFUL BARRIER AFTER I EAT A BEAN.
SURE, BUT THAT'S A BAR OF *CHOCO-LATE.*
OH NO!
OMF OMF
MY SWEET TOOTH GOT THE BEST OF ME!
HA HA HA, NO WORRIES, FRIEND!
HA HA HA, CHOCOLATE! THAT'S *RICH!*
LAID-BACK FOOLS.
IF YOU'RE CASTING A BARRIER, THEN BE QUICK WITH IT.
THESE THINGS KEEP GROW-ING IN NUMBER.
MY APOLOGIES. ALLOW ME TO SHOW YOU WHAT I AM *TRULY* CAPABLE OF.

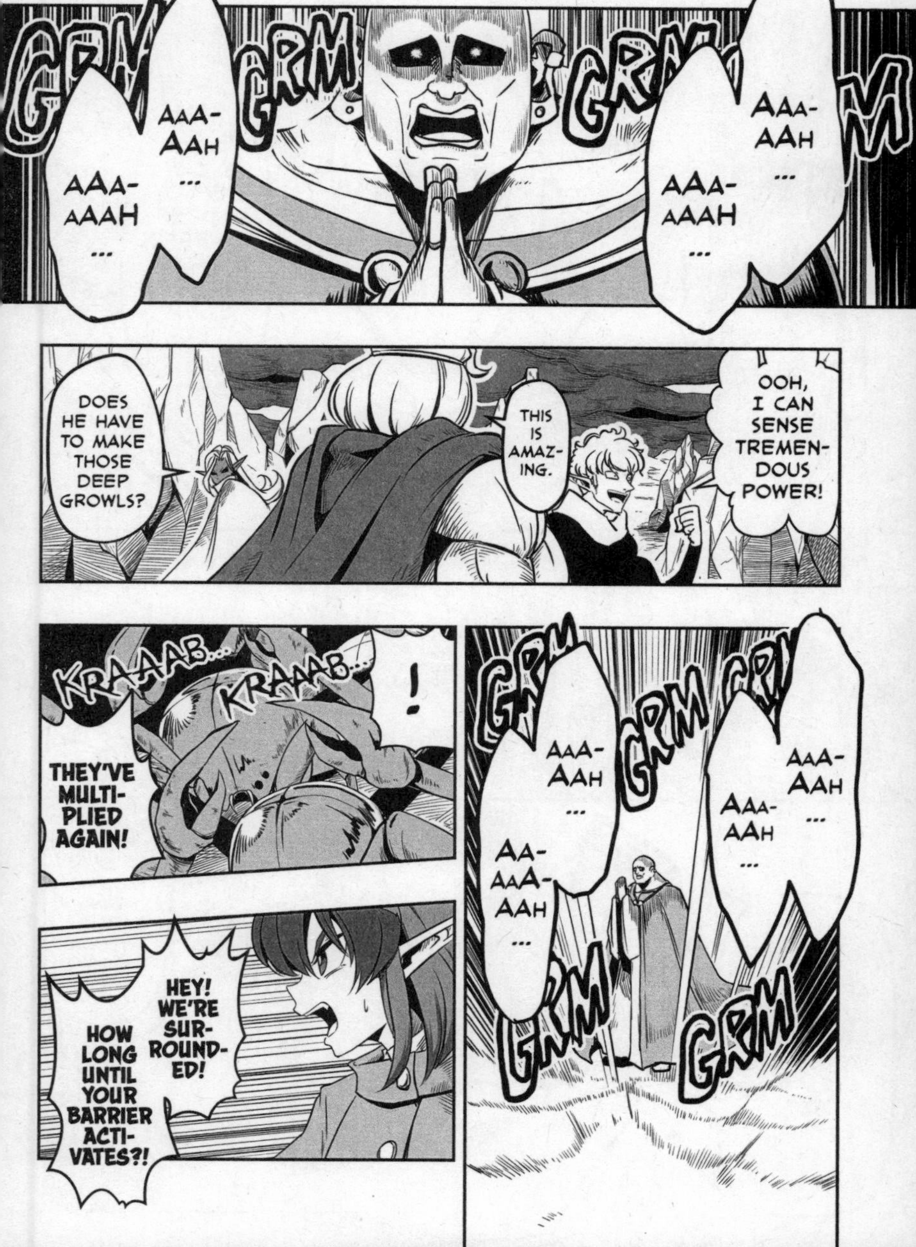
GRM GRM GRM GRM
AAA-AAH ...
AAA-AAAH ...
AAA-AAH ...
AAA-AAAH ...
OOH, I CAN SENSE TREMEN-DOUS POWER!
THIS IS AMAZ-ING.
DOES HE HAVE TO MAKE THOSE DEEP GROWLS?
GRM GRM GRM GRM GRM
AAA-AAH ...
AAA-AAH ...
AAA-AAH ...
AA-AAA-AAH ...
KRAAAB... KRAAAB...
!
THEY'VE MULTI-PLIED AGAIN!
HEY! WE'RE SUR-ROUND-ED!
HOW LONG UNTIL YOUR BARRIER ACTI-VATES?!

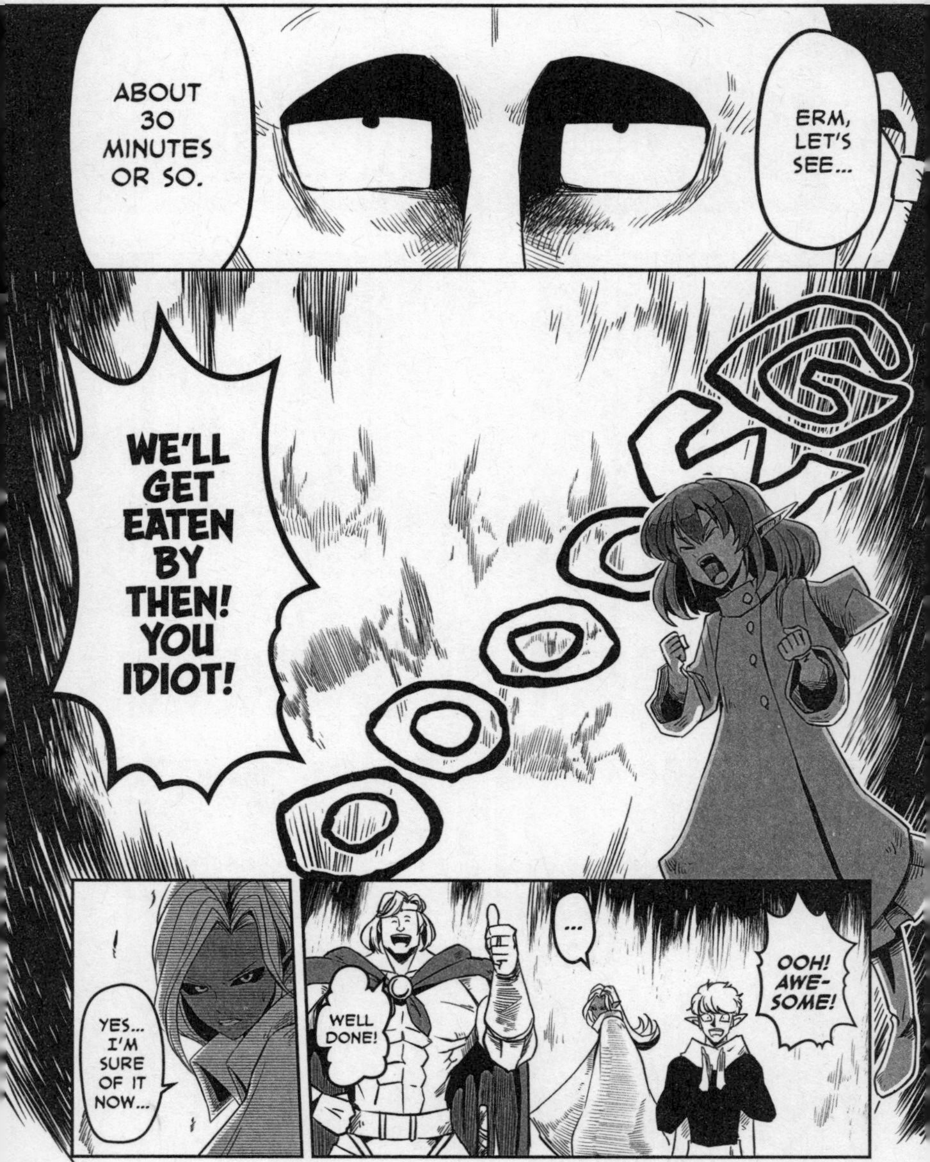
ERM, LET'S SEE...
ABOUT 30 MINUTES OR SO.
WE'LL GET EATEN BY THEN! YOU IDIOT!
OOH! AWE-SOME!
...
WELL DONE!
!
YES... I'M SURE OF IT NOW...

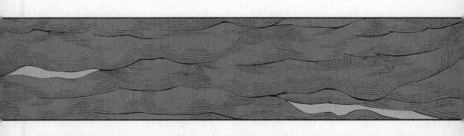

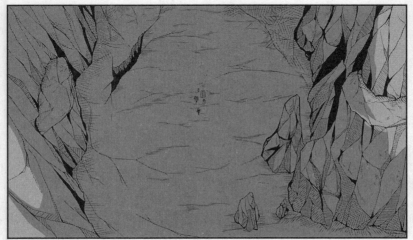

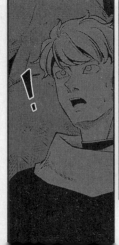

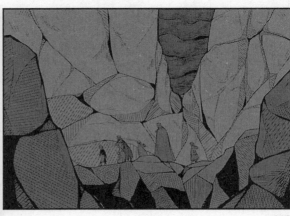

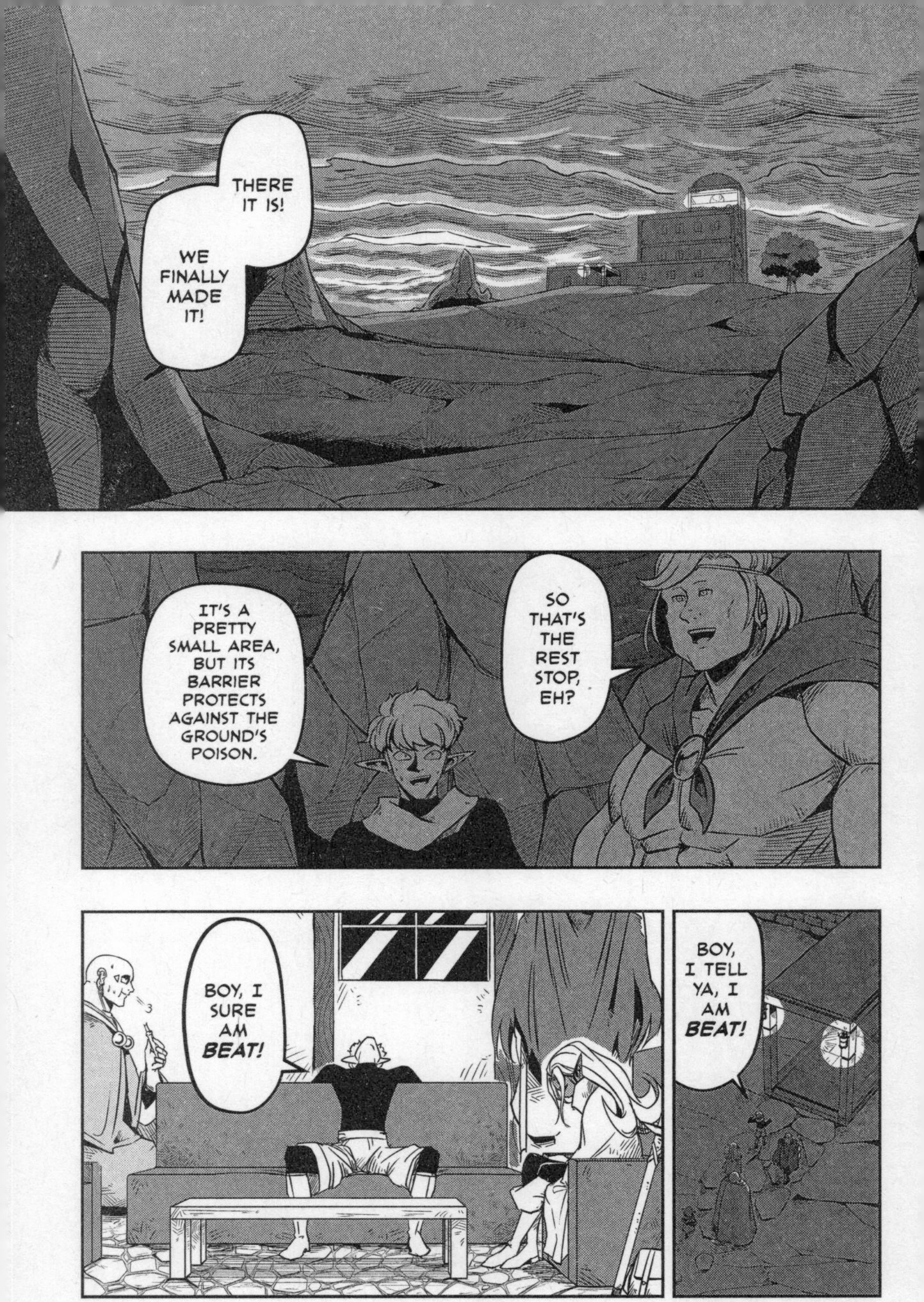
THERE IT IS!
WE FINALLY MADE IT!
SO THAT'S THE REST STOP, EH?
IT'S A PRETTY SMALL AREA, BUT ITS BARRIER PROTECTS AGAINST THE GROUND'S POISON.
BOY, I TELL YA, I AM *BEAT!*
BOY, I SURE AM *BEAT!*

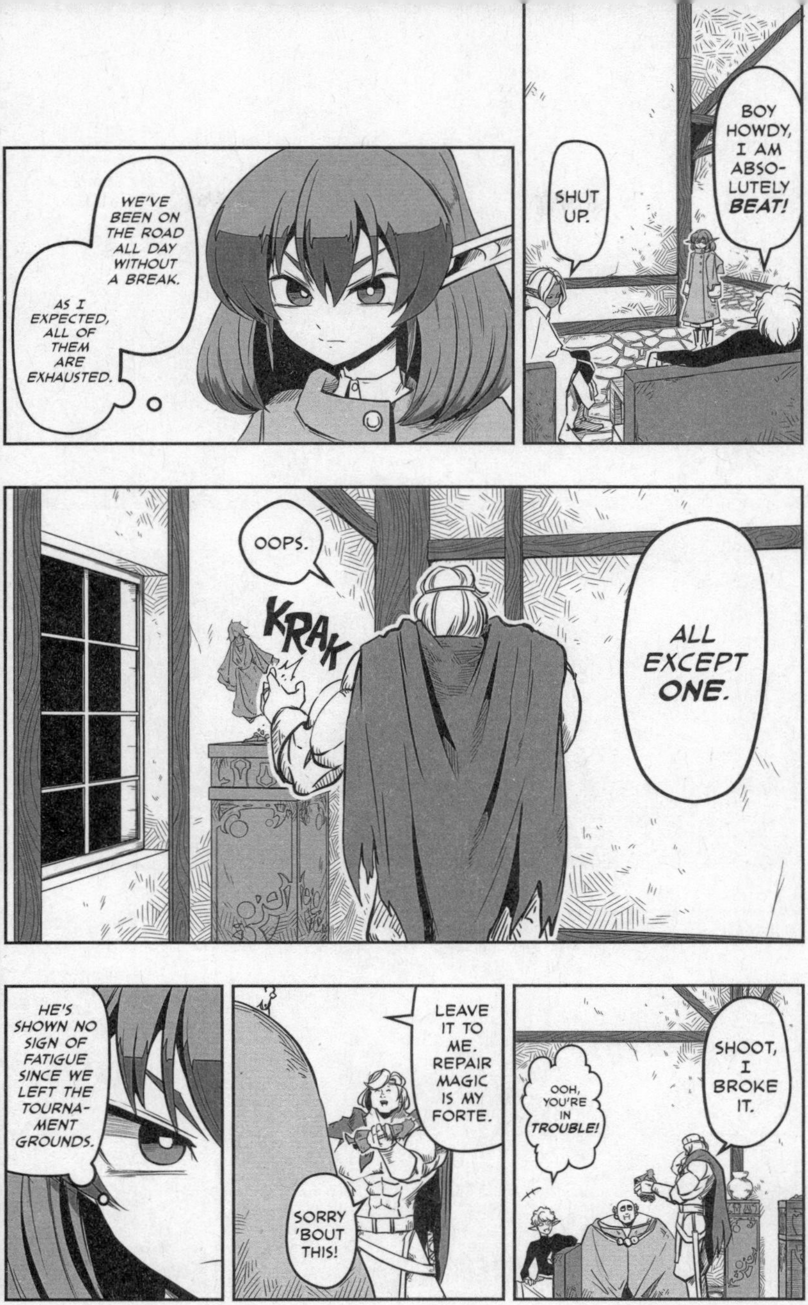
BOY HOWDY, I AM ABSOLUTELY **BEAT!**
SHUT UP.
WE'VE BEEN ON THE ROAD ALL DAY WITHOUT A BREAK.
AS I EXPECTED, ALL OF THEM ARE EXHAUSTED.
ALL EXCEPT **ONE.**
OOPS.
KRAK
SHOOT, I BROKE IT.
OOH, YOU'RE IN ***TROUBLE!***
LEAVE IT TO ME. REPAIR MAGIC IS MY FORTE.
SORRY 'BOUT THIS!
HE'S SHOWN NO SIGN OF FATIGUE SINCE WE LEFT THE TOURNAMENT GROUNDS.

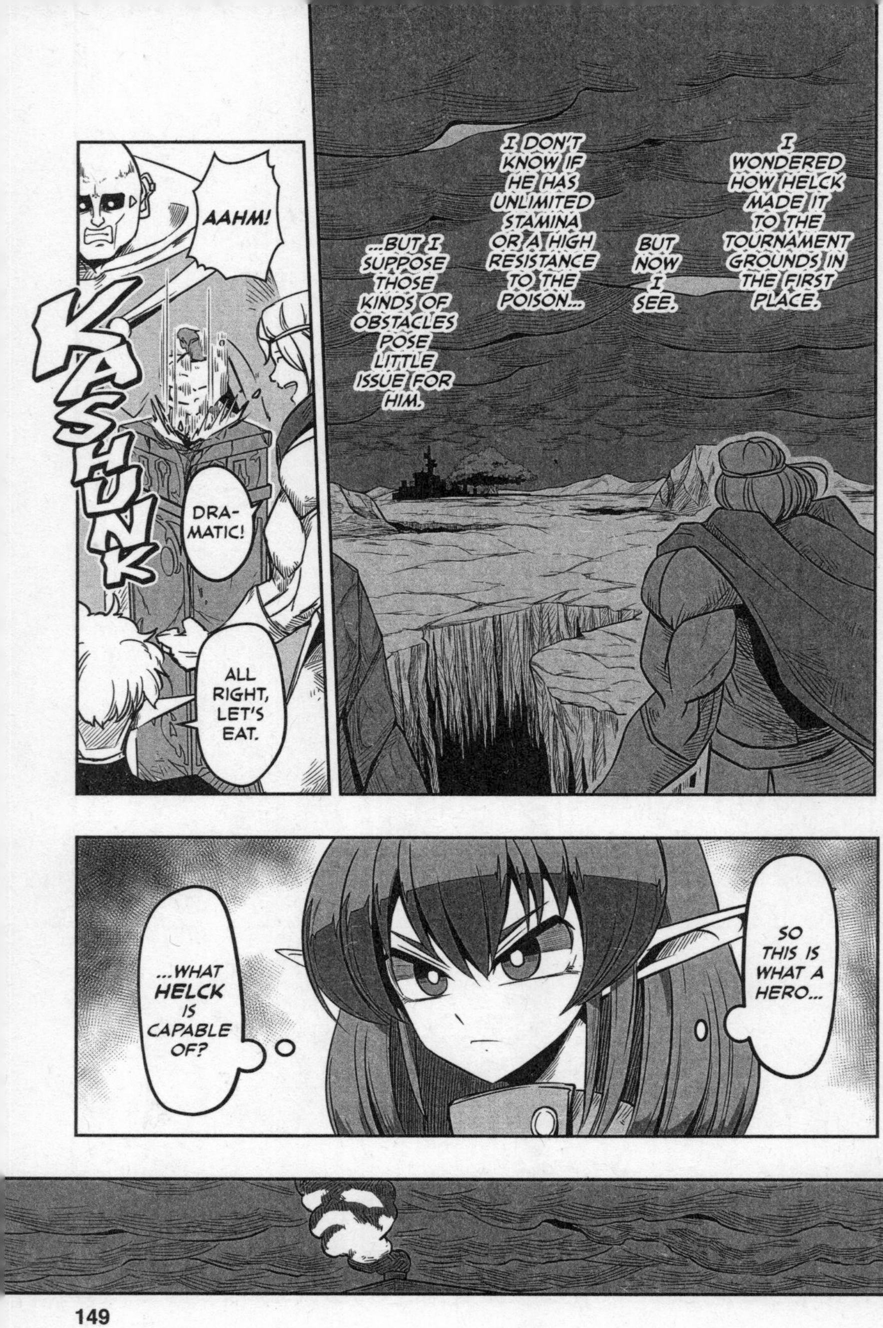
I WONDERED HOW HELCK MADE IT TO THE TOURNAMENT GROUNDS IN THE FIRST PLACE.
BUT NOW I SEE.
I DON'T KNOW IF HE HAS UNLIMITED STAMINA OR A HIGH RESISTANCE TO THE POISON...
...BUT I SUPPOSE THOSE KINDS OF OBSTACLES POSE LITTLE ISSUE FOR HIM.
AAHM!
KASHUNK
DRA-MATIC!
ALL RIGHT, LET'S EAT.
SO THIS IS WHAT A HERO...
...WHAT HELCK IS CAPABLE OF?

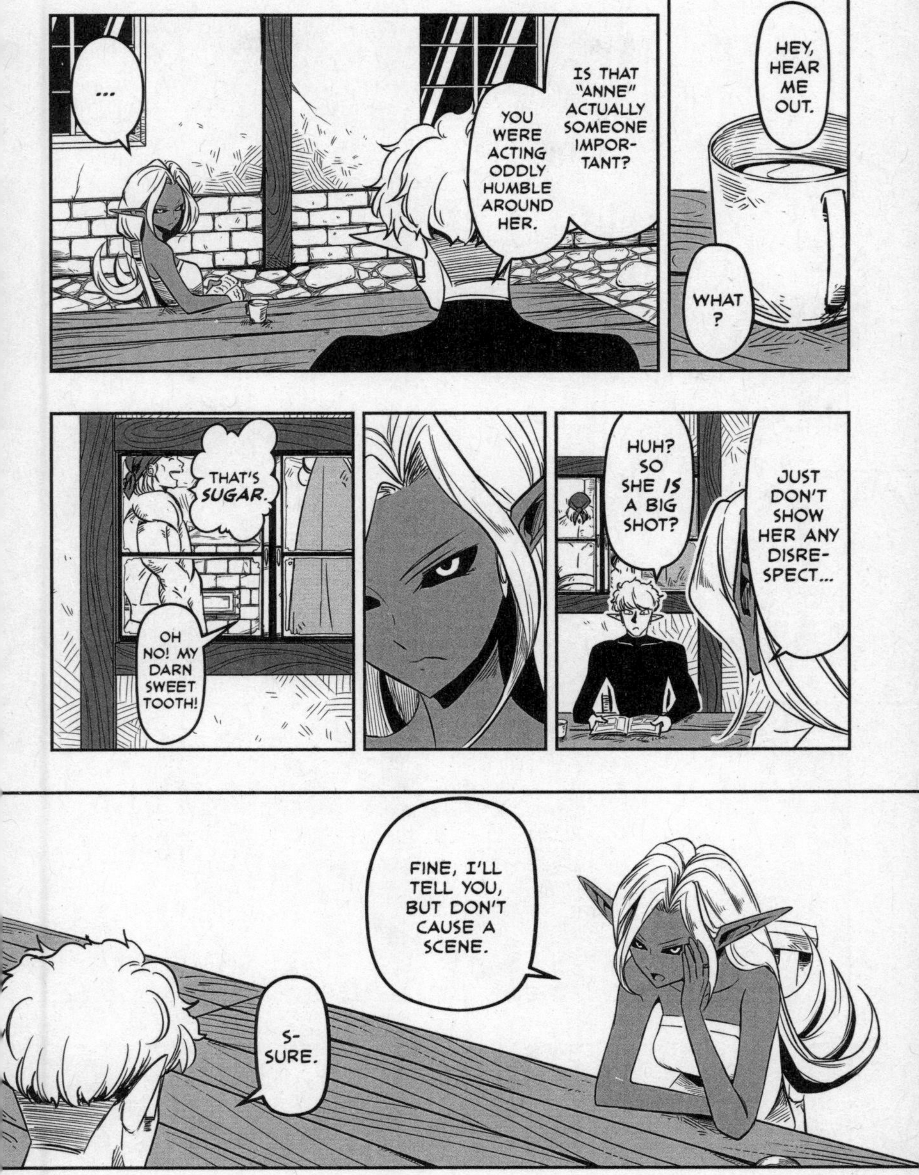
HEY, HEAR ME OUT.
WHAT?
IS THAT "ANNE" ACTUALLY SOMEONE IMPORTANT?
YOU WERE ACTING ODDLY HUMBLE AROUND HER.
...
JUST DON'T SHOW HER ANY DISRESPECT...
HUH? SO SHE *IS* A BIG SHOT?
THAT'S **SUGAR**.
OH NO! MY DARN SWEET TOOTH!
FINE, I'LL TELL YOU, BUT DON'T CAUSE A SCENE.
S-SURE.

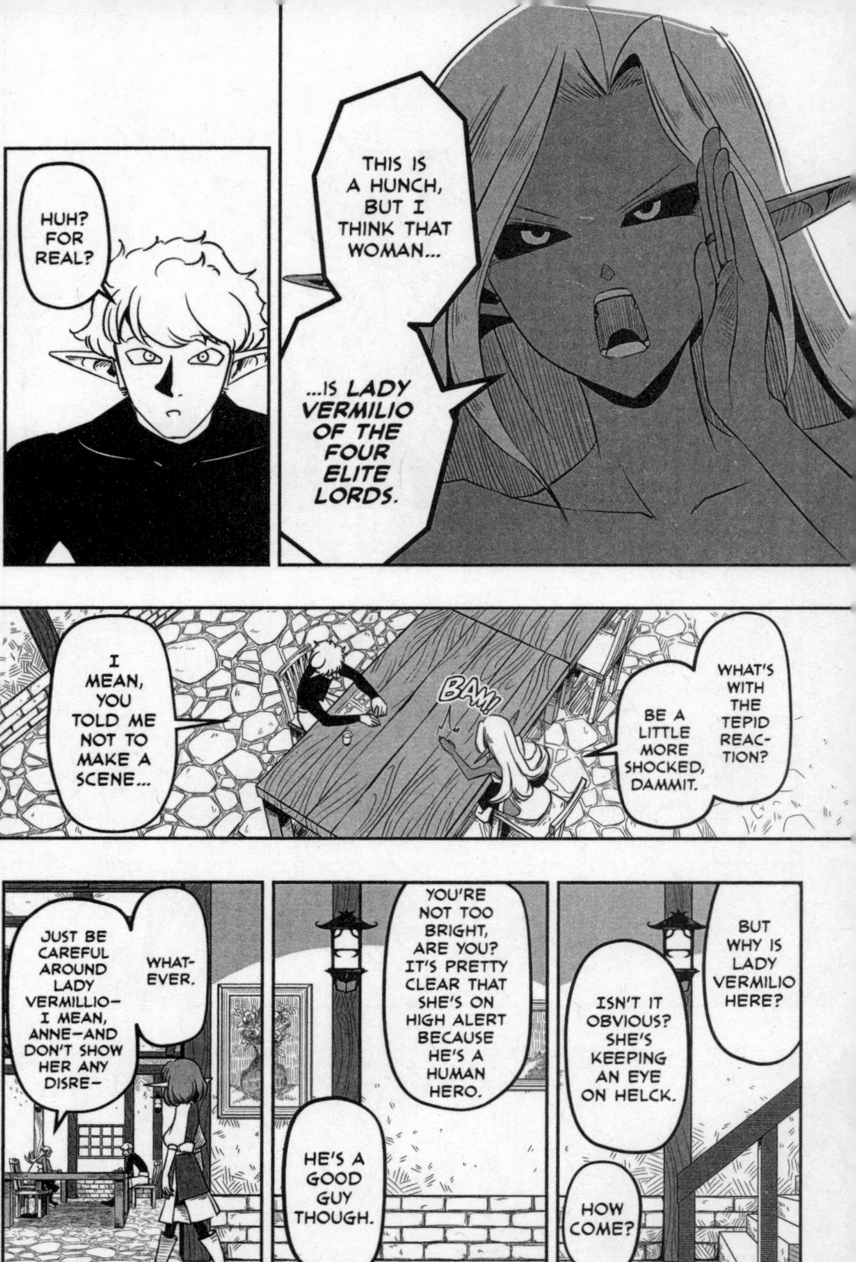
THIS IS A HUNCH, BUT I THINK THAT WOMAN...
...IS LADY VERMILIO OF THE FOUR ELITE LORDS.
HUH? FOR REAL?
WHAT'S WITH THE TEPID REACTION?
BE A LITTLE MORE SHOCKED, DAMMIT.
BAM!
I MEAN, YOU TOLD ME NOT TO MAKE A SCENE...
BUT WHY IS LADY VERMILIO HERE?
ISN'T IT OBVIOUS? SHE'S KEEPING AN EYE ON HELCK.
HOW COME?
YOU'RE NOT TOO BRIGHT, ARE YOU? IT'S PRETTY CLEAR THAT SHE'S ON HIGH ALERT BECAUSE HE'S A HUMAN HERO.
HE'S A GOOD GUY THOUGH.
WHAT-EVER.
JUST BE CAREFUL AROUND LADY VERMILLIO—I MEAN, ANNE—AND DON'T SHOW HER ANY DISRE—

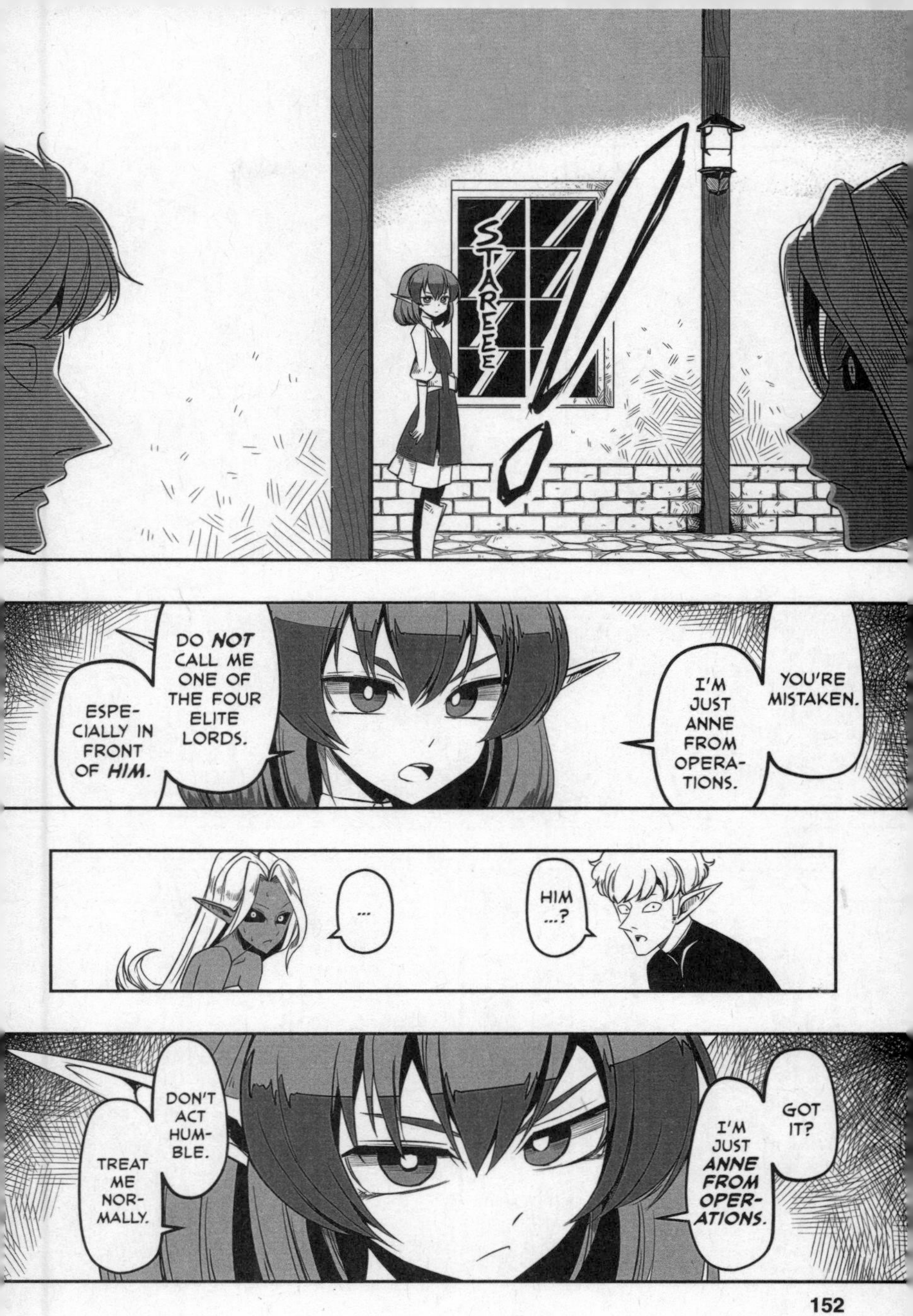
STAREEE
YOU'RE MISTAKEN.
I'M JUST ANNE FROM OPERATIONS.
DO NOT CALL ME ONE OF THE FOUR ELITE LORDS.
ESPECIALLY IN FRONT OF HIM.
HIM ...?
...
GOT IT?
I'M JUST ANNE FROM OPERATIONS.
DON'T ACT HUMBLE.
TREAT ME NORMALLY.

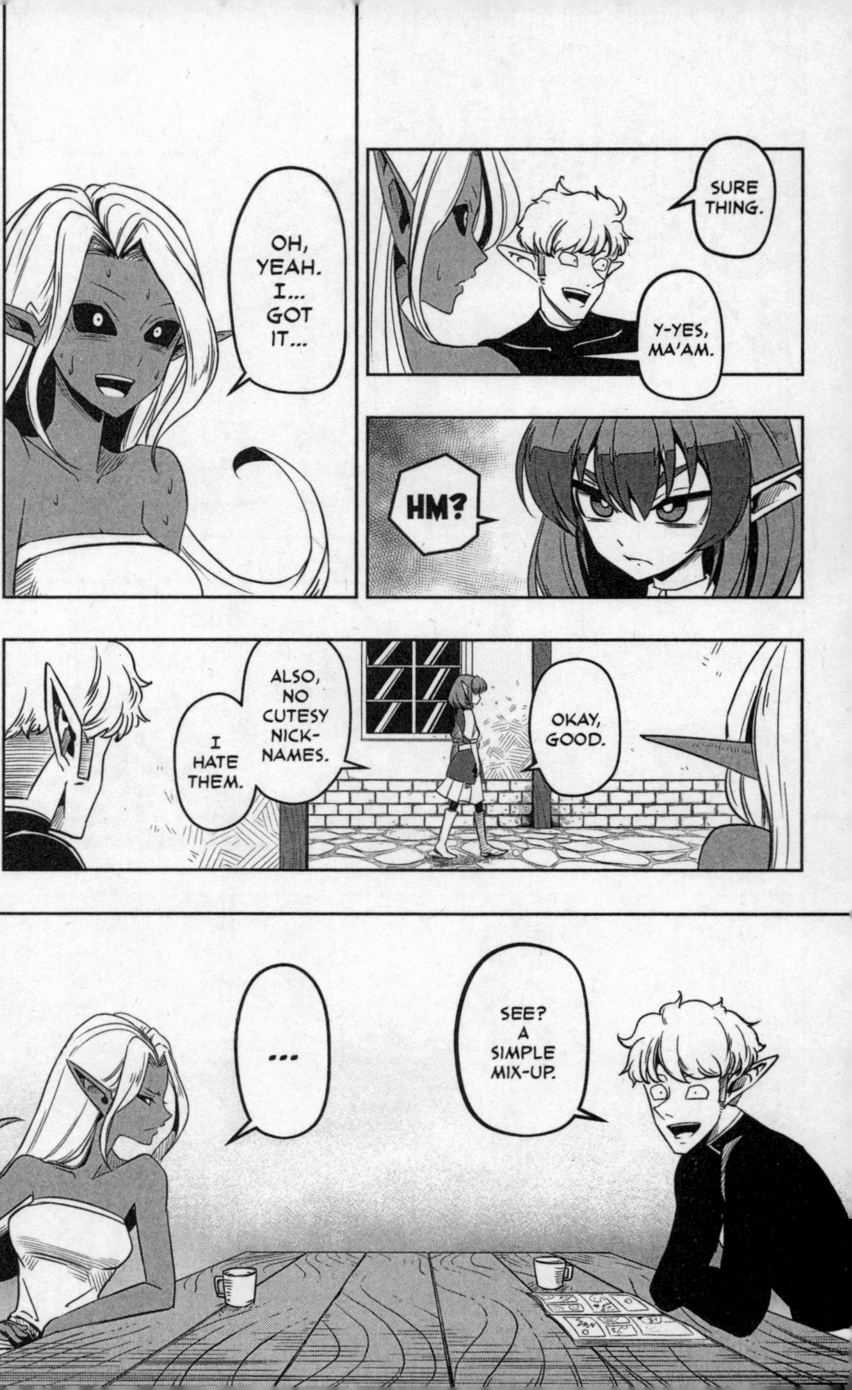
SURE THING.
Y-YES, MA'AM.
HM?
OH, YEAH. I... GOT IT...
OKAY, GOOD.
ALSO, NO CUTESY NICK-NAMES.
I HATE THEM.
SEE? A SIMPLE MIX-UP.
...

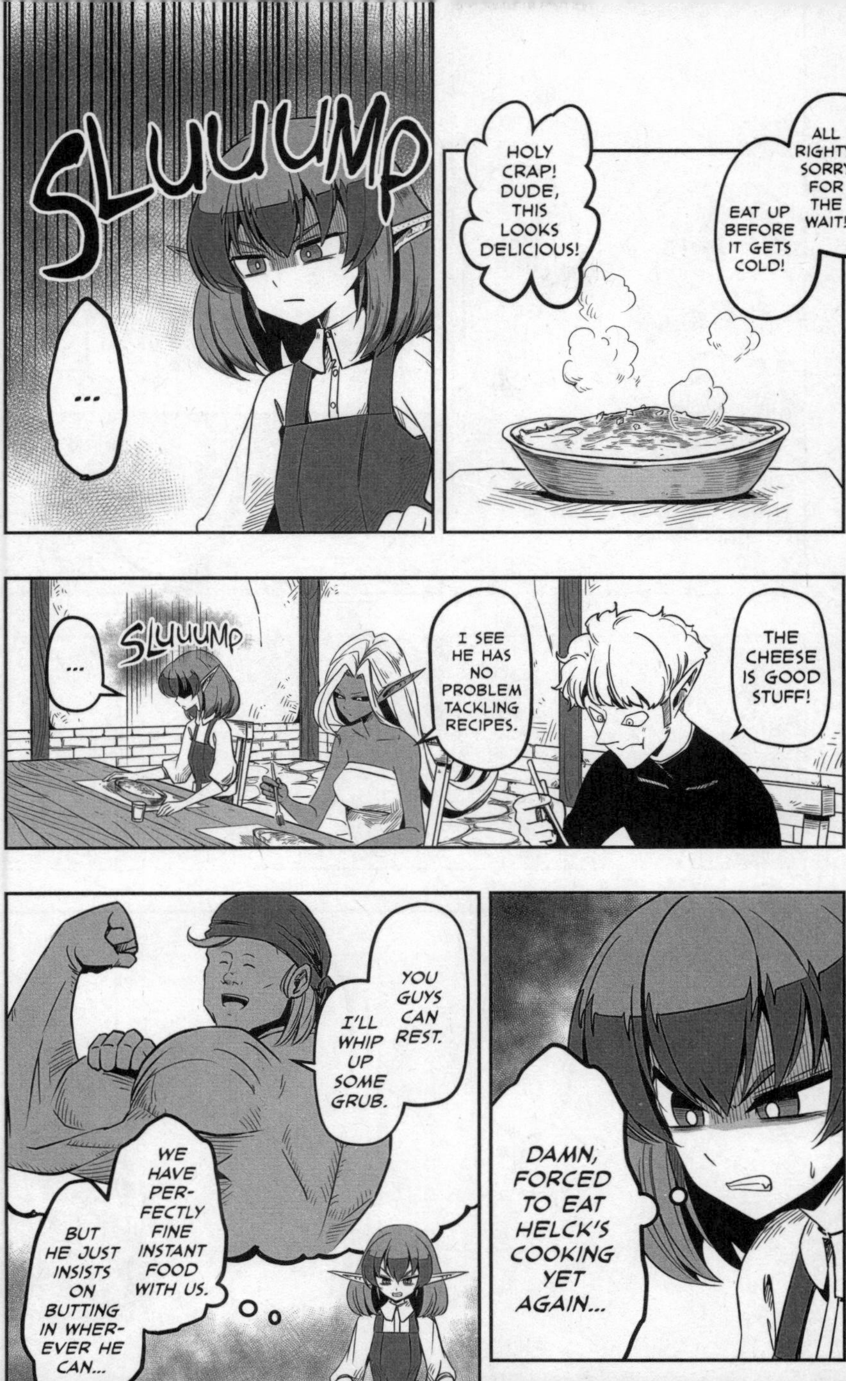
ALL RIGHTY! SORRY FOR THE WAIT!
EAT UP BEFORE IT GETS COLD!
HOLY CRAP! DUDE, THIS LOOKS DELICIOUS!
SLUUUMP
...
THE CHEESE IS GOOD STUFF!
I SEE HE HAS NO PROBLEM TACKLING RECIPES.
SLUUUMP
...
DAMN, FORCED TO EAT HELCK'S COOKING YET AGAIN...
YOU GUYS CAN REST.
I'LL WHIP UP SOME GRUB.
WE HAVE PER-FECTLY FINE INSTANT FOOD WITH US.
BUT HE JUST INSISTS ON BUTTING IN WHER-EVER HE CAN...

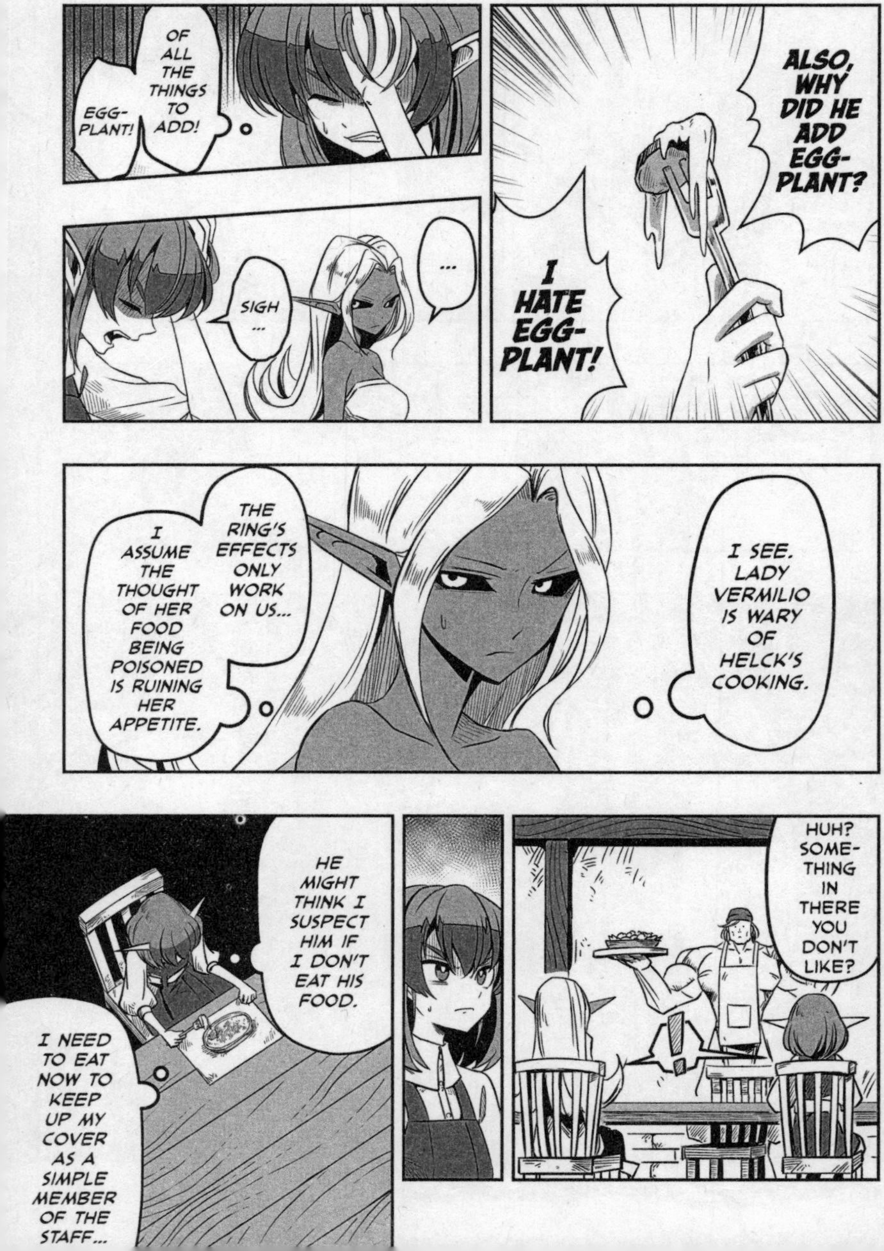
ALSO, WHY DID HE ADD EGG-PLANT?
I HATE EGG-PLANT!
OF ALL THE THINGS TO ADD!
EGG-PLANT!
...
SIGH ...
I SEE. LADY VERMILIO IS WARY OF HELCK'S COOKING.
THE RING'S EFFECTS ONLY WORK ON US...
I ASSUME THE THOUGHT OF HER FOOD BEING POISONED IS RUINING HER APPETITE.
HUH? SOME-THING IN THERE YOU DON'T LIKE?
HE MIGHT THINK I SUSPECT HIM IF I DON'T EAT HIS FOOD.
I NEED TO EAT NOW TO KEEP UP MY COVER AS A SIMPLE MEMBER OF THE STAFF...

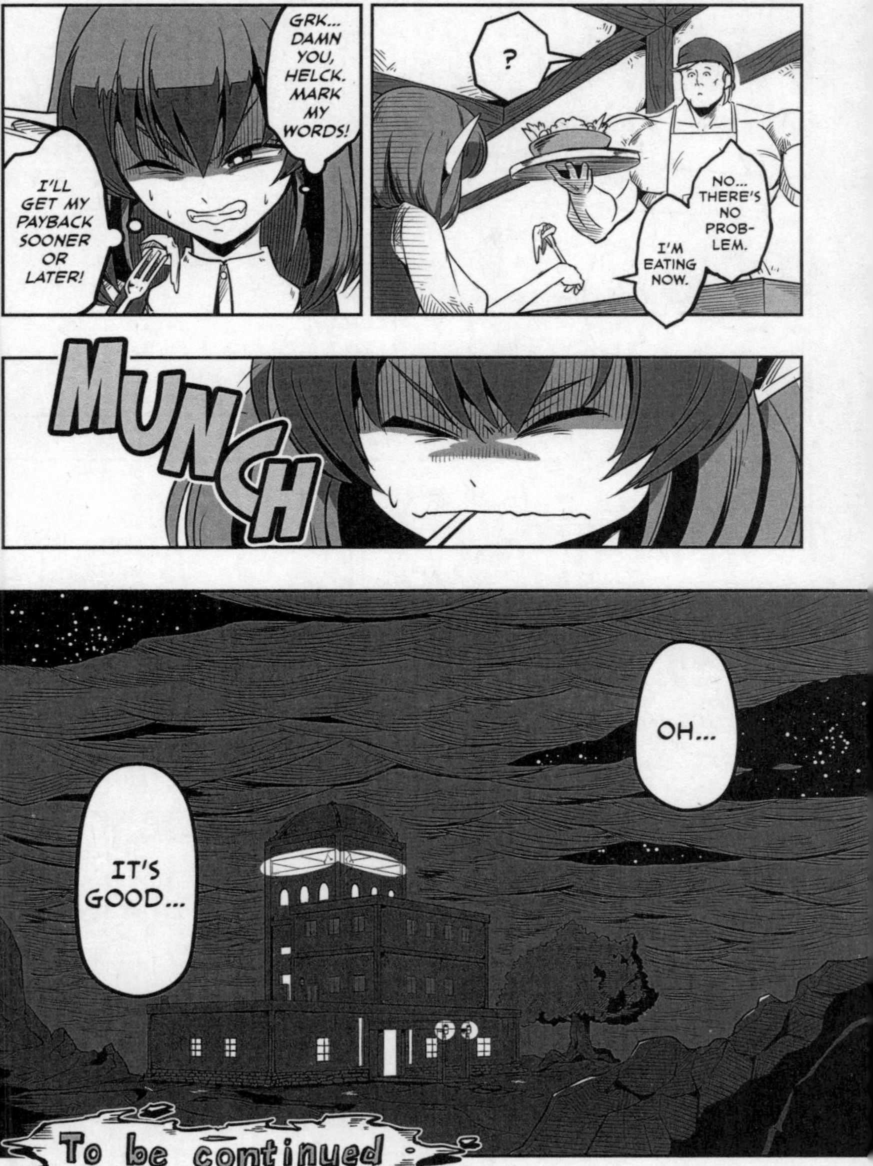
?
NO... THERE'S NO PROB-LEM.
I'M EATING NOW.
GRK... DAMN YOU, HELCK. MARK MY WORDS!
I'LL GET MY PAYBACK SOONER OR LATER!
MUNCH
OH...
IT'S GOOD...
To be continued

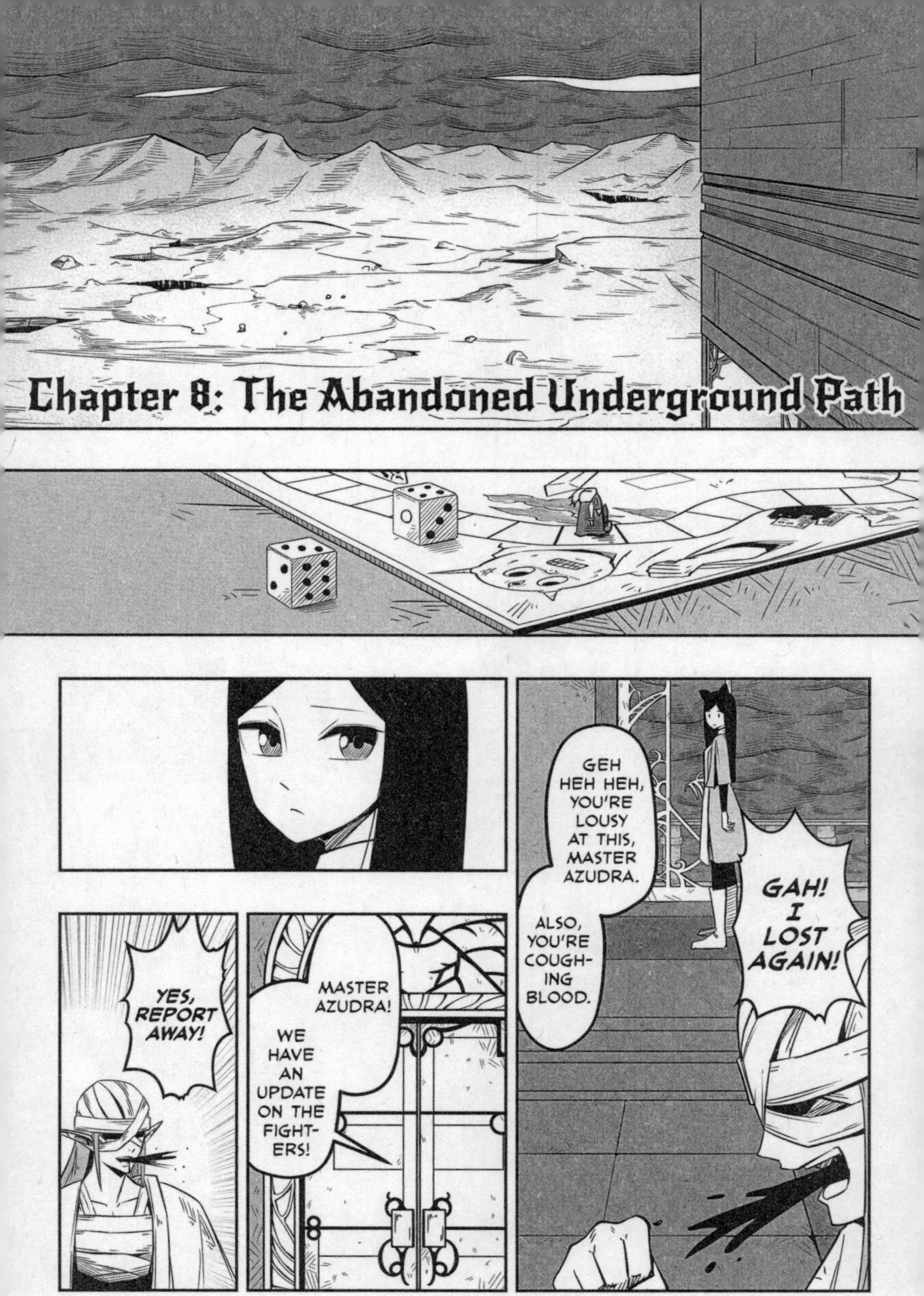
Chapter 8: The Abandoned Underground Path
GEH HEH HEH, YOU'RE LOUSY AT THIS, MASTER AZUDRA.
ALSO, YOU'RE COUGHING BLOOD.
GAH! I LOST AGAIN!
MASTER AZUDRA!
WE HAVE AN UPDATE ON THE FIGHTERS!
YES, REPORT AWAY!

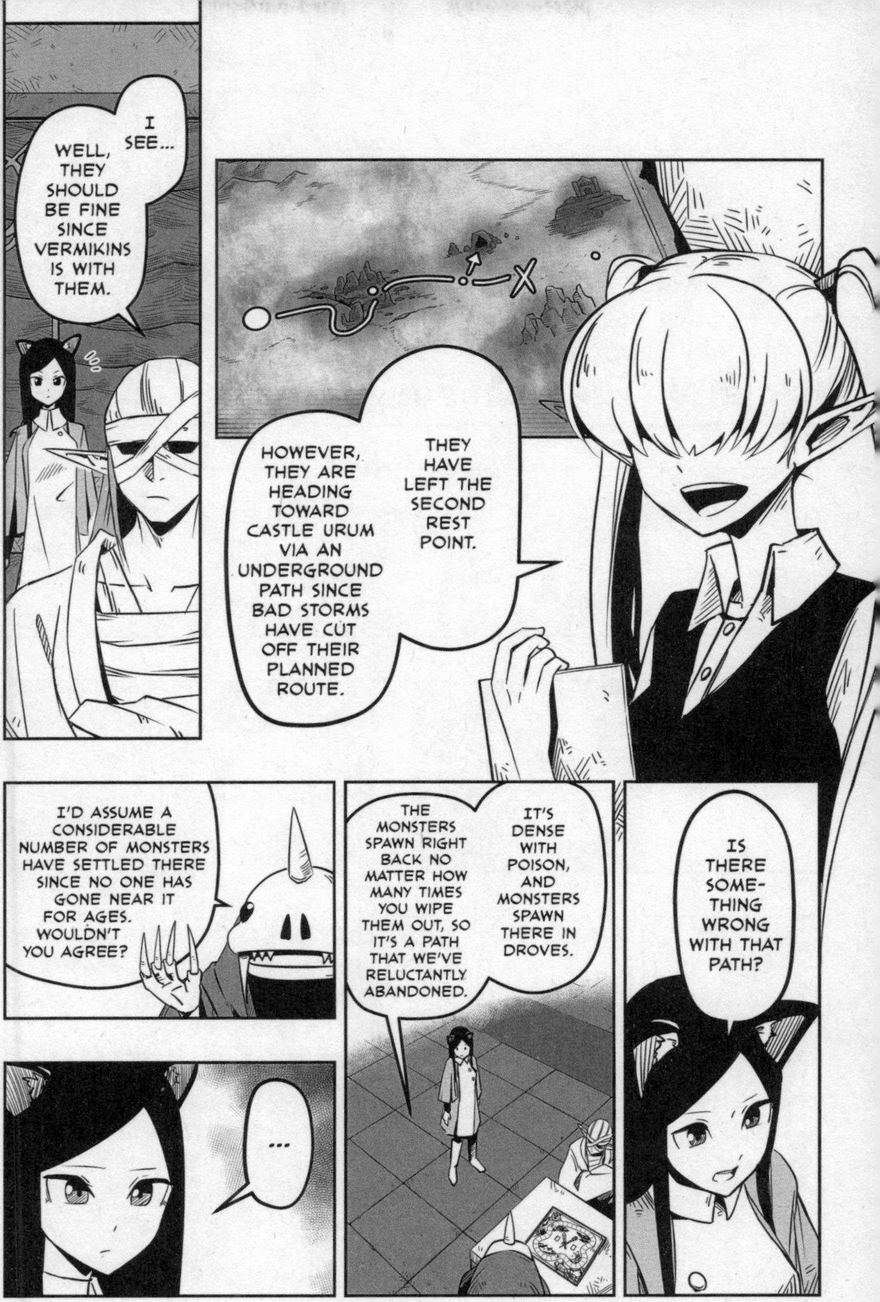
THEY HAVE LEFT THE SECOND REST POINT.
HOWEVER, THEY ARE HEADING TOWARD CASTLE URUM VIA AN UNDERGROUND PATH SINCE BAD STORMS HAVE CUT OFF THEIR PLANNED ROUTE.
I SEE...
WELL, THEY SHOULD BE FINE SINCE VERMIKINS IS WITH THEM.
IS THERE SOME-THING WRONG WITH THAT PATH?
IT'S DENSE WITH POISON, AND MONSTERS SPAWN THERE IN DROVES.
THE MONSTERS SPAWN RIGHT BACK NO MATTER HOW MANY TIMES YOU WIPE THEM OUT, SO IT'S A PATH THAT WE'VE RELUCTANTLY ABANDONED.
I'D ASSUME A CONSIDERABLE NUMBER OF MONSTERS HAVE SETTLED THERE SINCE NO ONE HAS GONE NEAR IT FOR AGES. WOULDN'T YOU AGREE?
...

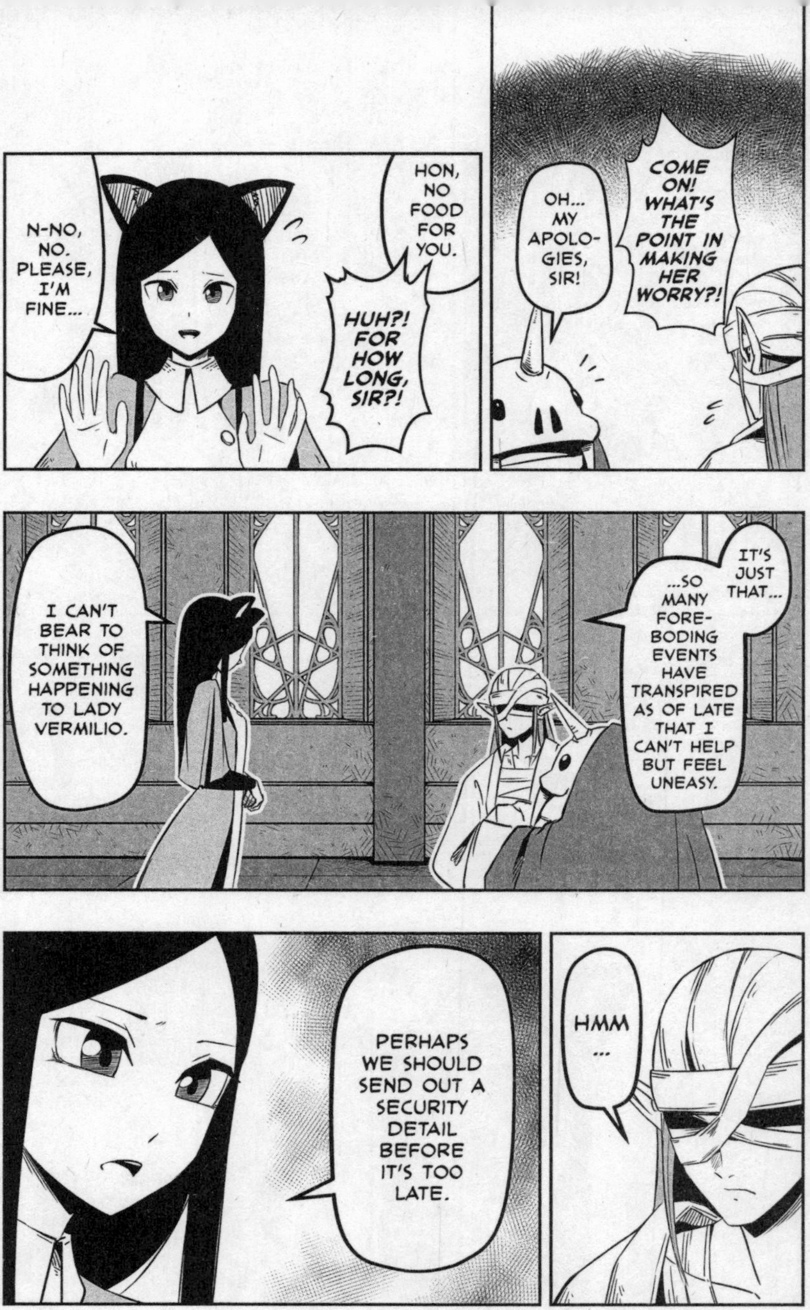
COME ON! WHAT'S THE POINT IN MAKING HER WORRY?!
OH... MY APOLOGIES, SIR!
HON, NO FOOD FOR YOU.
HUH?! FOR HOW LONG, SIR?!
N-NO, NO. PLEASE, I'M FINE...
IT'S JUST THAT...
...SO MANY FOREBODING EVENTS HAVE TRANSPIRED AS OF LATE THAT I CAN'T HELP BUT FEEL UNEASY.
I CAN'T BEAR TO THINK OF SOMETHING HAPPENING TO LADY VERMILIO.
HMM ...
PERHAPS WE SHOULD SEND OUT A SECURITY DETAIL BEFORE IT'S TOO LATE.

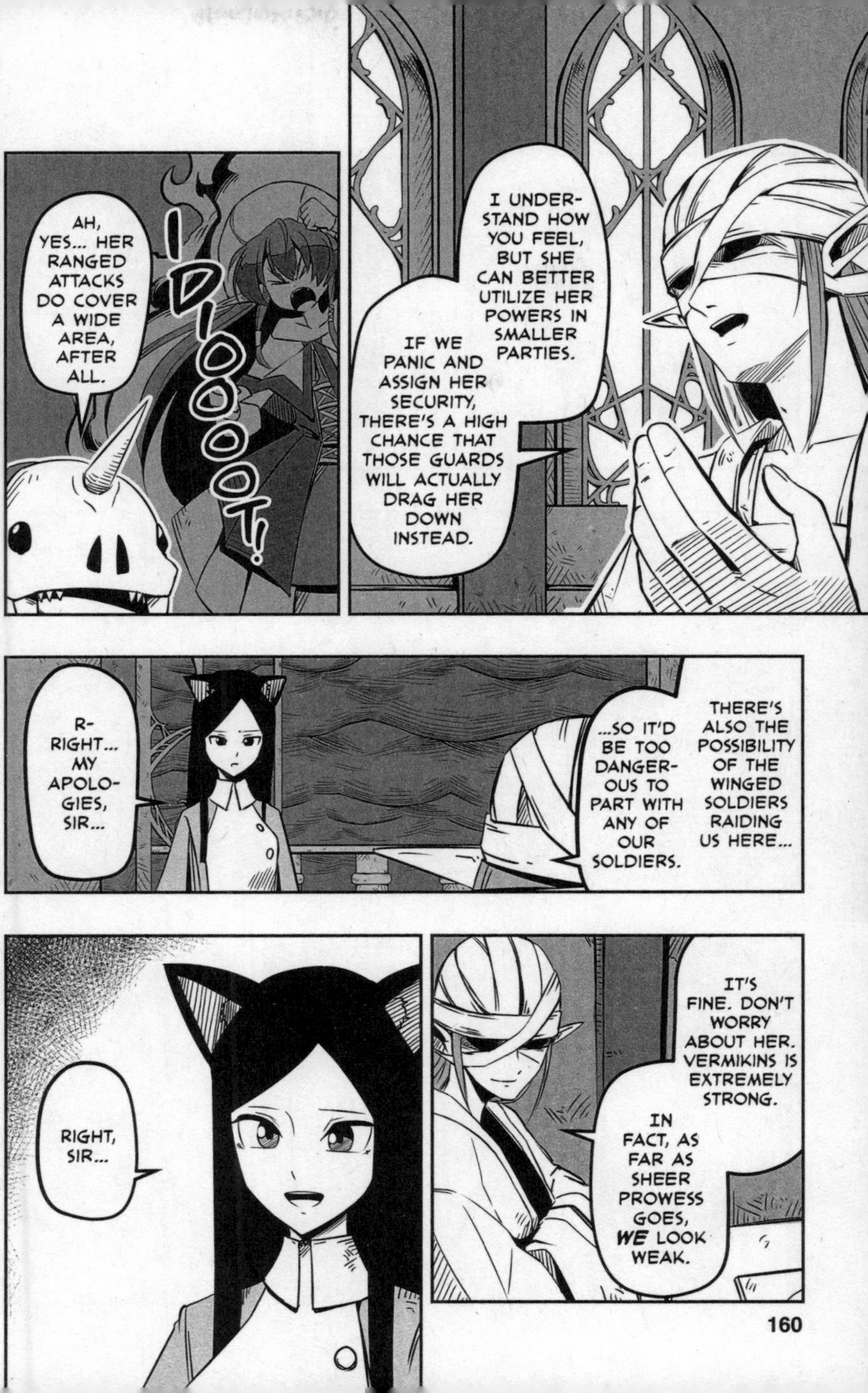
I UNDERSTAND HOW YOU FEEL, BUT SHE CAN BETTER UTILIZE HER POWERS IN SMALLER PARTIES.
IF WE PANIC AND ASSIGN HER SECURITY, THERE'S A HIGH CHANCE THAT THOSE GUARDS WILL ACTUALLY DRAG HER DOWN INSTEAD.
AH, YES... HER RANGED ATTACKS DO COVER A WIDE AREA, AFTER ALL.
IDIOOOOT!
THERE'S ALSO THE POSSIBILITY OF THE WINGED SOLDIERS RAIDING US HERE...
...SO IT'D BE TOO DANGEROUS TO PART WITH ANY OF OUR SOLDIERS.
R-RIGHT... MY APOLOGIES, SIR...
IT'S FINE. DON'T WORRY ABOUT HER. VERMIKINS IS EXTREMELY STRONG.
IN FACT, AS FAR AS SHEER PROWESS GOES, *WE* LOOK WEAK.
RIGHT, SIR...

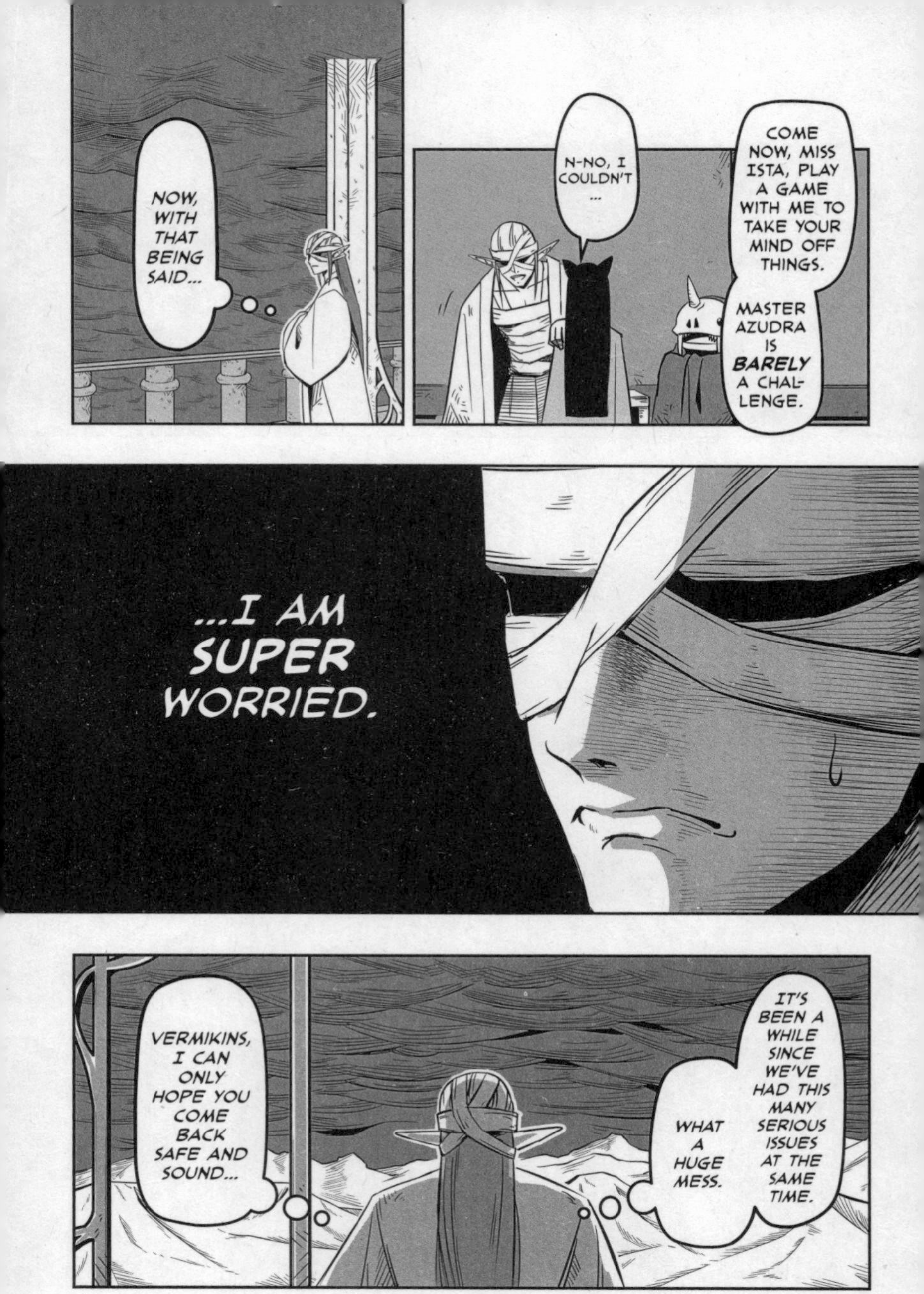
COME NOW, MISS ISTA, PLAY A GAME WITH ME TO TAKE YOUR MIND OFF THINGS.
MASTER AZUDRA IS BARELY A CHAL-LENGE.
N-NO, I COULDN'T ...
NOW, WITH THAT BEING SAID...
...I AM SUPER WORRIED.
IT'S BEEN A WHILE SINCE WE'VE HAD THIS MANY SERIOUS ISSUES AT THE SAME TIME.
WHAT A HUGE MESS.
VERMIKINS, I CAN ONLY HOPE YOU COME BACK SAFE AND SOUND...

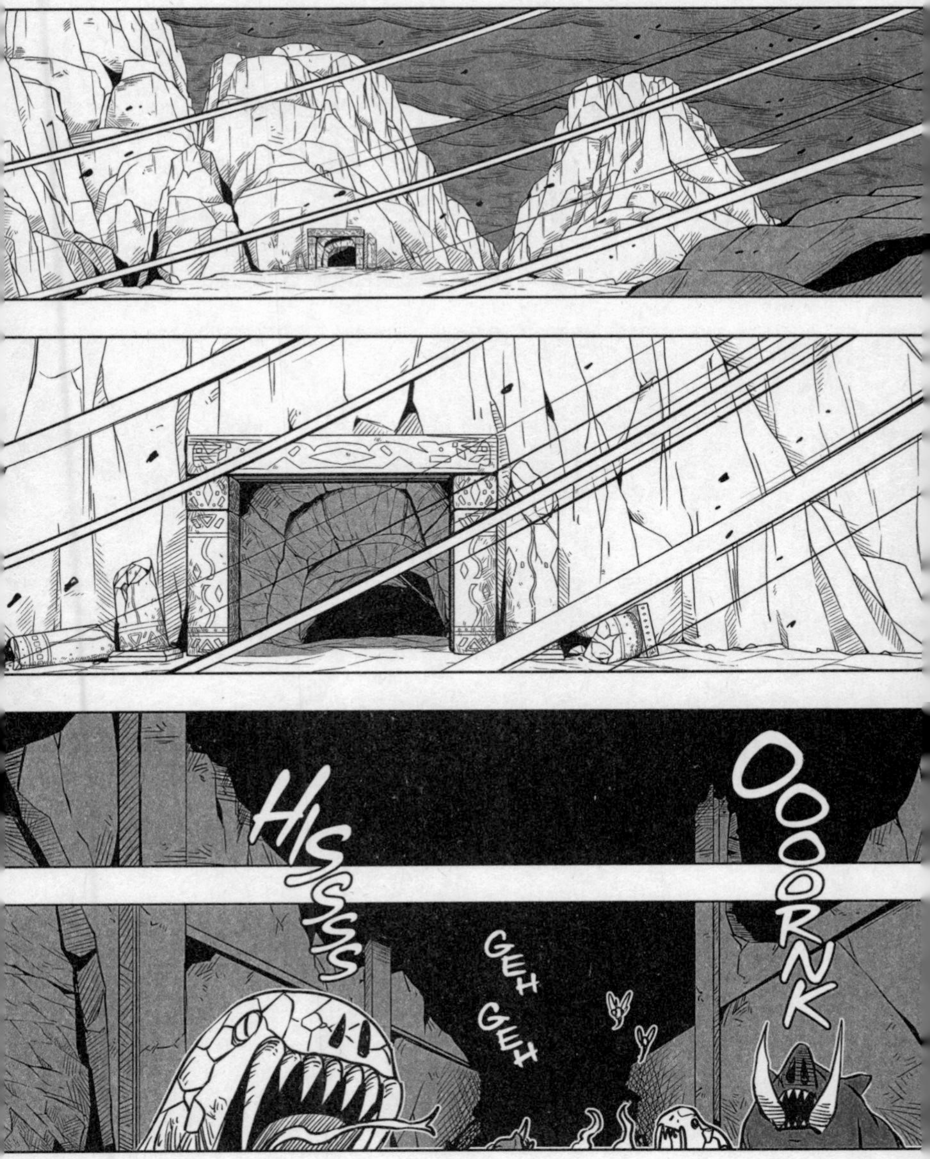
OOOORNK
HISSSS
GEH GEH

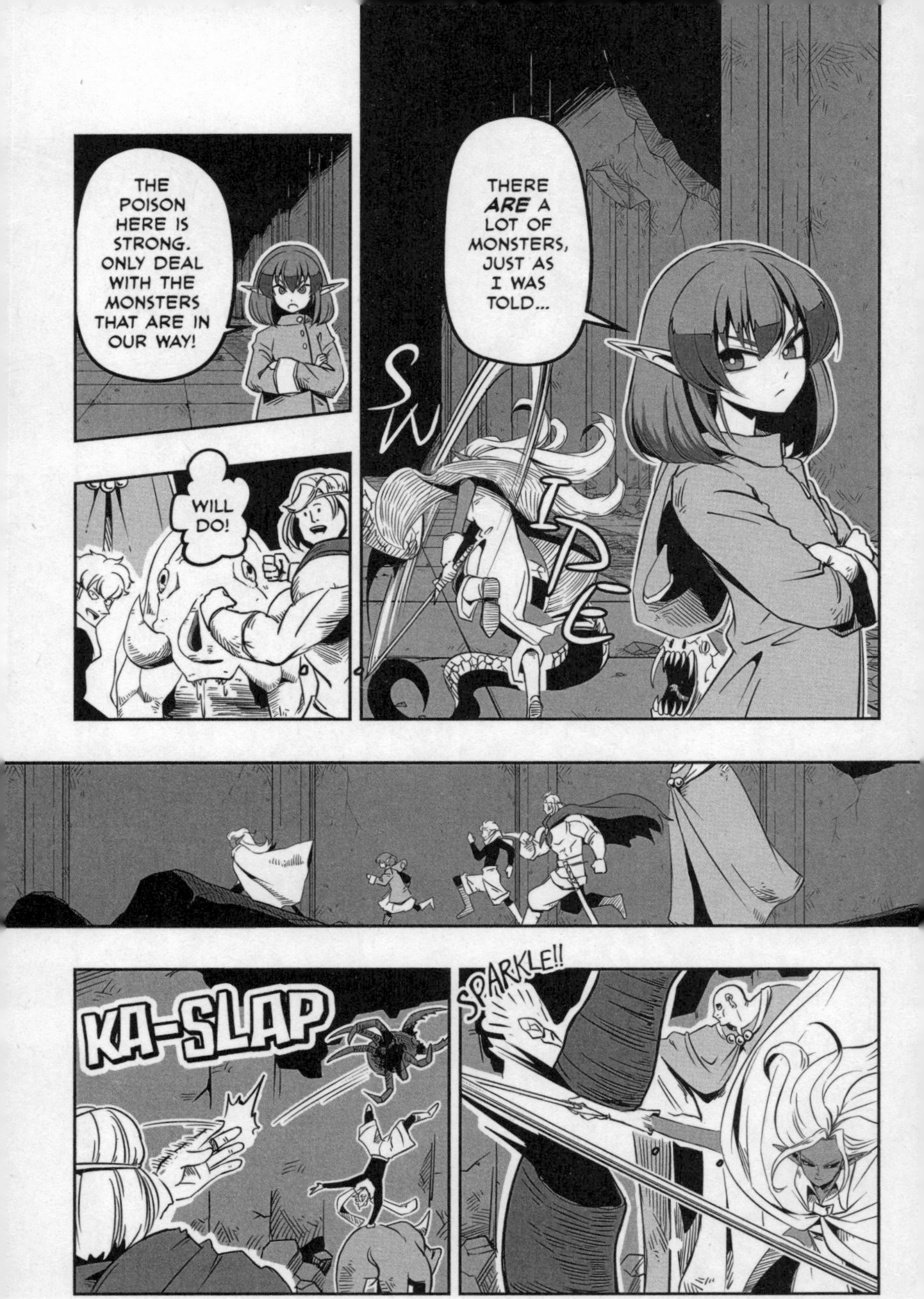
THERE *ARE* A LOT OF MONSTERS, JUST AS I WAS TOLD...
SWIPE
THE POISON HERE IS STRONG. ONLY DEAL WITH THE MONSTERS THAT ARE IN OUR WAY!
WILL DO!
SPARKLE!!
KA-SLAP

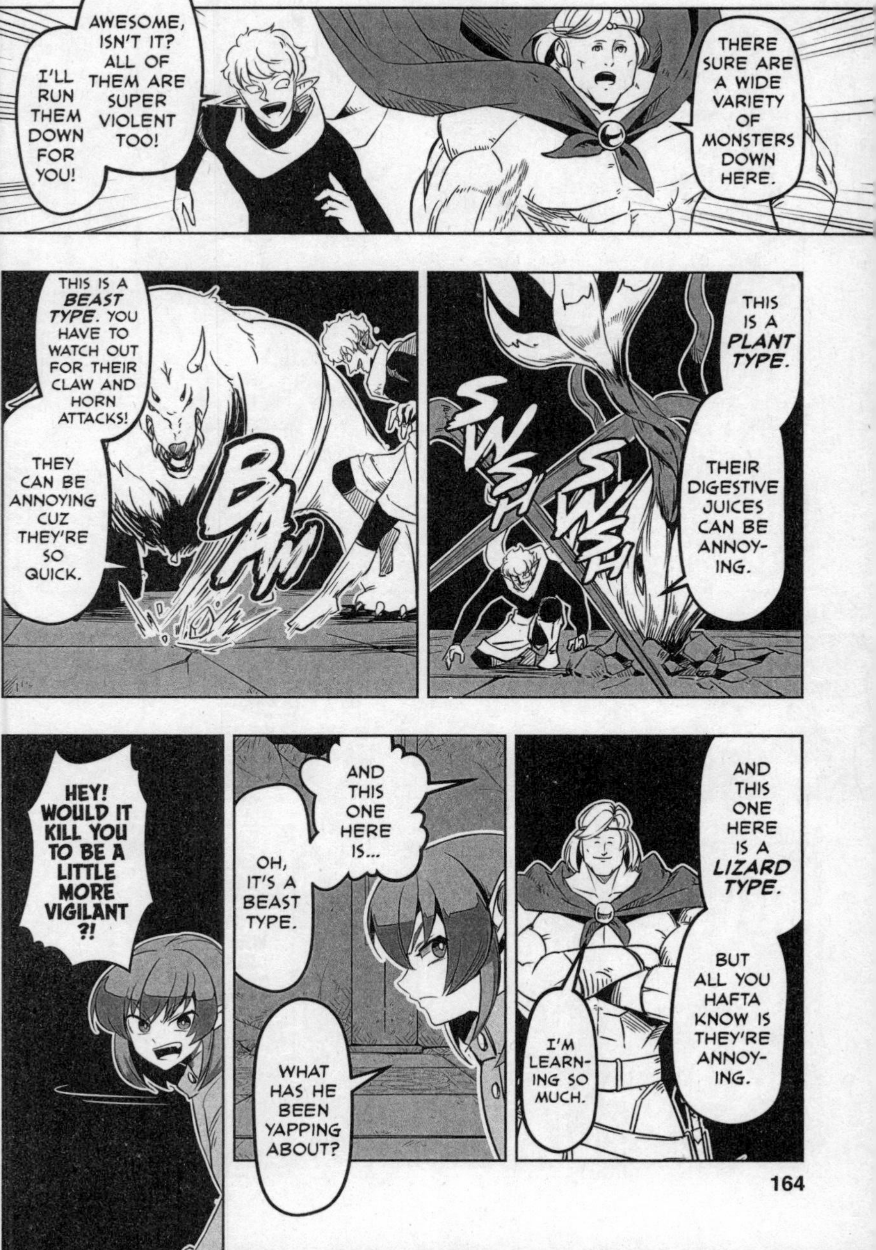
THERE SURE ARE A WIDE VARIETY OF MONSTERS DOWN HERE.
AWESOME, ISN'T IT? ALL OF THEM ARE SUPER VIOLENT TOO!
I'LL RUN THEM DOWN FOR YOU!
THIS IS A *PLANT TYPE*.
THEIR DIGESTIVE JUICES CAN BE ANNOY-ING.
SWSH
SWSH
THIS IS A *BEAST TYPE*. YOU HAVE TO WATCH OUT FOR THEIR CLAW AND HORN ATTACKS!
THEY CAN BE ANNOYING CUZ THEY'RE SO QUICK.
BAM
AND THIS ONE HERE IS A *LIZARD TYPE*.
BUT ALL YOU HAFTA KNOW IS THEY'RE ANNOY-ING.
I'M LEARN-ING SO MUCH.
AND THIS ONE HERE IS...
OH, IT'S A BEAST TYPE.
WHAT HAS HE BEEN YAPPING ABOUT?
HEY! WOULD IT KILL YOU TO BE A LITTLE MORE VIGILANT?!

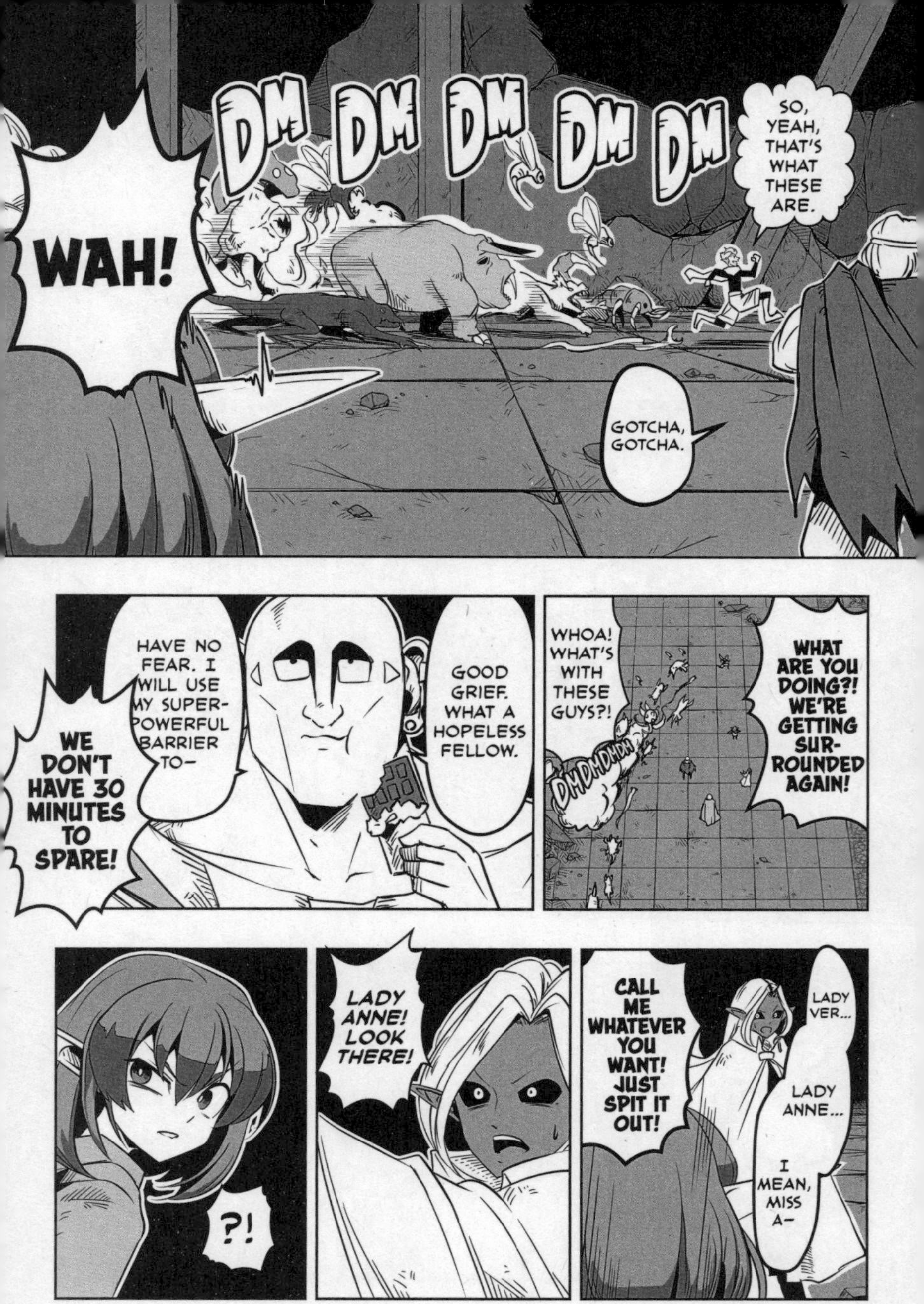
SO, YEAH, THAT'S WHAT THESE ARE.
DM DM DM DM DM
GOTCHA, GOTCHA.
WAH!
WHAT ARE YOU DOING?! WE'RE GETTING SUR-ROUNDED AGAIN!
WHOA! WHAT'S WITH THESE GUYS?!
DMDMDMDM
GOOD GRIEF. WHAT A HOPELESS FELLOW.
HAVE NO FEAR. I WILL USE MY SUPER-POWERFUL BARRIER TO—
WE DON'T HAVE 30 MINUTES TO SPARE!
LADY VER...
LADY ANNE...
I MEAN, MISS A—
CALL ME WHATEVER YOU WANT! JUST SPIT IT OUT!
LADY ANNE! LOOK THERE!
?!

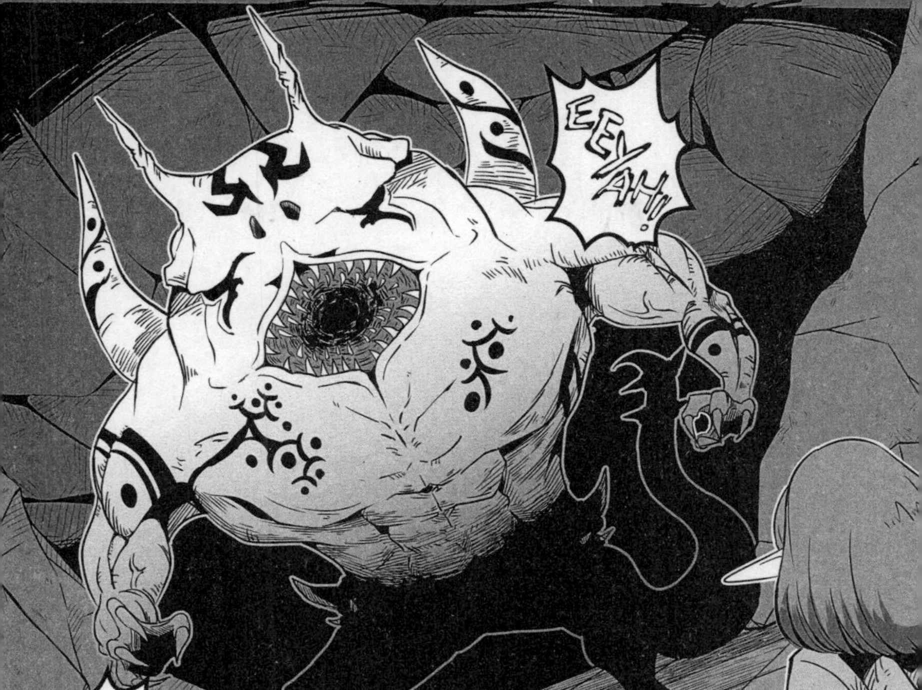
EEYAH!
EEYAH!

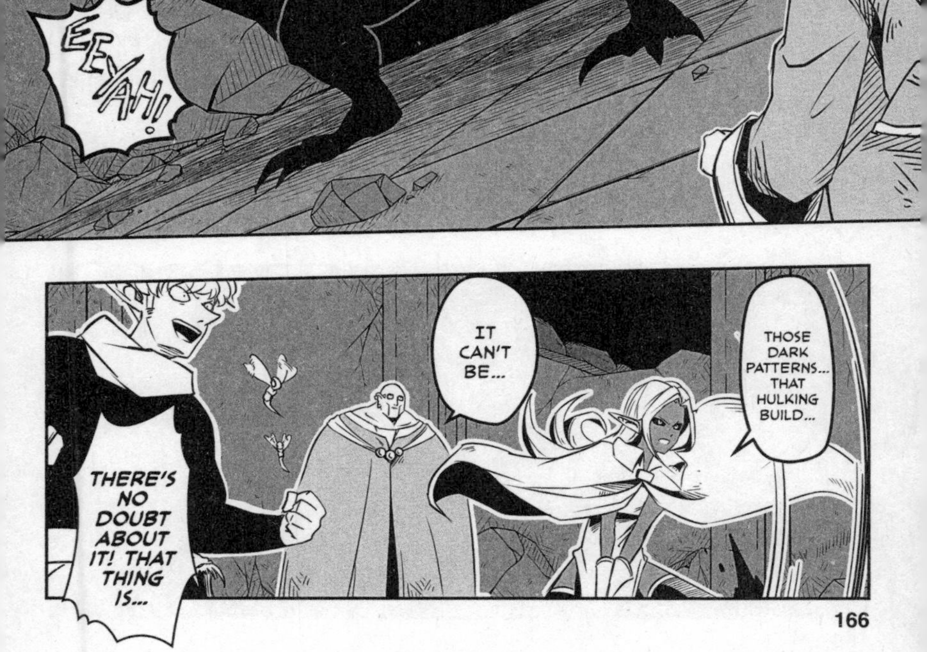
THOSE DARK PATTERNS... THAT HULKING BUILD...
IT CAN'T BE...
THERE'S NO DOUBT ABOUT IT! THAT THING IS...

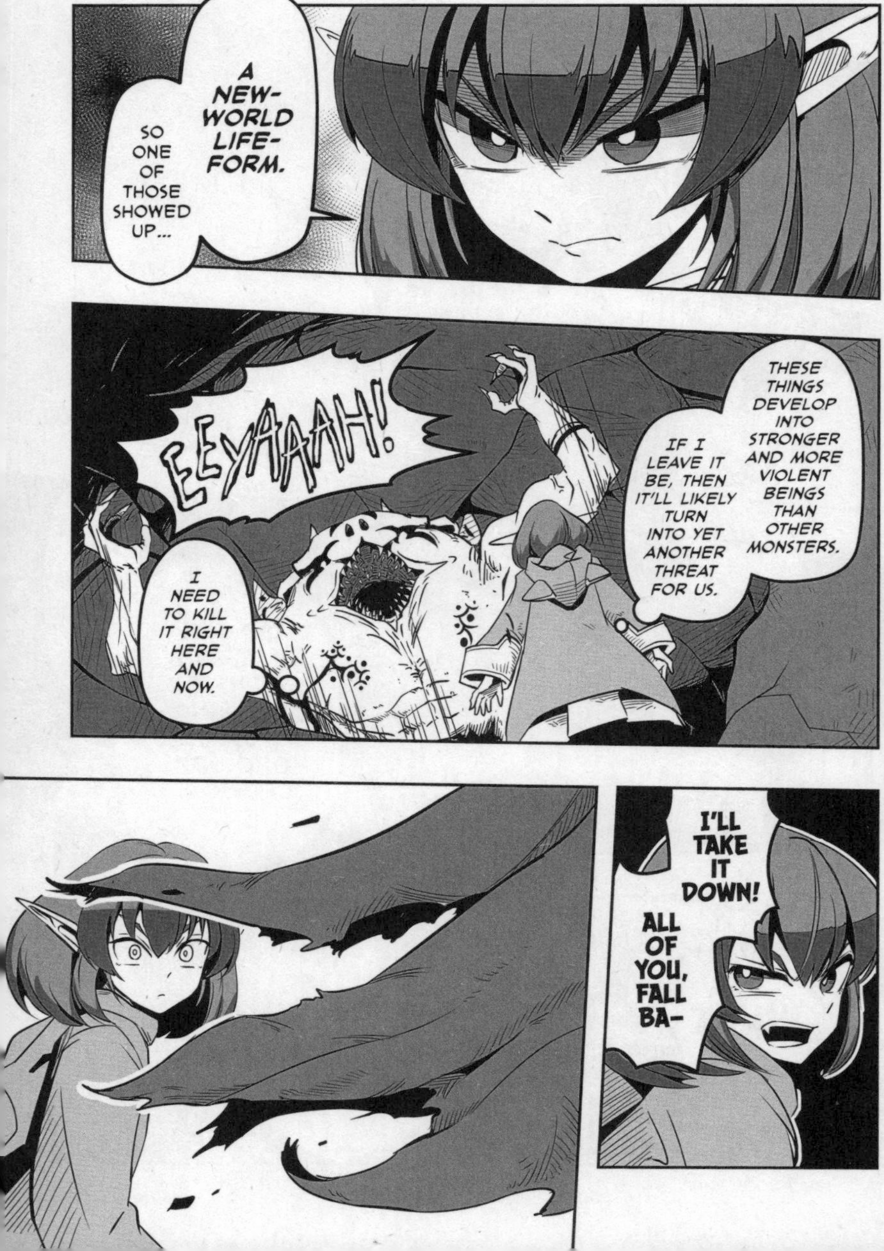
A NEW-WORLD LIFE-FORM.
SO ONE OF THOSE SHOWED UP...
THESE THINGS DEVELOP INTO STRONGER AND MORE VIOLENT BEINGS THAN OTHER MONSTERS.
IF I LEAVE IT BE, THEN IT'LL LIKELY TURN INTO YET ANOTHER THREAT FOR US.
EEYAAAH!
I NEED TO KILL IT RIGHT HERE AND NOW.
I'LL TAKE IT DOWN!
ALL OF YOU, FALL BA-

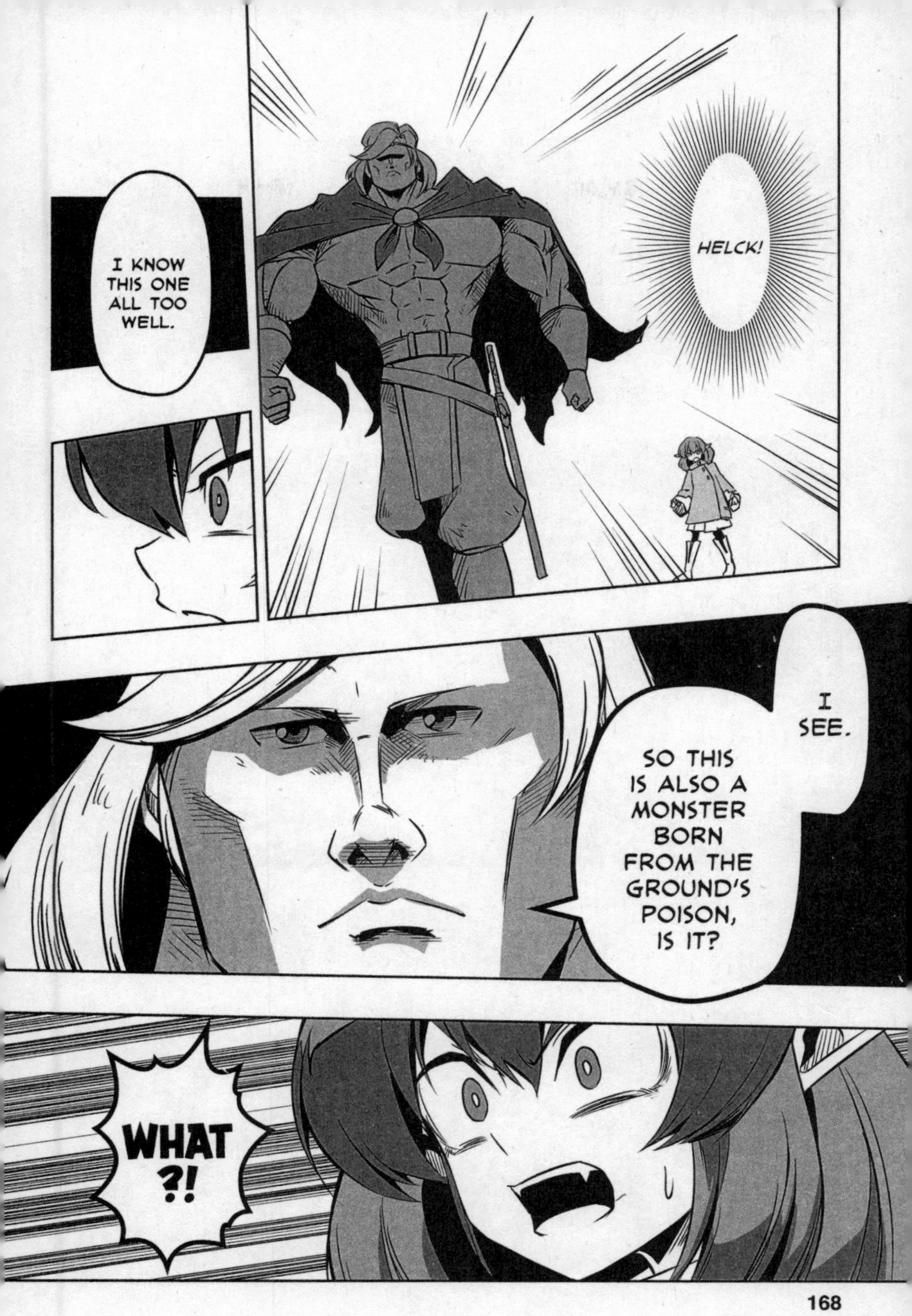
HELCK!
I KNOW THIS ONE ALL TOO WELL.
I SEE.
SO THIS IS ALSO A MONSTER BORN FROM THE GROUND'S POISON, IS IT?
WHAT?!

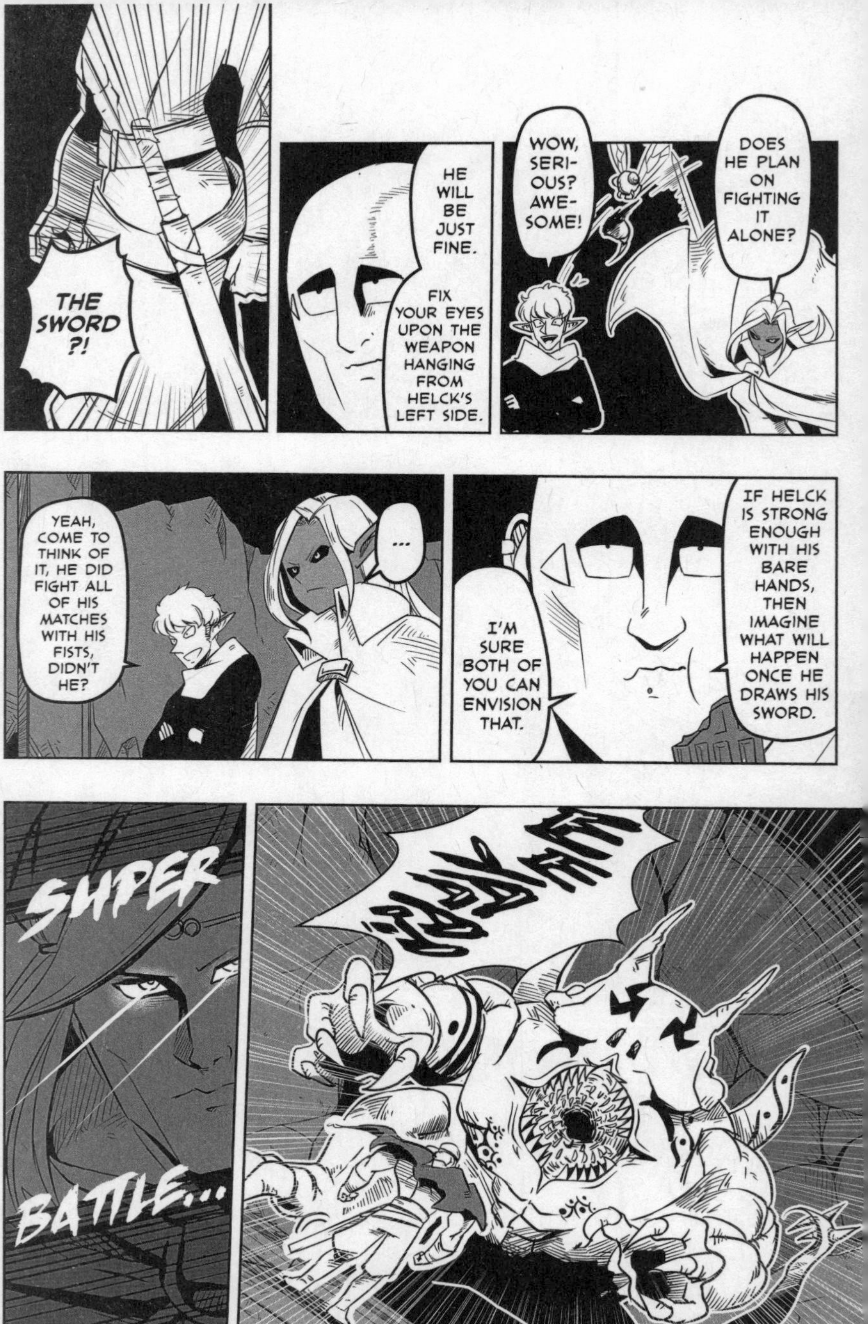
DOES HE PLAN ON FIGHTING IT ALONE?
WOW, SERIOUS? AWESOME!
HE WILL BE JUST FINE.
FIX YOUR EYES UPON THE WEAPON HANGING FROM HELCK'S LEFT SIDE.
THE SWORD ?!
IF HELCK IS STRONG ENOUGH WITH HIS BARE HANDS, THEN IMAGINE WHAT WILL HAPPEN ONCE HE DRAWS HIS SWORD.
I'M SURE BOTH OF YOU CAN ENVISION THAT.
...
YEAH, COME TO THINK OF IT, HE DID FIGHT ALL OF HIS MATCHES WITH HIS FISTS, DIDN'T HE?
SUPER BATTLE...

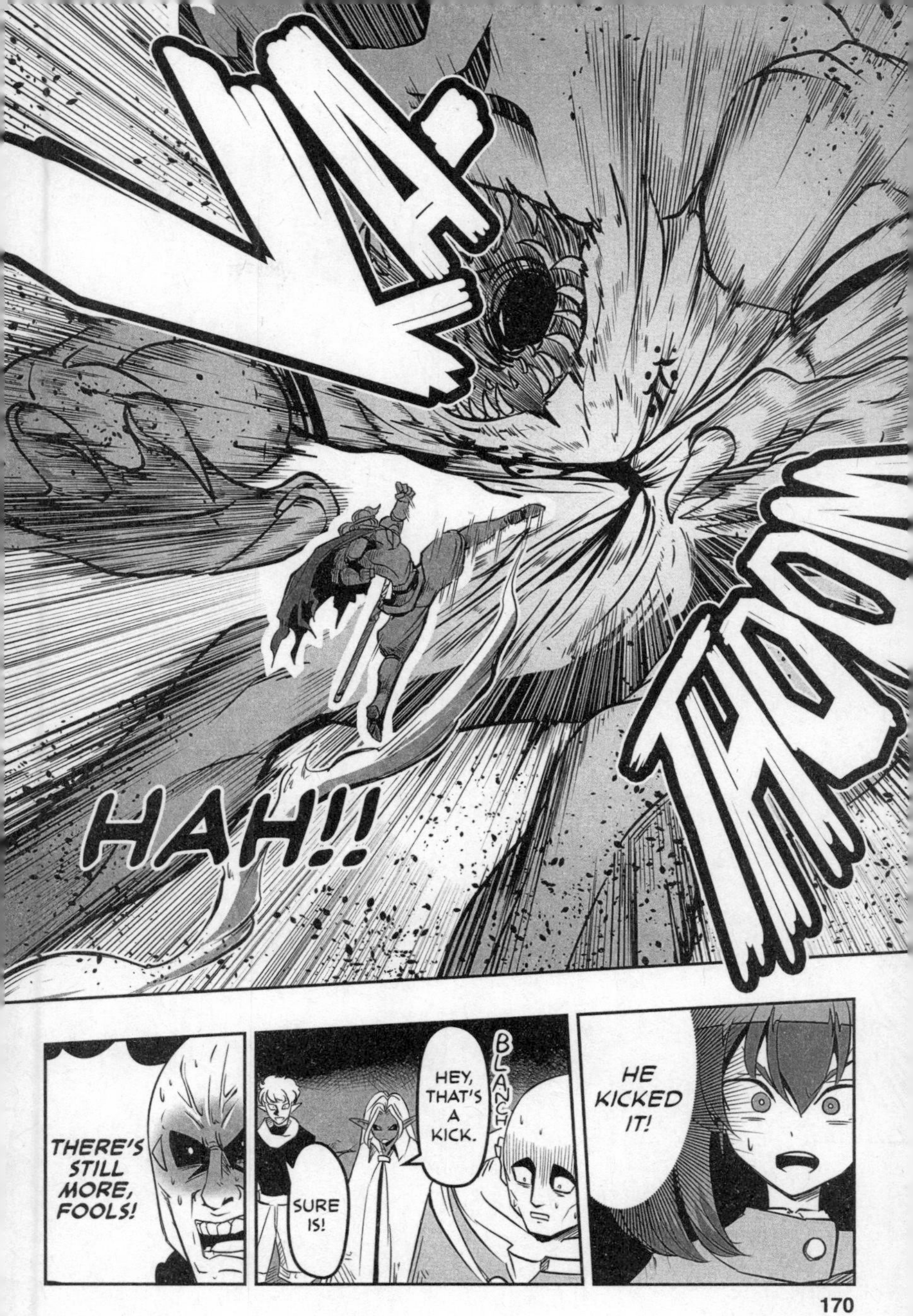
THOOM
HAH!!
HE KICKED IT!
BLANCH
HEY, THAT'S A KICK.
SURE IS!
THERE'S STILL MORE, FOOLS!

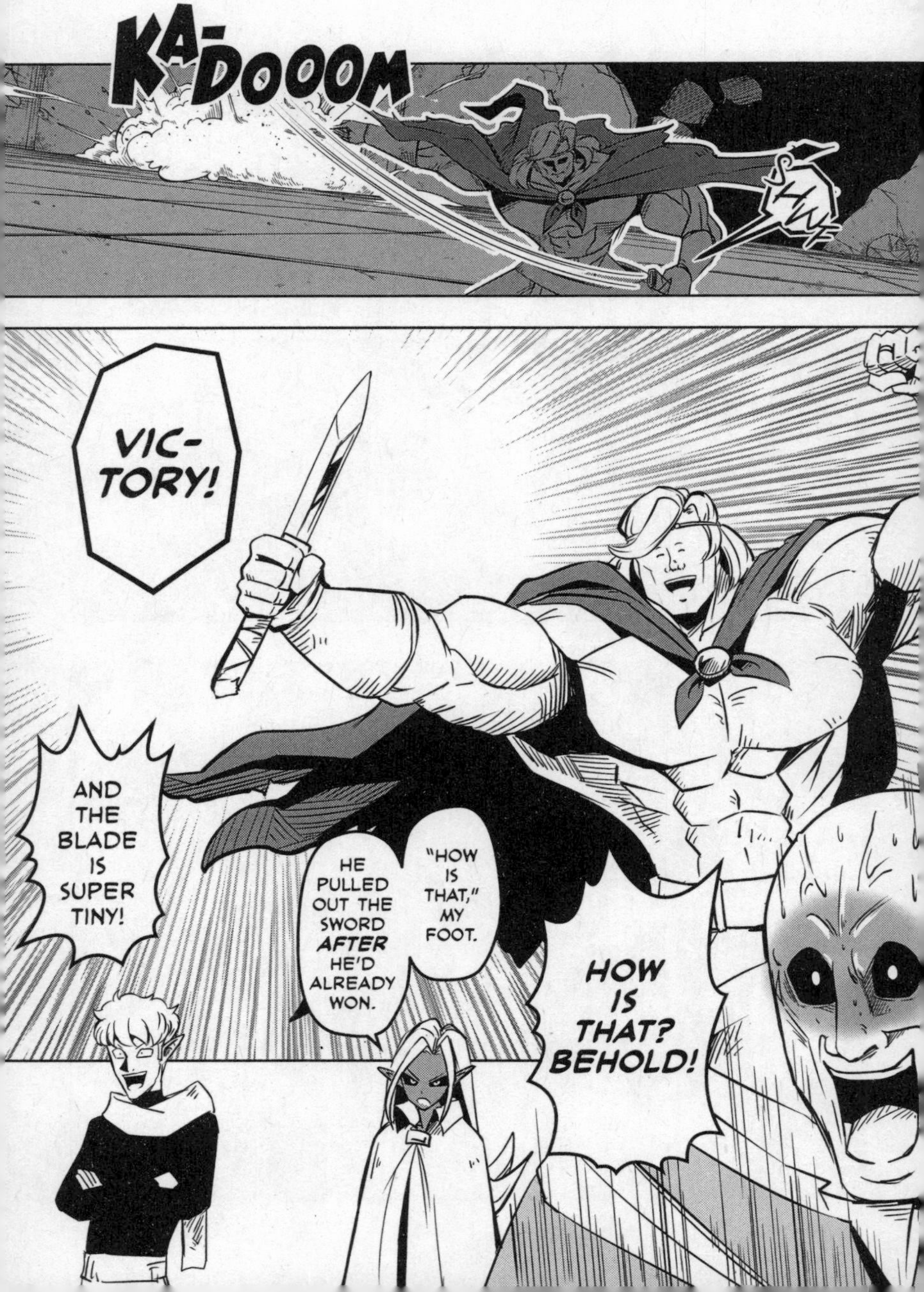
KA-DOOOM
VIC-TORY!
HOW IS THAT? BEHOLD!
"HOW IS THAT," MY FOOT.
HE PULLED OUT THE SWORD *AFTER* HE'D ALREADY WON.
AND THE BLADE IS SUPER TINY!

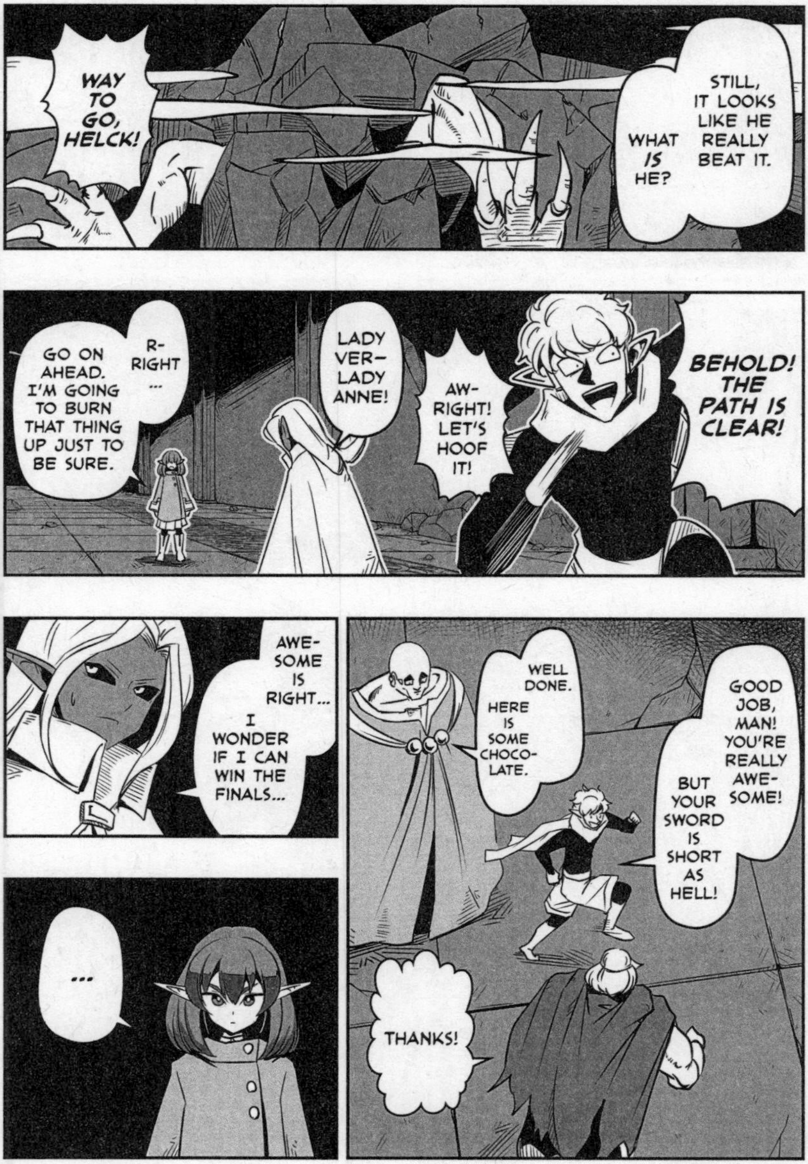

STILL, IT LOOKS LIKE HE REALLY BEAT IT.
WHAT *IS* HE?
WAY TO GO, HELCK!
BEHOLD! THE PATH IS CLEAR!
AW-RIGHT! LET'S HOOF IT!
LADY VER- LADY ANNE!
R-RIGHT ...
GO ON AHEAD. I'M GOING TO BURN THAT THING UP JUST TO BE SURE.
GOOD JOB, MAN! YOU'RE REALLY AWE-SOME!
BUT YOUR SWORD IS SHORT AS HELL!
WELL DONE.
HERE IS SOME CHOCO-LATE.
THANKS!
AWE-SOME IS RIGHT...
I WONDER IF I CAN WIN THE FINALS...
...

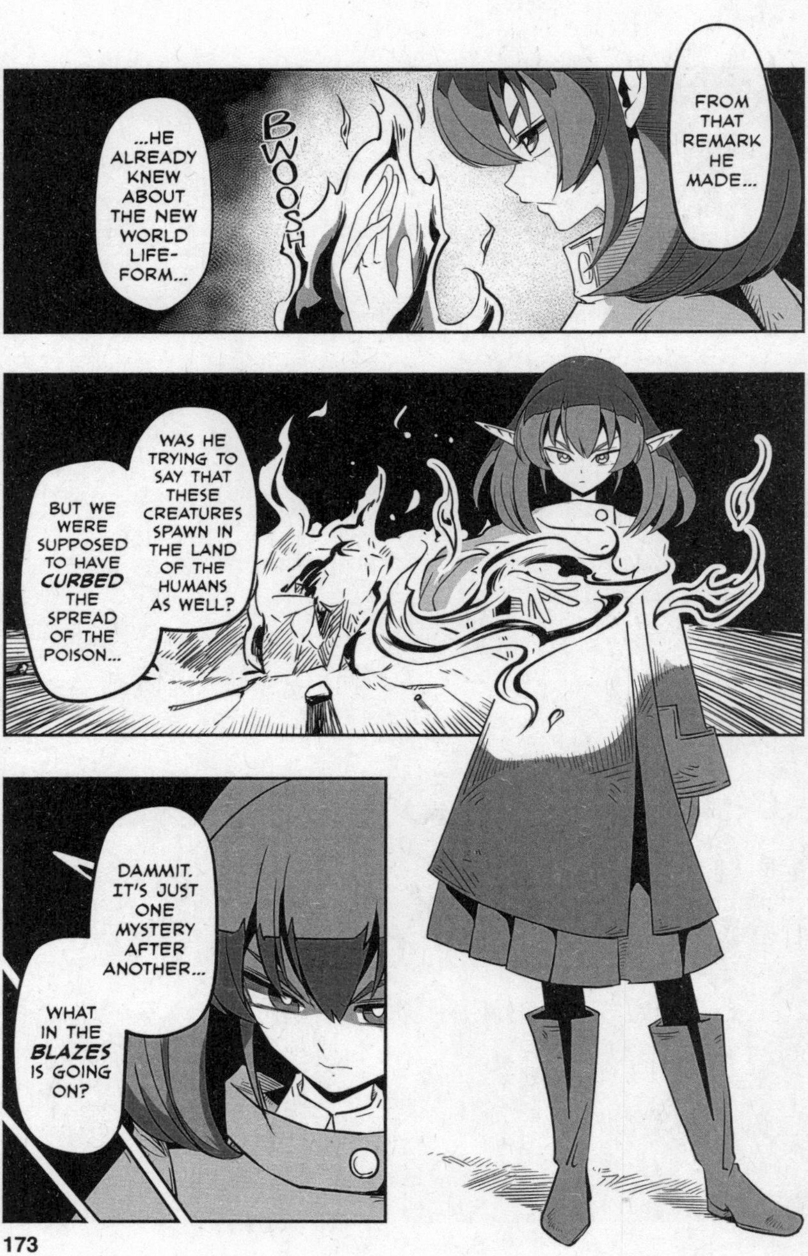
FROM THAT REMARK HE MADE...
BWOOSH
...HE ALREADY KNEW ABOUT THE NEW WORLD LIFE-FORM...
WAS HE TRYING TO SAY THAT THESE CREATURES SPAWN IN THE LAND OF THE HUMANS AS WELL?
BUT WE WERE SUPPOSED TO HAVE *CURBED* THE SPREAD OF THE POISON...
DAMMIT. IT'S JUST ONE MYSTERY AFTER ANOTHER...
WHAT IN THE *BLAZES* IS GOING ON?

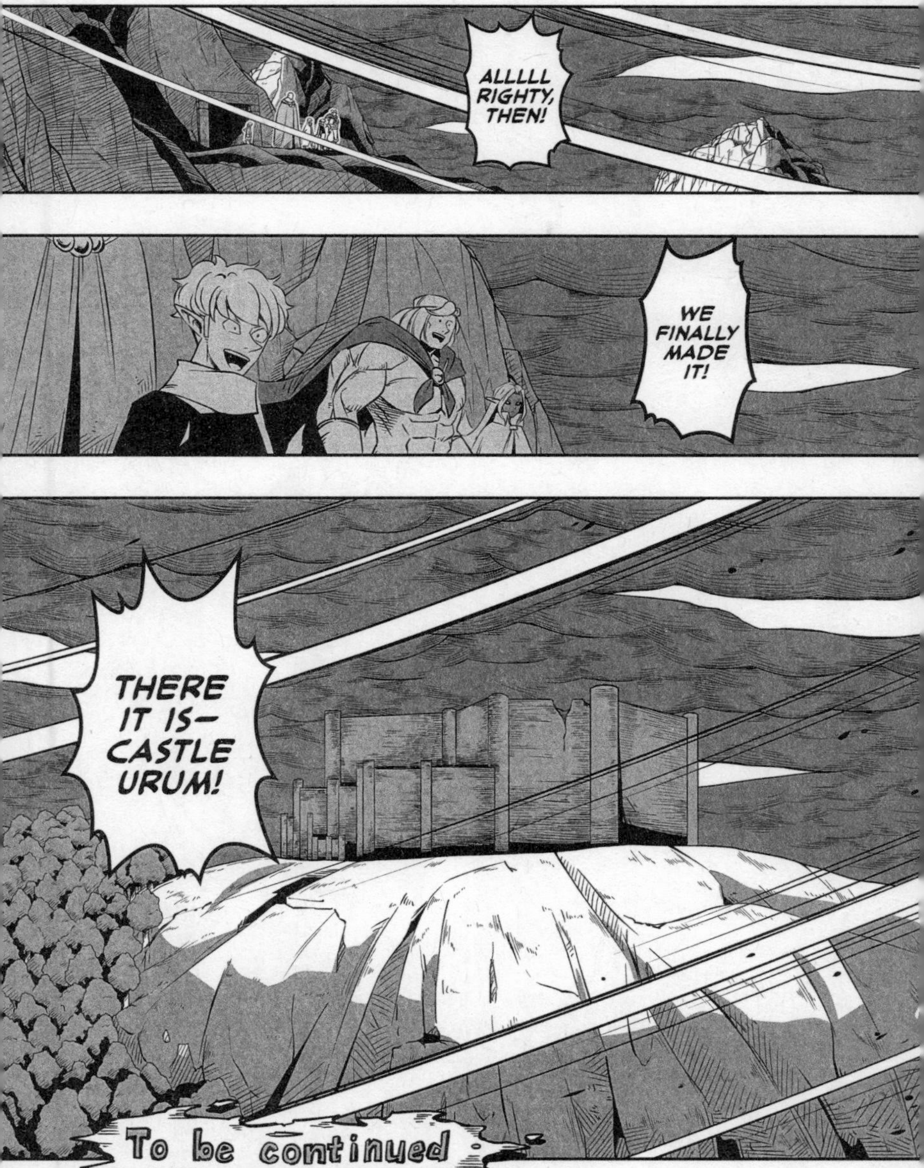
ALLLLL RIGHTY, THEN!
WE FINALLY MADE IT!
THERE IT IS— CASTLE URUM!
To be continued

Chapter 9:
Winged Soldiers, the Unknown Enemy

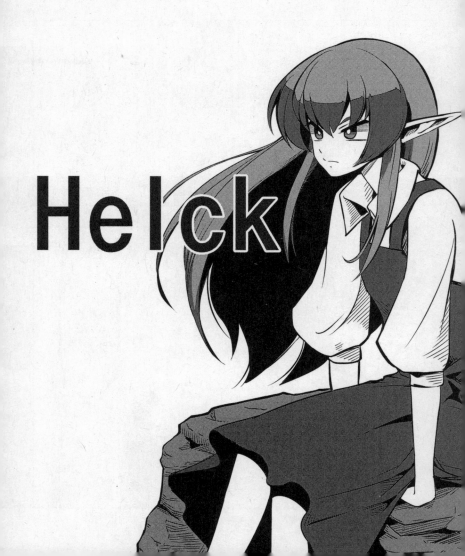

Helck

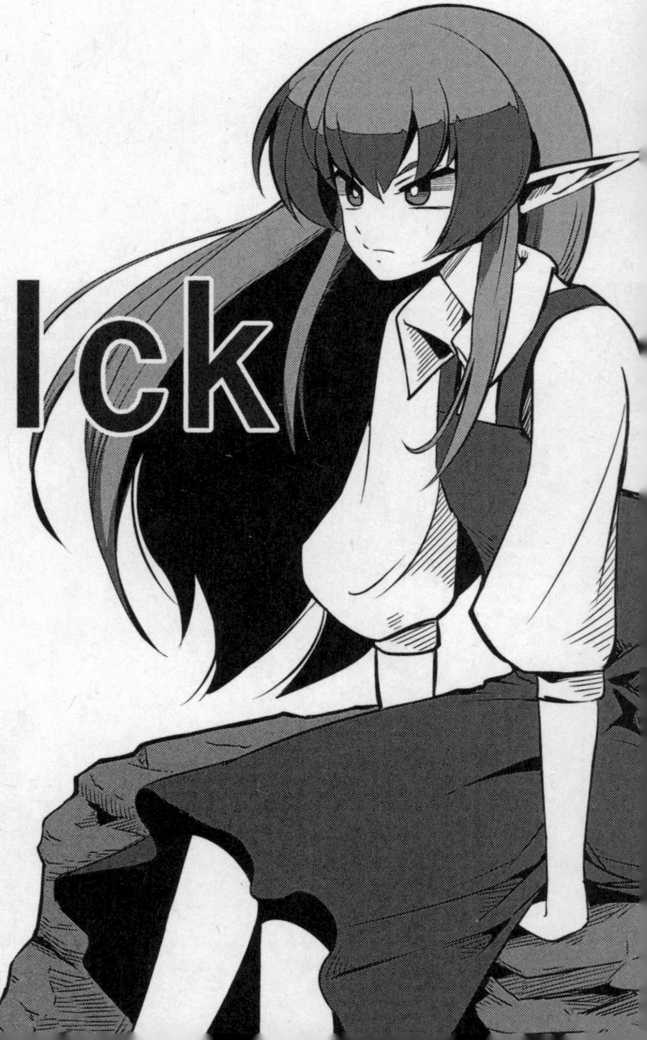

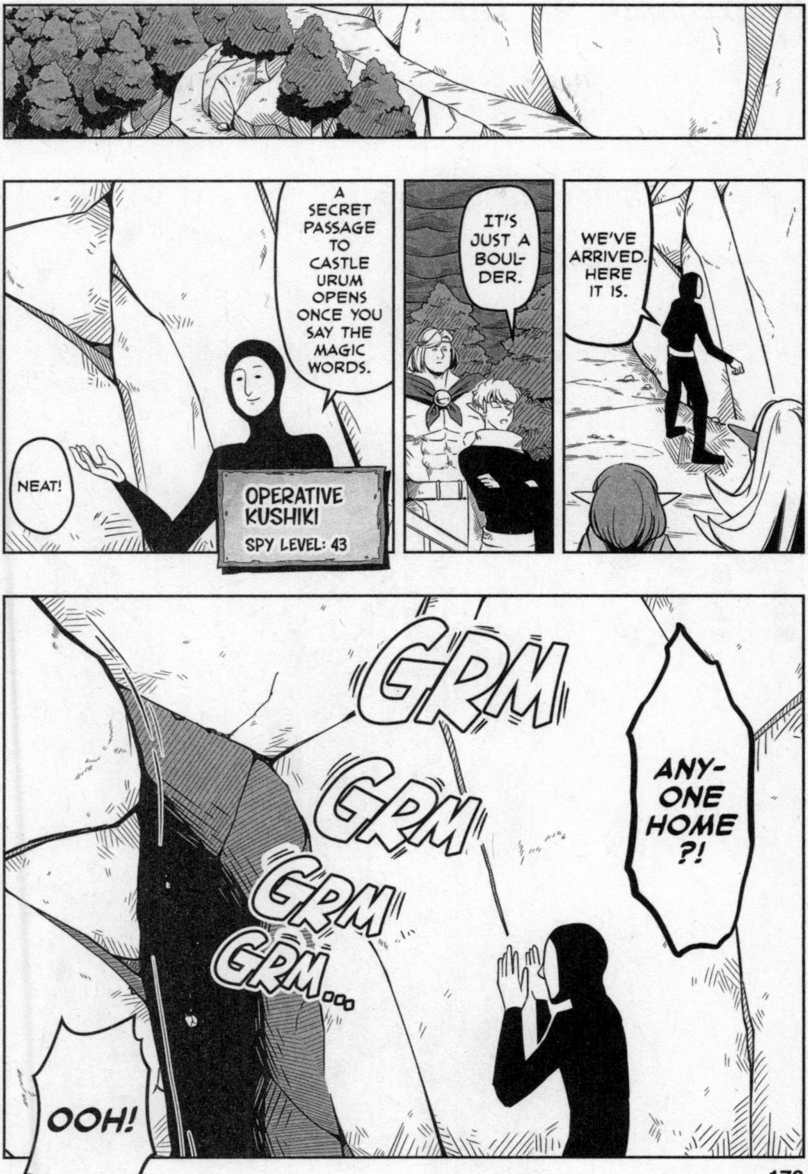
WE'VE ARRIVED. HERE IT IS.
IT'S JUST A BOUL-DER.
A SECRET PASSAGE TO CASTLE URUM OPENS ONCE YOU SAY THE MAGIC WORDS.
NEAT!
OPERATIVE KUSHIKI
SPY LEVEL: 43
ANY-ONE HOME ?!
GRM
GRM
GRM
GRM...
OOH!

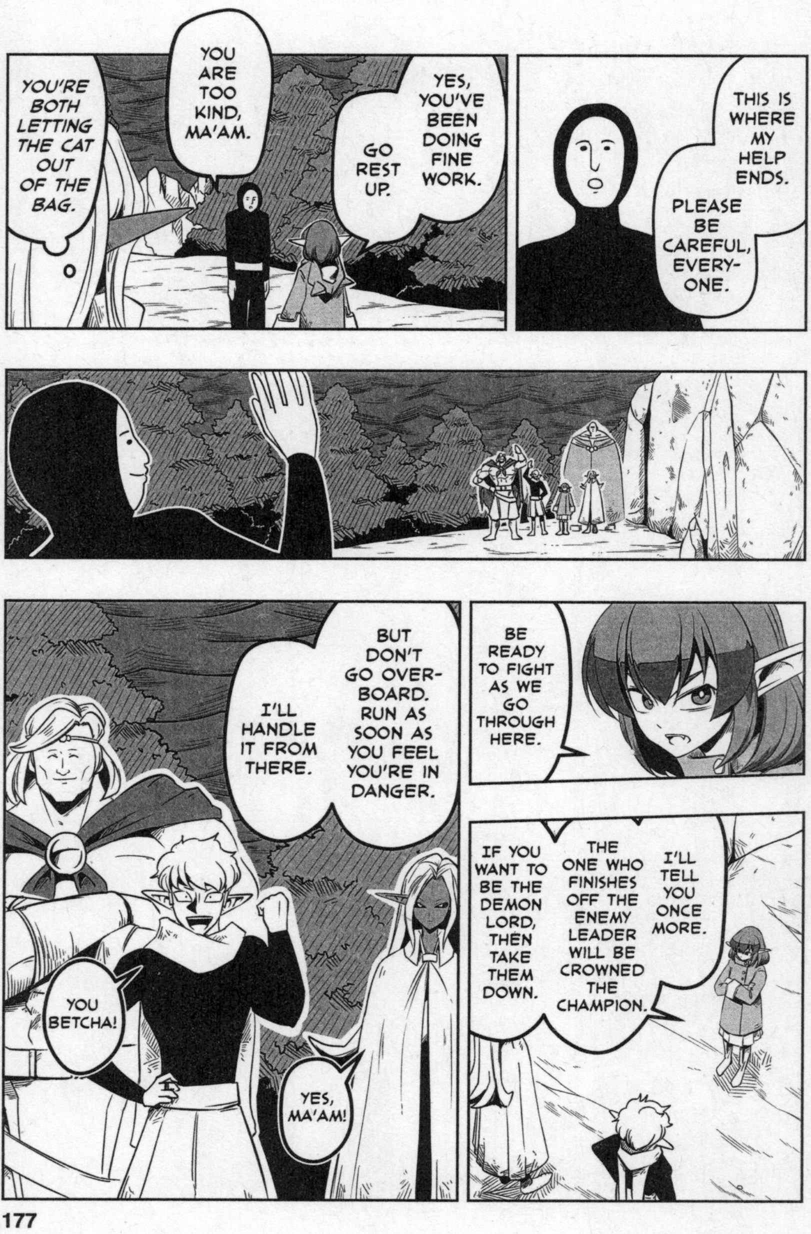
THIS IS WHERE MY HELP ENDS.
PLEASE BE CAREFUL, EVERYONE.
YES, YOU'VE BEEN DOING FINE WORK.
GO REST UP.
YOU ARE TOO KIND, MA'AM.
YOU'RE BOTH LETTING THE CAT OUT OF THE BAG.
BE READY TO FIGHT AS WE GO THROUGH HERE.
I'LL TELL YOU ONCE MORE.
THE ONE WHO FINISHES OFF THE ENEMY LEADER WILL BE CROWNED THE CHAMPION.
IF YOU WANT TO BE THE DEMON LORD, THEN TAKE THEM DOWN.
BUT DON'T GO OVER-BOARD. RUN AS SOON AS YOU FEEL YOU'RE IN DANGER.
I'LL HANDLE IT FROM THERE.
YES, MA'AM!
YOU BETCHA!

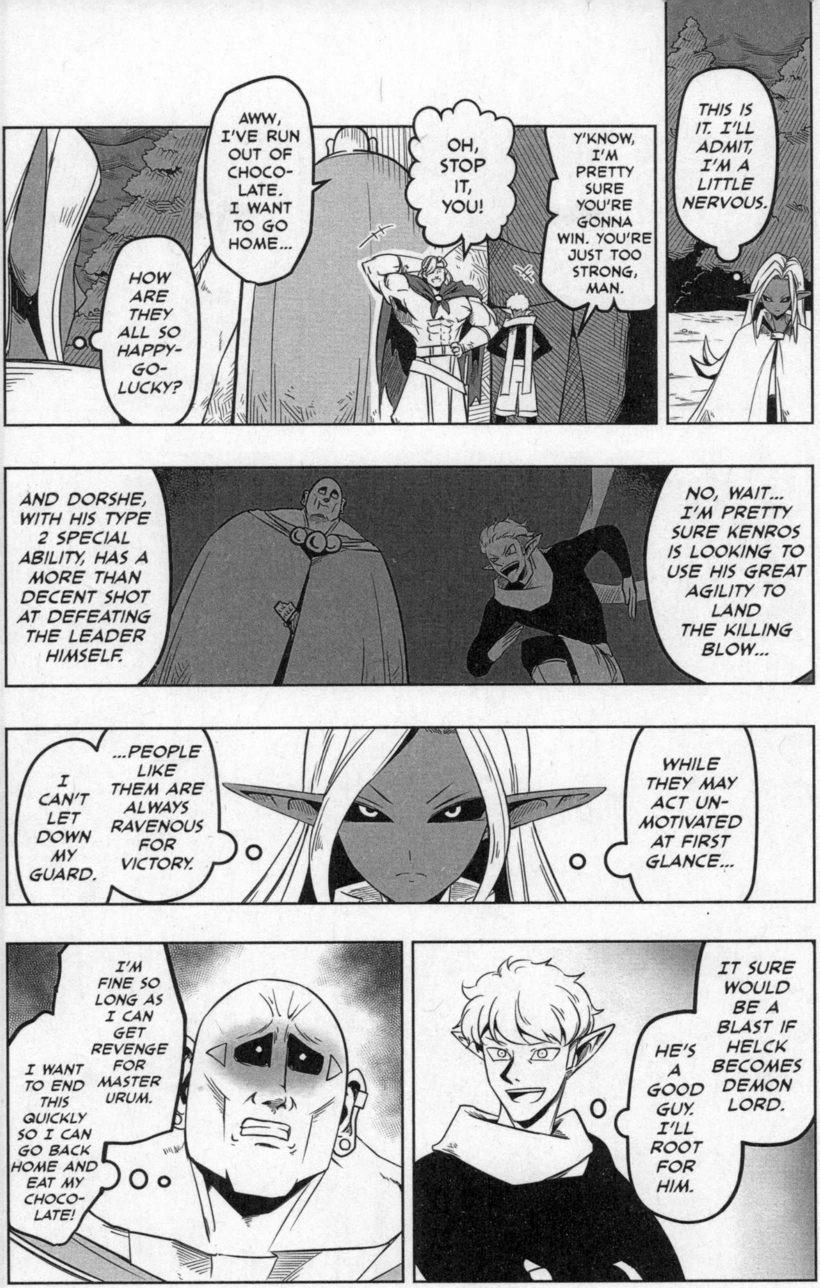
THIS IS IT. I'LL ADMIT, I'M A LITTLE NERVOUS.
Y'KNOW, I'M PRETTY SURE YOU'RE GONNA WIN. YOU'RE JUST TOO STRONG, MAN.
OH, STOP IT, YOU!
AWW, I'VE RUN OUT OF CHOCO-LATE. I WANT TO GO HOME...
HOW ARE THEY ALL SO HAPPY-GO-LUCKY?
NO, WAIT... I'M PRETTY SURE KENROS IS LOOKING TO USE HIS GREAT AGILITY TO LAND THE KILLING BLOW...
AND DORSHE, WITH HIS TYPE 2 SPECIAL ABILITY, HAS A MORE THAN DECENT SHOT AT DEFEATING THE LEADER HIMSELF.
WHILE THEY MAY ACT UN-MOTIVATED AT FIRST GLANCE...
...PEOPLE LIKE THEM ARE ALWAYS RAVENOUS FOR VICTORY.
I CAN'T LET DOWN MY GUARD.
IT SURE WOULD BE A BLAST IF HELCK BECOMES DEMON LORD.
HE'S A GOOD GUY. I'LL ROOT FOR HIM.
I'M FINE SO LONG AS I CAN GET REVENGE FOR MASTER URUM.
I WANT TO END THIS QUICKLY SO I CAN GO BACK HOME AND EAT MY CHOCO-LATE!

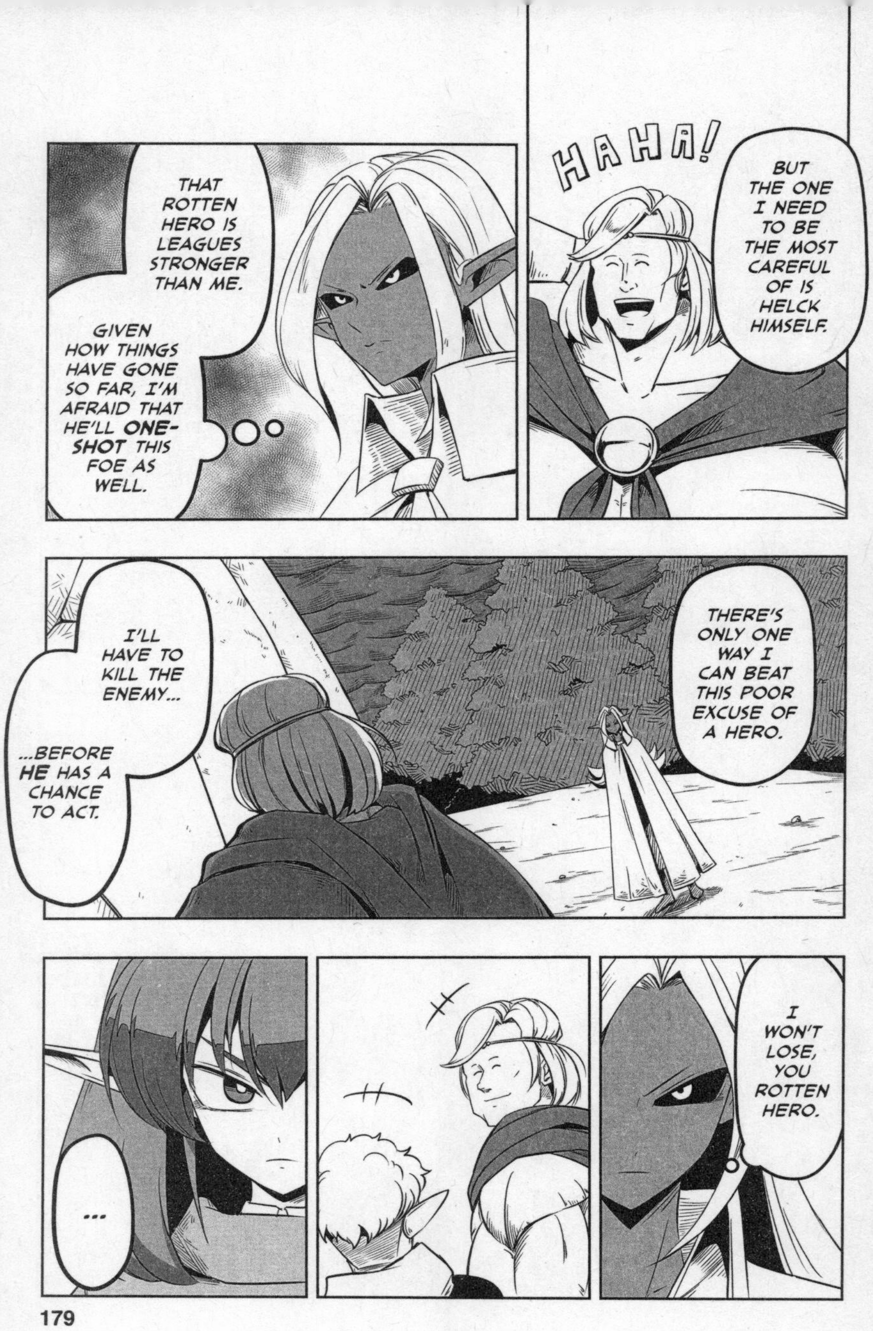
HAHA!
BUT THE ONE I NEED TO BE THE MOST CAREFUL OF IS HELCK HIMSELF.
THAT ROTTEN HERO IS LEAGUES STRONGER THAN ME.
GIVEN HOW THINGS HAVE GONE SO FAR, I'M AFRAID THAT HE'LL **ONE-SHOT** THIS FOE AS WELL.
THERE'S ONLY ONE WAY I CAN BEAT THIS POOR EXCUSE OF A HERO.
I'LL HAVE TO KILL THE ENEMY...
...BEFORE **HE** HAS A CHANCE TO ACT.
I WON'T LOSE, YOU ROTTEN HERO.
...

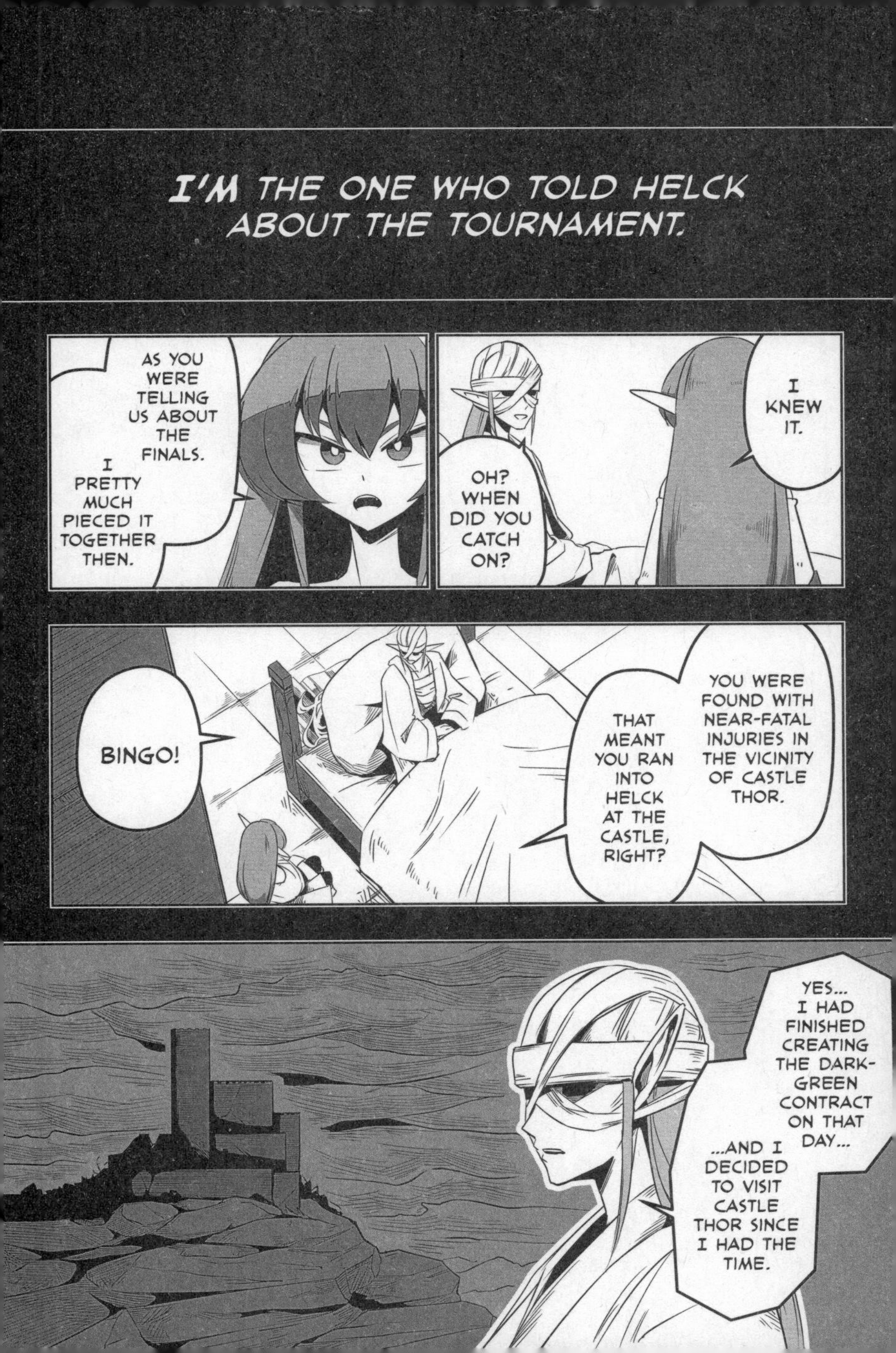
I'M THE ONE WHO TOLD HELCK ABOUT THE TOURNAMENT.
I KNEW IT.
OH? WHEN DID YOU CATCH ON?
AS YOU WERE TELLING US ABOUT THE FINALS.
I PRETTY MUCH PIECED IT TOGETHER THEN.
YOU WERE FOUND WITH NEAR-FATAL INJURIES IN THE VICINITY OF CASTLE THOR.
THAT MEANT YOU RAN INTO HELCK AT THE CASTLE, RIGHT?
BINGO!
YES... I HAD FINISHED CREATING THE DARK-GREEN CONTRACT ON THAT DAY...
...AND I DECIDED TO VISIT CASTLE THOR SINCE I HAD THE TIME.

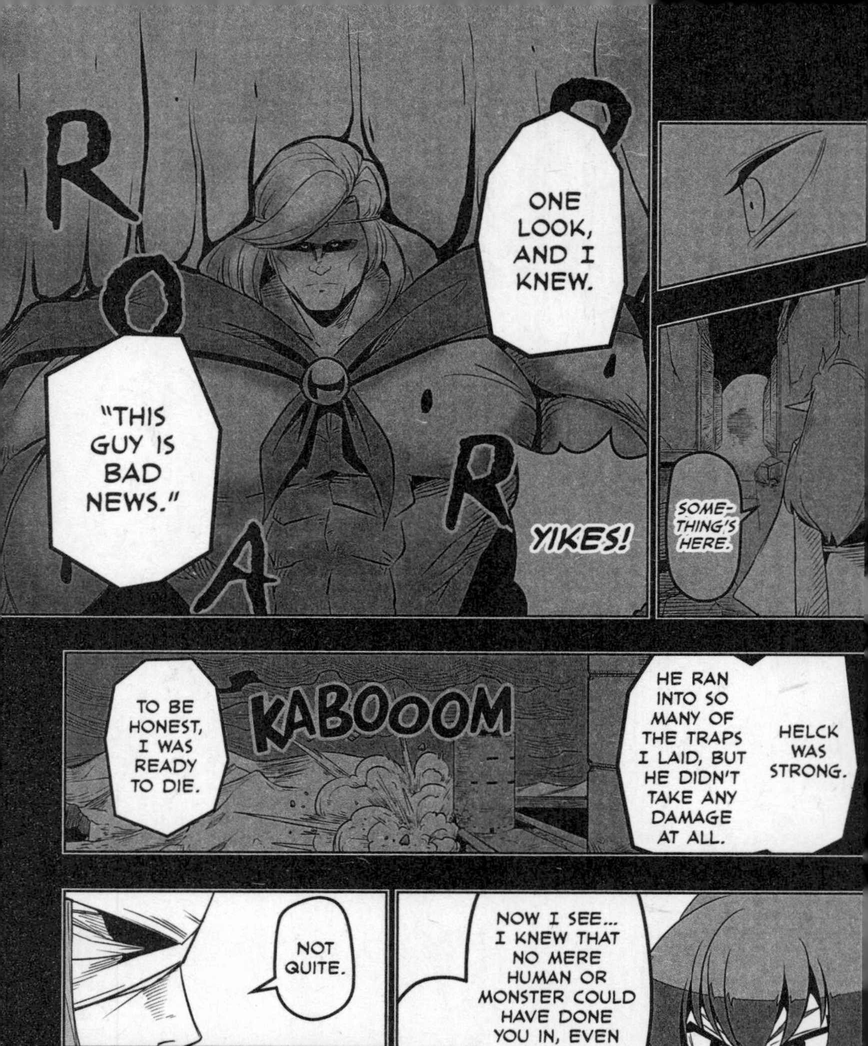
SOME-THING'S HERE.
ONE LOOK, AND I KNEW.
ROAR
"THIS GUY IS BAD NEWS."
YIKES!
HELCK WAS STRONG.
HE RAN INTO SO MANY OF THE TRAPS I LAID, BUT HE DIDN'T TAKE ANY DAMAGE AT ALL.
KABOOOM
TO BE HONEST, I WAS READY TO DIE.
NOW I SEE... I KNEW THAT NO MERE HUMAN OR MONSTER COULD HAVE DONE YOU IN, EVEN WITH YOUR REDUCED STRENGTH.
THOSE INJURIES ARE A RESULT OF YOUR FIGHT WITH HELCK THEN.
NOT QUITE.
HM?

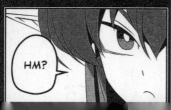

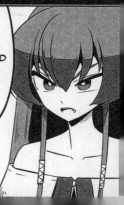

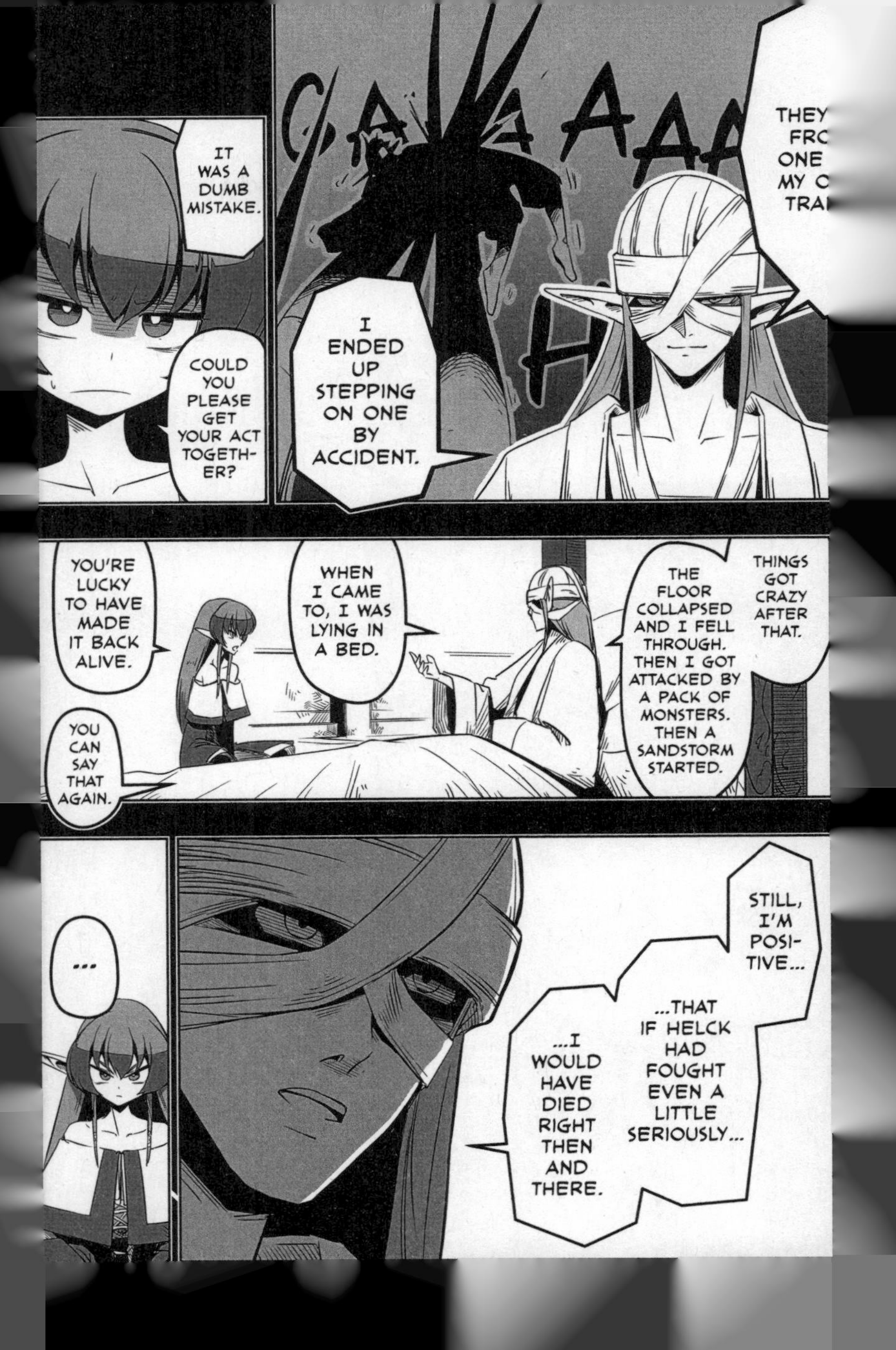
THEY FRO ONE MY O TRA
GAAAAAH
I ENDED UP STEPPING ON ONE BY ACCIDENT.
IT WAS A DUMB MISTAKE.
COULD YOU PLEASE GET YOUR ACT TOGETHER?
THINGS GOT CRAZY AFTER THAT.
THE FLOOR COLLAPSED AND I FELL THROUGH. THEN I GOT ATTACKED BY A PACK OF MONSTERS. THEN A SANDSTORM STARTED.
WHEN I CAME TO, I WAS LYING IN A BED.
YOU'RE LUCKY TO HAVE MADE IT BACK ALIVE.
YOU CAN SAY THAT AGAIN.
STILL, I'M POSITIVE...
...THAT IF HELCK HAD FOUGHT EVEN A LITTLE SERIOUSLY...
...I WOULD HAVE DIED RIGHT THEN AND THERE.
...

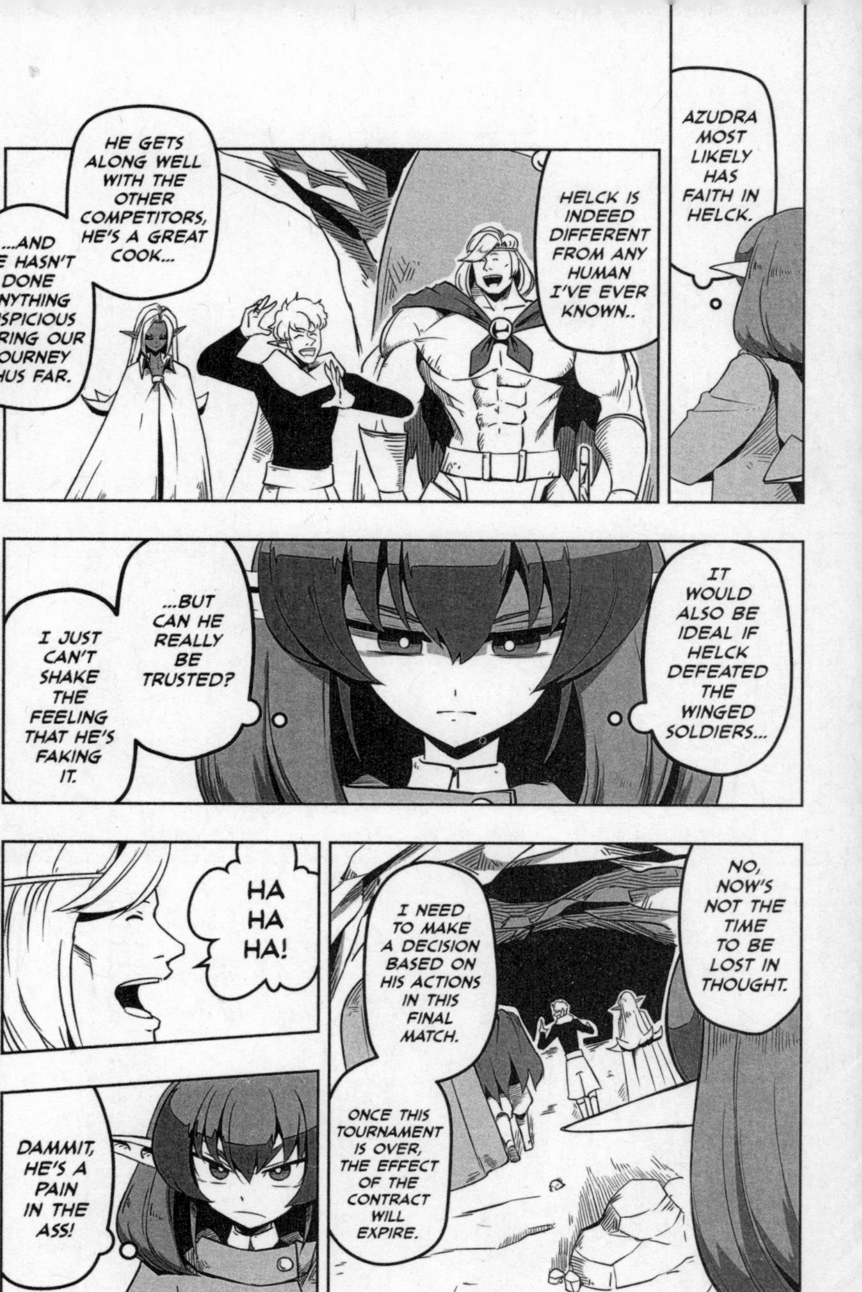
AZUDRA MOST LIKELY HAS FAITH IN HELCK.
HELCK IS INDEED DIFFERENT FROM ANY HUMAN I'VE EVER KNOWN..
HE GETS ALONG WELL WITH THE OTHER COMPETITORS, HE'S A GREAT COOK...
...AND HE HASN'T DONE ANYTHING SUSPICIOUS DURING OUR JOURNEY THUS FAR.
IT WOULD ALSO BE IDEAL IF HELCK DEFEATED THE WINGED SOLDIERS...
...BUT CAN HE REALLY BE TRUSTED?
I JUST CAN'T SHAKE THE FEELING THAT HE'S FAKING IT.
NO, NOW'S NOT THE TIME TO BE LOST IN THOUGHT.
I NEED TO MAKE A DECISION BASED ON HIS ACTIONS IN THIS FINAL MATCH.
ONCE THIS TOURNAMENT IS OVER, THE EFFECT OF THE CONTRACT WILL EXPIRE.
HA HA HA!
DAMMIT, HE'S A PAIN IN THE ASS!

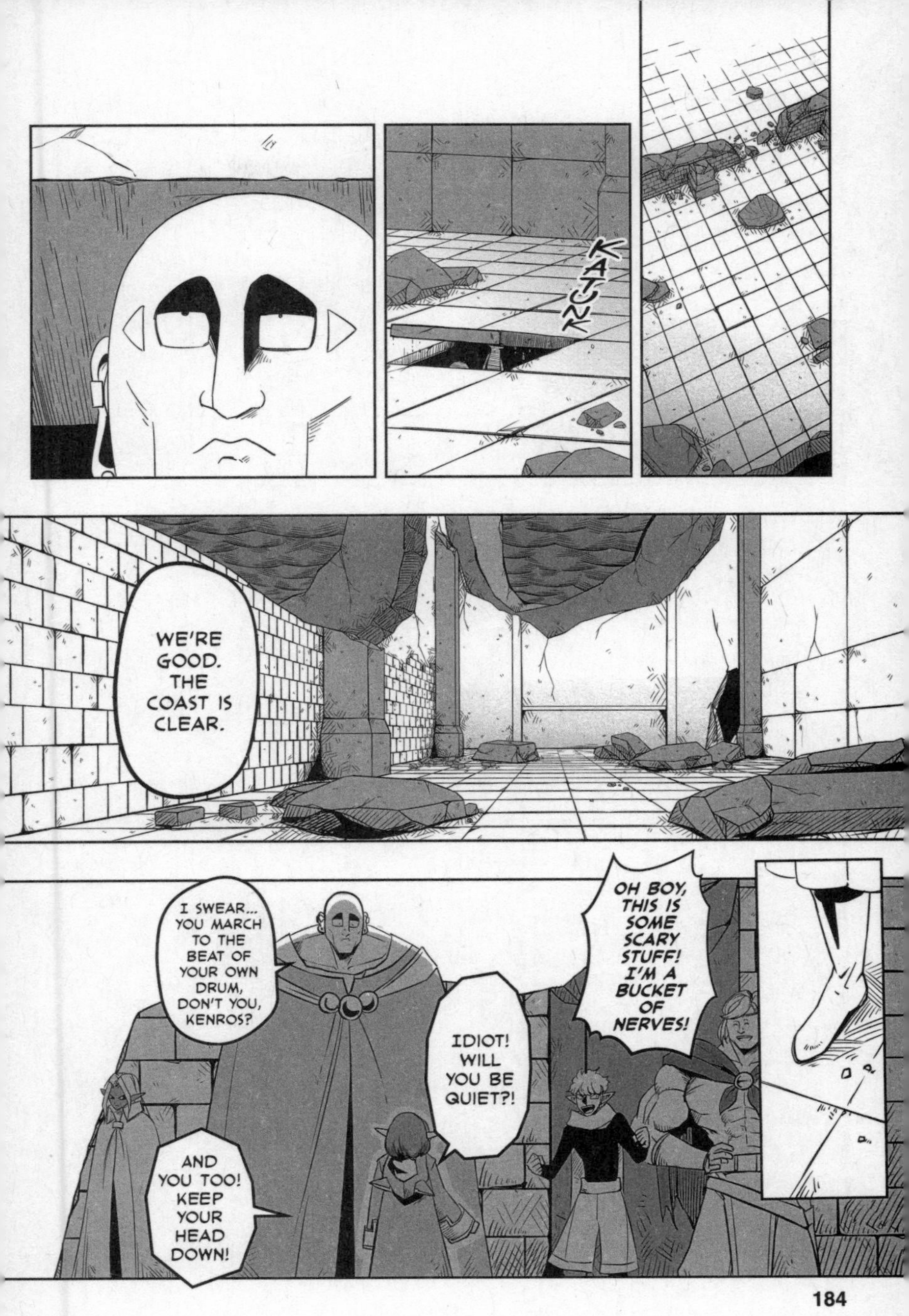
KATUNK
WE'RE GOOD. THE COAST IS CLEAR.
OH BOY, THIS IS SOME SCARY STUFF! I'M A BUCKET OF NERVES!
IDIOT! WILL YOU BE QUIET?!
I SWEAR... YOU MARCH TO THE BEAT OF YOUR OWN DRUM, DON'T YOU, KENROS?
AND YOU TOO! KEEP YOUR HEAD DOWN!

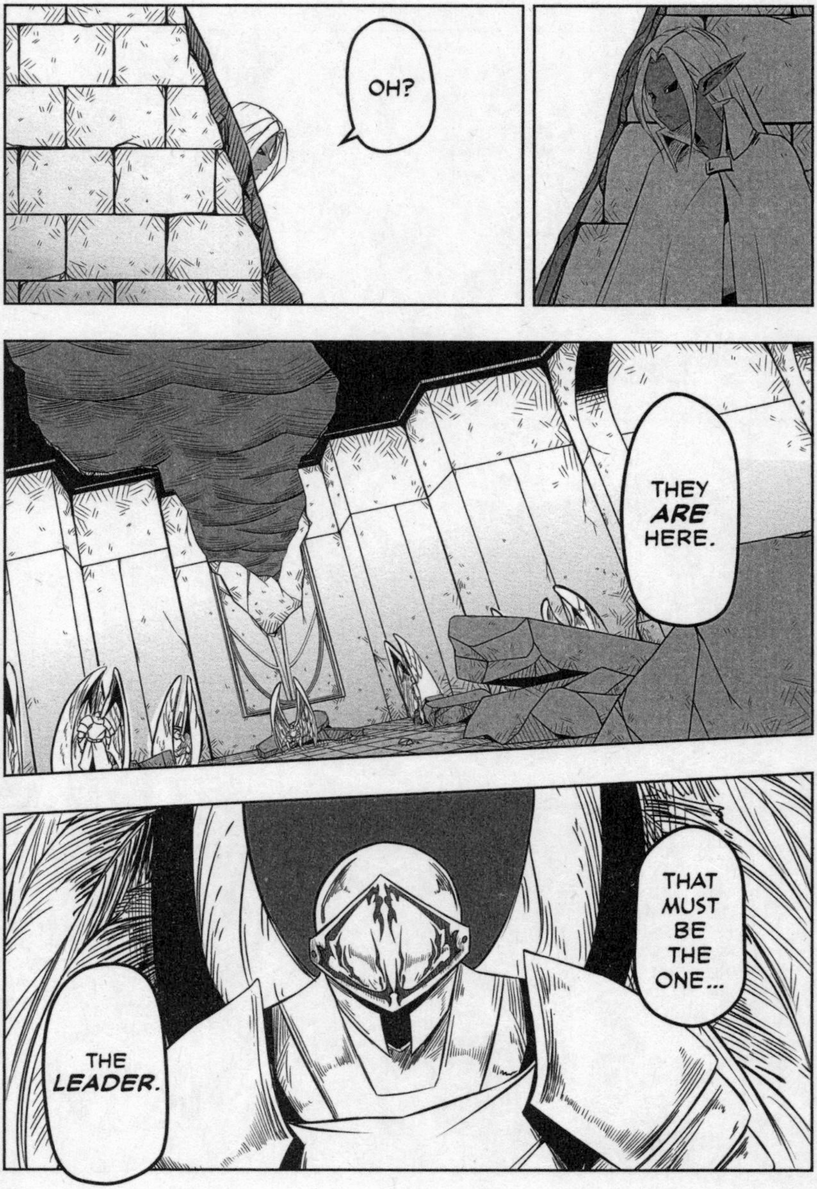
OH?
THEY *ARE* HERE.
THAT MUST BE THE ONE...
THE *LEADER*.

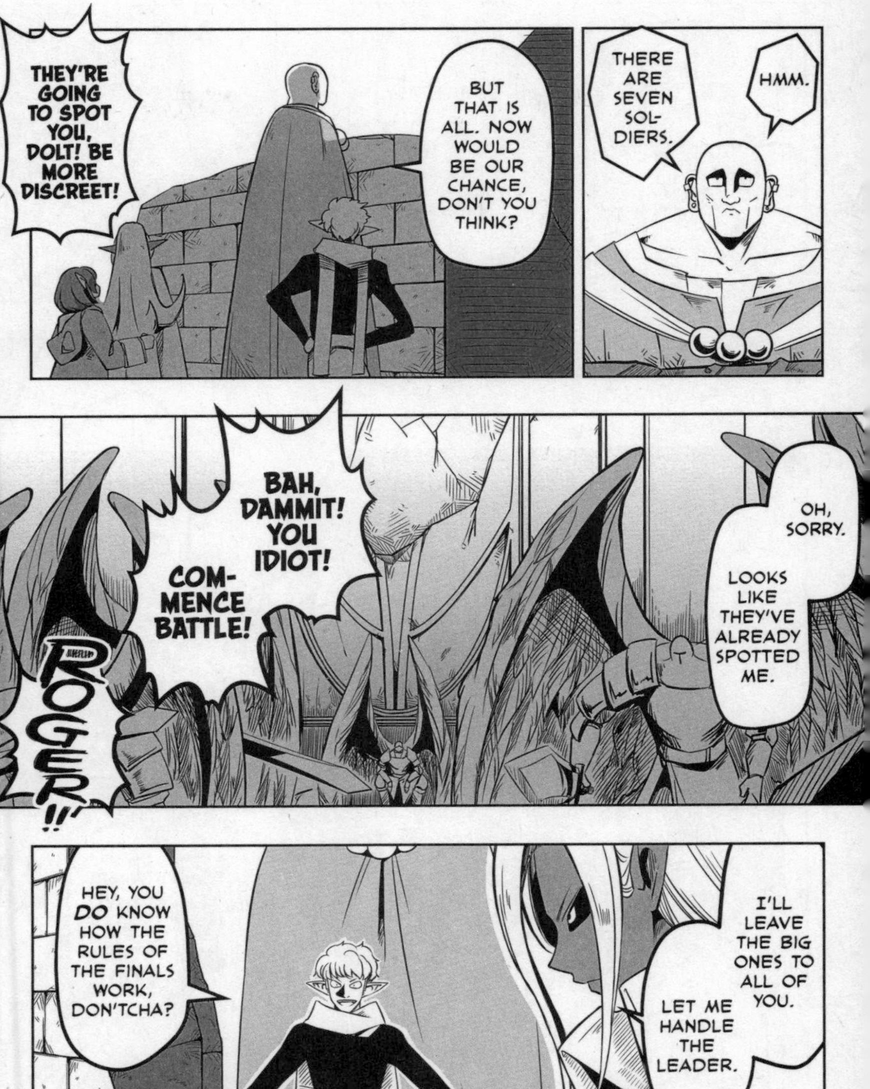
HMM.
THERE ARE SEVEN SOL-DIERS.
BUT THAT IS ALL. NOW WOULD BE OUR CHANCE, DON'T YOU THINK?
THEY'RE GOING TO SPOT YOU, DOLT! BE MORE DISCREET!
OH, SORRY.
LOOKS LIKE THEY'VE ALREADY SPOTTED ME.
BAH, DAMMIT! YOU IDIOT!
COM-MENCE BATTLE!
ROGER!!
I'LL LEAVE THE BIG ONES TO ALL OF YOU.
LET ME HANDLE THE LEADER.
HEY, YOU *DO* KNOW HOW THE RULES OF THE FINALS WORK, DON'TCHA?

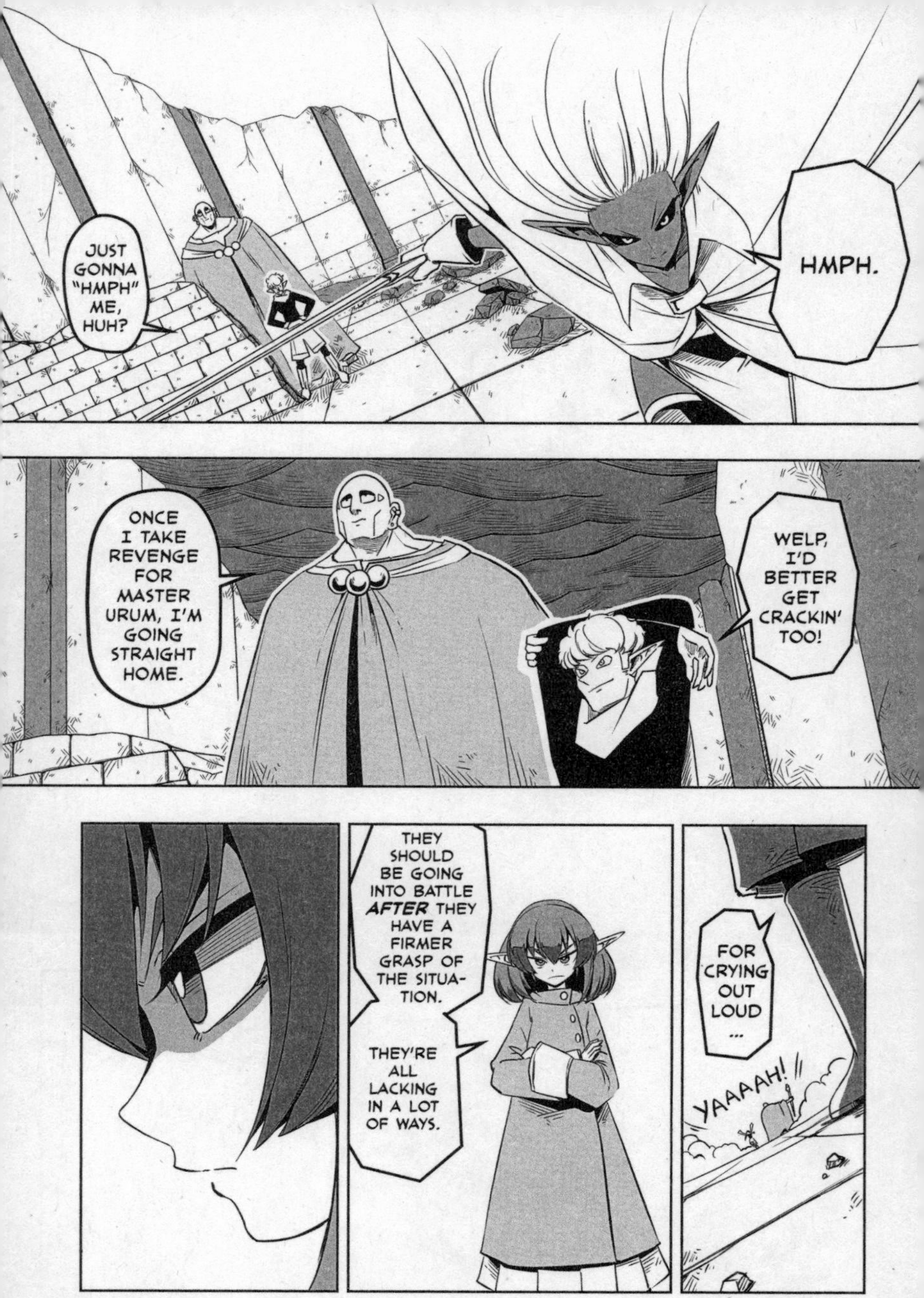
HMPH.
JUST GONNA "HMPH" ME, HUH?
WELP, I'D BETTER GET CRACKIN' TOO!
ONCE I TAKE REVENGE FOR MASTER URUM, I'M GOING STRAIGHT HOME.
FOR CRYING OUT LOUD ...
YAAAAH!!
THEY SHOULD BE GOING INTO BATTLE *AFTER* THEY HAVE A FIRMER GRASP OF THE SITUATION.
THEY'RE ALL LACKING IN A LOT OF WAYS.

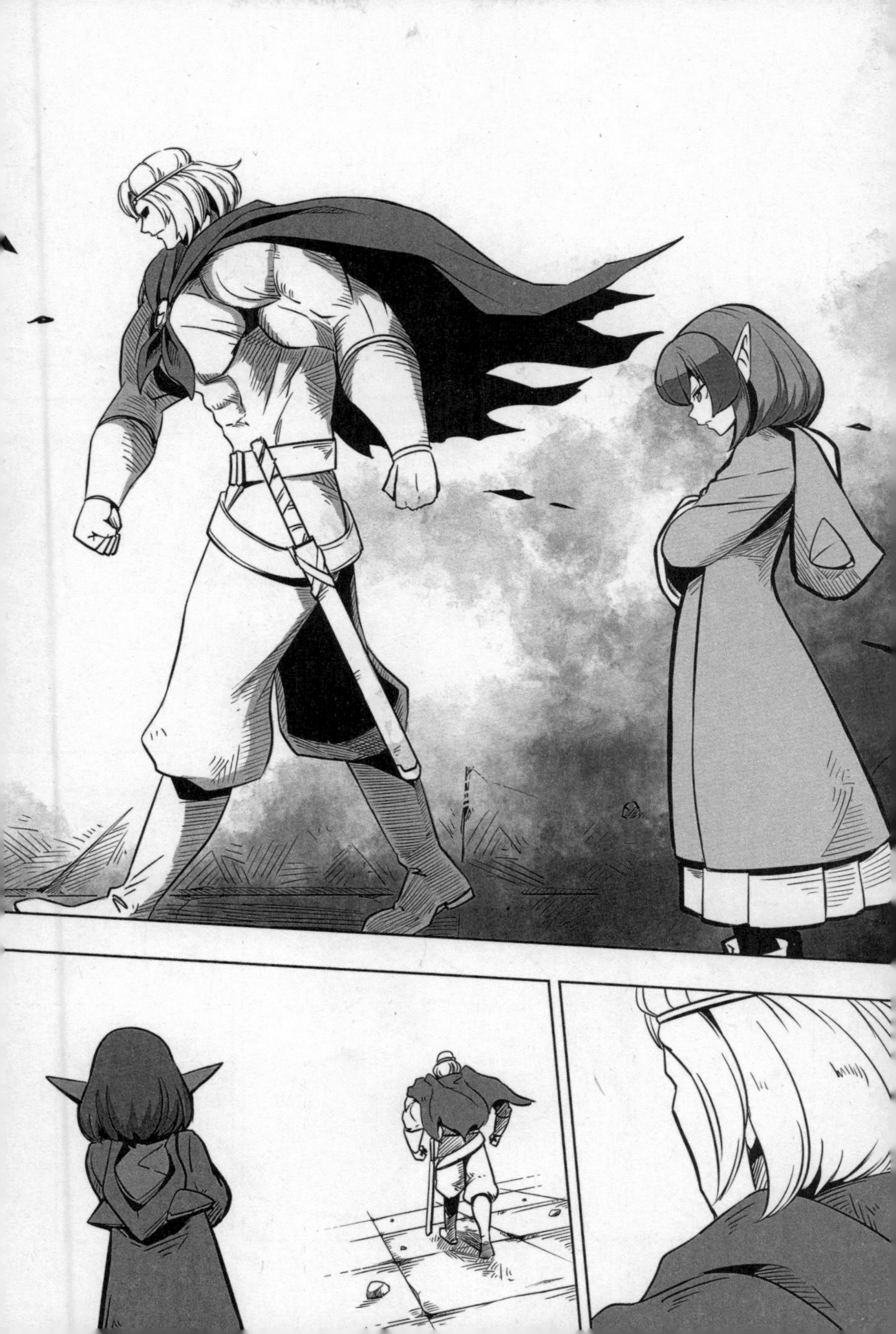

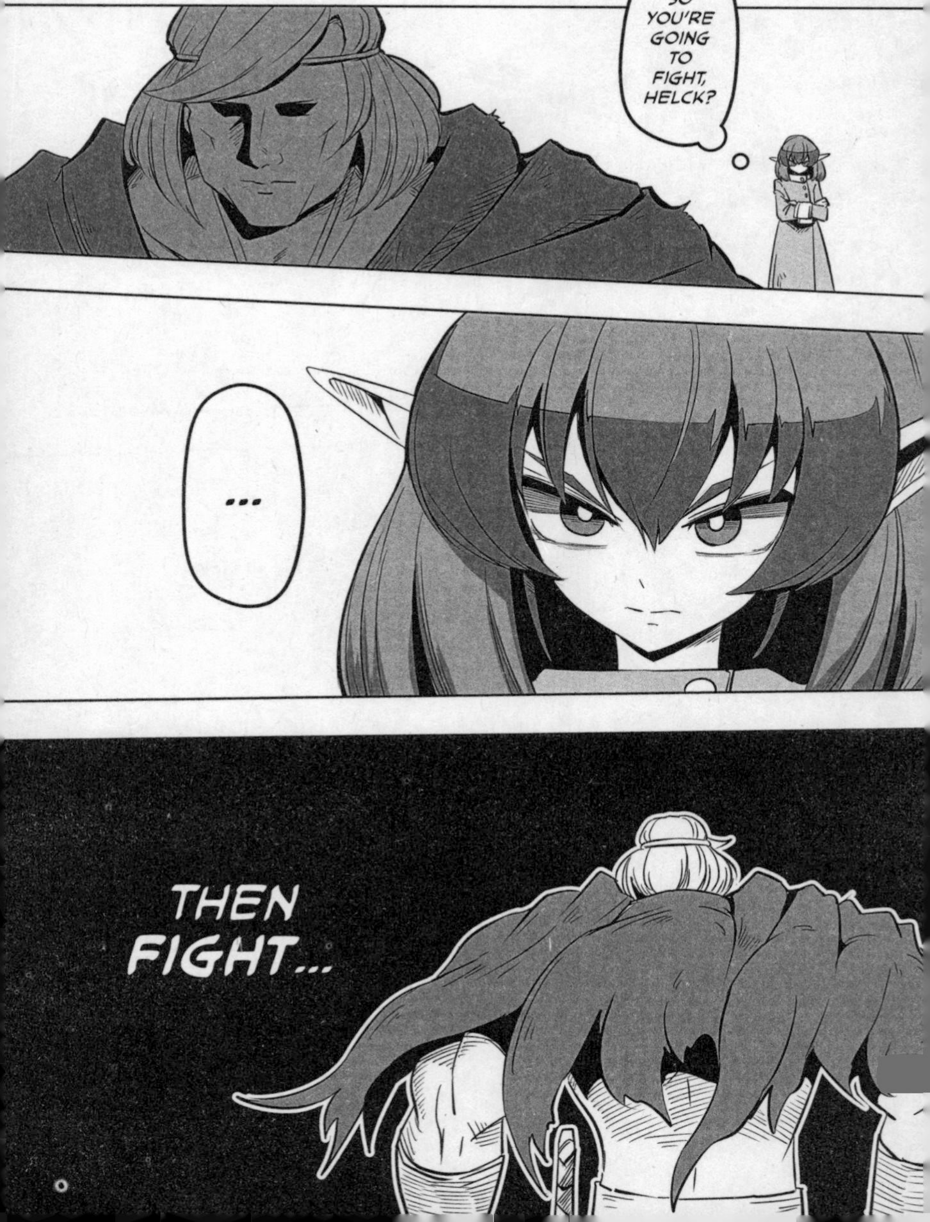
SO YOU'RE GOING TO FIGHT, HELCK?
...
THEN FIGHT...

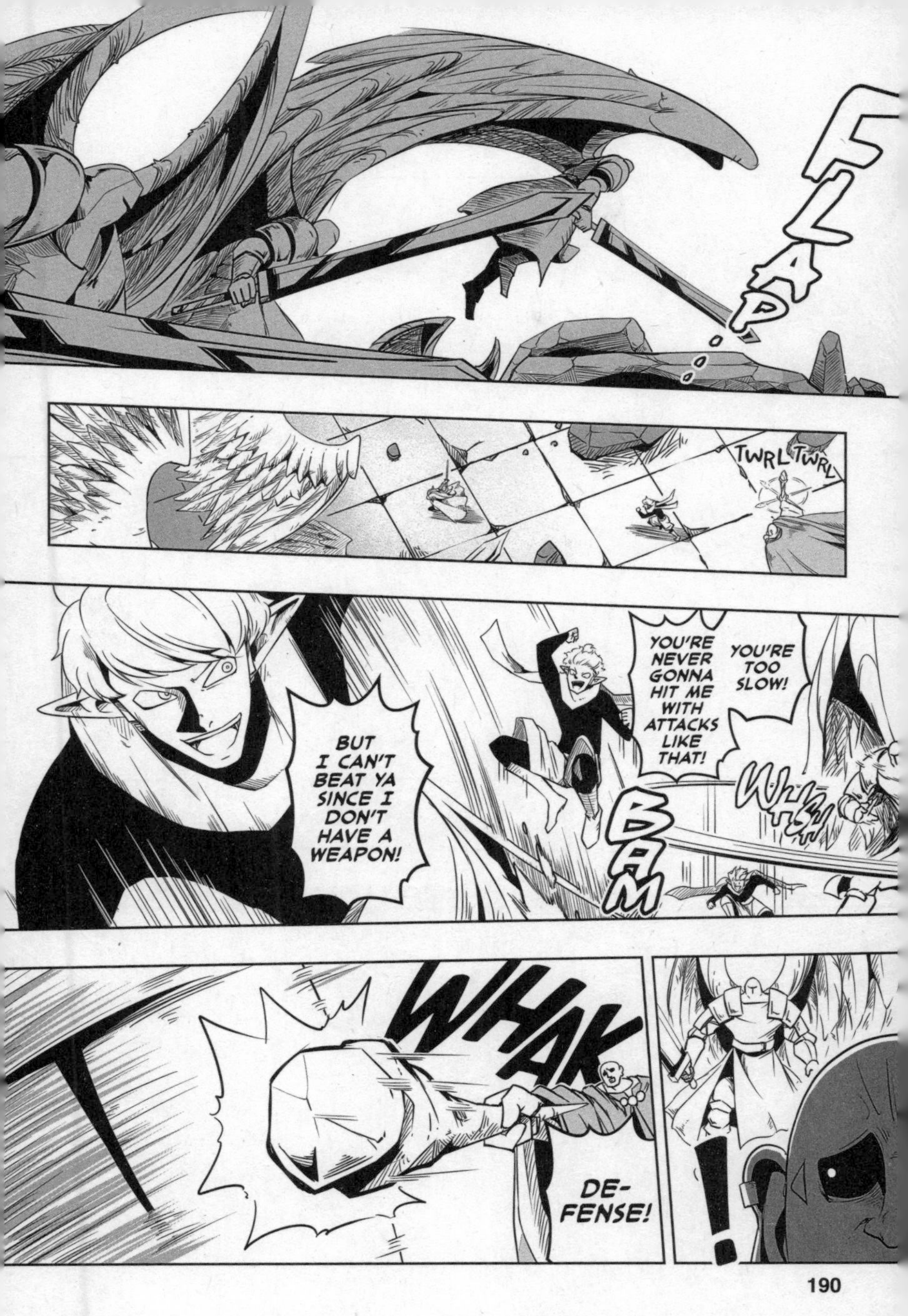
FLAP
TWRL TWRL
YOU'RE TOO SLOW!
YOU'RE NEVER GONNA HIT ME WITH ATTACKS LIKE THAT!
WHSH
BAM
BUT I CAN'T BEAT YA SINCE I DON'T HAVE A WEAPON!
!
WHAK
DE-FENSE!

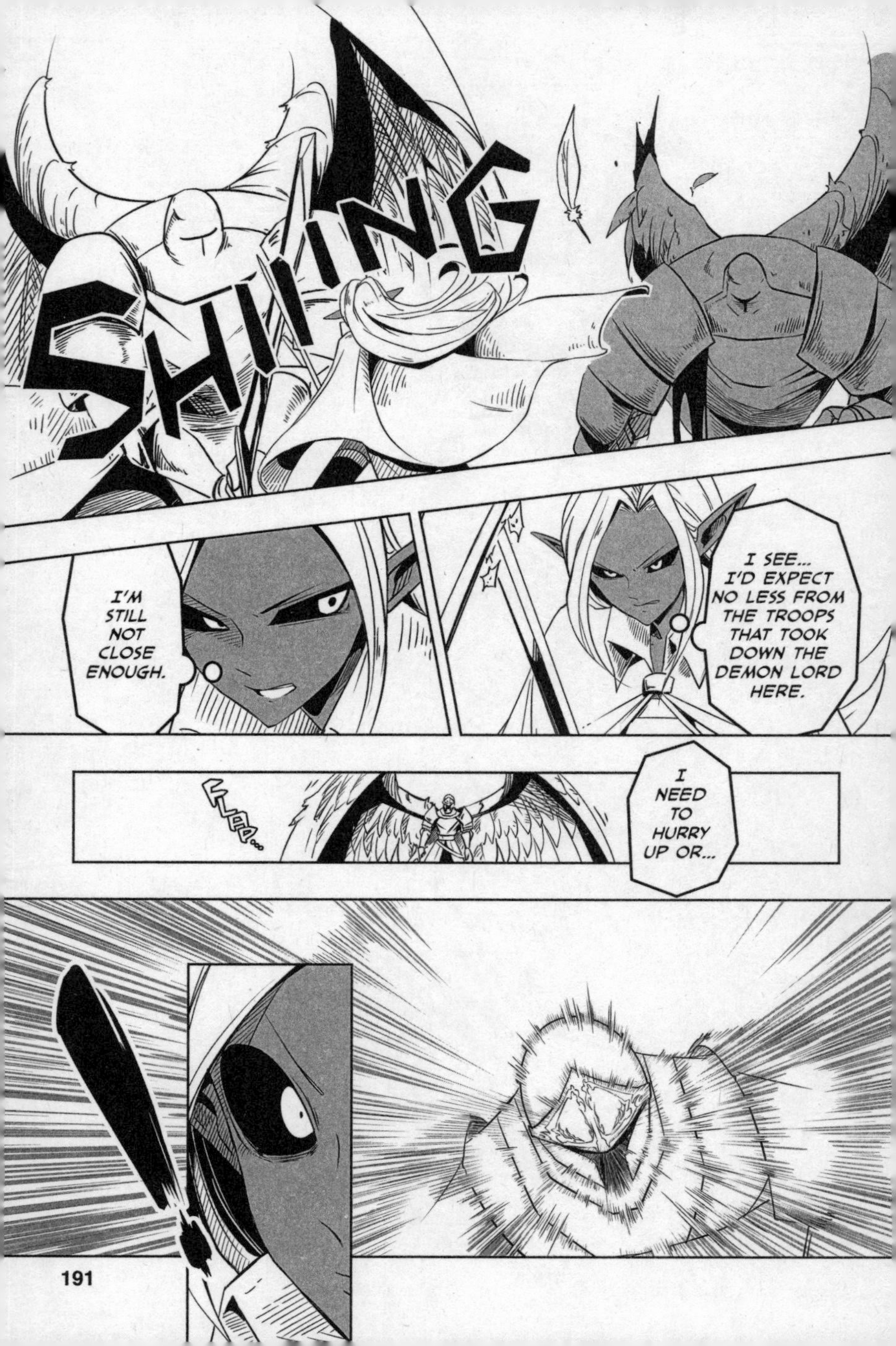
SHIIING
I SEE... I'D EXPECT NO LESS FROM THE TROOPS THAT TOOK DOWN THE DEMON LORD HERE.
I'M STILL NOT CLOSE ENOUGH.
I NEED TO HURRY UP OR...
FLAP...

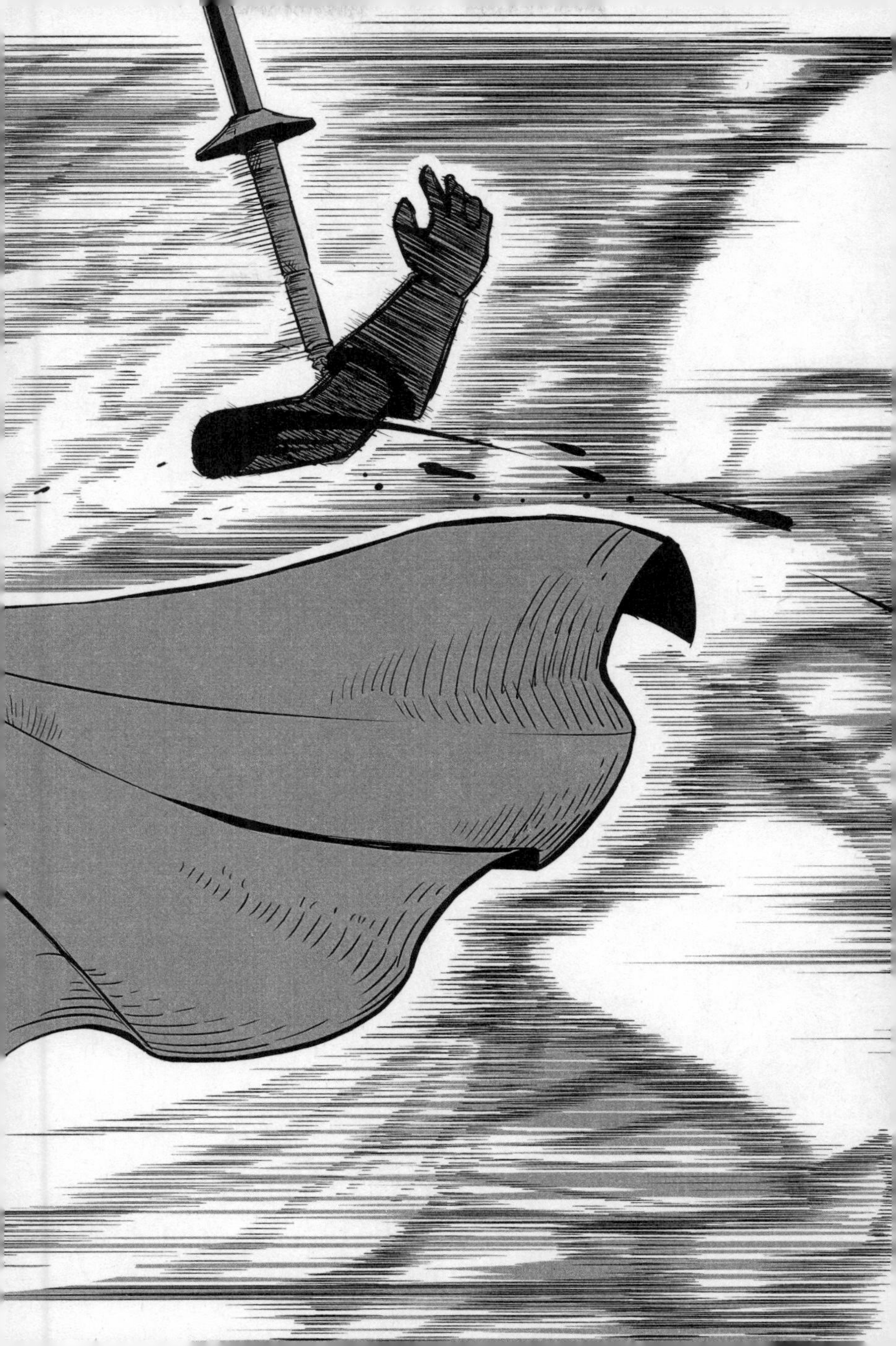

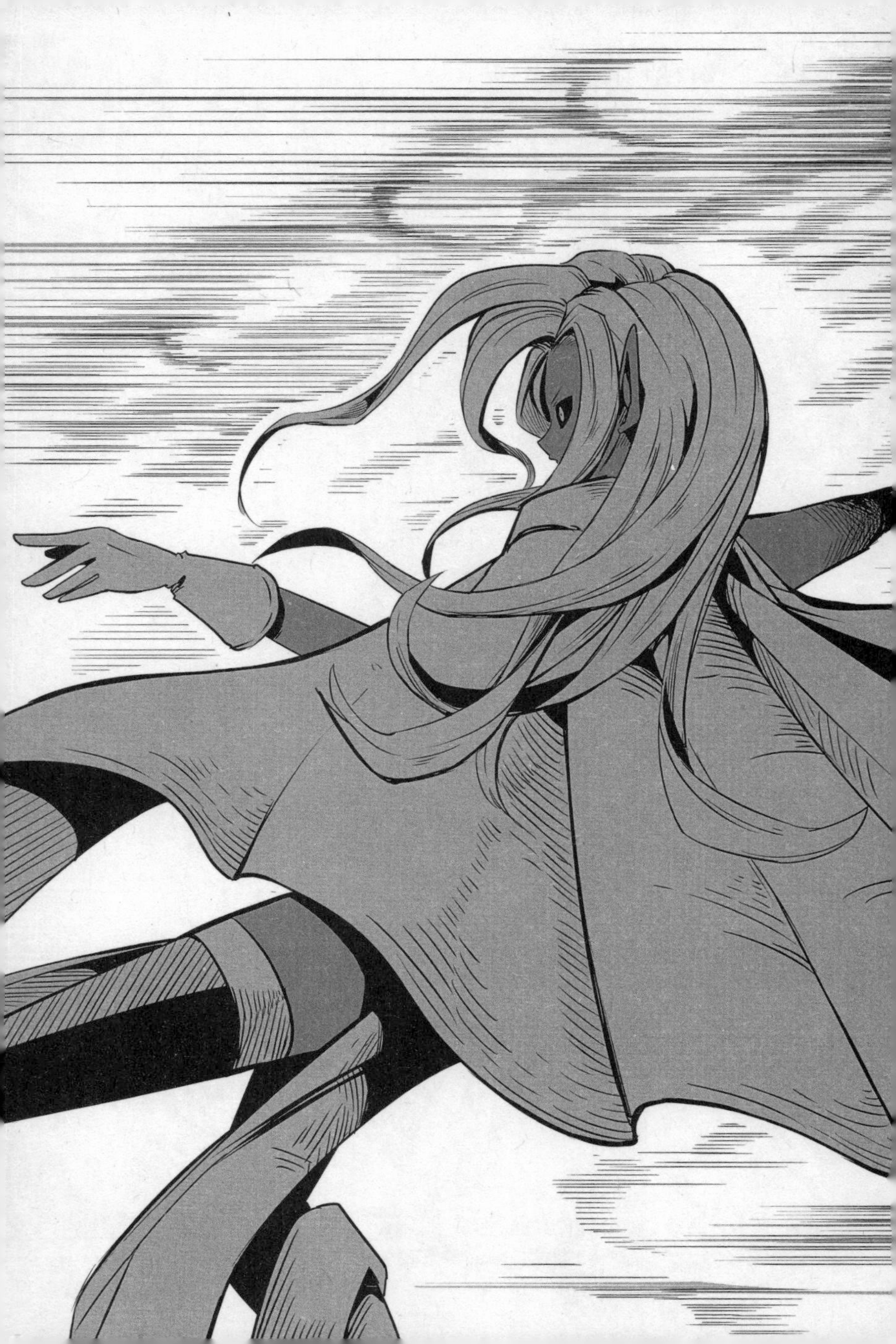

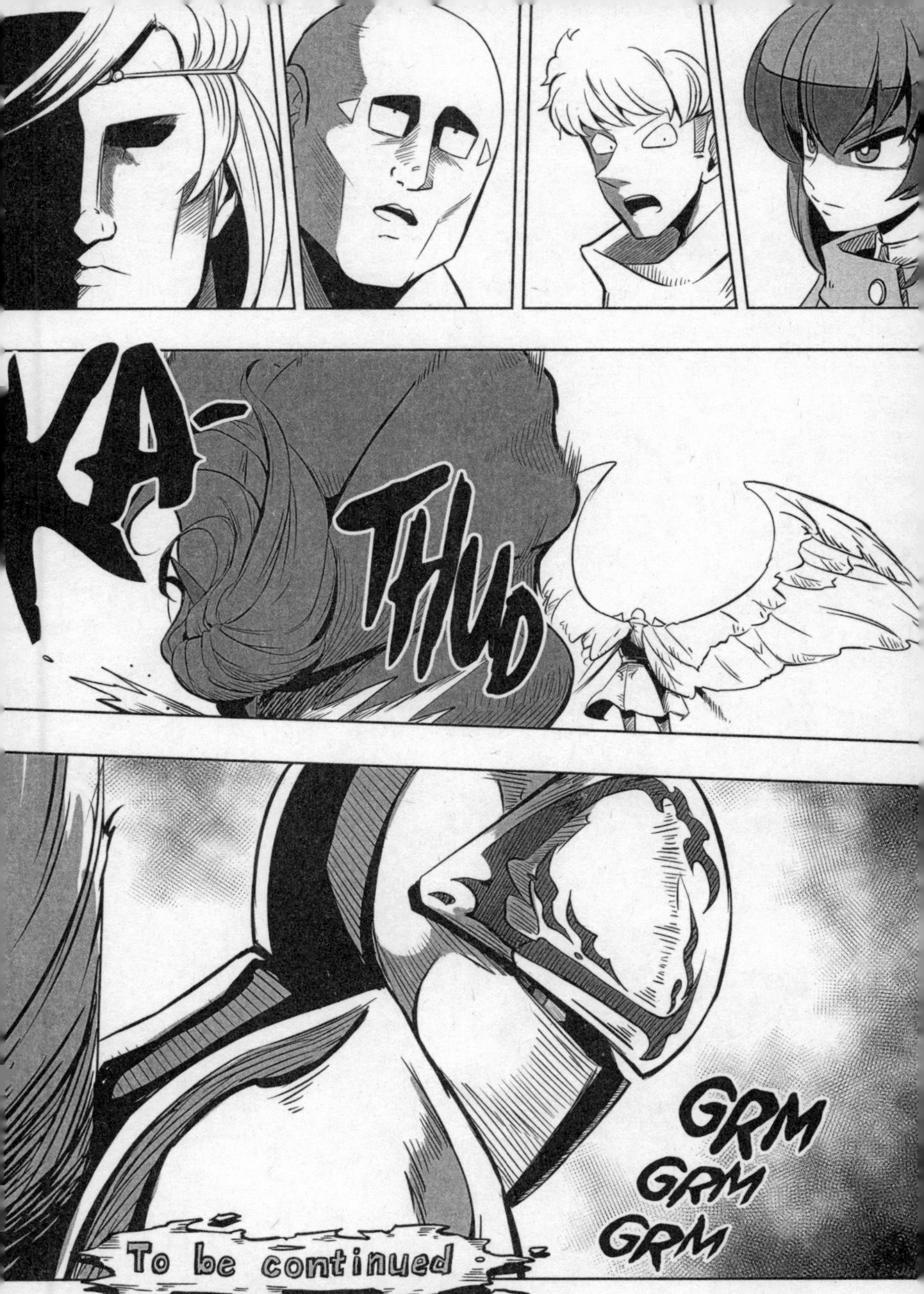
KA-THUD
GRM GRM GRM
To be continued

HELCK 1 [END]

BONUS COMIC

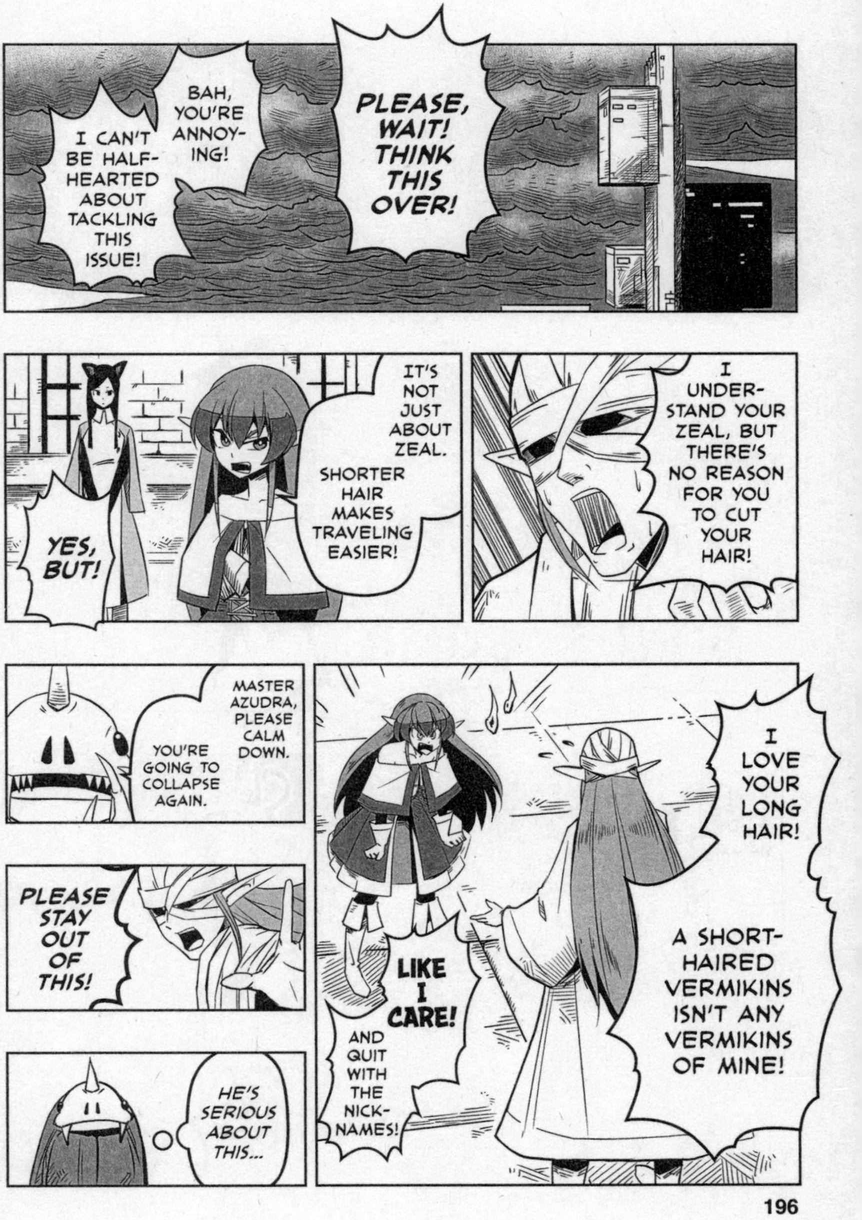
PLEASE, WAIT! THINK THIS OVER!
BAH, YOU'RE ANNOYING!
I CAN'T BE HALF-HEARTED ABOUT TACKLING THIS ISSUE!
I UNDERSTAND YOUR ZEAL, BUT THERE'S NO REASON FOR YOU TO CUT YOUR HAIR!
IT'S NOT JUST ABOUT ZEAL.
SHORTER HAIR MAKES TRAVELING EASIER!
YES, BUT!
I LOVE YOUR LONG HAIR!
A SHORT-HAIRED VERMIKINS ISN'T ANY VERMIKINS OF MINE!
LIKE I CARE!
AND QUIT WITH THE NICK-NAMES!
MASTER AZUDRA, PLEASE CALM DOWN.
YOU'RE GOING TO COLLAPSE AGAIN.
PLEASE STAY OUT OF THIS!
HE'S SERIOUS ABOUT THIS...

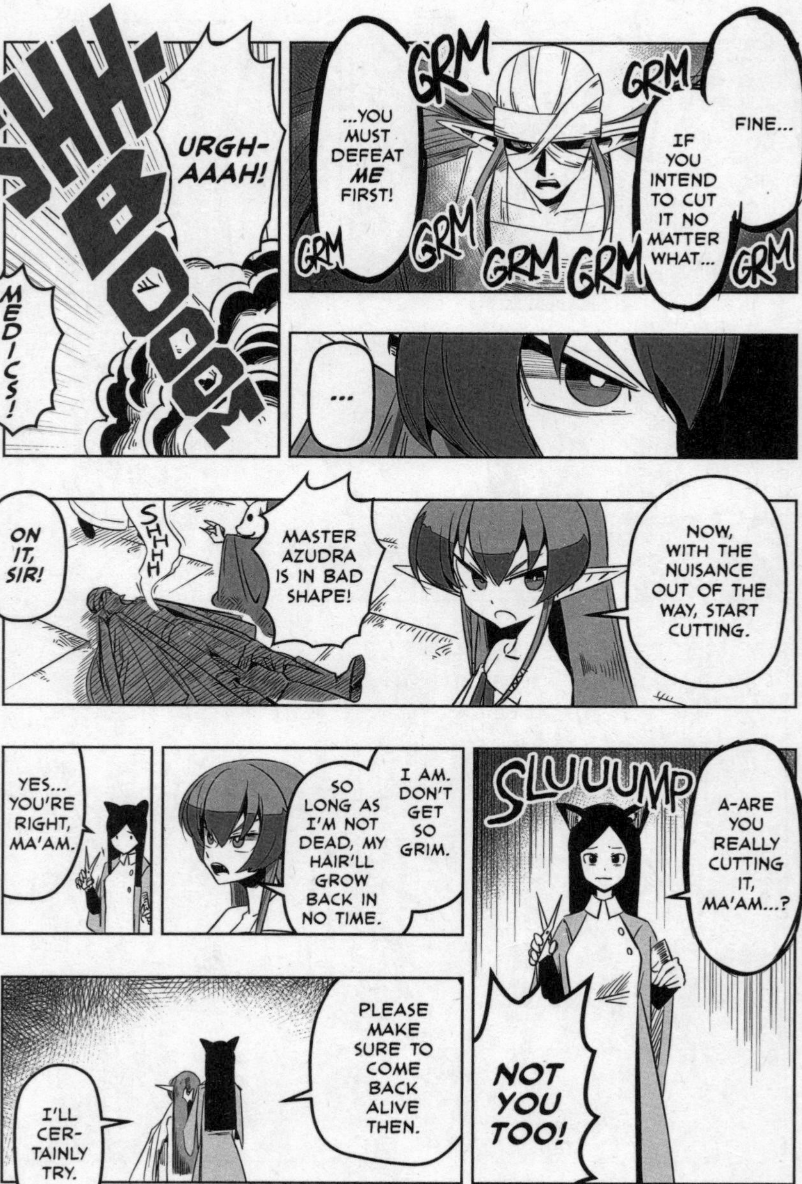
GRM
GRM
FINE...
IF YOU INTEND TO CUT IT NO MATTER WHAT...
GRM
...YOU MUST DEFEAT *ME* FIRST!
GRM GRM GRM GRM
GRM
...
URGH-AAAH!
SHH-BOOM
MEDICS!
NOW, WITH THE NUISANCE OUT OF THE WAY, START CUTTING.
MASTER AZUDRA IS IN BAD SHAPE!
SHHHH
ON IT, SIR!
SLUUUMP
A-ARE YOU REALLY CUTTING IT, MA'AM...?
NOT YOU TOO!
I AM. DON'T GET SO GRIM.
SO LONG AS I'M NOT DEAD, MY HAIR'LL GROW BACK IN NO TIME.
YES... YOU'RE RIGHT, MA'AM.
PLEASE MAKE SURE TO COME BACK ALIVE THEN.
I'LL CER-TAINLY TRY.

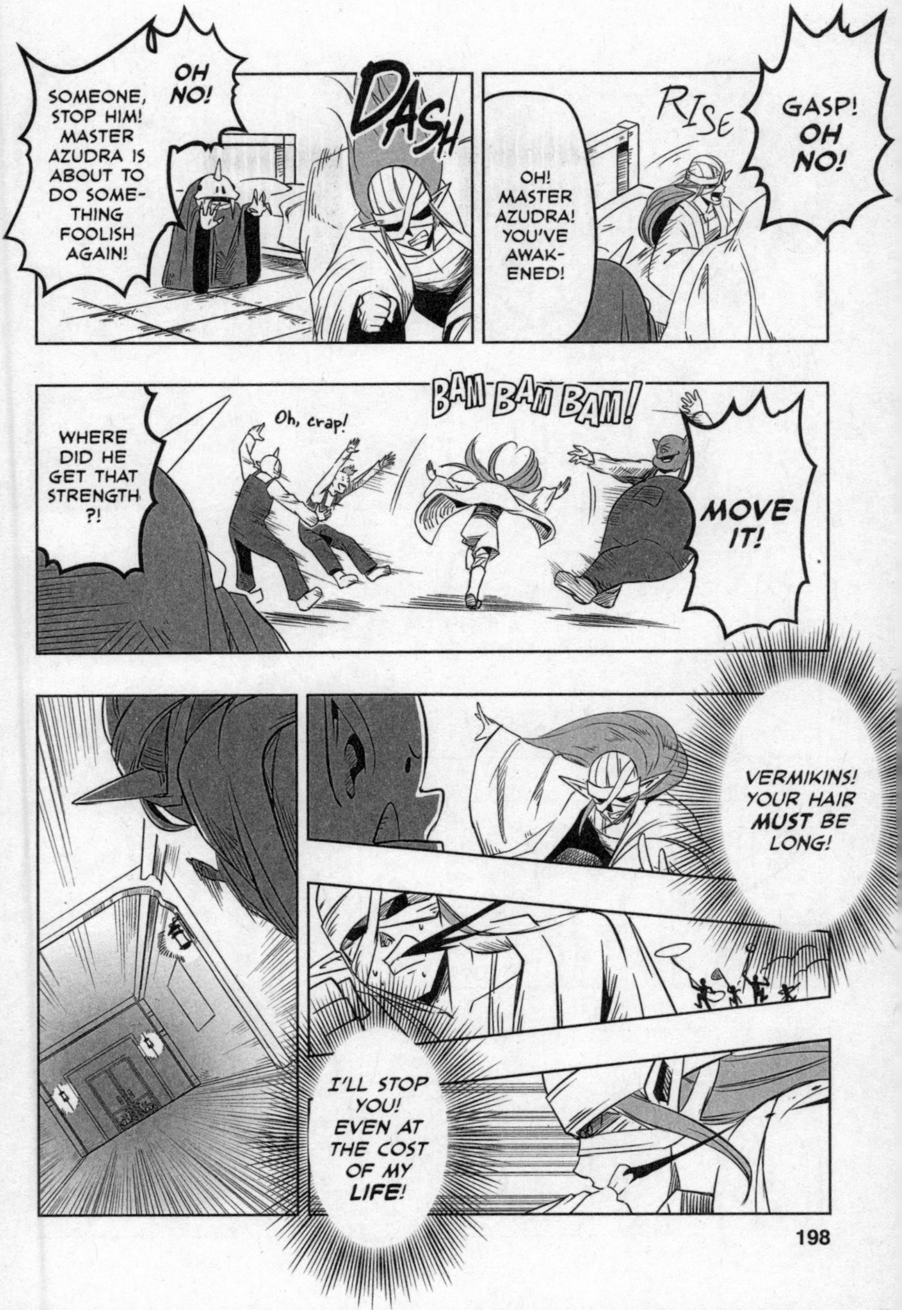
RISE
GASP! OH NO!
OH! MASTER AZUDRA! YOU'VE AWAK-ENED!
DASH
OH NO!
SOMEONE, STOP HIM! MASTER AZUDRA IS ABOUT TO DO SOME-THING FOOLISH AGAIN!
MOVE IT!
BAM BAM BAM!
Oh, crap!
WHERE DID HE GET THAT STRENGTH?!
VERMIKINS! YOUR HAIR MUST BE LONG!
I'LL STOP YOU! EVEN AT THE COST OF MY LIFE!

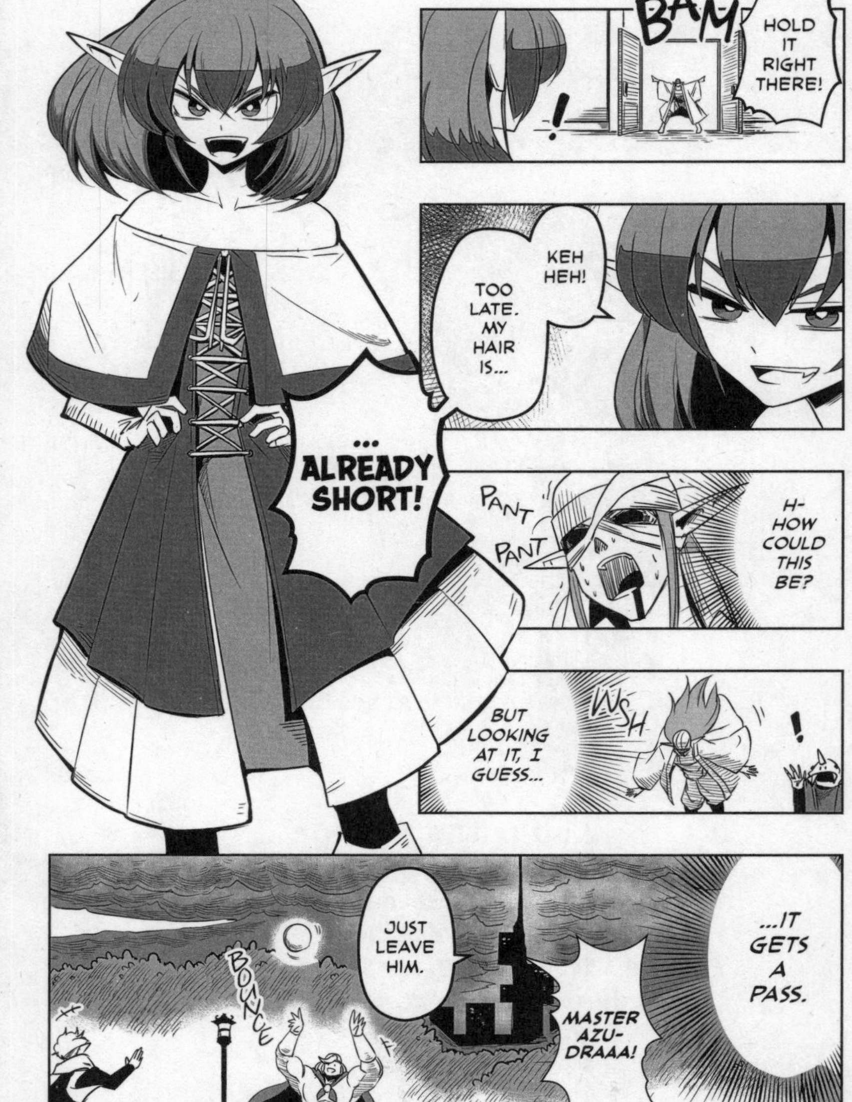
BAM
HOLD IT RIGHT THERE!
!
KEH HEH!
TOO LATE. MY HAIR IS...
...ALREADY SHORT!
PANT PANT
H-HOW COULD THIS BE?
!
WSH
BUT LOOKING AT IT, I GUESS...
...IT GETS A PASS.
MASTER AZU-DRAAA!
JUST LEAVE HIM.
BOUNCE
BONUS END

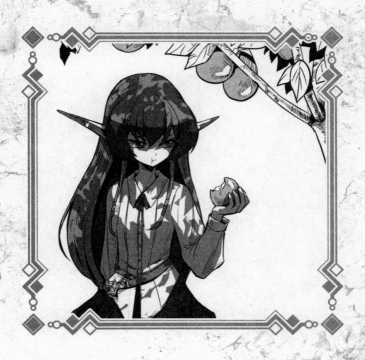

About the Author

Nanaki Nanao is best known for the manga *Helck*, originally published in 2014 and re-released in 2022. Nanao's other works include *Piwi* and *Völundo: Divergent Sword Saga*, both set in the world of *Helck*, as well as *Acaria*.

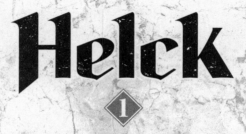

Helck

1

Story and Art by NANAKI NANAO

Translation: **DAVID EVELYN**
Touch-Up Art & Lettering: **ANNALIESE "ACE" CHRISTMAN**
Design: **KAM LI**
Editor: **JACK CARRILLO CONCORDIA**

HELCK SHINSOBAN Vol. 1
by Nanaki NANAO
© 2022 Nanaki NANAO
All rights reserved.
Original Japanese edition published by SHOGAKUKAN.
English translation rights in the United States of America, Canada, the
United Kingdom, Ireland, Australia and New Zealand arranged with
SHOGAKUKAN.

Original Cover Design: Masato ISHIZAWA + Bay Bridge Studio

Printed in the U.S.A.

Published by VIZ Media, LLC
P.O. Box 77010
San Francisco, CA 94107

10 9 8 7 6 5 4 3 2 1
First printing, January 2023

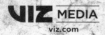 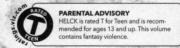

The adventure is over but life goes on for an elf mage
just beginning to learn what living is all about.

Frieren
Beyond Journey's End

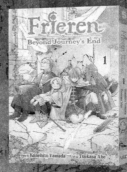

Decades after their victory, the funeral of one
of her friends confronts Frieren with her own
near immortality. Frieren sets out to fulfill the
last wishes of her comrades and finds herself
beginning a new adventure...

Story by **Kanehito Yamada**
Art by **Tsukasa Abe**

VIZ

Kidnapped by the Demon King and imprisoned in his castle, Princess Syalis is...bored.

SLEEPY PRINCESS IN THE DEMON CASTLE

Story & Art by
KAGIJI KUMANOMATA

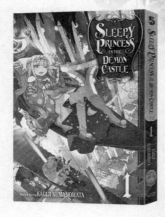

Captured princess Syalis decides to while away her hours in the Demon Castle by sleeping, but getting a good night's rest turns out to be a lot of work! She begins by fashioning a DIY pillow out of the fur of her Teddy Demon guards and an "air mattress" from the magical Shield of the Wind. Things go from bad to worse—for her captors—when some of Princess Syalis's schemes end in her untimely—if temporary—demise and she chooses the Forbidden Grimoire for her bedtime reading...

A new feudal fairytale begins!

YASHAHIME
— PRINCESS HALF-DEMON —

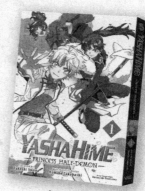

Story and Art
Takashi Shiina

Main Character Design
Rumiko Takahashi

Script Cooperation Katsuyuki Sumisawa

Can the three teenage daughters of demon dog half-brothers Inuyasha and Sesshomaru save their parents, themselves, and both realms from the menace of the seven mystical Rainbow Pearls?

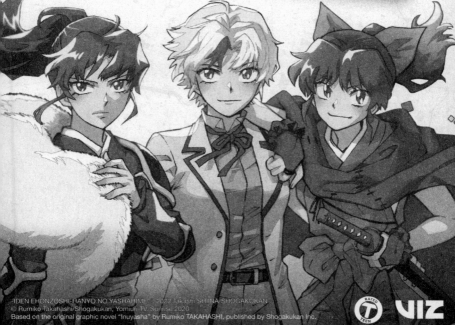

RATED TEEN

VIZ

MAGI
The labyrinth of magic

Story & Art by
SHINOBU OHTAKA

A **fantasy adventure** inspired by
One Thousand and One Nights

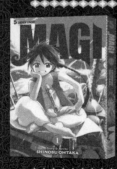

Deep within the deserts lie the mysterious Dungeons, vast stores of riches there for the taking by anyone lucky enough to find them and brave enough to venture into the depths from where few have ever returned. Plucky young adventurer **Aladdin** means to find the Dungeons and their riches, but Aladdin may be just as mysterious as the treasures he seeks.

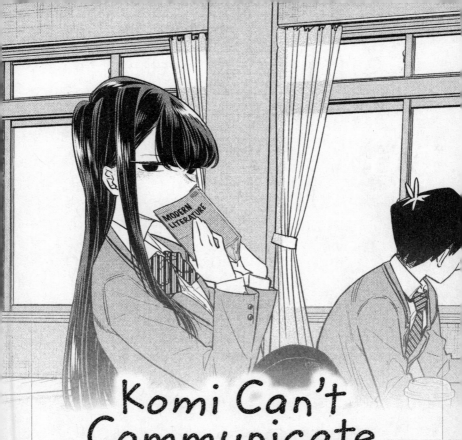

Komi Can't Communicate

Story & Art by Tomohito Oda

The journey to a hundred friends begins with a single conversation.

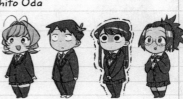

Socially anxious high school student Shoko Komi's greatest dream is to make some friends, but everyone at school mistakes her crippling social anxiety for cool reserve. With the whole student body keeping its distance and Komi unable to utter a single word, friendship might be forever beyond her reach.

  COMI-SAN WA, COMYUSHO DESU. © 2016 Tomohito Oda/SHOGAKUKAN

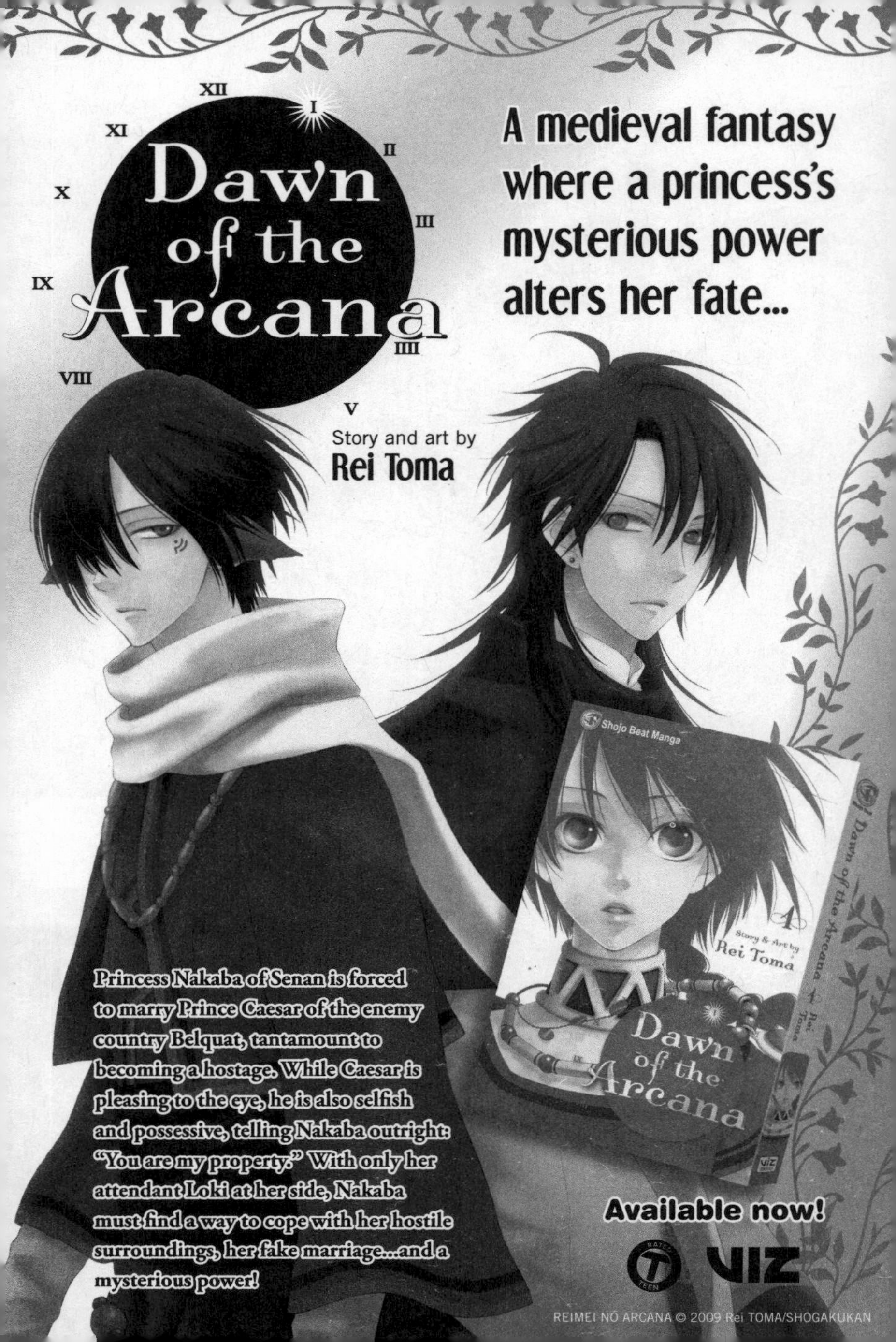
Dawn of the Arcana
A medieval fantasy where a princess's mysterious power alters her fate...
Story and art by
Rei Toma
Shojo Beat Manga
1
Story & Art by Rei Toma
Dawn of the Arcana
Princess Nakaba of Senan is forced to marry Prince Caesar of the enemy country Belquat, tantamount to becoming a hostage. While Caesar is pleasing to the eye, he is also selfish and possessive, telling Nakaba outright: "You are my property." With only her attendant Loki at her side, Nakaba must find a way to cope with her hostile surroundings, her fake marriage...and a mysterious power!
Available now!
T TEEN RATED
VIZ
REIMEI NO ARCANA © 2009 Rei TOMA/SHOGAKUKAN

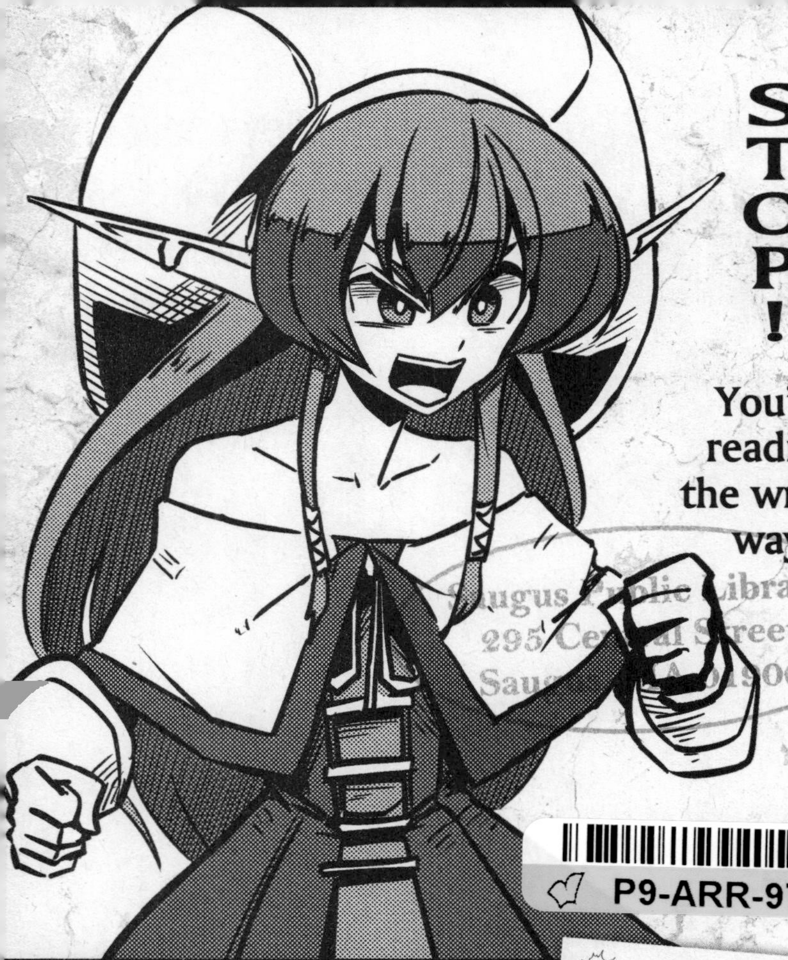

STOP!

You're reading the wrong way!

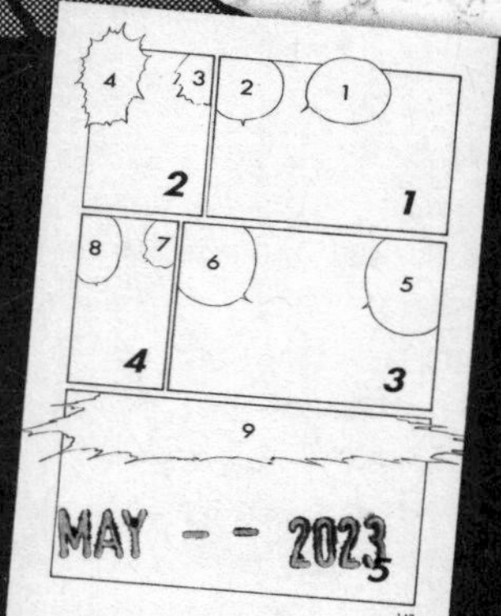
1
2
3
4
1
2
5
6
7
8
3
4
9
5
142

In keeping with the original Japanese comic format, this book reads from right to left—so action, sound effects and word balloons are completely reversed to preserve the orientation of the original artwork.

Check out the diagram shown here to get the hang of things, and then turn to the other side of the book to get started!